**ALEXANDER STEWART** read English and History at Leeds University. Born in England, he left for Kenya aged only three months and spent the next fifteen years shuttling between Africa, Australia and Europe. The wanderlust instilled during his formative years has never left him and he has now visited more than thirty countries on six continents. He has followed Peruvian spirits over high Andean passes, seen the sunrise from the Roof of Africa, been airlifted from the Alps and fallen through the floor of a Vietnamese hostel. He's been spat at by llamas and assaulted by orang-utans but undeterred, he continues to explore, producing articles and photographs for various magazines and newspapers. He is also the author of *The Inca Trail* and *The Walker's Haute Route* for Trailblazer. Currently based in London, he is Group Product Manager at Stanfords, the travel bookshop.

**New Zealand – the Great Walks**
First edition: 2004; this second edition 2009

**Publisher**
Trailblazer Publications
The Old Manse, Tower Rd, Hindhead, Surrey, GU26 6SU, UK
Fax (+44) 01428-607571, info@trailblazer-guides.com
www.trailblazer-guides.com

**British Library Cataloguing in Publication Data**
A catalogue record for this book is available from the British Library

**ISBN** 978-1-905864-11-9

© **Alexander Stewart** 2004; 2009
Text, maps and photographs

The right of Alexander Stewart to be identified as the author of this work has been
asserted by him in accordance with the Copyright, Designs and Patent Act 1988

**Editor**: Henry Stedman
**Series editor**: Patricia Major
**Layout**: Anna Jacomb-Hood
**Proof-reading**: Nicky Slade
**Cartography**: Nick Hill
**Index**: Anna Jacomb-Hood

# New Zealand
## THE GREAT WALKS
### includes
### Auckland and Wellington city guides

ALEXANDER STEWART

**Lake Waikaremoana Track
Tongariro Northern Circuit
Whanganui River Journey
Abel Tasman Coast Track
Heaphy Track
Routeburn Track
Milford Track
Kepler Track
Rakiura Track**

**TRAILBLAZER PUBLICATIONS**

Dedicated to my Mum and Dad, who gave me the world;
and to the memory of my Grandpa

## Acknowledgements

First, I'd like to say thank you to the countless Department of Conservation (DOC) staff and hut wardens who freely gave their time to answer my questions and kept me fully informed as to developments concerning the Great Walks. I'd also like to thank the many locals who showed me such kindness and offered advice or encouragement. Many thanks as well to Gus, Joey and Stu who journeyed around the world in the course of the various editions of this book to keep me company and blindly agreed to help tackle various tramps.

Closer to home, special thanks to Martin for his support whilst living through the creation of the first edition of this book, and of course, as ever, a massive, heartfelt thanks to Katie who's been there through all of them and whose encouragement made it all possible in the first place. Also, an enormous thank you to all the people at Trailblazer whose hard work contributed to the completion of this book: Henry Stedman for again editing the text so diligently, Nick Hill for making my maps legible, Anna Jacomb-Hood for typesetting, layout and index and Nicky Slade for proof-reading. Lastly, thanks to Bryn Thomas for giving me the initial opportunity to write this guide and for his continued, unstinting support throughout this second incarnation of the project.

## A request

The author and publisher have tried to ensure that this guide is as accurate and up to date as possible. Nevertheless, things change even on well-worn routes. If you notice any changes or omissions that should be included in the next edition of this book, please write to Alexander Stewart at Trailblazer (address on p2), or email him: 🖥 alex.stewart@trailblazer-guides.com. A free copy of the next edition will be sent to persons making a significant contribution.

Updated information will shortly be available on the internet at
**www.trailblazer-guides.com**

**Front cover**: View back south over the glorious beaches and forested inlets north of Totaranui on the Abel Tasman Coast Track.
Photo © Alexander Stewart

The symbol used in the boxed text sections throughout this book is the *koru*. This is a traditional Maori design, a young uncurling fern frond that represents the vitality of life, vigorous growth and good health.

# CONTENTS

# INTRODUCTION

*'When you see someone putting on big boots, you can be sure adventure is about to happen'*
**AA Milne**, *Winnie the Pooh*

In the Northern Hemisphere the practice of walking in the wilderness for several days carrying a loaded pack and being self-sufficient is known as trekking or hiking; Australians refer to it as bushwalking; in New Zealand you go **tramping**.

People have been tramping in New Zealand since 1889, when Quintin Mackinnon first led groups up the Clinton Valley on the Milford Track. Since then the numbers of trampers reaching remote corners of the country has increased dramatically, and no wonder. The country is similar in size to the UK but has only around four million inhabitants. Consequently there are vast tracts of unspoilt, empty, natural coastline, forest and mountainous land. Furthermore, there is now more than 12,000km of track criss-crossing this wilderness.

The **Great Walks** represent some of the finest walks in the country. These nine routes, each of which takes between two and five days to complete, have been selected by New Zealand's Department of Conservation (DOC; see box p37) on the basis of their outstanding scenery, diversity and universal appeal. So fêted and exceptional are these tracks that they have taken their place in the pantheon of famous footpaths worldwide. Bold, square-jawed tramps over high mountain passes are featured alongside much easier boardwalked trails through native forest or tramps along the country's varied coastline. And because of the excellent network of tracks and huts that comprise the Great Walks, people of all levels of experience can enjoy the wilderness without the trials usually associated with travelling in such remote areas. The uncompromising terrain has been tamed but its drama remains undiminished.

The eight walking tracks and (bizarrely) one canoe trip that make up the Great Walks draw on the country's rich history and culture. The tracks were mainly carved out by the early inhabitants of New Zealand, first Maori and then European, and are steeped in both Maori heritage and colonial history. By walking them slowly with your eyes open you should gain a much broader understanding of New Zealand's evolution. They also encompass a huge array of landscapes: the verdant native forests of the North Island, the smouldering volcanic moonscape of the Central Plateau, the glorious beaches of the South Island, the glacier-sculpted landscape of Fiordland and the remote haven of Stewart Island. All are unique, profoundly interesting parts of the country. The indigenous flora and fauna is equally exotic.

Tramping will give you unsurpassed access to this natural beauty. New Zealand is a country that demands to be experienced rather than merely viewed and tramping offers the most intimate way of getting to know this exceptional, untainted land.

**PART 1: PLANNING YOUR TRAMP**

# With a group or independently?

*That night was typical of a stop at a trail hut. Over dinner we discussed murder, race relations, AIDS, nuclear testing, the greenhouse effect, Third World economies, the Maori claim to New Zealand and Martin Luther King Day.*

**Paul Theroux**, *The Happy Isles of Oceania*

New Zealand has an outstanding network of tracks and trails that are well managed and preserved. By tramping you are able to get to some of the finest wilderness left in the country and experience a host of landscapes. The Great Walks are some of New Zealand's premier walking tracks. Well cut, clearly defined and well maintained, they are relatively easy to follow, thus enabling people of all abilities to attempt a tramp. For those who like hot showers and other home comforts, there is the option of taking luxury guided walks on some of the tracks. Or, if you don't mind roughing it a bit, independent tramping, where you carry your own pack and remain self-sufficient, is a very rewarding way of seeing New Zealand.

## INDEPENDENT TRAMPING

Tramping independently is the cheapest way to explore the wilderness and offers you the greatest freedom. You can either camp, or stay in huts provided along the tracks which, in some cases, you must book and pay for in advance (see p283) and receive a hut pass in return. Toilet facilities are often basic but modern flushing versions have been installed along the most popular tracks.

The Great Walks are exceptionally easy to arrange and most can be booked when you arrive in New Zealand. The Lake Waikaremoana, Milford, Routeburn, Kepler and Abel Tasman tracks may have to be booked well in advance but, with a little forethought and planning, this is simple to do. On these you will be obliged to stay in your pre-booked hut on a specified date. On other tracks, however, you are afforded a greater degree of flexibility than if you were tramping as part of an organised group and are able to make changes to your itinerary as you wish, choosing to stop early or push on as the mood takes you.

Even if tramping alone, you are only rarely entirely on your own. There will almost certainly be other trampers out on the track with you and you all congregate in the same huts at the day's end. Tramping is a remarkably social pastime that enables you to interact with like-minded individuals and the striking things you see and do on the way are usually enough to spark a conversation.

For most, the ideal way to tramp is in small, independent groups. This way you retain your freedom to do as you please, will minimise your impact on the

All the Great Walks are clearly signed. Unlike this one, however, most signboards aren't decorated with abandoned boots.

countryside, are far less likely to disturb flora or fauna unduly and you improve your chances of seeing various species. You are also safer, since if one person gets into difficulties there will be others immediately on hand to help.

## GUIDED WALKS

Most people sign up for a guided walk (tramp) because it is perceived as easier to arrange than an independent one. Some, however, may be doing so because they don't realise that arranging an independent tramp is equally straightforward. Others join guided walks for the companionship, higher level of comfort and the security of being led by someone who has been there before.

The main drawback to joining a guided walk is the cost. It can be a substantially more expensive way of seeing exactly the same tract of wilderness. For example, an independent walker will expect to pay around NZ$280-350 for their Milford Track experience, whilst joining a guided group can cost in the region of NZ$2000.

Although most tramping groups will stay in the same accommodation as the independent walkers, there are exclusive, **private lodges** for guided groups on the Routeburn and Milford tracks which provide a degree of luxury never seen in a hut run by the Department of Conservation (DOC; see box p37). The divide between guided and independent walkers is most pronounced on the Milford Track where even the emergency shelters are split between the two.

### Tramping agencies

There are several agencies in New Zealand who can organise a Great Walk for you. For all the relevant prices, dates of departure and to find out more about what each company offers, contact them directly. For companies operating guided trips on the Whanganui River see pp154-6.

### On North Island

● **Adrift Guided Outdoor Adventures** (☎ 07-892 2751, 💻 www.adriftnz .co.nz; PO Box 19, National Park Village) Organises one- to five-day tramps in Tongariro National Park. Also leads one- to six-day canoe trips on the Whanganui River or can organise jet-boat excursions.

● **New Zealand Nature Safaris** (☎ 025-360268 or in NZ tollfree ☎ 0800-697232, 💻 www.hikingnewzealand.com; PO Box 93, Lyttelton 8033) Runs four-day tramps around Tongariro National Park, where you stay in DOC huts.

● **Walking Legends** (NZ tollfree ☎ 0800-925569, 💻 www.walkinglegends .com; PO Box 267, Whakatane) Runs four-day circuits around Lake Waikaremoana and four-day hikes on the Tongariro Circuit, in addition to multi-day tramps exploring Te Urewera National Park.

## On South Island

● **Abel Tasman Kayaks** (☎ 03-527 8022 or in NZ tollfree ☎ 0800-732529, 🖥 www.abeltasmankayaks.co.nz; Main Rd, Marahau)  Specialist operator offering half- and multi-day outings on the Abel Tasman Coastal Track incorporating tramping and kayaking (see box p179).

● **Bush and Beyond** (☎ 03-528 9057, 🖥 www.bushandbeyond.co.nz; PO Box 376, Motueka)  Focuses on five-day/five-night tramps on the Heaphy Track but also operates a guided day trip on the Abel Tasman Coastal Track.

● **Kahurangi Guide Walks** (☎ 03-525 7177, 🖥 www.abel-tasman-track.co.nz; Dodson Rd, Takaka)  Operates one- to five-day guided walks on the Abel Tasman Coastal Track but also leads five-day outings on the Heaphy Track and a number of half- and multi-day tramps elsewhere in the region.

● **Kiwi Wilderness Walks** (☎ 03-442 6017 or in NZ tollfree ☎ 0800-733549, 🖥 www.nzwalk.com; PO Box 2125, Queenstown)  Probably the best for organised group tramps on Stewart Island.

● **Real Journeys** (☎ 0800-656 501, 🖥 www.realjourneys.co.nz; Te Anau). Runs guided day walks along an 11km stretch of the Milford Track.

● **Southern Wilderness** (☎ 03-545 1308, 🖥 www.heaphytracknz.com; PO Box 1821, Nelson). Offers a range of tramps on the Heaphy Track and also leads trips to the Nelson Lakes region.

● **Ultimate Hikes** (☎ 03-441 1138 or in NZ tollfree ☎ 0800-659255, 🖥 www .milfordtrack.co.nz; PO Box 259, Queenstown)  Arranges guided Milford tramps lasting five days/four nights as well as guided three-day/two-night treks on the Routeburn Track. Both tramps are all-inclusive, Queenstown to Queenstown trips and involve staying in private, guided walks accommodation. Also runs 'Encounter' day walks on stretches of each track for people short of time. Its 'Classic' eight-day/seven-night tramp combines both routes.

● **Wilsons Abel Tasman** (☎ 03-528 2027, in NZ tollfree ☎ 0800-223582 or 🖥 www.abeltasman.co.nz; 265 High St, Motueka)  Lead one- to five-day tramps on the Abel Tasman Coastal Track, staying in private lodges and using boats to transfer your gear. Can also arrange sea kayaking (see box p179).

## On Stewart Island

● **Stewart Island Wilderness Walks** (☎ 03-226 6739, 🖥 www.sigw.co.nz; PO Box 108, Halfmoon Bay)  Personalised guiding service exploring elements of the island's history and wildlife in the course of half-, one- or two-day outings.

## Tramping clubs

Because tramping is such a popular pastime in New Zealand, a number of clubs have developed. Some have quite long and illustrious histories. If you are inclined to join some sort of group but still want to tramp independently these can be a good alternative to the tramping agencies.

The **Federated Mountain Club of New Zealand** (☎ 04-233 8244, 🖥 www .fmc.org.nz, PO Box 1604) is located in Wellington. It is a national association of more than 100 tramping clubs that can be found throughout New Zealand. The website has the largest list of clubs in the country posted on it and some 14,000

members. Some of the main clubs include **Auckland Tramping Club** (🖳 www
.aucklandtramping.org.nz), **Wellington Tramping and Mountaineering Club**
(🖳 www.wtmc.org.nz), **Nelson Tramping Club** (🖳 www.nelsontrampingclub
.orcon.net.nz) and **Massey University Alpine Club** (🖳 www.massey.ac.nz/
muac). **New Zealand Alpine Club** (🖳 www.alpineclub.org.nz) is one of the
oldest and most respected clubs of its kind in the world.

# Getting to New Zealand

## BY AIR

New Zealand has three major international airports: **Auckland** (🖳 www.auck
land-airport.co.nz) and **Wellington** (🖳 www.wellington-airport.co.nz) are on
North Island; **Christchurch** (🖳 www.christchurch-airport.co.nz) is on South
Island. The vast majority of flights arrive in Auckland, which is probably the
cheapest entry point to the country. There are also airports at **Palmerston
North**, **Hamilton** and **Dunedin** that receive flights from Australia as well as
domestic flights.

New Zealand is a long way from nearly everywhere. Auckland is 18,355km
from London, 10,450km from Los Angeles and even from Sydney it's 2165km.
Consequently it will require a long-haul flight to reach New Zealand. The flight
times are lengthy, taking around $3^1/_2$ hours from Eastern Australia, $10^1/_2$ hours
from countries on the Pacific Rim such as Singapore and Hong Kong, 12 hours
from the west coast of America and up to 27 hours from the UK.

This usually means that the flight ticket will be expensive. There are various ways of trying to minimise the cost, such as by booking well in advance or
using the internet to search out cheap deals. Take time to consider the various
options before making a final choice; the flight ticket is likely to be the single
biggest expense of your trip so consider it thoroughly. One popular option to
consider if you are planning to travel through the country is an open-jaw ticket

---

### ❛ Climate change and long-distance travel

Climate change is a serious threat to the planet and to ecosystems required for
survival. Air travel is one of the contributors to the problem, with greenhouse
gases released high into the atmosphere. Long-distance travel is correspondingly
more damaging. New Zealand is a long way from anywhere, being 1600km from
Australia and some 19,000km from the UK. Although travel is still massively bene-
ficial, this threat cannot be ignored and you should aim to travel responsibly at all
times. To offset your emissions and reduce your personal impact on global warming
visit 🖳 www.climatecare.org, where a 'carbon calculator' will work out the 'cost' of
your flight after which you can make a financial contribution to sustainable travel
schemes and projects aimed at reducing global warming, which will 'neutralise' the
greenhouse gases you are responsible for generating in the course of your flight.

> **Departure tax**
> When leaving New Zealand from Auckland airport you do not have to pay departure tax – the tax is instead charged to the airlines. However, there is an international departure tax of NZ$25 payable by anyone aged 12 or over from all other New Zealand airports. The tax is not incorporated into the price of an airline ticket and must be paid separately at the airport prior to departure. You can pay using either cash or credit card.

that allows you to fly into one airport (say Auckland) and out of another (for instance Christchurch), usually at no extra cost, meaning that you do not have to retrace your steps.

The price of your ticket also depends on the **season** in which you are travelling. The busiest, most expensive time of year is from December to February. The cheapest time of year to travel is June to August. The shoulder seasons from March to May and September to November are slightly cheaper and availability is slightly better than in the high season.

## From the UK

There is a multitude of airlines operating flights from the UK to New Zealand (though note that there are no direct flights from Ireland to New Zealand). The following all operate daily services: **Air Canada** (☎ 0871-220 1111, 🖳 www .aircanada.ca); **Air New Zealand** (☎ 0800-028 4149, 🖳 www.airnewzealand .co.nz); **British Airways** (☎ 0870-850 9850, 🖳 www.britishairways.com); **Qantas** (☎ 0845-7747 767, 🖳 www.qantas.com.au); **Singapore Airlines** (☎ 0844-800 2380, 🖳 www.singaporeair.com).

In addition, **Thai Airways International** (☎ 0870-606 0911, 🖳 www.thai air.com), **Japan Airlines** (☎ 0845-774 7700, 🖳 www.jal.co.jp), **Aerolineas Argentinas** (☎ 0845-601 1915, 🖳 www.aerolineas.com.ar), **Malaysia Airlines** (☎ 0870-607 9090, 🖳 www.mas.com.my), **Korean Air** (☎ 0800-0656 2001, 🖳 www .koreanair.com), and **Cathay Pacific** (☎ 020-7747 8888, 🖳 www.cathaypacific .com) fly several times per week, the exact frequency depending on the season.

The majority of flights depart from Heathrow, although Singapore Airlines also fly from Manchester. You are faced with two choices as to which way to fly around the world: airlines either fly east via Asia, stopping in one or more of India, Thailand, Indonesia, Singapore or Australia; or west via Buenos Aires, New York, Los Angeles and/or Honolulu and the Pacific islands.

**Buying a ticket**  London is one of the cheapest places to buy international plane tickets. Prices begin at just under £700 and rise from there to some astronomical amounts. The cheapest seats sell out very quickly and need to be booked well in advance.

The following **travel agents** are good places to begin finding out about fares: Trailfinders (☎ 020-7628 7628, 🖳 www.trailfinders.co.uk); STA Travel (☎ 0870-1600 599, 🖳 www.statravel.co.uk); Flight Centre (☎ 0870-890 8099, 🖳 www.flightcentre.co.uk); Thomas Cook (☎ 0870-5666 222, 🖳 www.thomas

PLANNING YOUR TRAMP

cook.co.uk); Travel Bag (☎ 0870-900 1350, 💻 www.travelbag.co.uk); North South Travel (☎ 01245-608291, 💻 www.northsouthtravel.co.uk).

The **internet** is a good source of discounted tickets and a handy means of comparing what is available: 💻 www.cheapflights.co.uk gives a summary of the various offers available to your destination from lots of different agents. Other internet sites worth looking at include 💻 www.cheaptickets.com, 💻 www.expedia.com, 💻 www.travelocity.com or 💻 www.opodo.co.uk. Another useful resource is the Sunday newspapers and travel supplements, which list airfares from different agents. Magazines such as *TNT*, *Time Out* and some of the dedicated travel magazines also list basic fares.

## From the USA and Canada

Only Auckland receives direct, non-stop flights from the **USA**. Most of these originate from Los Angeles or occasionally San Francisco. If you are flying from elsewhere in the States you'll have to purchase an additional ticket to either of these departure points. The majority of flights originating in **Canada** and bound for Auckland pass through the west coast of the USA too, although Air New Zealand operate a direct flight from Vancouver to Auckland.

**Air New Zealand** (💻 www.airnewzealand.com) and **Qantas** (💻 www.qantas.com) are the only airlines operating planes from the USA but various code share partners such as **Air Canada** (💻 www.aircanada.ca), **American Airlines** (💻 www.aa.com) and **British Airways** (💻 www.britishairways.com) will also sell you a ticket. As an alternative, **Korean Airlines** (💻 www.koreanair.com) fly east via Asia, changing at Seoul.

Air New Zealand and Qantas operate daily non-stop flights from Los Angeles to Auckland. A standard return fare during peak season from the west coast to Auckland costs around US$1700. This drops slightly during the quieter periods of the year.

**Buying a ticket** In the **US**, the cheapest tickets can be bought through one of the hundreds of offices of Council Travel (💻 www.counciltravel.com), or STA Travel (💻 www.statravel.com) who have offices in all the major cities. Both specialise in fares for students but sell tickets to everyone.

The cheapest tickets from **Canada** to New Zealand tend to be around 10% more expensive than the equivalent ticket from the USA. Vancouver to Auckland costs upwards of C$1500 whilst a ticket from the eastern side of Canada, from Toronto for example, costs upwards of C$2100. Canada's national student agency Travel Cuts (💻 www.travelcuts.com), STA Travel (💻 www.statravel.com) and the Flight Centre (💻 www.flightcentre.com) are the best places to try to secure cheap tickets.

## From Australia

Flights to and from Australia arrive in New Zealand at one of six airports: Auckland, Christchurch, Wellington, Dunedin, Palmerston North and Hamilton.

The following airlines all operate flights to New Zealand: **Aerolineas Argentinas** (💻 www.aerolineas.com.au); **Air New Zealand** (💻 www.airnz.com.au); **Emirates** (💻 www.emirates.com); **Jetstar** (💻 www.jetstar.com);

**Pacific Blue** (🖳 www.flypacificblue.com); **Qantas** (🖳 www.qantas.com.au); **Singapore Airlines** (🖳 www.singaporeair.com); **Thai Airways** (🖳 www.thai air.com).

Air New Zealand and Qantas are the main carriers and the only major airlines to offer frequent flights from Australia. They operate several daily direct flights from major cities to Auckland. Pacific Blue and Jetstar are no-frills budget-airline offshoots of Virgin Blue (Australia's second biggest airline) and Qantas respectively. They operate several flights from the Gold Coast and key Australian cities (Sydney, Brisbane, Cairns and Melbourne) to Auckland, Wellington, Dunedin, Palmerston North and Hamilton for around A$300-350 return.

**Buying a ticket** Discount-ticket travel agents can offer flights with the main carriers from Sydney to Auckland for around A$500 return, Sydney to Christchurch or Wellington for A$600 return and from Melbourne to either Auckland, Christchurch or Wellington for A$700 return. Flights from Perth cost around A$1000. During the peak season return fares go up by A$200 or so. For cheap tickets try the Flight Centre (🖳 www.flightcentre.com.au), STA Travel (🖳 www.statravel.com.au), Thomas Cook (🖳 www.thomascook.com.au) or Trailfinders (🖳 www.trailfinders.com.au), all of which have offices nationwide.

### From South Africa
Flying to New Zealand from South Africa usually involves going via Australia. Qantas operate regular flights from Johannesburg to Sydney that then connect with onward flights to Auckland, Wellington or Christchurch. South African Airlines (🖳 www.flyssa.com) operates the same route. Tickets will set you back around R20,000 depending on the season.

# When to go

It is possible to visit New Zealand at almost any time of year. Summer and winter temperatures vary by only about 10°C across much of the country. There are regional variations in temperature, with the south generally being cooler. The areas of the country at higher altitude are also likely to be cooler, of course, and to experience more severe weather. New Zealand's seasons are the reverse of those in the Northern Hemisphere, which means that the warmest months are December to February whilst the coldest are June to August.

However, if you are travelling to New Zealand with the intention of tramping some of the Great Walks there a few things to take into consideration. During periods of good weather the Great Walks are safe and passable. Unpredictable and highly changeable weather can cause problems, though, as the sudden onset of bad weather can make a track more hazardous or even impassable. Furthermore, it is not uncommon for some of the tracks in the mountains to experience a drop in temperature of up to 10°C in as many minutes.

PLANNING YOUR TRAMP

## AUCKLAND

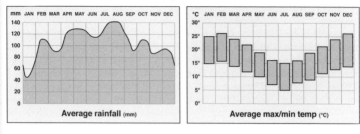

Average rainfall (mm)

Average max/min temp (°C)

## WELLINGTON

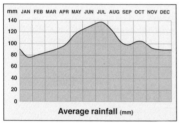

Average rainfall (mm)

Average max/min temp (°C)

## CHRISTCHURCH

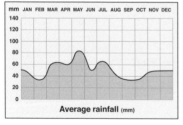

Average rainfall (mm)

Average max/min temp (°C)

## QUEENSTOWN

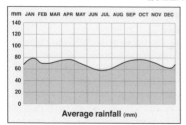

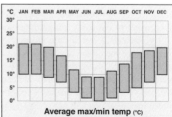

Average rainfall (mm)

Average max/min temp (°C)

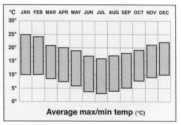
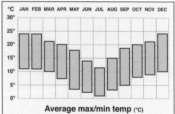

Although you can tramp some of the tracks all year round, such as those at the top of South Island like the Abel Tasman Coast Track, some of the higher routes are closed during the winter season as snow tends to make certain sections impassable. This is particularly true for those Great Walks found in Fiordland, namely the Routeburn, Milford and Kepler tracks. Equally, rain can turn parts of Stewart Island into a quagmire at certain times of year, making the Rakiura track more of a struggle to complete.

If you wish to give yourself the most flexibility and choice over which Great Walk to undertake, the best time to visit is in the **summer season**, from December to April. Within this time the tracks are at their busiest over Christmas, during the New Zealand school holidays which run from early/mid December to the end of January, and again over the Easter holidays. Therefore, the ideal time to visit is probably **February to March**, when the crowds have thinned slightly but the weather remains stable and summery.

# Budgeting and costs

The New Zealand economy is currently fairly stable but, having enjoyed high growth in recent years, it slipped towards recession at the tail end of 2008 in line with many of the world's economies affected by the global credit crunch. However, despite a relatively strong New Zealand dollar (which means that New Zealand is no longer the bargain destination it once was), things will still seem comparatively cheap compared to prices in Europe or the USA. The goods and services are also all of a very high standard, so you still receive excellent value for money.

It is possible to live relatively cheaply whilst travelling through New Zealand. The country is set up for backpacking with hordes of cheap hostels, a good communication network and a reasonably priced public transport system. Activities cost a little more, and how much of these you do will affect how expensive or otherwise your trip becomes. A realistic budget estimate of the **daily cost of living** in New Zealand is NZ$70-90. This sum allows you to eat, travel on public transport, camp or stay in hostels and enjoy some of New Zealand's many attractions. If planning on more activities, staying in budget accommodation or eating out more often, then expect to spend NZ$120-150 per day. Stay in a decent B&B or hotel or eat out at a better class of restaurant and you can easily spend in excess of NZ$300 per day.

**Accommodation** ranges in price depending on the level of comfort. Tent pitches on campsites cost around NZ$10, dorm rooms between NZ$20 and NZ$27, whilst simple double rooms go for NZ$40-70. Motel units are a little pricier at NZ$100-150 and B&B-style accommodation will set you back somewhere between NZ$70 and $180. An international-standard hotel charges anything from NZ$150-350 for a room. See the box on p18 for accommodation prices on the trail.

❏ **Great Walk hut and campsite fees – see also p283**

The Great Walks vary in price depending on their popularity. The following table illustrates the **summer-season fees** for using the huts and campsites along the Great Walks. They were correct at the time of writing but should be checked and confirmed before you make any bookings. Variations in prices or discounts may be available and there are different fees for off-season tramping on some of the routes. For full details see the relevant Great Walk section in Part 5.

| | Adult hut/night | Adult campsite/night |
|---|---|---|
| Lake Waikaremoana Track | NZ$25 | NZ$12 |
| Tongariro Northern Circuit | NZ$25 | NZ$20 |
| Whanganui River Journey | NZ$45 (for use of all huts or campsites up to four nights) | |
| Abel Tasman Coast Track | NZ$30 | NZ$12 |
| Heaphy Track | NZ$25 | NZ$12.50 |
| Routeburn Track | NZ$45 | NZ$15 |
| Milford Track | NZ$45 | Not available |
| Kepler Track | NZ$45 | NZ$15 |
| Rakiura Track | NZ$15 | NZ$5 |

Obviously where you eat will also affect your budget. The **food** is generally robust fodder and excellent value. Supermarkets are usually well stocked and reasonably priced. Takeaway prices range from NZ$5 to NZ$15 and meals in cafés or pubs cost upwards of NZ$15-25; restaurants charge NZ$40 or more for a three-course meal. **Travelling** through New Zealand is relatively easy and cheap since it is a fairly small country and the prime destinations are all a short hop from one another. However, once you've made several short trips the costs start to mount up. If you choose to forsake buses in favour of airplane tickets, no matter how 'low-cost', then you must expect to pay slightly more.

**Activities** and one-off trips are the major expenses. The costs for these activities vary considerably and it is worth shopping around. New Zealand's adrenaline sports such as bungy-jumping and parachuting will set you back around NZ$150 and NZ$250 respectively.

# What to take

*Think of everything you could possibly want on a climbing expedition, say, of thirty hours. Cut out from this all that you think might be fairly easily dispensed with. Take with you fifty percent of the remainder.* **Harold Raeburn**, *Mountaineering Art*

Careful consideration as to what to take on your tramp is vital. How much you pack will depend a lot on the type of tramp, how far you're going, what sort of terrain you'll have to cover and in which season you are planning to go. The key point to remember is to be equipped to deal with every eventuality.

It is impossible to overstate the importance of getting your choice of equipment right. Tramping in New Zealand, regardless of which track you choose to tackle, should not be undertaken lightly. The slightest thing – an ill-fitting boot, an inadequate sleeping bag, a rucksack that won't sit properly – can cause discomfort and a premature end to your trip.

The key to sensible packing is to take only what you need to make the tramp comfortable and enjoyable. However, this varies from person to person. Many people take far too much. Weight is an important consideration on multi-day tramps since no matter which walk you choose there will be some lengthy ascents at some stage. Men shouldn't carry more than 15-18kg, or a quarter of their body weight, whilst women will usually be more comfortable carrying 10-12kg. There are all sorts of ways to keep the weight of your pack to a minimum. Unfortunately, whilst tramping gear has become considerably more sophisticated over the years, it has also become markedly more expensive; light, strong, good quality, durable trekking equipment doesn't come cheap but the benefits of having the right gear on your tramp will outweigh the expense.

## RUCKSACK

For multi-day tramps, comfort is the key when choosing a rucksack. Modern internal-frame backpacks are readily available in a variety of sizes. Get the help of an experienced shop assistant to fit you with the right-sized pack.

The hip belt should support about a third of the weight of the pack, with the rest being carried by your shoulders. Make sure that the straps are adjustable so you can alter them to suit the terrain: when climbing it is better to take the weight on your shoulders, whilst when descending it is often more comfortable if you release the shoulder straps slightly and tighten the waistband.

Once you have found a backpack that fits, compare capacities and features. You should be aware that if you buy too large a pack you may be tempted to fill it simply because the space is there. The pack should be equipped with easily accessible compartments for the items you want most often, such as water bottles, guidebooks, maps and snacks. You might also find that buckles and straps on the outside of the pack are useful for securing roll-mats or tents, although these will obviously be less protected on the outside of the pack than inside. All materials should be robust and long lasting. Stitching on the pack must be high quality and any zips need to be resilient and smooth running.

All packs will inevitably leak slightly in heavy rain and it is almost certain that you will encounter at least one downpour on your tramps. Consequently it is important that you use a heavy-duty, **waterproof inner liner** to protect your gear. For further protection, you can split your things into **plastic shopping bags** or waterproof 'stuff sacks', which should ensure that everything remains dry.

## SLEEPING BAG

You will need a sleeping bag for all the huts along the Great Walks and for camping out. There are three main considerations when choosing a sleeping bag: shape, filling and temperature rating. Mummy-shaped bags are better than rectangular-shaped ones as the tapered shape reduces weight and increases warmth. These can be a little claustrophobic in warmer conditions though. Down insulates far better than synthetic fibre but ceases to be as efficient once wet and can take a very, very long time to dry out. Sleeping bags are rated by temperature. Since temperatures in New Zealand are usually moderate and none of the Great Walks has overnight accommodation at particularly high altitude, a sleeping bag offering two- to three-season comfort in temperatures of –5°C to –10°C ought to be sufficient. You should consider taking a **sheet sleeping-bag** – essentially a sheet folded and sewn along two sides – to use as an inner liner for your main bag, since they offer an extra layer of warmth, are easy to wash and keep the inside of the sleeping bag cleaner. They are also useful on some of the warmer coastal tramps where the night-time temperatures are much higher.

If you are staying in the huts along the tracks you will have no need for a **sleeping mat** since mattresses are provided on all bunks. However, if you are tramping during the busiest seasons and arrive late at a hut, the beds may be taken and you may have to sleep on the floor. If you plan to camp, a mat or Thermarest can provide a layer of insulation between yourself and the cold ground, offering a degree of warmth and improving your chances of a good night's sleep.

## FOOTWEAR

Your top priority whilst tramping ought to be the condition of your feet. This will have the single biggest impact on your enjoyment of the track. Many people manage in a pair of stout trainers, though these will not support your ankles, are not waterproof, and you could get bruised and sore feet after a hard day's tramp over rocky terrain. The tracks are of rough, uneven ground and you will have to negotiate patches of loose scree, scramble over smooth, wet rocks, wade through mud and ford the occasional stream. Therefore, you will need footwear that is supportive without being too restrictive or rigid, is waterproof, has sewn-in tongues and soles that can grip even in wet conditions. What you really need is a pair of sturdy **boots** that will support your feet properly and keep them dry as well as blister free. Buy boots that have a little room at the toe end to assist blood circulation, keep your feet warmer in cold conditions and ensure that your toes don't get crushed or bruised on steep descents. It is essential to buy and break your boots in well ahead of your tramp, otherwise you may find yourself with blisters and a limp. Three- to four-season close-fitting boots are ideal.

Take a pair of **sandals** or flip flops as well. These are ideal for relieving your feet in the evenings or during long breaks on the track; they might also prove useful if you need to ford a river or tramp along a beach.

Some people choose to wear **gaiters** on some of the tougher tracks to help keep water, mud and other debris out of their boots. They also stop shins from being scratched or hooked by the undergrowth.

Wear two pairs of **socks** in order to combat blisters. Thinner silk socks should be worn under thicker hard-wearing outer socks. The under-layer prevents friction and rubbing, whilst the outer layer provides insulation. This is less important if you are wearing close-fitting modern boots as long as you continue to use good quality hiking socks. For more details on preventing and treating blisters, please see box p35.

## CLOTHES

Since most of the Great Walks take you through a range of landscapes and altitudes you will need to carry clothes that are appropriate for a range of temperatures and conditions. Adopt the simple technique of layering, remembering that it is always possible to take clothes off but impossible to put them on if you don't have them. The **base layer** should keep the skin comfortable and dry. The second, **insulation layer** should trap and retain body heat in order to provide extra warmth, whilst the **outer layer** must protect you against the wind, rain, snow and even sun.

It is vitally important that the base layer dries easily and helps to conduct sweat away from the body. Polypropylene is a popular undergarment material as it absorbs very little and so remains relatively warm when wet. **T-shirts** made of synthetic materials do the best job of 'wicking' moisture away from the body. Wool, silk or cotton are less useful for this layer.

**Fleece** is the most desirable material for the insulation layer since it is light, wind-resistant and quick-drying. Wool is also a good insulator but dries very slowly and becomes surprisingly heavy once wet. Since you will be stretching and bending forward a lot whilst scrambling or tramping over uneven ground you should try to wear something that covers your lower back adequately.

Your legs need to have as much freedom of movement as possible. **Shorts**, especially Lycra-style shorts, offer the most flexibility. Lightweight, tough **trousers** are vital on any Great Walk. Ideally these should be made of rip-stop fabric. 'John Wayne never wore Lycra,' the climber Ron Kauk may well have quipped whilst competing in blue jeans and commenting on the proliferation of Lycra-clad sport climbers. But in general avoid thick trousers, especially denim jeans, as they restrict your movement and are very heavy and difficult to dry.

New Zealand gets a lot of rainfall and good **waterproofs** are absolutely essential in any season. The weather is highly unpredictable and rain can occur pretty much all year round. Modern **raincoats** are made from lightweight, waterproof, highly breathable fabrics such as Gore-Tex that allow water vapour to pass through the jacket from the inside to the outside but don't allow water to leak in. In this way condensation is prevented from forming on the inside of the coat which would quickly drain away body heat. The coat ought to have a roomy hood that can be drawn tight but that still provides you with peripheral vision. A variety of pockets in which to store maps, snacks, etc are also useful. The sleeves need to be long enough to fit over warm under-layers and the coat needs to have a long body so that your lower back isn't exposed when you stretch, bend forward or sit down.

Wind-proof, **waterproof over-trousers** are also a sound investment. Make sure they can be put on and removed easily without the need to unlace your boots.

A **hat** provides important protection against the elements. A wide-brimmed version is a good idea to shield your eyes from the harsh sun of the mountains. A woolly **balaclava** is useful for warmth even during the summer when evening temperatures along the coast or in the mountains drop quite dramatically. Take a pair of **gloves** to keep your hands warm and your fingers flexible.

## TOILETRIES AND MEDICAL KIT

Take only those toiletries that you think you will actually need. You should aim to be well equipped but don't bring bulky items: take the smallest bottles. That said, before you set out on the actual tramp make sure that you are fully equipped with all the toiletries that you may require. Whilst New Zealand is well stocked with chemists and shops that can supply you with tampons or contraceptives, you are unlikely to encounter too many of these once you reach the trailhead and certainly won't once you've begun your tramp.

A checklist of toiletries could include:
- **A bar of soap**  Keep it in a bag or container. Liquid soap is a good idea for washing clothes. Shampoo is largely redundant. Unless you are particularly masochistic you are unlikely to be washing all that regularly in the icy cold rivers or mountain lakes. You should be aware that there are bans on using soaps and detergents, even biodegradable ones, in some waterways and lakes in New Zealand in a bid to protect the flora and fauna that live in and around them.
- **Towel**  Most outdoor shops sell special low-bulk, highly absorbent towels.
- **Toothbrush** and **toothpaste**  Take only as much toothpaste as you'll need. Buy a small tube or take a part-used one to save on space and weight.
- **Toilet paper**  Some of the most popular Great Walks have toilet paper provided at the huts but bring a roll just in case.
- **Pre-moistened tissues**  For example 'Wet-Ones'; useful.
- **Nail scissors**  Useful for trimming sharp or snagged nails.
- **Earplugs**  May help if sharing a hut with a crowd of snorers.
- **Lip balm**  Essential on higher altitude tramps where the track is exposed or on tramps where the atmosphere is drier.
- **Tampons**
- **Contraceptives**

### Medical kit

Your medical kit should cover most eventualities though hopefully you won't have to use any of it. However, most people will find they need to dip into their supplies sooner or later to sort out everyday ailments caused by tramping such as blisters. Perhaps most importantly, do not forget to take an adequate supply of any **prescription drugs** that you might need.

A basic medical kit should comprise **hydrocolloid blister pads** and **zinc-oxide tape** with a strong adhesive for securing dressings or bandages. **Plasters** are good for covering and protecting minor cuts and injuries. **Sterilised gauze** is useful should you need to soak up blood or pus from a cut or graze. It is also useful in keeping a cut clean and free from infection. **Antiseptic cream** or spray will prevent minor infections from developing. **Anti-inflammatory painkillers** such as Ibuprofen are helpful in easing the discomfort of bruises or sprains. **Hydrocortisone cream** is a good aid if you suffer from heat rash. **Mosquito repellent** is also vital to protect you from bugs and sandflies; to be really effective it needs to be at least 30% DEET. **Deep-heat spray** will ease minor sprains and help to loosen or warm-up sore muscles.

**Hypodermic needles** are essential tools for piercing blisters and removing splinters, whilst **tweezers** can be helpful for less delicate work. A pair of small, sharp **scissors** is also a good idea. **Bandages** may be needed to cover more substantial wounds or to support damaged joints. An **elasticated knee support** is helpful for week knees and useful on long, pounding descents.

High-factor **sun-cream** is vital, no matter which Great Walk you're on. **Aloe vera** is also useful in the wake of sunburn and to ease the discomfort of windburn, rashes or grazes.

Although not strictly necessary, you may wish to take **multivitamin tablets** with you on the longer tramps.

## MISCELLANEOUS ITEMS

As well as the essential items you may want to bring a few other bits and pieces on your tramp. A **watch** is very useful, for keeping track of time and gauging how far or fast you have travelled. **Sunglasses** help to cut out the sun's glare and will protect you from reflected light. A **penknife** with all of its various blades and tools is a valuable item. A reliable, compact, waterproof **torch** is a good idea since the majority of huts have no lighting, as are extra **batteries** for it. A head torch is even better as it means that both your hands are still free. **Matches** and a **lighter** are necessary to ignite cooking gear or start a fire. A **whistle** may prove to be a vital survival aid should you get lost or injured and need to attract attention. A stretch of **string** has several uses – to fasten things to the outside of your pack, for example, or to act as an impromptu washing line. A **compass** or **GPS unit** might be of interest although they are unnecessary on these well-defined tracks. Furthermore, remember that a Northern Hemisphere compass will not function properly in the Southern Hemisphere.

Some of the huts along the more popular Great Walks are equipped with gas stoves. However, some aren't, so a **portable stove and fuel** are essential. Even on those tracks where the huts are equipped with hobs, a portable stove enables you to cook hot food on the track or boil up water for soup or tea whenever you choose. In the most popular huts competition for the hobs can be fierce and you might find that having your own stove is an advantage in this situation too. Most people settle for cheap, cartridge-based stoves, where a flame burner screws onto a small, pressurised gas canister. Some brands of canister have a valve that allows you to detach the canister from the stove before it is finished in order to pack it more easily without losing any gas. Gas cartridges and stoves are widely available in outdoor shops and equipment stores throughout New Zealand. Finally, you must remember to take (degradable) **rubbish bags** with you since it is obligatory that you pack out all your litter.

## PHOTOGRAPHIC EQUIPMENT

Mountains and landscapes are notoriously difficult to photograph well. The results often don't capture the scale or grandeur of the view and the powerful sweep and subtle colours very rarely translate well to prints. Equally, the gloomy forest interiors are a very sizeable challenge to reproduce accurately.

Good quality, compact 'point and shoot' cameras are light, tough and take adequate pictures. **Digital SLR cameras** and a couple of lenses offer more scope for creativity and increase your chance of capturing the delicate light and effects found in the mountains. A 28-300mm **zoom lens** will afford you a greater degree of compositional flexibility without adding too much weight to your bag. A **lens hood** will reduce the glare from the sun, whilst a **UV filter** will cut through the high-altitude haze. A **polariser** will also cut through the haze and deepen the blue of the sky as well as add colour and depth to lakes and coasts. For self-timer or longer exposure shots a small, lightweight, sturdy **tripod** is a good idea and a remote **shutter-release cable** is a good investment too.

A **carrying case** that can be attached to your belt or waist strap is useful since it means that your equipment will be well protected and still be readily accessible. If you have to stop, drop your pack and rummage about for your camera you may be less inclined to use it. Make sure that your camera bag is waterproof since there is a very high likelihood that you'll encounter rain, especially in Fiordland or on Stewart Island.

For film users, the best all-round **film speeds** to use whilst tramping are 100 or 200ISO since the mountain light can be very bright. The native forest in New Zealand tends to be dense and the resultant light levels can be very low. In this instance you might want to use a more sensitive film, such as a 400ISO, in order to avoid the need for longer exposures. Fuji, Kodak and Agfa are the most popular brands and these can be found throughout New Zealand.

## MONEY

**Travellers' cheques** are still the safest way of carrying quantities of money abroad. They also attract a slightly better exchange rate than cash. American Express, Visa and Thomas Cook travellers' cheques are all widely recognised and accepted. These can be readily exchanged at banks and bureaux de change throughout New Zealand. At most banks you won't incur a service charge for converting travellers' cheques into cash. Keep a separate record of your travellers' cheque numbers so that you can obtain a refund if they're stolen or lost.

**Credit or debit cards** are a good alternative to travellers' cheques. The ATMs of most New Zealand banks will allow you to access your account at home. Stick to using your own bank's ATMs and you should avoid any nasty hidden charges.

New Zealand also operates an EFTPOS scheme (Electric Funds Transfer at Point of Sale). An EFTPOS card is akin to a switch/debit card except you pay for goods and services by entering a PIN number rather than giving a signature.

## MAPS

New Zealand is well covered by detailed maps. Look at websites 🖥 www .linz.govt.nz and 🖥 www.maps.co.nz in order to see exactly what is available.

The Parkmap 273 series consists of a single sheet for each national park. The scale varies between 1:50,000 and 1:250,000 depending upon the size of the national park, an insufficient scale for tramping though it is useful during the preparation stages of a trip. The Parkmap 274 series covers the 20 forest parks (or conservation parks) in the same manner.

The NZMS Topographic Map (aka Topomaps) 262 series covers areas of land measuring 150km by 200km at 1:250,000 scale. Eighteen maps cover the entire country and are again useful in terms of putting places in context and helping you plan your trip.

The Topographic Map 260 series has been designed primarily for outdoor use, with 300 maps at 1:50,000 scale covering almost the entire country. The maps feature 20m contour intervals, shading and colour coding in order to assist with the visualisation of the terrain. However, these maps are rarely updated and can be quite old; maps of the more popular areas tend to be the more accurate. From these have grown a series of specialised maps that cover the national parks and other features of note. They vary in scale from 1:50,000 to 1:80,000.

There is also a series of Info Trackmaps that have been produced especially for trampers. This limited series covers many of the most popular tramps at a scale of between 1:50,000 and 1:75,000.

For people using digital mapping, the program to try is Map Toaster Topo (🖥 www.maptoaster.com), which offers the user every 1:50,000 scale map for the entire country, or for each island. It also has search tools, integrated aerial photography and is GPS compatible. Although the program may sound expensive at several hundred New Zealand dollars, it is still considerably cheaper than buying every paper map.

## RECOMMENDED READING

There is a wealth of material published about New Zealand. Practical and illustrated guides abound and there are many fiction titles that are very firmly rooted in New Zealand and consequently give an excellent impression of certain aspects of the country. Whilst there you should try to pick up a copy of *New Zealand Wilderness*, a magazine featuring a host of articles on tramping and the countryside.

### Guidebooks

All the major travel publishers produce practical guides to New Zealand. Rough Guide, Lonely Planet and Footprint all have credible, well-researched guides. Insight and Eyewitness both produce more heavily illustrated books. Craig Potton publishes a range of very attractive photographic guides to New Zealand. His *Moment and Memory* and *Lost in New Zealand*, as well as *New Zealand Photographs* by Scott Freeman, and *New Zealand Landscapes* and

*New Zealand Horizons*, both by Andris Apse, are superb and beautiful pictorial representations of the country. Craig Potton also publishes an innovative range of books aimed at people travelling through New Zealand that uses digital imaging and virtual reality mapping technology from Geographx to create incredible, almost 3-D representations of the countryside and enabling the near-photographic quality presentation of landscape features. Titles include *Travelling New Zealand* by Simon Henshaw, which is a guide to 45 top visitor destinations throughout the country.

There are several high quality books that are more specifically about tramping in New Zealand. The majority of these are published in the country and are widely available there. Some of the titles can also be found in specialist travel bookshops such as Edward Stanfords (12-14 Long Acre, Covent Garden; ☎ 020-7836 0189, 🖥 www.stanfords.co.uk) or New Zealand specialist Kiwifruits (☎ 020-7930 4587, 🖥 www.kiwifruitsnzshop.com, 6-7 Royal Opera Arcade, Pall Mall), both in London.

The lavishly illustrated *Classic Walks of New Zealand* by Craig Potton and *Classic Tramping in New Zealand* by Shaun Burnett, both published by Craig Potton, are over-sized photographic route guides that capture the essence of the wilderness. *The Trampers Guide to New Zealand National Parks* by Robbie Burton and *101 Great Tramps in New Zealand* by Mark Pickering, both published by Reed New Zealand, are good introductions to the tramping options in the country. Lonely Planet also publishes *Tramping in New Zealand*.

There is also a selection of books concerned with only certain areas of the country. *The Restless Land: Stories of Tongariro National Park* (DOC) is a good introduction to the natural and social history of the park. *A Park For All Seasons*, produced by the Abel Tasman National Park, provides the best insight into the area. The *North-West Tramping Guide* by Derek Shaw (Nikau Press) is a comprehensive guide to this region of South Island. *Moir's Guidebook: South* (New Zealand Alpine Club) is essential reading for those wishing to tramp in Fiordland. Hodder Moa Beckett also publishes slim guides to walking the Abel Tasman, Routeburn and Milford tracks.

There are several excellent guides to New Zealand's flora and fauna. Geoff Moon is the author of the *Reed Guide to New Zealand Wildlife* and the *Reed Guide to New Zealand Birds*. Also by Reed, John Salmon wrote *Native Trees of New Zealand* and *Native New Zealand Flowering Plants*; whilst Murdoch Riley is responsible for the excellent *New Zealand Trees and Ferns* (Viking Sevenseas).

### Fiction

New Zealand's most internationally renowned author is probably Katherine Mansfield. Her concise, penetrating examinations of human behaviour set in New Zealand provide a good insight into the country at the end of the nineteenth and beginning of the twentieth centuries. *The Collected Stories of Katherine Mansfield* contains more than 70 of her short stories as well as a number of unfinished fragments.

Equally distinguished in New Zealand is Frank Sargeson, whose novels from the 1930s to 1980s are characterised by incisive, sharp dialogue that captures the essence of the country: for a good introduction to his work try *The Stories of Frank Sargeson*, an anthology of his finest short stories. Maurice Gee is also highly rated and his *Plumb Trilogy* novels cover three generations of New Zealanders. As an introduction to the current literary crop, try the *Picador Book of Contemporary New Zealand Fiction*, containing extracts and short stories by the best living authors in the country.

There are several authors who provide searing insights into what life is like in contemporary New Zealand for the Maori. The highly prolific Maori author Witi Ihimaera is one such. His novels *The Matriarch*, *Tangi*, *Bulibasha*, *Pounamu, Pounamu* and *The Whale Rider* are all widely available. The last of these has also been made into a well-received film. Another is Patricia Grace, whose novel *Potiki* is an emotive, poetic account of a Maori community coming to terms with its place in modern New Zealand whilst its land is threatened by developers. Her other novels, *Baby no Eyes*, *Tu* and *Dogside Story* also consider and portray events from the Maori perspective.

Keri Hulme's haunting tale, *The Bone People*, set on the South Island's west coast, blends myth, mysticism and reality into a visionary fable and won the 1985 Booker Prize. Lloyd Jones was Booker-shortlisted for his novel *Mister Pip* that dealt with an unreported war on a Pacific Island. His other books, including *Here at the End of the World We Learn to Dance*, a sensuous story about dance and love, and *The Book of Fame*, which fictitiously chronicles the All Black rugby tour to Britain at the start of the 20th century, also provide engrossing insights into aspects of New Zealand. Ian Cross's account of a boy trapped between two warring parents, *The God Boy,* is rated as New Zealand's equivalent to *Catcher in the Rye*. Alan Duff is another acclaimed author whose books have been translated into film. His brutal, passionate tale of 1970s Maori living in South Auckland, *Once Were Warriors*, is probably his best-known title.

### Film

Although best known for the *Lord of the Rings* trilogy, which was shot in New Zealand, the country's film industry has enjoyed limited success, with resources, infrastructure and money all missing. However, there are a number of notable exceptions. Peter Jackson, the man behind *Lord of the Rings,* has made a number of well-received flicks including *Bad Taste*, *Forgotten Silver* and the Oscar nominated *Heavenly Creatures*.

Jane Campion, another of the country's best-known directors, has produced the inspiring *Angel at my Table* and the moody *The Piano*. Brad McGann's emotionally draining *In My Father's Den* is based on a novel by Maurice Gee, whilst Alan Duff's story of poor Maori in Auckland, *Once Were Warriors*, was made into a hard-hitting film by Lee Tamahori.

Vincent Ward's *The Navigator* garnered praise for its stylistic approach whilst Roger Donaldson's *The World's Fastest Indian*, about Kiwi Burt Munro, is a genuinely heart-warming tale. Comedies include Robert Sarkies' blackly funny *Scarfies*, Ian Mune's *Came a Hot Friday* and Taika Waititi's *Eagle versus Shark*, proving that not all the films to make it out of New Zealand have to be sombre affairs.

## ❏ USEFUL WEBSITES

There is a multitude of websites that can help you plan every aspect of your trip. Below is just a selection of some of the more useful ones.

### General New Zealand websites

❏ **www.newzealand.com** 100% Pure New Zealand official tourism site; ❏ **www .purenz.com** New Zealand Tourism Board site; ❏ **www.immigration.govt.nz** Visa details; ❏ **www.destination-nz.com** New Zealand listings site; ❏ **www.nz.com** New Zealand guide and news resource; ❏ **www.govt.nz** General information on New Zealand; ❏ **www.kiwinewz.com** News resource; ❏ **www.new-zealand.com** Comprehensive online guide to the country.

### Tramping

❏ **www.doc.govt.nz** Department of Conservation site; ❏ **www.fmc.org.nz** Federated Mountain Club of New Zealand site; ❏ **www.mountainsafety.org.nz** Designed to promote outdoor skills; ❏ **www.nzalpine.org.nz** New Zealand Alpine Club site; ❏ **www.gorp.com** Outdoors recreation site; ❏ **www.wildtrek.com** *New Zealand Wilderness* magazine site; ❏ **www.walksofnz.com** Tramping site; ❏ **www .tongarirocrossing.co.nz** Site dedicated to the one-day crossing; ❏ **www.abeltas man.co.nz** Site devoted to the national park; ❏ **www.backpack-newzealand.com** General site on travelling around New Zealand with some good detailed information on the Great Walks; ❏ **www.tramper.co.nz** Online tramping guide including noticeboard advertising for tramping companions.

### City guides

The following websites are the official sites to the gateway towns and cities: ❏ **www .aucklandnz.com**; ❏ **www.wellingtonnz.com**; ❏ **www.queenstown-nz.co.nz**; ❏ **http://nelsonnz.co.nz**.

### Transport

❏ **www.intercitycoach.co.nz** Coach timetable and routes; ❏ **www.newmans coach .co.nz** Coach timetable and routes; ❏ **www.tranzrail.co.nz** Rail and ferry details; ❏ **www.stewartislandexperience.co.nz** Ferry details to Stewart Island; ❏ **www .stewartislandflights.com** Flight times to Stewart Island; ❏ **www.drivingnz.com** Full of information from road rules to estimated journey times and distances; ❏ **www .aatravel.co.nz** Suggested itineraries, time and distance planners and directions; ❏ **www.transit.govt.nz/road** Section dedicated to motoring tourists; ❏ **www .tourism.net.nz** Range of car, motorbike and bicycle hire companies listed.

### Accommodation

The following websites offer pictures and information on some of the many hundreds of campsites, B&Bs, homestays, hotels and motels throughout the country:
❏ **www.backpack.co.nz**; ❏ **www.heritagehotels.co.nz**; ❏ **www.heritageinns.co .nz**; ❏ **www.nzhomestay.co.nz**; ❏ **www.aaguides.co.nz**; ❏ **www.bnb.co.nz**.

### Birdlife

These websites offer images, descriptions and information on the country's avifauna: ❏ **www.nzbirds.com**; ❏ **www.forest-bird.org.nz**.

# Route options

New Zealand is justifiably known amongst walkers as an outstanding destination renowned for its remarkable diversity of scenery and land-forms. The Great Walks take you to some of the most remote, beautiful places in the country. It is very difficult to compare the walks with each other since they are incredibly varied and your experience of them can be affected by so many factors: the time of year, the weather, the people that you encounter and share the track with and your own mood. Each Great Walk has its own defining characteristics but between them they encompass some of the finest tramping routes in the world.

## FACTS AND FIGURES

A considerable number of people descend on the New Zealand countryside with the intention of tackling the Great Walks. However, some walks are more popular than others. Attracted at least in part by its accessibility and its reputation for being easy, around 30,000 trampers tackle the **Abel Tasman Coast Track** each year, with another 150,000 visiting on day trips. The **Routeburn Track** is the second most popular route, with around 14,500 independent trampers each year. The two other Great Walks in Fiordland are also very popular: 14,000 independent trampers complete the **Milford Track**, whilst approximately 8500 people walk the **Kepler Track**. Around 5000 people follow the **Tongariro Northern Circuit** although many, many more tackle the walk's most spectacular section, the one-day Tongariro Alpine Crossing.

The **Heaphy** and **Lake Waikaremoana** tracks each attract approximately 5000-5500 trampers every year, while 4000 canoeists paddle the length of the **Whanganui River Journey**, although plenty more complete part of it or simply enjoy day trips. The **Rakiura Track** is comparatively deserted, with only 1500-2000 people travelling to Stewart Island to tramp the path.

---

### Te Araroa – The Long Pathway

New Zealanders have dreamed of constructing a track the length of the country since the 1970s. In recent years a private group, the Te Araroa Trust, in consultation with local authorities, regional groups, *iwi* and other interested groups have begun to construct and connect 2900km worth of trails with the aim of producing just such a path. The impressive, epic route (🖳 www.teararoa.org.nz) is slated to open in 2010, when especially built sections of trail will join existing tracks or forestry roads to form a continuous route running the length of the country. Although designed to explore remote sections of countryside, the path detours via small communities so trampers will be able to restock en route. The idea is that people will be able to walk from Cape Reinga (northern tip of North Island) to Bluff (southern tip of South Island) in one go, but in reality most people will probably tackle only shorter sections.

## PROS AND CONS OF EACH ROUTE

The enchanting **Lake Waikaremoana Track** lies amidst a vast unbroken mantle of forested ridges and valleys. This moderate three- to four-day, 46km tramp skirts the moody waters of Lake Waikaremoana, climbs the precipitous bluffs of the Panekiri Range and meanders through eerie moss-draped forest. The track can be walked in either direction and offers an insight into an isolated, unspoilt area. Its remoteness means it's difficult to get there, but is also part of its appeal.

The three- to four-day, 49km **Tongariro Northern Circuit** cuts an arc around the perfect cone of Mt Ngauruhoe through probably the most spectacular and colourful part of Tongariro National Park, a volcanically active 'moonscape'

---

### OTHER ACTIVITIES IN NEW ZEALAND
Although synonymous with tramping, New Zealand is in fact an outdoor enthusiast's paradise, with a multitude of options to consider.

**On rivers and waterways** To take advantage of the country's many rivers and waterways try **canoeing** or **whitewater rafting**. The numerous rapids, stunning scenery and remote locations mean that from October to May this is an excellent, adrenaline-fuelled way of exploring chunks of the land not readily accessible by road. The Shotover and Kawarau rivers near Queenstown are perhaps the best known but there are plenty of other options, including rivers around Rotorua and the Whanganui River; see 🖥 www.nz-rafting.co.nz for more information.

If you want to let the boat take the strain, try **jetboating** in specially designed boats capable of planing in as little as 100mm of water and reaching speeds of 80km/hr: the Shotover River adjacent to Queenstown is particularly popular, whilst there are also good options on the Whanganui River on North Island.

For a more relaxing alternative consider **fishing** for rainbow or brown trout, quinnat or salmon: Taupo is world famous, although the waterways running off the eastern side of the Southern Alps are also hard to beat. You will, however, need a licence (see 🖥 www.fishandgame.org.nz) to take part legitimately.

**In and on the sea** With so much coastline it was inevitable that the beach would become a focal point for so many Kiwis.

**Swimming** can be a little hazardous on the West Coast as there are strong currents and pounding waves. However, there are numerous pristine white-sand beaches and great swimming spots, such as those found along the Abel Tasman Coast Track at the northern end of South Island. The big waves and breakers mean that there's good **surfing** throughout the country, with boarders to be found hanging out at most of the major beach resorts, although Raglan, the Bay of Plenty and some of the beaches around Wellington are particularly popular. For more information check out 🖥 www.surf.co.nz.

**Sea kayaking** is available in the Hauraki Gulf, Abel Tasman National Park, Marlborough Sounds and throughout Fiordland. **Sailing** is a national passion, which goes some way to explaining the country's success in, and fascination with, the America's Cup. The summer months (Dec-Mar) are ideal but sailing is a year-round activity. It's often possible to hire a boat at any major harbour, for day trips or longer charters, although your best bets are Auckland and Nelson. **Scuba diving** off North Island is superb in the Hauraki Gulf and Bay of Islands, whilst the Poor Knights Islands off the east coast are rated as having some of the best dive sites in the world.

of tortured rock, dramatic lava formations and craters. The hordes of people pouring over the Tongariro Crossing are the only drawback to this unique tramp.

The **Whanganui River Journey** is not a traditional tramp – or, indeed, a tramp at all. Instead, it is an exhilarating 145km canoe trip that takes up to five days to complete, taking you through stunning scenery past fascinating relics of Maori and colonial history. It's an intriguing alternative to tramping.

Droves of people are attracted to the gorgeous golden beaches and granite coastline of the **Abel Tasman Coast Track**. Much of the three- to five-day, 51km track involves leisurely strolls along coarse sand beaches, making it ideal for trampers of all abilities. Huts and campsites are positioned alongside pic-

The Poor Knights Islands also afford you the chance to dive the wreck of the Greenpeace flagship *Rainbow Warrior*. At the other end of the country, Milford Sound also offers some unusual diving opportunities.

**On land**  Land-based activities include **mountain biking**, especially around Rotorua, Nelson, Queenstown and Mount Cook (check out 🖥 www.mountainbike.co .nz) and **horse riding**, through tracts of native bush, along some of the country's beaches and across vast swathes of farmland (see 🖥 www.ridenz.com).

**Canyoning** and **coasteering** are great ways of getting adrenaline flowing, with the best spots around Auckland, Queenstown and Wanaka. For the single biggest rush try **bungy jumping**, pioneered as a commercial sport in New Zealand, or the increasingly popular variation **bridge swinging**, which is like bungy jumping but with a swing rather than simply a vertical fall. Essentially it's a gut-wrenching fall and superfast swing along a gorge whilst harnessed to a cable. Queenstown is the spiritual home of the sport, but Taupo and Rotorua are also very popular.

**On the mountains**  To revel in the country's mountains or follow in the footsteps of one of the country's most famous sons Sir Edmund Hillary, consider **mountaineering** or **climbing**, either on the relatively straightforward summits of Mount Ruapehu or Mount Taranaki, or as part of a guided expedition up the classic peaks of Aoraki Mount Cook, New Zealand's highest mountain, and Mount Aspiring. Details and climbing information can be found at 🖥 www.climb.co.nz. **Skiing** and **snowboarding** are increasingly popular from June to November, with North Island's volcanoes and the Southern Alps gaining an international reputation for their facilities and good quality powder. If you're after remote, off-piste experiences consider **heli-skiing** in the Southern Alps. For more information see the annual guide available at 🖥 www.brownbear.co.nz or 🖥 www.snow.co.nz.

**In the air**  Even the skies above New Zealand offer opportunities for adventure, with tandem **skydiving**, particularly in Fiordland, a popular way of raising your heart rate. Tandem **paragliding** is also usually available.

**For those who prefer to observe**  If exhausted by participating in any or all of the above, you can catch your breath as a spectator at one of the many rugby matches played throughout the winter. Beginning with the Super 14 series from Feb to May, you can also catch the tri-nations matches between the All Blacks and South Africa and Australia in July and August. During the summer cricket takes over, and the Black Caps, as the national team are known, become the focus for the country's sports fans.

turesque coves and inlets. This is the easiest, safest, sunniest Great Walk, although it is also the busiest. Not a track for those who don't like crowds, this is nonetheless coastal walking at its finest.

The 82km **Heaphy Track** is the longest and most diverse tramp of all the Great Walks. This moderately hard, four- to five-day tramp climbs through lush forest, winds across haunting alpine downs and then drops to the rugged west coast where it ambles alongside the pounding Tasman Sea. Since each end of the track is remote it's relatively difficult to reach and also to leave, especially by private transport as, being a linear trek, you have to go back to where you left your vehicle to collect it. The west-coast weather is also highly unpredictable.

The **Routeburn Track** usually takes two or three days. The 33km traverse linking Mt Aspiring and Fiordland national parks is gloriously remote. The encircling panorama of snow-capped mountains is astonishing and the serenity and stillness of Lake Mackenzie and Lake Harris is exquisite.

The accumulation of natural beauty and the endless variations of shape and colour make this an exceptional tramp. However, the trek is exposed in places and in bad weather can become treacherous. You must also book the track in advance.

The world-famous **Milford Track** is 53.5km long and takes four days to complete. It enjoys enormous popularity so you must book well in advance in order to secure a place. Located in the heart of dramatic Fiordland National Park it is a relatively easy tramp save for the testing climb to Mackinnon Pass and the steep descent into the Arthur Valley. The glacier-gouged scenery is breathtaking and the views from the top of the pass awe-inspiring. Although the track is heavily regulated and over-popular, it has a well-deserved, worldwide reputation. It is, however, the only trek where camping is not allowed.

Fiordland's third Great Walk, the 67km, three- to four-day **Kepler Track** is unique in its custom-made design as a circular route. This is one of the best-planned Great Walks. It circles Lake Te Anau before climbing stiffly onto Mt Luxmore, from where it makes an amazing alpine traverse of the Kepler tops before dropping to the tranquil shores of Lake Manapouri. The sheer immensity of the landscape and mountain splendour is breathtaking. The track is quite tough and an increase in popularity means that a booking scheme has been introduced.

The 36km, two- to three-day **Rakiura Track** is an appealing introduction to the subtle charms and unspoilt wilderness of Stewart Island. This relatively simple circular track passes through several areas of historical interest including settlements occupied by Maori and Europeans. This truly remarkable place is sufficiently isolated to ensure far fewer trampers than on other Great Walks. However, it can also suffer from atrocious weather that turns the track into a complete quagmire.

# Health: precautions and inoculations

New Zealand is one of the safest holiday destinations in the world, with high standards of health and hygiene. However, any form of outdoor physical activity carries with it the possibility of accidents and tramping is no exception. There are certain golden rules to follow on the track that will help to minimise the risk of accidents or getting lost such as always filling out the intentions books at each hut (see box below). These rules are outlined on pp39-41.

## PRE-DEPARTURE PREPARATION

### Fitness
Most people launch into the Great Walks without too much training. However, if you lead a mostly sedentary existence it may be wise to do a little pre-departure exercise before tramping. Any type of exercise is better than none at all. Alternatively, make sure that you ease into the tracks once you reach New Zealand. Start with some gentler, shorter routes before building up to the more arduous multi-day tramps.

If you need a particular type of **medication**, acquire an adequate supply in advance as it may not be as readily available once you get to New Zealand. If you are carrying a quantity of medication into the country you should bring a doctor's certificate to avoid any potential problems at New Zealand customs.

### Inoculations
No inoculations are officially required to enter New Zealand. However, it is wise to make sure that your **tetanus** vaccination is up to date. Tetanus boosters are required every ten years. You may also wish to consider getting vaccinated against **hepatitis A and B**.

---

**Intentions Book**
Each Great Walk hut has an 'Intentions Book' in it. These are usually used to record who is using the hut and where they are heading, thus helping wardens in their search for any missing trampers. They also have a comments section allowing trampers to express their thoughts, compliments and criticisms. This can sometimes lead to a running debate between trampers over a period of time.

For example, the DOC (see box p37) is responsible for cutting overgrown vegetation from the tracks. One ungrateful tramper observed in the hut book, 'Whoever trimmed the bottom kilometre of the track should go back and sweep it! It is dangerous with off-cuts strewn over the track – the track is knee-wrenching enough without the added problem.' Some wag had later added 'I agree, DOC staff should also get up and sweep the head of the valley – it's very messy with avalanche debris.'

If you require further advice, travel clinics are good sources of information. In the UK, Nomad Travellers Store and Medical Centre (☎ 020-7833 4114, 🖥 www.nomadtravel.co.uk; 40 Bernard St, Russell Square, London) has a clinic that can carry out on-the-spot vaccinations. There are other branches at London's Turnpike Lane (☎ 020-8889 7014), Bristol (☎ 0117-922 6567) and Southampton (☎ 023-8023 4920).

Alternatively, consult the official website of the World Health Organisation (🖥 www.who.ch) for the latest health recommendations for international travel.

## Insurance

A comprehensive policy that covers theft, loss and medical problems is recommended. You are strongly advised to consider health insurance if you are undertaking any outdoor activity such as tramping.

That said, personal injury is covered by the local **Accident Compensation Scheme**. Benefits include some medical and hospital expenses but do not include the loss of earnings outside of New Zealand. For this reason ensure your insurance policy covers accidents.

Make sure, too, that you check to see what activities are covered by your insurance and, even more importantly, what aren't, as 'dangerous activities' including tramping may not be automatically included. Your policy should also cover ambulances and emergency medical evacuations by air.

A private company, **Accident Info Services** (☎ 09-529 0488 or ☎ 0800-263 345), has been established to advise travellers in New Zealand on how best to find medical attention. This is a 24hr service.

## HEALTH

The most common complaint in New Zealand is **sunburn**. The country's clear, unpolluted atmosphere and proximity to a hole in the ozone layer means that the sunlight here is much stronger than in Europe or the USA. It is possible to get burnt surprisingly quickly, even on apparently overcast days. Wear a hat and high-factor sun-cream to avoid getting burnt. Sun can do just as much damage to your eyes, so protect them by wearing sunglasses.

The cold can also be a hazard when you are tramping. The weather in New Zealand is highly changeable and you should be prepared for sudden drops in temperature. Cold, wet and windy conditions can sometimes be the cause of **hypothermia**, and several people die from it in New Zealand every year. General awareness, being properly equipped and the ability to react to any symptoms promptly should prevent a serious incident.

New Zealand is free of snakes. It is also largely free of venomous insects. The katipo is New Zealand's only **poisonous spider**. This diminutive arachnid is a relative of the infamous black widow spider. It has a potentially fatal bite although in reality very few deaths ever occur. The katipo can be found in coastal areas, where it spins small webs in the forest or in driftwood. It is likely to bite only if disturbed or provoked. There is an effective antivenom, which can be successfully administered even a few days after the bite.

You are much more likely to be bitten by **sandflies**, particularly in Fiordland or along the west coast. These tiny insects leave an irritating, itchy swelling that takes a couple of days to go down. The use of insect repellents or DEET-based lotions should prevent bites.

## Giardia

Giardia is a parasite that lives in the intestine. Invisible to the naked eye it can cause severe diarrhoea that in turn may lead to chronic dehydration.

Giardia can be spread by any mammal. It can occur in humans as the result of poor personal hygiene, the unhygienic handling of food and by drinking water contaminated by the hardy cysts of the parasite. Symptoms usually appears about a week after the body has been exposed to the parasite. These include explosive, foul-smelling diarrhoea, stomach cramps, bloating, dehydration, nausea and weight loss since the infection prevents food from being absorbed properly in the upper part of the gut.

In order to be absolutely safe on the Great Walks you should **treat all drinking water**. Although much of the water is perfectly safe, even clear-flowing streams may carry the parasite. Before drinking the water you should either boil it vigorously for more than three minutes to kill the cysts, treat it with iodine or chlorine tablets or filter the water through a giardia-rated filter.

Treatment is quick and easy. If you suspect that you have contracted the infection seek medical advice. The usual cure is a course of antibiotics, either 250mg of metronidazole three times a day for five to ten days or a single 2g dose of tinidazole. You ought to be able to find one of these drugs in pharmacies.

---

### Blisters

Blisters are the bane of trampers and their most common complaint. Friction between the boot and the foot causes a protective layer of liquid to develop beneath the skin. This can take four or five days to heal properly. As with so many things, prevention is far better than cure. By taking the necessary steps and precautions in advance you ought to be able to avoid them altogether. Firstly, make sure that you break in all footwear well in advance of the tramp. Wear two pairs of socks, for the inner layer will prevent rubbing. Never tramp with wet feet as this is a sure-fire way of getting blisters. If your boots get soaked wear plastic bags over dry socks in order to prevent them becoming damp too. Change into dry socks when you take a break on the trail. Most importantly, never ignore the feeling that your boots may be rubbing; cover the sore area with zinc-oxide tape, a plaster or a specialised blister pad. This will act as an additional layer of skin and should stop the chafing. Vaseline or, at a push, lip salve or even butter, when rubbed onto a sore toe or heel, can also stop abrasion and delay the onset of a blister.

There are minor adjustments that you can make to your boots, depending on the terrain, that will help to stave off blisters. Whilst going uphill tighten the upper section of your boot and loosen the laces slightly across the foot. Conversely, when descending, loosen the upper part a little and tighten the laces across the foot.

Should you develop blisters use a clean hypodermic syringe to burst them. Allow the blister to dry out, then apply antiseptic cream and a dressing to keep it covered and free from infection. Salt water is particularly good at hardening blistered skin.

# PART 2: MINIMUM IMPACT & SAFE TRAMPING

## Minimum impact tramping

New Zealand's national parks are coming under increasing amounts of pressure from escalating visitor numbers. The continued tourist boom and the sustained advertising of New Zealand's natural wonders has inevitably led to a relentless rise in the number of people who wish to explore the wilderness and experience some of the country's beauty for themselves.

The Department of Conservation (DOC; see box opposite) is charged with managing and preserving New Zealand's national parks and wild places. In a bid to minimise the impact that visitors have on the landscape, the DOC has produced a countrywide Environmental Care Code and everyone who ventures into the wilderness is expected to abide by it. In order to ensure that the parks remain clean and unspoilt and to prevent the authorities having to take more draconian measures, all trampers must adopt this code of practice whilst in the wilderness. You must also be aware that some activities and practices are banned or require a permit; furthermore, domestic pets must not be taken into national parks. Hunting and fishing are allowed in most areas, but an up-to-date permit must be obtained from the DOC before you enter the park.

### ENVIRONMENTAL IMPACT

'Hutia te rito o te pu harakeke       *From where*
Kei whea te komako e ko?'            *Will the bellbird sing?*

A traditional Maori plea for conservation, ie if you destroy the flax plant, from where will the bellbird sing?

### *Toito te whenua* – Leave the land undisturbed

Damaged vegetation, litter, polluted waterways, deteriorating facilities and an increase in erosion are all indications that trampers have had a negative impact on a landscape. Luckily people are now much more conscious of the potential impact that they can have on the environment and are more likely to adopt a considerate, responsible attitude whilst tramping in or otherwise enjoying the national parks. It's important we maintain this new-found responsibility.

### Protect plants and wildlife

Take care of habitats and wildlife. Many of New Zealand's flora and fauna species are unique, vulnerable or endangered. Do not disturb or remove anything that you find in the national parks. If you wish to observe wildlife or birds use a pair of binoculars and maintain your distance.

> **The Department of Conservation**
> The Department of Conservation (DOC) is a central government organisation that is responsible for conserving the natural and historic heritage of New Zealand. The organisation's Maori name, Te Papa Atawhai, encapsulates its mission: *Te Papa* literally means 'Our Place', and *atawhai* is the art of preserving or caring.
> The DOC was formed in 1987 when the New Zealand Department of Lands and the New Zealand Forest Service merged. The organisation now oversees and manages the running of New Zealand's national parks, conservation areas, protected lands and waterways, minimising threats to native species and habitats and ensuring the maintenance and protection of historic places on conservation land. As such, the DOC is responsible for the running and maintenance of each of the Great Walks.

### Remove rubbish

Human detritus is one of the most significant threats to the natural environment. Litter is unsightly and a potential hazard for wildlife. An accumulation of rubbish encourages vermin such as rats, mice and possums. It is also a breeding ground for disease, which can affect wildlife and people equally.

There used to be rubbish pits adjacent to each hut along the tracks but this practice has been discouraged and trampers are now obliged to carry any litter they generate out of the national park with them when they leave. You should **carry (degradable) rubbish bags** with you for this very purpose and be conscious of the amount of litter that you are likely to create when preparing to tramp. Where possible reuse bags or containers rather than simply throwing them away.

If you come across litter in the park you should remove it if at all possible.

Toilet facilities are provided on all the Great Walks. However, if you do have to dispose of **toilet waste** bury it in a shallow hole, making sure that it isn't near the track, waterways, huts or places where people camp. Ideally all toilet-paper waste should be burnt or at the very least buried in the same hole.

### Keep streams and lakes clean

New Zealand's waterways and lakes are fragile ecosystems. Contamination can easily lead to a deterioration of water quality. In order to reduce the chance of polluting these important habitats there are several practices that you should adopt. Wherever possible use the toilet facilities that are provided. If no facilities are to hand make sure that all waste is buried in a shallow hole away from any waterways.

For washing yourself, clothes or utensils, collect some water and carry it away from the source; soaps and detergents can be highly detrimental to water-based flora and fauna, so should not be used in rivers or lakes. Don't throw used water back into a stream or lake; rather pour it onto the soil so that it has a chance to be filtered before re-entering the water system.

For your own health you should treat water before drinking (see p35). This should minimise the chances of contracting waterborne illnesses such as giardia, which although rare are occasionally present in New Zealand's waterways.

MINIMUM IMPACT & SAFE TRAMPING

## Take care with stoves and fires

Fire can have a devastating impact on the natural environment. Camp fires, matches and cigarettes all have the potential to start a fire. This is particularly true during the summer season when much of the countryside can be tinder dry. You must also adhere to any **fire regulations** and any bans that have been put in place.

When cooking, use a **portable stove** rather than build a fire. Take all empty gas canisters out of the national park with you. If you have to build a fire see Fires opposite before you start.

## Camp carefully

On the Great Walks you must pitch your tent at designated campsites only. Resist the urge to spread yourself out and instead try to keep your campsite as small as possible. Once you have finished with your tent pitch leave the area undisturbed.

## Keep to the track

The Great Walks usually follow clear, well-cut tracks. Try to stay on these established trails wherever possible in a bid to reduce any potential damage to the landscape. Don't be tempted to take short-cuts, particularly on long sections of track that include switchbacks. Laborious as it may seem, stick to the path as it winds downhill. Some habitats are very fragile and can suffer irreparable damage very easily. Take particular care when crossing wetland areas, moss bogs, alpine herb fields or whilst tramping along coastal areas.

## CULTURAL IMPACT

Whilst you are tramping try to be considerate to other visitors and users of the countryside. Try to keep noise to a minimum. As a general rule, be selfless and remember that you are only *visiting*.

## Respect the cultural heritage

New Zealand is awash with sites of special cultural and historical importance. The Maori hold that a few natural sites and features are *tapu*, sacred. There are also a host of important European historical sites. Treat these locations with the respect that they deserve. To fully appreciate and understand the cultural value of the place that you are visiting you ought to spend some time learning about its people (see p59) and history (p47-58).

## ECONOMIC IMPACT

Tourism is a major industry in New Zealand and contributes quite significantly to the country's economy. It is a good source of foreign revenue.

Tramping in New Zealand is a relatively cheap way of seeing the country and experiencing the wilderness. In return for the small investment of a hut or campsite pass you are entitled to stay in good quality back-country huts or on campsites in some truly outstanding areas.

These facilities can be maintained only if people continue to pay the requisite fees and give the DOC a much needed cash injection. Although sometimes there are wardens in the most popular huts to check passes, it is every tramper's obligation to make sure that they abide by the rules and contribute to the upkeep of the facilities. By paying your hut and campsite fees you are helping to ensure that staples such as mattresses and gas for stoves are provided and that repairs are carried out to ageing huts.

As any tramper in New Zealand will soon notice, the Great Walks are superbly maintained and kept to a very high standard. A little thought and consideration should ensure that they remain that way.

# Safe tramping

The New Zealand wilderness can be an unforgiving environment. However, since it is free from predatory animals, poisonous snakes and other dangerous creatures, the most significant threat to trampers is the weather ... and their own foolhardiness. As long as you are well-prepared, properly equipped and know what you are doing, you should be able to enjoy the countryside with the minimum of risk to yourself or others. Nonetheless, a few people do die in the mountains every year. By learning a few basic survival techniques you can avoid being one of them.

Make sure that you select a track that is appropriate for your level of fitness and ability. Inexperienced trampers should choose easier routes, such as the Lake Waikaremoana or Abel Tasman tracks, that don't involve long days or particularly tough sections. Give yourself plenty of time to complete each day's tramp and aim to finish well before dark. Before setting out check on the weather forecast and current track conditions; the local DOC office or information centre are the most useful sources. Bear in mind that the weather is very changeable.

Every hut along the Great Walks is equipped with an **intentions book** (see box p33). It is good practice to fill these in upon arrival at the huts. As well as enabling the DOC to gauge how popular the hut is, the books are useful tools in keeping track of people in the wilderness. If an individual gets lost, these books often provide rescue services with the best indication of where the tramper was headed and consequently where to begin searching for them.

There are also several general rules that should be adhered to in the wilderness with regard to both personal safety and the prevention of damage to the environment, as follows:

## FIRES

Lighting fires is generally discouraged because of the potential danger and the detrimental effect it can have on the environment. Even dead wood is an essential part of the bush ecology and shouldn't be burnt without at least first considering the consequences. However, a fire can be a very useful tool in the wilderness, for cooking, comfort and warmth.

Only build a fire if it's essential and you have no stove. When it comes to lighting a fire try to use a designated place or an existing fireplace. Ideally, light a fire on a beach between the low and high tide marks. Failing that, a gravel bank alongside a river is a safe spot. At the very least look for a sheltered spot where the fire will not be able to spread to surrounding vegetation. Use rocks to create a three-sided fireplace to prevent it spreading and do not make it unnecessarily large. Use only dry, dead wood taken from areas where it is plentiful. Do not cut branches from trees since living, green wood burns poorly. Arrange the wood in a pyramid form to create a natural chimney. Light the fire and add small pieces of kindling to it until it has begun to catch properly. Blowing at the base or fanning may encourage a stubborn fire. Once you have finished with your fire, make sure that it is properly extinguished. and douse the embers with water and cover them. Cool heated rocks with water and return them to their original place.

## RIVERS

When New Zealand was being explored by European settlers, drowning was a common cause of death. The lack of bridges in remote areas meant that fording rivers was necessary. The rivers in New Zealand are prone to frequent flooding and can be deceptively powerful. The explorer Charlie Douglas famously quipped in the 1860s that 'not being able to swim has saved my life many a time' since he was never tempted to ford a fast-flowing river.

On the Great Walks there are plenty of foot, swing and log bridges across streams and rivers. In extreme conditions these may be damaged or destroyed and you may be required to cross the river by alternative means.

**Never attempt to cross a river that is in flood or surging**. If you can see trees or other debris being swept downstream or hear the sound of rocks tumbling underwater, do not enter the water. If the river is flowing faster than walking pace it is potentially dangerous.

In general, you shouldn't try to ford the river if you can't see the bottom clearly. If you have any doubts, sit the storm out and wait for the river to subside.

If you choose to ford a river prepare in advance of entering the water. Keep your boots on or wear sandals to protect your feet; don't go barefoot. Make sure that the contents of your pack are sealed inside waterproof bags and tie any external bags to the top of the pack rather than the bottom to minimise drag. Undo the chest straps and loosen the shoulder straps so that you can jettison the pack quickly if necessary. If you don't have a reliable quick-release waist strap you should unfasten this too so the pack is hanging loosely from you.

Swing bridges (suspension bridges) span many of the rivers along the Great Walks.

Try to find a spot to cross between two gently sloping banks where the water is shallow and flowing less swiftly. Steeply inclined banks generally indicate deep water. Check further downstream for any dangers such as rapids or large boulders which you may encounter if you lose your footing and are swept away. Try to gauge the depth of the water and the speed at which it is flowing: if the river is higher than your knees and flowing at any sort of pace you will struggle to make a safe crossing – so don't try.

When actually crossing the river keep your body side-on to the current to create as little resistance as possible. Take only short, even steps, using your feet to feel the way. Try to head diagonally across the river, veering downstream so as to conserve energy during the crossing. If there are a number of you crossing the river, do so as a group. The strongest member should stand furthest upstream. Each person should grasp the clothing of the individual next to them at the hip and the group should move steadily as one.

If you do lose your footing, the best position to maintain is on your back. Lift your feet to avoid underwater snags and use them to push you away from any boulders or other hazards. By angling your body across the current you should be channelled towards the bank. Your pack will act as a natural buoyancy aid and should help to keep you afloat.

## IN THE EVENT OF AN ACCIDENT

Should you or one of your party be unlucky enough to be involved in an accident, remain calm and don't panic. If the injured person can't be moved, leave somebody with them whilst another member of the party goes for help. Try to ensure that they are as warm and comfortable as possible, with as much food and water as you can leave. Try to make sure that they are as conspicuous as possible too, and, if you can, leave them with a whistle or other means of attracting attention.

### Summoning help
The standard international emergency signal is six short blasts on a whistle (or shouts, if you don't have a whistle) or six flashes with a torch, each at ten-second intervals. Wait for a minute then repeat. If someone hears the call and responds accordingly, you should hear three signals at 20-second intervals, followed by a pause and then a second set of three signals.

### Helicopter rescue
Should a helicopter be required to evacuate an injured member of your party, you should be prepared to signal to the pilot. By standing with your arms raised above your head in a 'V' shape you signal that you need help or assistance. By standing with one arm raised above your head and the other by your side, as if one axis of the letter 'X', you are signalling that everything is okay. When the helicopter does attempt to land, make sure that you are clear of the rotors.

You should be aware of the fact that mountain rescue can be very costly and consequently you should make sure that you are properly insured before setting off on your tramp.

MINIMUM IMPACT & SAFE TRAMPING

# PART 3: NEW ZEALAND

# Facts about the country

## GEOGRAPHY

*The land has no rest, but is continuously steep up and down, as if nature had determined to try how much mountain she could place upon a given space.* Writer and explorer **Samuel Butler**, 1861, as quoted by Warren Jacobs in *The Birth of New Zealand*

New Zealand was born from the vast Pacific Ocean and lies between latitude 34°S and 47°S. Millennia of violent upheavals meant that the landmass was pushed out of the seabed. From the earliest history, volcanoes have shaped New Zealand's landscape. Eruptions have moulded the country and left a legacy of spectacular land-forms. The landscape presents a wild juxtaposition of jagged mountains and peaceful rolling hills, mysterious volcanic craters and almost tropical coastlines, tranquil fiords and lonesome islands, desolate lava fields and lush forests. It is seemingly tamed but occasionally, as with the eruptions of Mt Ruapehu in 1995-6, chooses to remind people that it is still wild at heart.

The country runs roughly north–south and is 1600km from top to bottom. The North and South Islands are the two major land masses and between them cover 266,200 sq km, making New Zealand slightly larger than Britain and roughly the same size as California. It is some 35 times smaller than the entire United States. However, its massively indented coastline is disproportionately long in comparison to its overall landmass. New Zealand equates to a world in miniature. Simply by driving across South Island you can witness an astonishing number of climatic and physical variations.

**North Island** sits on the southern edge of the 'Ring of Fire', where the Pacific plate is sliding under the Indo-Australian plate and generating a large amount of volcanic activity. Volcanic cones, both extinct and active, riddle North Island. The largest is the crater which now houses Lake Taupo, which was formed following a huge eruption in AD186. A line of volcanoes extends from White Island in the Bay of Plenty through the thermal area of Rotorua to the central volcanic plateau where Mts Tongariro, Ngauruhoe and Ruapehu are found. Further south-west is the perfect cone of Mt Taranaki.

**South Island** is characterised by the sinuous spine of grand mountains that run virtually its whole length. These have been forced up out of the sea by the collision of the two tectonic plates. The process is ongoing and the mountains are still growing slowly. Mt Cook/Aoraki (3753m/12,310ft) rises majestically out of the Southern Alps and is New Zealand's highest peak.

Natural erosion from extended periods of glaciation has further sculpted the landscape, forming the country's defining characteristics such as U-shaped valleys, moraines and deep lakes. Spectacular glaciers are still scattered throughout the country, with the most readily accessible being the Fox and Franz Josef glaciers on the west coast.

New Zealand receives a lot of rainfall and this has inevitably resulted in the landscape being covered in lakes and rivers. The longest river in the country is the Waikato, which stretches 425km from Lake Taupo to the Tasman Sea.

## National parks

*The mountains of the south wind have spoken to us for centuries. Now we wish them to speak to all who come in peace and in respect of their tapu.*

**Te Heuheu Tukino IV**, paramount chief of the Tuwharetoa, upon gifting the sacred summits of Mts Tongariro, Ngauruhoe and Ruapehu to the Crown for the creation of Tongariro National Park, 1887

New Zealand is acutely aware of the need to preserve its natural heritage. To this end 14 national parks (see map p44), three maritime reserves, two World Heritage areas, hundreds of nature reserves and ecological areas, a network of marine reserves and wetlands and further protection for special rivers and lakes have been established.

At the heart of this environmental protection scheme are the national parks. The National Park Act passed in 1980 defines these parks as 'areas of New Zealand that contain scenery of such distinct quality, ecological systems, or natural features so beautiful, unique, or scientifically important that their preservation is in the national interest' and further declares that they are to be preserved 'in perpetuity as national parks, for their intrinsic worth and for the benefit, use and enjoyment of the public'. More than 10% of the country has been set aside for the 14 national parks, which incorporate a huge diversity of landscape and vegetation offering unrivalled opportunities for outdoor activities. The best way to experience the unspoilt landscape is by tramping and all nine designated Great Walks can be found within these protected areas.

**North Island**  There are four national parks on North Island. Immense, remote **Te Urewera National Park** in the north-east is home to the largest forested wilderness remaining on North Island and the site of the spectacular Lake Waikaremoana Track. **Tongariro National Park** is the oldest national park in New Zealand and the fourth oldest in the world. Tongariro is unusual in that it has been granted dual World Heritage status in recognition of both its natural features and cultural importance. It covers the volcanic central plateau and is the site of some of New Zealand's largest and most active volcanoes as well as the Tongariro Northern Circuit.

**Egmont National Park**, on the west coast, is one of the most readily accessible parks and is centred on the dormant volcano of Mt Taranaki (also known as Mt Egmont, as christened by Captain Cook in 1770). **Whanganui National Park** encompasses the Whanganui River and surrounding forest and is the home of the memorable Whanganui River Journey.

**South Island**  On South Island the national parks capture an even more diverse range of scenery. **Abel Tasman National Park** at the top of South Island is the smallest national park. It is famous for its golden beaches, seclud-

NEW ZEALAND

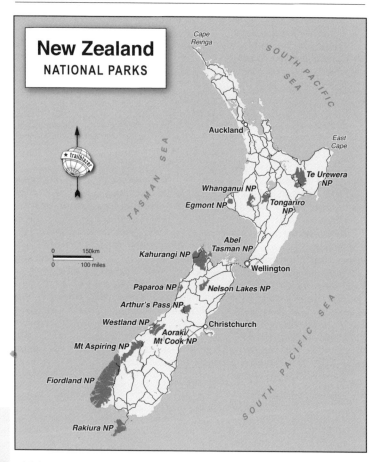

**New Zealand**
NATIONAL PARKS

Cape Reinga

SOUTH PACIFIC SEA

Auckland

East Cape

TASMAN SEA

Te Urewera NP

Whanganui NP

Egmont NP

Tongariro NP

Abel Tasman NP

Kahurangi NP

Wellington

Paparoa NP

Nelson Lakes NP

Arthur's Pass NP

Westland NP

Christchurch

Aoraki/ Mt Cook NP

Mt Aspiring NP

SOUTH PACIFIC SEA

Fiordland NP

Rakiura NP

0   150km
0   100 miles

ed inlets, sunny climate and the massively popular Coastal Track. **Kahurangi National Park** is a much less visited, more rugged area that abuts the west coast and is the site of the Heaphy Track.

   **Nelson Lakes National Park** is set at the northern end of the Southern Alps, while **Arthur's Pass National Park** lies midway down South Island on an historic link between the east and west coasts. The narrow **Westland** and the compact **Paparoa National Parks** protect the high peaks of the Southern Alps and stretch to the west coast.

   **Mount Aspiring National Park** is a World Heritage Area straddling the southern tip of the Southern Alps. **Aoraki Mount Cook National Park** is located in the central part of South Island, deep in the heart of the Southern Alps and is home to the highest peak and the longest glacier in New Zealand. One end of the Routeburn Track lies here.

**Fiordland National Park** is the largest national park and covers a vast, virtually uninhabited wilderness in the south-west corner of South Island. The importance of the park is emphasised by its designation as a World Heritage Area. It is also the site of the Routeburn, Milford and Kepler tracks. **Rakiura National Park** on Stewart Island is the newest national park and the first to be established outside the two main islands. It covers almost 90% of the island and is home to the Rakiura Track.

## CLIMATE

### Seasons

The Maori used to determine the seasons with regard to the cultivation and harvest of *kumara*, a type of Pacific sweet potato that formed part of their staple diet. During *mahura*, spring, they would till the soil and plant the seeds. The warm conditions during *raumati*, summer, would cause the crop to grow and in *ngahuru*, autumn, the crop would be harvested. The Maori would then be sustained through *takurua*, winter, by the harvest. The Maori believe that once upon a time there was no kumara on earth, rather it belonged in the sky and was jealously guarded by Whanui, the God of the Kumara. The male God of the Moon, Rongomatane, stole some kumara from Whanui's storehouse and distributed it amongst mortals. Ever since the Maori have always gathered the first kumara tubers, cooked them in a sacred fire and ceremoniously offered them up to the gods of the harvest moon.

**Winter** occurs between June and August when the weather is at its wettest and coldest whilst **summer** takes place between December and February when the days are, by and large, crisp and dry.

**Spring** officially begins on 1 September when the land is stirred into rebirth. The Maori refer to this season as '*Ka whakaniho ngo mea katoa o te whenua i konei*', the time when 'All things of the earth begin to sprout'. The forests receive a steady stream of rain and the bloom of life that follows results in a glorious floral display. The build-up to summer is slow and erratic and the weather is subject to sudden changes. The official beginning of summer is 1 December. **Autumn** traditionally starts on 1 March with a blaze of colour. Gradually the weather becomes colder and wetter as a prelude to the winter storms in July.

### The weather

*...one moment enveloped in thick darkness, the next dazzled by flashes of lightning...The Sounds below, the naked peaks above, and the realm of bush between were lit up in marvelous detail. I could see an enormous waterspout dancing with insane speed...This storm was...sublime.* **Yesterdays in Maoriland: New Zealand in the 1880s**, Andreas Reischek

New Zealand is a mountainous country and has a mountainous country's weather patterns. These are frequently dynamic and volatile. The shape and size of the country also affects the climate. Since it is relatively small and surrounded by sea, New Zealand has a maritime climate as opposed to a continental climate;

NEW ZEALAND

this ensures that the weather is temperate, with few extremes of hot and cold, but does mean that it is highly fickle.

New Zealand straddles 40° South latitude and lies within the **Roaring Forties**, a name given to this part of the world by sailors as a result of the region's very strong westerly winds. New Zealand's weather is dominated by these westerly airflows. The airflow gusts in from the Tasman Sea, gathering moisture as it goes. When it arrives at the west coast of New Zealand the airflow hits a long, narrow ridge of mountains and is forced to rise, cooling as it does so until it releases its load on the western slopes in the form of rain or snow. Once the air has rid itself of moisture it descends to the east as a drier breeze.

On South Island the Southern Alps form a dramatic and comprehensive obstacle which ensures that the majority of rain is deposited on the western side and the eastern side lies in a dramatic rain shadow. The annual rainfall on the west coast is 7500mm per year and Fiordland is one of the wettest places in the world. In contrast, the eastern side of South Island receives as little as 500mm of rain per year. On North Island the variation is less dramatic since the mountainous barrier is less complete. The western slopes of the high volcanoes running down North Island receive most rainfall but in general rain is much more evenly distributed. The island as a whole receives around 1300mm of rain per year.

New Zealand weather tends to follow a cycle that takes six to ten days to complete. The westerly airflow is generated by areas of depression to the south of the country, which create cold fronts. Between these depressions are periods of high pressure that typically bring light winds and frequently fine weather.

New Zealand is renowned for its highly changeable weather conditions. For trampers, this can be a cause for concern. It is quite possible for the weather to change dramatically in the course of a morning or afternoon, and on Stewart Island you can experience different types of weather every couple of hours. However, prolonged periods of bad weather are by and large infrequent and after a particularly bad spell you should get a few days of more stable, fine weather.

---

❑ **Weather patterns**

● **Easterly**  An easterly airflow is quite unusual. It tends to result in light rain falling on the east coast whilst the west coast enjoys fine weather.

● **North-easterly**  A north-easterly airflow causes heavy rainfall on the east coast, particularly on North Island. It is quite a rare occurrence.

● **North-westerly**  A north-westerly airflow tends to bring rainfall and storms to the west coast and causes high winds on the ridges and mountain tops. The further east you go the clearer, warmer and drier the weather will get.

● **Southerly**  A southerly airflow will probably carry rain or snow with it. This particular pattern never lasts very long and in the wake of this cool spell you can expect clouds to clear and fine weather to follow.

● **Westerly**  A westerly airflow causes the build-up of cloud on the western side of the mountains. Usually this will break up during the early evening and a clear night will follow. However, it can deteriorate and morph into a 'nor'westerly', which results in an increase in wind speed and the development of denser, more menacing cloud.

As a general rule, North Island has less temperamental weather patterns than South Island and is a couple of degrees warmer. Low-lying areas are also warmer than those at altitude as the temperature drops by around 7°C every 1000m climbed. Certain areas have very characteristic weather. Wellington is often very windy, the far north doesn't really experience winter, Canterbury is dry and barren, Nelson and Blenheim enjoy the most hours of sunshine, Otago has blistering summers and bitter winters whilst the west coast and Fiordland are infamous for their high rainfall.

## Watching the weather

When tramping you will need to pay close attention to what the weather is doing. Be aware of changes in temperature, an increase in wind speed and the onset of cloud cover. All DOC offices and national park headquarters receive twice-daily **weather forecasts** and updates. You should check with these offices to see what the forecast holds before starting out on your tramp. On the tougher, higher altitude Great Walks hut wardens should post daily weather forecasts in the huts. In bad weather consider remaining in the hut and sitting it out rather than trying to rush a section and putting yourself at risk.

Alternatively you can get forecasts and **long-range predictions** from several sources. The Meteorological Service, abbreviated to MetService, has a specialised, state-of-the art weather computer prediction model that is designed to cope with New Zealand's unique weather. MetPhone provides recorded forecasts for the whole of New Zealand including all national parks and mountainous areas.

To access a **regional forecast** phone ☎ 0900-999 plus the area code of the region that you are interested in: thus to check the forecast in the Mt Tongariro area you would ring ☎ 0900-999 15. Calls last around one minute and will cost about NZ$1.30. Or visit the MetService website (🖳 www.metservice.co.nz) which features five-day outlooks and has hazardous-weather warnings posted on it. Otherwise you could try *The Press* website (🖳 www.press.co.nz), one of New Zealand's leading search engines, which carries short and extended forecasts. National radio features a five-day forecast at 12.30pm every weekday and has a detailed forecast after the 4pm news programme. National newspapers also carry full and regular forecasts, as does Teletext page 465.

## HISTORY

*Towards noon we saw a large high-lying land bearing south-east of us.*
**Abel Tasman** in his diary, 13 December, 1642

New Zealand was the last inhabitable landmass discovered by mankind. Consequently it has the shortest human history of any major land area. The two main islands were perfectly habitable but remained lost in a far-flung corner of the world's largest ocean. People didn't arrive on these distant shores until long after whole civilisations had appeared and crumbled in all of the other major inhabitable areas of the world. Nonetheless, New Zealand's short history is rich and fascinating. More than a thousand years have passed since the earliest

### In the beginning

In the beginning there was no light and the world was shrouded in darkness. Te Kore, the 'Nothingness', was all pervasive. Te Po, the Night, was long and impossibly gloomy. Out of this darkness the beginnings of life were fashioned. Rangi-nui, the Sky Father, was bound to Papa tua nuku, the Earth Mother, in a secure embrace. The numerous children of Rangi-nui and Papa tua nuku dwelt in the darkness between their parents, amidst creeping plants and rank low weeds. Over time the children of Rangi-nui and Papa tua nuku resolved to do something about their parents so that they could stretch and grow. They debated whether to kill their parents or to separate them.

The fiercest child, Tu-matauenga, the God of War, declared that they had no choice but to kill their parents. However, Tane-mahuta, the God of the Forests, protested and proposed that they should separate their parents so that Rangi-nui could stand high above them and Papa tua nuku could remain close by and nurture them.

After much discussion all of the children were agreed that they should separate their parents, except for Tawhiri-matea, the God of Winds and Storms, who threatened to wage war endlessly on anyone who prised his parents apart.

Rongo-matane, the God of Cultivated Food, was the first to try to force his parents apart, but he failed to separate them. Tangaroa, the God of Everything that Lives in the Sea, tried valiantly but was also forced to concede defeat. Haumia-tike-tike, the God of Uncultivated Food, was also thwarted in his attempts to prise them apart.

Tu-matauenga, the God of War, then stepped up to try. He hacked viciously at the sinews that tied the Earth to the sky, causing them to bleed. The blood seeped into the soil and created the red clay, ochre, which is considered sacred. Yet even the ferocious Tu-matauenga couldn't force the children's parents apart.

Finally, Tane-mahuta took over and slowly grew, braced with his back against the earth and his feet against the sky until the sky began to yield. The parents cried out and demanded to know why their children were doing this to their great love. The sinews that tied the two together stretched and then tore apart so that Rangi-nui was hurled high above Papa tua nuku.

Outraged, Tawhiri-matea, who had been holding his breath in anger, rose up and joined his father. Out of a desire for revenge he vented his rage on his siblings. The great trees of Tane-mahuta were blown over and the waters of Tangaroa were lashed and churned up. Fortunately, Papa tua nuku snatched her peaceful sons Rongo-matane, the fern root, and Haumia-tike-tike, the kumara, and hid them within her soils. Only Tu-matauenga was able to stand up to his irate brother.

Once Tawhiri-matea had calmed down peace returned to the skies. Yet Rangi-nui still wept for Papa tua nuku and his tears fell like rain. Papa tua nuku also still yearned for Rangi-nui and she too cried. Their combined tears threatened to swamp the land. In a bid to prevent their parents from always seeing each other's grief, some of the children agreed to turn Papa tua nuku over. This they duly did. As Papa tua nuku was turned over, another of her sons, Ruaumoko, was found still at her breast. In order to keep his mother warm he became the God of Earthquakes and Volcanoes. When he strides about his rumblings manifest themselves as earthquakes.

In order to clothe his mother's nakedness, Tane-mahuta caused trees and plants to spring forth. He encouraged birds to sing in a bid to cheer his mother up. He also sought to illuminate the darkness of his father who sprawled cold and grey in the vastness above. He put the sun on his father's front and the moon on his back. He summoned the stars and scattered them across the dark blue mantle. Lastly he took five stars, Ao-tahi, Puaka, Tuku-rua, Tama-rereti and Te-Waka-a-Tama-rereti, and he formed a cross in the sky. Then he sat back to admire the beauty of the Earth below and the sky above.

NEW ZEALAND

Polynesian explorers arrived on this mountainous land and went on to establish one of the world's most sophisticated Stone Age cultures. Their world was subsequently shaken when European explorers landed on these shores, paving the way for further migrants to settle here. New Zealand's modern history has thus been forged from a unique combination of Polynesian and European heritage.

## The discovery of New Zealand and the first settlers

Maori legend records that it was the great chief Kupe who sailed from their mythical homeland of Hawaiki and arrived on New Zealand's shores first. One day he is said to have declared '*He ao, he aotea he aotearoa*' ('It is a cloud, a white cloud, a long white cloud'). Such a cloud was a sure indication of land. New Zealand subsequently became known as Aotearoa, the Land of the Long White Cloud. Kupe is alleged to have returned to Hawaiki and encouraged others to make the journey with him. Another Maori legend tells the story of a grandfather, Whatonga, who set out to find his grandson, Toi, who had been lost at sea. The two of them were eventually reunited and came to settle in New Zealand, which was by now populated.

The occupation of New Zealand by **Polynesian travellers** between AD800 and 1000 was the culmination of a migration started around 5000BC, when the inhabitants of the coast and islands of South-East Asia set out to explore the Indian and Pacific oceans. By 1200BC these explorers had arrived on Fiji, by the time Christ is said to have been born they had filtered down to Tonga and Samoa and a few hundred years later they descended on the islands of Eastern Polynesia, still some 2500km away from New Zealand. The exact reason why they set out to explore the oceans is unclear although a popular theory is that their homeland was becoming overcrowded and a shortage of food and resources necessitated a search for new land. It is unlikely that the early migrants crossed the vast expanse of water by mistake as they were skilled navigators and took care to sail with livestock and provisions, including yams and kumara, presumably in the hope of settling somewhere. War or religious dissent may also have inspired these settlers to search for new land.

In their history, different Maori tribes trace their lineage to ancestors who sailed from Hawaiki over a period of 200-300 years. It is likely that the Victorian story of a legendary fleet of giant canoes descending on New Zealand in one go is a mistranslation of Maori oral tradition that has been passed off as actual history. Whilst the canoes named, including *Te Arawa*, *Aotea* and *Tainui*, probably existed it is unlikely that they journeyed together. The East Polynesian culture that they brought with them slowly evolved into a distinct Maori culture, which in turn became one of the most complex Stone Age cultures in the world. Archaeological evidence suggests that there was a cessation of contact between the Polynesian Islanders and Aotearoa before AD1500.

By the 18th century the Maori had evolved from nomadic hunters into settled gardeners. **Fortified villages**, *pa*, were built on strategic headlands and hills. These consisted of wooden and reed huts protected by great palisades, ditches and ramparts. Unfortified settlements, *kainga*, were constructed adjacent to fields and fishing grounds. Protective sites remained essential to the

NEW ZEALAND

> ### The legend of Maui and the creation of New Zealand
> The demi-god Maui boasted that he could catch a fish larger than anything his fishermen brothers could land. The brothers took him out fishing in a bid to test his claim. They set sail from Hawaiki and sailed far out to sea. Once they were a long way out at sea Maui took out an enchanted fishhook that he had fashioned from a piece of the jawbone of his ancestress Muri-ranga-whenua. His brothers refused to allow him to share their bait, so Maui struck himself on the nose and smeared his own blood onto the fishhook. He then cast it into the sea.
>
> Once he felt that something was caught on his hook, Maui hauled with all his might and a huge fish rose to the surface. Maui returned to the shore to give thanks to the gods and instructed his brothers not to touch the fish whilst he was gone. However, no sooner had Maui left than his brothers set about the giant fish, hacking at its flesh, gouging and cutting it. The gods reacted angrily and turned the fish to stone.
>
> The great fish became North Island of New Zealand, and was known as Te Ika a Maui, 'The Fish of Maui'. Wellington Harbour is the fish's mouth, the Tarankai and east coast area are its fins and the Northland Peninsula is its tail. South Island of New Zealand was created from the canoe that Maui used to haul the great fish up from the sea floor. It came to be known as Te Waka o Maui, 'The Canoe of Maui'. Stewart Island had anchored the canoe when Maui struggled with his great catch and became known as Te Punga o te Waka a Maui, 'The Anchor Stone of the Canoe of Maui'.

Maori since warfare played an integral part in their pre-European lifestyle. Battles were fought between tribes to settle land disputes, win food or for the sake of honour. These were often bloody affairs, conducted hand to hand.

**Maori society** was made up of **tribes**, *iwi*, whose genealogy was traced back to the arrival of a particular canoe from Hawaiki. Each iwi could be broken down into sub-tribes, *hapu*, which numbered up to 500 people. Each hapu could be further distilled into *whanau*, or clans, which consisted of direct and extended family members. The focus of people's communal and daily lives was the *marae*, a complex of buildings comprising a meeting-house, *whare hui*, dining hall, *whare kai*, and an open area within the *pa* (a fortified village) or *kainga* (an unfortified village or home) where the community would gather for social and ritual occasions. Life is generally considered to have been democratic with responsibility shared. Social control was achieved by the voluntary acceptance of an individual's obligation to the iwi. The Maori believed in a plethora of gods who featured heavily in everyday life.

By the early 18th century the Maori culture was well established and had mutated slowly over the course of a thousand years to suit their needs. The next hundred years were to see the Maori subjected to much more rapid and far-reaching changes.

### The Europeans arrive

In 1642 the Dutchman **Abel Tasman** set sail from Batavia in the Dutch East Indies (now called Jakarta, the capital of modern-day Indonesia) to discover the great southern continent that many Europeans believed must lie in the distant reaches of the Pacific Ocean alongside recently discovered Australia, in order to counterbalance the land masses of the Northern Hemisphere.

On 13 December, 1642, he sighted a ridge of mountainous land that marked the west coast of South Island of New Zealand. Believing that this was part of a larger continent, he sailed north, mapping part of the coastline as he went. He rounded the top of South Island and on 18 December made his first contact with the local Maori. This encounter did not go well. Confusion and misunderstanding led to an attack on the Dutch by the Maori. Four Dutch sailors were killed in what Tasman dubbed Moordenaers ('Murderers') Bay. Tasman promptly weighed anchor without ever setting foot on land and sailed away in the belief that this unreceptive country was hostile and held no treasure. The new land mass was christened Staten Landt but was later renamed Nieuw Zeeland after the Dutch maritime province.

Abel Tasman left only an enticing line on the map. It wasn't until 130 years later that **Captain James Cook** was to reach this land and complete the picture. In 1769 Cook set sail from England for Tahiti. He then sailed south to search for the supposed southern continent that people still believed must exist. If he could not find it he was instructed to explore New Zealand. In October 1769 land was sighted and on 9 October Cook dropped anchor in Poverty Bay and duly became the first European to stand on New Zealand soil. Cook remained in New Zealand waters for the next six months, during which time he circumnavigated most of the country, accurately charting the coastline. In doing so he was able to dispel the notion of the great southern continent. He returned twice more during the 1770s and relied upon New Zealand harbours in the Marlborough Sounds and at Dusky Sound for rest and restocking during his exploration of the Pacific. During this time he formed a detailed impression of the country and its inhabitants. He described the country as 'rude and craggy', noting that it was hilly, thickly covered in forests and well inhabited. He enjoyed mostly amicable encounters with the Maori and formed a high opinion of the local inhabitants, declaring in his journals that 'I have allways [sic] found them of a Brave, Noble, Open and benevolent disposition'.

Several other European explorers followed in Cook's wake. In 1772 the Frenchman Marion du Fresne arrived in New Zealand, only to be killed in the Bay of Islands. Later Vancouver, D'Entrecastaux, Malaspina and D'Urville contributed to the exploration and mapping of New Zealand's long coastline.

Cook and his botanists, Banks and Solander, made several astute observations. They observed that the islands supported excellent timber for masts and a type of broad-bladed grass, **flax**, that could be turned into ropes and canvases. During the 1790s the first cargo of timber was collected from New Zealand's vast native forests. The sailors relied on the Maori to dress the fibre of the flax, which they then traded for cloth, nails and guns. Cook also noted the abundant sealife, which in turn led to the arrival of sealing gangs on North Island. So much slaughter was conducted that by as early as 1810 the trade in sealskins was in decline. At much the same time whalers began to arrive in New Zealand waters, initially to hunt sperm whales and later to focus on southern right or black whales. They set up bases in the Bay of Islands from where they traded blankets, knives and guns for food and favours from Maori women.

NEW ZEALAND

Small, rough European settlements began to spring up along the coast. Inter-racial marriages and the adoption of each other's customs and ways of life duly followed. Around 1830, Kororareka, now Russell, in the Bay of Islands became New Zealand's first proper European town. At this time there were around 300 Europeans living in New Zealand. By the end of the decade this number had swelled to almost 2000. This was still a trifling amount in comparison to the number of Maori, but their impact was profound.

Relations between Maori and Europeans were mostly cordial. There were occasional skirmishes but in the main the Maori fought amongst themselves. With the advent of early trade and the use of guns as a means of barter, these battles inevitably became more lethal. In the 1820s Hone Heke led the Northland **Nga Puhi iwi** south to ravage lands owned by other tribes. The Nga Puhi were one of the first to acquire quantities of guns from the Europeans. Elsewhere, Te Ruaparaha fought to establish his tribe, the Ngati Toa, on the coast of North Island before taking a band of armed warriors over to South Island to attack the Ngai Tahu tribe. Thousands were killed in these and other tribal conflicts.

Europeans were also responsible for introducing new diseases to the islands. With no immunity to them, epidemics raged amongst the Maori tribes, decimating their numbers. At the time of Cook's arrival in New Zealand there were probably 200,000 Maori living there. By 1840 this figure had been nearly halved.

## The reluctant colonisation

Many of the goods exported from New Zealand at this time found their way to Australia. In return the desire to bring European-style civilisation and religion flowed from Australia to New Zealand.

**Samuel Marsden**, a prison chaplain in Sydney, succeeded in persuading the authorities to allow him to take the gospel to the Maori. On Christmas Day 1814 he landed in the Bay of Islands and began to preach. Other missionaries including Wesleyans, Anglicans and Catholics subsequently followed. Initially they all had little impact on the traditional Maori beliefs, relying instead on Maori evangelists converted and trained to take the gospel to their brethren. One of the benefits of the introduction of Christianity was a decline in the number of inter-tribal wars and the near disappearance of cannibalism from the islands.

There was also a widely held belief in Australia that European towns in New Zealand were lusty, lawless and violent. The Bay of Islands was considered unruly and full of unprincipled rogues. Traders and missionaries prevailed upon the British government to intervene, sparking the debate as to whether to formally colonise New Zealand or not. Unsure of what action to take, the government sent **James Busby** to be British Resident in New Zealand in 1833. Busby was charged with keeping law and order and encouraging trade yet he was given little real authority or muscle with which to implement or enforce his suggestions.

Shortly after Busby's arrival, Baron Charles de Thierry, a Briton of French descent, declared his intention of becoming chief of New Zealand. This caused Busby to panic and persuade 35 Maori chiefs to sign a **Declaration of**

**Independence**, proclaiming themselves the 'United Tribes of New Zealand' in 1835. This declaration stated that the Maori chiefs were sovereign in New Zealand and the Maori people were the owners of the country, which was to be placed under British parentage for the purpose of protection.

The sound reasoning behind this document was that the Maori needed to be protected from exploitation by the European settlers. The British government had realised that colonisation could not be avoided, but also believed that unchecked colonisation would be calamitous for the Maori. To their credit, the British were keen to ensure that the Maori were neither subjugated nor wiped out and in a bid to protect both the interests of prospective settlers and the Maori, the government believed that annexation was the only logical option.

The Declaration of Independence ensured that in order to annex New Zealand, the British had to sign a treaty with the independent Maori chiefs before they could legally proclaim sovereignty. So in August 1839 William Hobson was ordered to sail to New Zealand and persuade the Maori to acknowledge the sovereignty of Queen Victoria; in return, they would receive guarantees of their rights to the land. He was formally instructed to obtain their 'free and intelligent consent' to the British annexation of New Zealand.

After a day of debate the **Treaty of Waitangi** was signed on 6 February, 1840. Forty-five Northland chiefs signed the document, which was then circulated throughout New Zealand. Over 500 Maori chiefs added their signatures to the document as it was carried around the islands for the next eight months. This figure by no means represented all the tribes present in New Zealand at that time. Nonetheless on 21 May Hobson proclaimed British sovereignty over the whole country and New Zealand became a British possession.

The Treaty of Waitangi remains central to New Zealand law and society. It is considered by many to be the country's founding document. However, ever since its signing the treaty has been at the centre of controversy with regard to its legal standing and whether it has been properly observed. One of the major problems has been the question of interpretation. The English and Maori versions of the treaty both contain three articles. However, there are discrepancies between the original text and the translated version presented to the Maori chiefs with the result that the Maori are unlikely to have fully grasped the importance of what they were being asked to sign.

The first article deals with the issue of sovereignty. The English version declares that the Maori willingly give up their *kawanatanga*, or sovereignty, to the British Crown. Whilst the English version states that this must be a complete transference of power, the Maori version suggests that power would be shared. The second article concerns *tino rangatiratanga*, or chieftainship. The English version offers the Maori control over their lands, forests and fisheries whilst the Maori version promises much broader, far-reaching rights to the protection of their culture and language.

The third article declares that the Maori be afforded the rights of British subjects, rights which have subsequently been neglected or ignored. It also meant that they would be bound by British law.

Thus, although the rights of the Maori were supposedly protected, the reality was rather different and the Maori went on to lose a considerable amount of land in dubious circumstances. This in turn led to vociferous protests. The rumblings of dissatisfaction that could be heard at the time the treaty was signed can still be heard today. In 1975 the **Waitangi Tribunal** was established to honour the treaty as a relevant document. Since then the tribunal has passed judgement on several land claims brought by Maori *iwi* (tribes). In many cases compensation in the form of land or money has been granted. Land claim cases continue to be presented to the tribunal to this day.

## Political developments and the Constitutional Act

In January 1841 Hobson moved the capital of New Zealand to Auckland, proclaiming the country a Crown Colony in May of that year. He died in office in 1842. His successor as Governor of New Zealand was Robert FitzRoy, who was in turn succeeded by the hugely influential George Grey in 1845.

Over the next few years a series of parliamentary acts gave New Zealand the constitution under which it was to be governed. In 1846 the Constitution Act provided for a representative government as elected by settlers. In 1852 a further Constitution Act divided New Zealand into six provinces, each with its own council and superintendent who was to oversee land purchases and sales. This act also established a central government with an elected House of Representatives and an appointed Upper House. The provinces survived until 1876 when they were abolished for being divisive and hindering the development of the country as a whole.

Essentially, settlers gained the right to govern themselves without any real struggle. The Constitution of 1852 provided for self-government and an act in 1855 guaranteed responsible government. To all intents New Zealand was politically independent of Britain whilst still a part of the British Empire. The Maori, meanwhile, were excluded from political decision-making and prevented from setting up their own government. The vote was given only to landowners and since the Maori didn't hold individual titles to the land but owned land collectively, they were denied suffrage. A growing sense of betrayal began to develop.

## The New Zealand Land Wars

As soon as annexation had been formalised, organised settlement began. Large numbers of settlers migrated to different parts of the country. Throughout the 1840s settlements were founded at Wellington, Nelson, New Plymouth, Dunedin and Christchurch. Initially coastal sites were chosen before inland areas were explored and claimed.

Settlers arrived hoping to be able to acquire land of their own. The Treaty of Waitangi clearly stated that the Maori could sell land only to the government and the government in turn could sell to settlers only that land that it had legally bought from its Maori owners. The whole process was complicated and time consuming since the Maori lands were governed by collective tribal rights. Furthermore, the Maori became increasingly unwilling to sell their land as they began to fear being overrun or pushed out. Misunderstandings compounded the tension between settlers and Maori tribes, which eventually spilt over into war.

The first serious clash of arms came in 1843 when the Maori owners of the Wairau Plains attempted to stop them being surveyed and purchased. Other skirmishes relating to disputed land sales took place in Wellington and Wanganui. At the same time war broke out in the Bay of Islands. This was precipitated by the Maori chief Hone Heke repeatedly cutting down the flagstaff, the symbol of royal authority, at Kororareka. It was an action borne of frustration and discontent at the loss of trading opportunities in the area as a direct result of the relocation of the capital to Auckland.

Typically expressive Maori carving, here found on Abel Tasman Coast Track

Old tribal rivalries were forgotten as the Maori became increasingly aware of a collective identity and shared interests. This was further heightened when the 1858 census revealed that Europeans outnumbered Maori in New Zealand for the first time. By the end of the 1850s there were 75,000 Europeans and around 55,000 Maori in New Zealand, although on North Island the Maori were still present in greater numbers than the settlers. As a symbol of their new unity in 1858 the Maori elected their first king, the Waikato chief **Te Wherowhero**.

Frustrated by the lack of land available for sale, the settlers in Taranaki attempted to speed up the process illegally. This led to first passive and then armed resistance. Several pitched battles occurred in 1860-61 before British and colonial troops secured victory.

In 1863 war again flared up in Taranaki, this time in the populous Waikato Valley. The crowning of a Maori king was seen as a direct challenge to the queen's authority and turned the Waikato Maori into rebels. Troops invaded the Waikato and key battles were fought at Rangiriri and Orakau in 1863 and 1864 respectively. With the final destruction of the Maori force the Land Wars, superficially at least, came to an end and by the mid-1860s much of the fighting was over, although sporadic **guerrilla incursions** continued into the 1870s. The rebel Te Kooti Rikirangi continued to wage bush and guerrilla warfare on the government until 1872 when he was forced to flee.

To the victor the spoils, and as a result of the conflicts large areas of fertile land were confiscated and made available for immediate settlement. These confiscations bred a sense of resentment and led the Maori to retreat into sullen isolation.

The **Native Land Act** passed in the 1860s waived the requirement that land be first sold to the government. It also provided for a Native Land Court to

NEW ZEALAND

determine which Maori individuals actually owned the land that the Europeans wanted to purchase, essentially making the Maori title to the land individual rather than communal or tribal.

In the aftermath of the war, European settlement continued apace. The European settler population grew dramatically and a European view came to dominate all aspects of New Zealand life. The Maori were increasingly marginalised and thought to be close to annihilation.

## Growth and social reform

The 1870s were characterised by a programme of development. Roads were improved, the rail network was expanded and communications were increased. Farming became more productive and the country's potential began to be realised. Wool became the main export and remained so until 1882 when the first refrigerated meat shipment set sail for Britain. This momentous event saw a shift in New Zealand's economy and the establishment of the country as an important supplier of foodstuffs for Britain.

There were also developments in political and human rights. In 1865 the capital was relocated to Wellington and shortly afterwards, in 1867, the government gave the vote to Maori men. In 1876 provincial governments were abolished and all power centralised in Wellington. Throughout the 1890s New Zealand became increasingly progressive with the introduction of compulsory arbitration, which led to numerous wage rises and graduated income tax. In 1893 New Zealand became the first nation in the world to endorse full women's suffrage, 25 years before Britain or the United States, and in 1898 legislation guaranteeing an old-age pension was ratified. However, this era could not last. Social unrest grew and manifested itself in a series of strikes. International socialists organised the New Zealand labourers and instigated prolonged strike action that boiled over into violence. This group was eventually smashed but further unrest was averted only by the outbreak of World War I.

## New Zealand between the wars

New Zealand rallied behind Britain during the war and committed more than 100,000 men, approximately ten per cent of the entire population, to the struggle. The New Zealand troops sustained huge losses and around 17,000 soldiers failed to return from the trenches. Fears regarding an increased rate of alcoholism inspired the Temperance Movement to promote national prohibition. This was averted but six o'clock closing was made law in 1918 and remained so until 1967. Returning European servicemen were rehabilitated on newly acquired land whilst Maori soldiers received nothing. The war at least ensured prosperous years for New Zealand as Britain's demand for food remained high.

Unfortunately, New Zealand was poorly prepared for the Wall Street Crash and the subsequent **Great Depression**, which caused national debt to rocket as export markets closed and the resultant income dried up. Initial prosperity gave way to an era of unemployment and poverty.

The year 1935 marked the onset of a second era of massive social change. The Labour Party swept to power. Salaries that had been cut during the

Depression were restored, public works programmes were restarted and the first ever welfare state offered a free health service, family benefits, state housing and increased pensions. **Maori welfare** was also on the agenda: their basic standard of living was improved with unemployment payments and greater pensions.

The outbreak of **World War II** forced New Zealand to reconsider its position in the world. When the Japanese bombed Pearl Harbour in 1941 they were forced to recognise that they were removed from Britain and needed to court their Pacific allies. Around a third of the male labour force was called up to fight, but fortunately casualties were much lower than in World War I.

## Prosperity and dissent

After the war New Zealand again enjoyed a period of prosperity. Between 1947 and 1975 more than 75,000 British men and women emigrated to New Zealand to fill job vacancies. The 1960s also saw the start of a wave of immigration of large numbers of Pacific islanders. The Maori also began to migrate to the large urban centres in search of work. At this time New Zealand was considered one of the most prosperous nations in the world. During the last years of the 1950s attempts were made to wean New Zealand off its dependence on imports. Improvements were made to steel mills, oil refineries and hydroelectric power schemes in a bid to make the country more self-sufficient.

Steps were also taken to secure the country's defence. New Zealand signed the anti-Communist **South-East Asia Treaty Organisation** (SEATO) document and in 1951 joined the **ANZUS military pact**, a reciprocal defence agreement between Australia, New Zealand and the United States.

Britain's entry into the Common Market in 1972 had a negative impact on New Zealand's exports. Although some new markets had been found, New Zealanders still felt betrayed. Oil prices increased exponentially later that same year and the country faced growing bills as its income decreased. Debt soared once more, unemployment rose and the standard of living began to fall. As a result, people began to leave in droves.

At the same time the Maori dissent began to increase again. They found expression through the formation of gangs such as Black Power, the Mongrel Mob and Highway 61, which unsettled many in the European community. Land disputes arose and the Waitangi Tribunal was convened to pass judgement on the claims and to ensure that the Treaty of Waitangi was seen to be a living, evolving agreement, and one with teeth. Although some settlements have been made, others have dragged on for many years.

## Recession and resurgence

In the mid-1980s the New Zealand dollar was devalued by 20 per cent, state industries were privatised and the protectionist economy largely deregulated. This temporary measure ensured that the economy recovered slightly until the stock market crash in 1987, at which time the country went into rapid decline.

In 1984 the Labour government refused to allow United States nuclear warships entry to New Zealand ports, which served to strain the relations between the two countries. The United States retaliated by withdrawing its support for the ANZUS pact. In 1985 French secret service agents bombed and sank the Greenpeace flagship *Rainbow Warrior* in Auckland Harbour in retaliation for its opposition to French nuclear testing in the South Pacific at Moruroa Atoll. In 1987 New Zealand announced that it was to become a nuclear-free zone.

In the grip of a recession in the mid 1990s, with dissatisfaction with both major parties running high, New Zealand voted for electoral reform. The traditional first-past-the-post system of elections was scrapped and replaced with mixed member proportional representation, which is designed to give smaller parties a voice. Since then there has been an increase in the Maori presence in parliament, New Zealand has elected its first female prime minister, the Green Party has enjoyed a resurgence and the first Rastafarian and transgender MPs have been installed.

The social democratic labour-led coalition under the guidance of Helen Clark won both the 2002 and 2005 elections, although they lost a number of traditional Maori supporters in the latter on the back of forcing through legislation to guarantee beach access to all. However, the reduced majority and over-riding sense that the party had out-stayed its welcome meant that in the run up to the 2008 elections the centre-right National Party managed to build up a commanding lead in the polls. Despite late setbacks, National topped the polls (59 seats) and their leader, John Key, was returned as prime minister. No party won an outright majority under New Zealand's complicated proportional voting system, so Key announced his intention to lead a National government with support from the ACT (5 seats), United Future (1 seat) and Maori parties (5 seats). The three minor parties are formally outside the minority National government but have agreed to support National on issues of confidence and supply. In the course of the election the Green Party (8 seats) became the third largest party in parliament behind the traditional giants National and Labour. Key's first challenge will be to tackle the recession that is looming for New Zealand and reverse the economic downturn the country has experienced by stimulating the economy.

Although New Zealand is still heavily influenced by its colonial heritage, the country now has a very strong sense of identity. The resurgence in Maori traditions, culture and language continues this trend. Whilst still a member of the British Commonwealth and close to the United States, New Zealand has developed into a far more independent nation.

## NEW ZEALAND TODAY

New Zealand is now a largely sophisticated, multicultural urban society. Its people are fiercely individual and self-reliant but have also embraced technology and modernity wholeheartedly. The diverse population is bound together by several uniting features.

Of the 4.2 million or so people who currently live in New Zealand, around seventy per cent are of European descent. Approximately ten per cent, some 450,000 people, are descended from the Maori, six per cent from Pacific island Polynesians and around eight per cent are from Asian backgrounds. Auckland is in fact the largest Polynesian city in the world. Meanwhile, New Zealand is consciously moulding a more bicultural society in a bid to correct some of the wrongs of the past. Although as a result of intermarriage there are few if any full-blooded Maori left in New Zealand, there is a general increase in the number of people acknowledging – and justifiably proud of – their Maori heritage and there may come a time in the 21st century when the Maori outnumber the European New Zealanders. This has led to a renaissance in *Maoritanga*, the Maori way of doing things and the Maori as a political force. The Maori party was founded in 2005 and is set to consolidate the gains made in recent years. Only time will tell how this shift in the balance of power will affect the country, how other native New Zealanders will react to this and what other repercussions there could be.

## ECONOMY

Over the last 20 years New Zealand has been transformed from a largely agrarian economy dependent on concessionary British market access to a more industrialised free market economy. The economy has been relatively buoyant over recent years, with strong exports to Australia, the USA, Japan and China supporting good growth. However, at the tail end of 2008 the country suffered an economic downturn and slipped towards recession, in line with many of the world's economies, as weak consumer spending, falling house prices and the global credit crisis began to bite. At the same time inflation hit an 18-year high. The new Prime Minister, John Key, announced tax cuts and a plan to stimulate the economy and promote growth but it remains to be seen if he can restore confidence.

Although on the up, exports still contribute significantly less to the overall GDP than they did at the turn of the century. The main commodities exported include dairy products, beef, lamb and mutton, wood and wood products, fish and machinery. Tourism has also made a significant contribution. Unemployment is very low, below 4%. The growth in the economy has boosted salaries, but left behind many at the bottom of the scale. The average annual wage is more than NZ$25,000, although this is unevenly spread and continuing to get more and more polarised: currently some 15% of the population earn twice that whilst around 45% subsist on less than NZ$20,000. Wellington is the wealthiest region.

## PEOPLE

Just over 4,250,000 people live in New Zealand, with around three-quarters of these making their home on the North Island. Some 80% of people live in cities and around a quarter of the total population live in Auckland alone. Although not particularly religious, the country is predominantly Christian; some 15% are Anglican, 12% Roman Catholic and 11% Presbyterian. A large percentage (25%) claims no affiliation at all.

# Flora and fauna

Until the Maori arrived around 1000 years ago, New Zealand had been left alone to evolve in its own way, untouched for more than 80 million years. This untainted isolation meant that unusual and unique species were able to develop.

New Zealand plants and animals, originally from the great southern continent of **Gondwanaland**, developed and evolved in their own way. A huge diversity of native birds resulted, including semi-flightless and ground-nesting species. There were virtually no land mammals on the islands save for some bats, so unusual birds, reptiles and insects developed to fill the niches usually occupied by mammals in other countries.

The waters off the New Zealand coastline teemed with fish, whales, seals and dolphins. Primeval swathes of conifer and rainforest covered much of North Island including the lower slopes of large volcanoes. Great swathes of beech forest covered lowland areas of South Island. Tussock grasslands and alpine gardens dominated the snow-capped higher ground.

**Human settlement**, both Maori and European, impacted on the nature of New Zealand. Some native forests were cleared to create farmland and exotic animals and plants were introduced that upset the balance of nature. In some cases species were wilfully brought over from Europe in a bid to create an economy for the settlers; in others the species were stowaways or mistakenly released onto the land. The loss and fragmentation of some habitats has had a detrimental effect on native species. The mistakes of the past have largely been recognised and New Zealanders today are very conscious of the need to conserve the original character of their country and to celebrate its differences. Although New Zealand's 'clean and green' tag owes more to a short human history and good fortune than design, steps have now been taken to secure the protection of the country's natural heritage.

Today more than five million hectares of land, around a third of New Zealand, is protected by national parks and reserves managed by the Department of Conservation (DOC; see box p37). The DOC is charged with conserving and caring for New Zealand's natural heritage. They work to restore damaged ecosystems, create reserves to save wildlife and its habitats and try to control the wide range of threats to native species of flora and fauna. Wildlife sanctuaries, breeding programmes and predator-control schemes have all helped to address the problems facing endangered species. Furthermore, all native species are now fully protected in a bid to safeguard their existence.

## FAUNA

Because New Zealand drifted away from Gondwanaland before mammals had a chance to colonise, it has virtually none that it can call its own. A small bat, of which there are two species, is the only native mammal. People rarely see the **short-** and **long-tailed bats**, even at sunset when they emerge to hunt. The Maori refer to the bat as *pekapeka* and associate it with the mythical flying bird *hokioi*, which foretells death or disaster.

Since the arrival of people, a variety of mammals have been introduced to the country. Charles Darwin, on a visit to New Zealand in 1835, predicted that the more dominant introduced species would lead to 'the destruction of the deliberate balance of the endemic productions which had reached a standard of perfection attained in long isolation'. All the deliberately introduced mammals have caused problems. **Stoats**, **weasels**, **ferrets**, **rabbits**, **rats**, **mice**, **cats**, **pigs**, **goats** and **deer** have all had a negative impact on the native flora and fauna. The worst reprobate is the **possum**. Brought across from Australia in a bid to establish a fur trade, they have flourished in New Zealand and there are now thought to be more than 70 million possums in the country. They destroy huge amounts of forest and eat bird eggs and chicks, depleting numbers hugely.

There is an impressive number of insect fauna found here. Several **butterfly** species, including the giant monarch butterfly, and many more **moth** species can be seen throughout the country. **Cicadas** can be heard in most of the forests, carrying on noisily. There are also more than 100 species of **weta**. These ancient insects look like large, intimidating grasshoppers and are found in a variety of sizes and habitats. The ground weta, tree weta and cave weta all pale in comparison with the giant weta which, at up to 10cm (4 inches) in length and weighing as much as a small bird, is the largest insect in the world.

There are several species of spider present in New Zealand. The only poisonous one is the **katipo**. This rare relative of the black widow spider can deliver a nasty nip but is rarely fatal. The katipo can be found along the coast, hidden within the forest undergrowth.

Perhaps the most obvious and unpleasant insect is the notorious **sandfly**. The enjoyment of the west coast and Fiordland can be overshadowed by this irritating distraction. Captain Cook described the sandfly as 'the most mischievous animal' his crew had encountered. The Maori would seek protection from this biting insect by sitting beside smoky fires or caking themselves in mud. New Zealand has a dozen or so species of sandfly, of which two bite humans. It is only the female of the species that bites people. She needs the blood for her eggs to mature. The victim of the bite is left with an itchy swelling. The Maori believed that the sandfly, *te namu*, was created by Te Hine nui te po, the Goddess of the Underworld, specifically to drive people out of Milford Sound.

The ancient **tuatara** is a remnant of the prehistoric era. This lizard-like reptile dates back to the age of the dinosaurs and roamed the earth some 225 million years ago. Once widespread they are now highly endangered. They are almost exclusively confined to offshore islands free from predators. The Southland Museum in Invercargill has a successful captive-breeding programme and represents your best chance of spotting one of these elusive creatures. New Zealand is one of the few temperate countries in the world that is free of snakes.

New Zealand's waterways teem with fish. The introduced **brown** and **rainbow trout** have flourished at the expense of some of the native species. However, the **kokopu** and **inanga**, which in its young state is whitebait, can be found here. **Eels** are also present.

New Zealand is also blessed with a wealth of marine mammals. Thirty-five different species of **whale** and **dolphin** can be seen off the coast of the islands. Common, bottlenose and dusky dolphins all pass through New Zealand waters, whilst Hector's dolphins are confined exclusively to these seas. Pods of sperm whale, humpback whale, southern right whale and orca are frequently spotted. The **New Zealand fur seal** is also prevalent along the coast.

## Birds

*This morn I was awakened by the singing of the birds ashore from whence we are distant not a quarter of a mile, the number of them were certainly very great who seemed to strain their throats with emulation perhaps; their voices were certainly the most melodious wild music I had ever heard, almost imitating small bells but with the most tuneable silver sound imaginable to which maybe the distance was no small addition. On enquiring of our people I was told that they had observed them ever since we have been here, and that they begin to sing at about 1 or 2 in the morn and continue till sunrise ...'*

**Joseph Banks** in his diary, 1770

The islands of New Zealand were originally part of the super-continent Gondwanaland. Eighty million years ago New Zealand began to separate and drift away from this landmass before mammals or snakes could populate its islands. Without any real predators, the bird species on the islands were able to develop in unusual and frequently unique ways. New Zealand still retains several unique birds that can be found nowhere else in the world. However, the arrival of humans, the destruction of habitats and the introduction of mammalian predators such as rats, stoats, possums and feral cats has had a devastating effect on the number of birds to be found on the islands. Birds such as the enormous, flightless moa and the New Zealand eagle, the largest bird of prey ever known, vanished completely, hunted into extinction.

The early Maori settlers brought with them a complex set of myths and traditions that related to birds. These were adapted in order to make them relevant and understandable in the context of their new homeland.

There are far too many species of bird to describe in detail here, but listed below are some of the more widespread or noteworthy species.

As you can see above, when Captain Cook first arrived off New Zealand's shores, Joseph Banks commented on the chorus of birdsong that could be heard. The chief performer in this chorus was almost certainly the **bellbird**, makomako. Whilst fairly drab in appearance, its melodic, bell-like call is beautiful. Traditionally, the Maori describe a great orator as *ka rite ki te kopara e ko nei I te ata*, 'someone who sounds like the bellbird singing in the morning'. Dark green with a curved bill, the bellbird is found all across New Zealand but nowhere else in the world.

New Zealand has many species of duck. The rarest of these is the highly endangered **blue duck**, or whio. This ancient inhabitant of New Zealand has steel grey plumage and brown flecks on its breast. The eyes are bright yellow. The blue duck lives around fast-flowing forest streams, leading to it also being referred to as the torrent duck. As its numbers have declined, so it has been forced to abandon the lowland and retreat to more isolated, upstream areas. The Maori onomatopoeically christened the bird 'whio' after the high whistle given by the male, pitched at the perfect frequency for carrying across a noisy stretch of white water. The female utters an unflattering croak in response. The birds are most active around dawn and dusk when they can sometimes be seen foraging for food. Strong clawed feet help the bird to scramble over rocks and keep its footing in the torrent as it searches for caddis fly larvae, its main foodstuff. Introduced trout competing for the same food supplies and the introduction of stoats, which eat their eggs, are largely responsible for the decline.

The flighty **fantail**, piwakawaka, is a tiny insect-eating bird living in forests, scrublands and suburban gardens all over New Zealand. The fantail is usually brown or black in colour, with a long set of tail feathers. They are perceived as a friendly bird because they will stick close to trampers, although they are in actual fact after the insects disturbed by the passage of people's feet. The Maori consider the fantail to be a harbinger of doom. The little bird features heavily in Maori mythology and was present when the demi-god Maui was slain by Te Hine nui te po, the Goddess of the Underworld.

The **kaka** is a large brown bush parrot with a crimson underbelly and underside of its tail and wings. It uses its large, rending beak to rip away bark and rotten wood to expose larvae and wood grubs upon which it feeds. They are also partial to nectar which they collect using brushes on the end of their tongues. Kaka numbers have been depleted by stoat predation. The Maori used to hunt kaka with long bird spears.

The largest parrot in the world, the **kakapo**, evolved into a flightless bird at a time when there were no predators. Now that predators have been introduced, it is severely endangered. The only remaining birds have been relocated to predator-free islands in the Marlborough Sounds and Codfish Island off Stewart Island. The kakapo is nocturnal, and its name literally translates as 'night parrot'. The male has a deep booming call that it uses to attract a mate.

The world's only mountain parrot, the **kea**, is a mischievous, inquisitive bird that has earned itself the nickname of the 'clown of the mountains'. It can be found in the upper margins of beech forests and above the treeline in the Southern Alps. This smart green parrot, a cousin to the kaka, has bright red underwings and subsists on large mountain daisies, low-growing plants and insects. They supplement their diet with fruit, seeds and flowers. However, they will eat almost anything and have been known to attack animal carcasses, DOC huts and rucksacks. The keas' boldness, destructiveness and curiosity stem from their high intelligence.

The **kereru** is New Zealand's native wood pigeon. They are dark green with a white breast and are quite large, sitting motionless and silent in the forest. When they fly their wings beat the air and make a distinctive thrumming sound. Entirely vegetarian, they feed almost exclusively on berries. Their conservation is vital since they play an important role in the regeneration of native forest by dispersing the seeds of trees and shrubs such as miro and tawa that are too large to be dispersed by other birds.

The best known of all New Zealand's birds is the **kiwi**, yet it remains a secretive, nocturnal species that is rarely seen in the wild. The kiwi is remarkably un-birdlike. Flightless (see box below), with loose, shaggy plumage, they wander through the forest at night using their long, slender bills to root out insects in the leaf litter and soft soil. The name is derived from the shrill call, heard most often an hour before dawn or dusk. When feeding the kiwi snuffles

---

### How the kiwi lost its wings

Tane-mahuta, the God of the Forest, was walking through the forest when he noticed that his children, the young trees, were starting to sicken as bugs ate them. He spoke to his brother Tanehokahoka, who in turn summoned all of his children, the birds. Tane-mahuta then spoke to them. He explained that something was eating his children and that he needed one of the birds to come down from the forest canopy and live on the floor in order to protect the young trees and preserve the forests. Not one of the birds responded to his plea.

Tanehokahoka turned to his children and addressed them individually. 'E Tui, will you come down from the forest roof?' The tui gazed at the sun filtering through the tree-tops and then looked down at the cold, dark forest floor and shook. 'No, Tanehokahoka, because it is too dark and I am afraid of the dark.' Tanehokahoka turned to the pukeko and asked the same question. The pukeko glanced at the cold, damp forest floor and shuddered. 'No, Tanehokahoka, for it is too damp and I do not want to get my feet wet.' The silence grew. In desperation Tanehokahoka turned to pipiwharauroa and asked the question once more. Pipiwharauroa glanced about and saw his family close by. 'No, Tanehokahoka, for I am busy building my nest.'

Tanehokahoka felt a great sadness settle on him as he realised that if none of the birds descended to the forest floor, not only would his brother lose his children but the birds would ultimately lose their homes. As a final act he turned to the kiwi and repeated his question. The kiwi looked all around, saw the sun filtering through the tree-tops, observed the cold, damp earth and looked at his family. 'I will,' he replied.

Both Tanehokahoka and Tane-mahuta were overcome with joy since the kiwi had given them hope. Tanehokahoka felt obliged to warn the kiwi what would happen. 'E kiwi, do you realise that if you do this you will have to grow thick, strong legs so that you can rip apart the logs on the ground and that you will lose your beautiful coloured feathers and wings and so will not be able to return to the forest canopy. You will never see the light of day again.' Once more he asked the kiwi, 'Will you come down from the forest roof?' The kiwi glanced about him and, saying a silent goodbye to the other birds, replied 'I will'.

Relieved, Tanehokahoka turned to the other birds and declared, 'E tui, because you were too scared to come down from the forest roof, from now on you will wear the two white feathers at your throat as the mark of a coward. Pukeko, because you did not wish to get your feet wet, you will live forever in the swamp. Pipiwharauroa, because you were too busy building your nest, from now on you will never build another nest of your own, but lay your eggs in the nests of other birds.' He then turned back to the kiwi and decreed, 'You kiwi, because of your great sacrifice, you will become the most celebrated and revered bird of them all.'

and when alarmed or frightened it hisses and snaps its beak together. They are experts at camouflage and their brown plumage blends in effortlessly with the forest. However, they have little defence against predators and large numbers of eggs and young chicks are lost to possums, stoats and rats. There are six varieties of kiwi including the brown kiwi, of which there are several subspecies, the little spotted kiwi and the great spotted kiwi. The Maori refer to the kiwi as *te manu huna a Tane*, 'the bird that Tane-mahuta hid'.

The only native owl is the **morepork**, or ruru, which can be heard throughout New Zealand. They are very difficult to see but their haunting cry, *more pork*, is one of the most distinctive night-time sounds in the forests. The morepork hunts silently at night taking insects and beetles on the wing. Mice, baby rats and small birds are also considered. The Maori associated the morepork with the spirit world and it featured heavily in their mythology.

**Oystercatchers** can most often be seen hunting for food on the beaches. These black-coloured birds have startlingly bright orange eyes and bills. They are noisy birds, strutting about the sands in search of crabs or worms. They feed on shellfish by prising the shells apart with their specially evolved bills.

There are two species of native parakeet in New Zealand, the **red-crowned** and the **yellow-crowned parakeet**. The red-crowned parakeet is found only on offshore islands but the yellow-crowned parakeet can be seen throughout the main islands. Their Maori name, *kakariki*, refers to their bright green plumage. The destruction of broadleaf forests, the introduction of stoats and weasels and an excess of hunting have all contributed to a rapid decline. Fortunately a captive breeding programme has been successful and birds have been re-released into the wild.

One of the most attractive New Zealand birds is the **pukeko**, which is a deep indigo blue and black. Their orange-red bill and legs complete a very striking picture. They are common throughout the country but are most likely to be found in pairs in wetland areas. In places where there is plenty of cover the pukeko prefers to run to safety but it is quite capable of flying, although it looks awkward and comical as its long legs dangle beneath it.

Similar in appearance to the pukeko and closely related to it is the much more endangered **takahe**. Darker and bulkier than the pukeko, it is also flightless. Thought to be extinct for several years, a number of birds were sighted in the Murchison Mountains in Fiordland in 1948. Although takahe chicks have a high mortality rate, an intensive campaign has ensured that these exquisite birds have escaped extinction for the time being although their population is still estimated to be only around 200.

One of the few birds to have thrived since the arrival of humans is the **tui**. This native bird is an attractive metallic green with bluish patches on its shoulders, tail and breast. Two tufts of snow-white feathers hang below its throat. Loud and noisy, tuis have a beautiful call and have been described as the nightingales of New Zealand. Widespread, they can be seen even in suburban areas. The tui was of great importance to the Maori, who incorporated it into their mythology. They also hunted and ate it.

The **weka**, or wood hen, is another of New Zealand's flightless birds. They are slim, brown birds that strut on long powerful legs over scrub and wetland areas. The weka is most active at dusk. Inquisitive and fractious, it feeds mainly on invertebrates and fallen fruit. It will, however, approach people and rucksacks in the hope of scavenging.

## FLORA

*The timber trees were the straightest, cleanest and I may say the largest I have ever seen...*
*it was not one but all these trees which were enormous.*
Captain Cook's botanist, **Joseph Banks**, in his diary, 30 March 1770

The early Maori inhabitants of New Zealand believed that the trees that covered the islands were the children of Tane-mahuta, the God of the Forests. If they needed to fell a tree for any reason it was necessary to first placate Tane-mahuta by uttering the appropriate prayers. After the tree had been cut down it was also the custom to replace it with a seedling.

The European explorers and settlers who arrived in the 18th century saw the forests differently. To them they were vast and seemingly endless supplies of timber. Rather than revel in their beauty the settlers considered the forests as lucrative hindrances that needed to be overcome in their quest to tame and colonise the landscape. The introduction of grazing animals also had a negative impact on the vegetation, resulting in a reduction in the extent of the forests. Before people arrived in New Zealand, forest is estimated to have covered over 80 per cent of the landscape. By the beginning of the 19th century this had been reduced to around 65 per cent and over the course of the next two hundred years the forest has been decimated to the extent that the forest cover is currently estimated to be only around 15-20 per cent.

Altogether, 112 native tree species grow in New Zealand and around 80 per cent of the country's flowering plants are not found anywhere else in the world. There are far too many species to describe in detail here, though some of the most widespread or unusual plants are detailed below.

### Trees and ferns

Beech trees dominate much of New Zealand's forest, with the exception of Stewart Island which is noticeably free of beech. There are five species in New Zealand. The **red beech** grows up to 30m high, its wide trunk often heavily buttressed. Red beech tends to be found in lowland and montane forests throughout the country. Beneath its dark, shaggy bark the wood is red and straight-grained, making it popular for use in furniture production. The highly distinctive **silver beech** is a native of New Zealand. A sturdy trunk up to 30m high supports a bushy, spreading mass of foliage. The bark is silvery-white but turns grey as the tree matures. Frequently it is festooned with mosses and lichens. Traditionally it has been used in the furniture industry, though it is a good all-purpose timber. The slightly shorter **black beech** gets its name from the dark, sooty fungus that can often be found growing on its trunk. The fungus grows on honeydew exuded by a small insect that is endemic to the tree. The dew itself is a major food source for several native birds that can often be seen flitting around the tree. Found throughout the centre of the country, black beech is markedly absent from Fiordland as well as Stewart Island. **Mountain beech** is the smallest species of beech tree, growing to merely 15m tall. It looks similar to black beech but is more widespread, being found throughout both North and South Island, particularly at higher altitudes. **Hard beech** has a much smaller range, being largely confined to North Island, although it can be seen as far south as the Marlborough Sounds and Nelson. Its rough, furrowed bark is dark in colour and protects a much harder wood than the other species. Historically its wood has been used for railway sleepers and bridges.

The ubiquitous **broadleaf** is found throughout the North and South Islands. Its territory ranges from sea level to over 1000m. Its rounded, bushy profile can most often be seen in open areas, especially amidst regenerating scrub. Its short, gnarled trunk rarely exceeds 15m high. Although the wood is tough and hard-wearing, it is usually too twisted to be of much practical use.

The distinctive **cabbage tree** is one of New Zealand's most easily recognisable native trees. The thick, corky bark of the trunk supports a series of branches adorned with a spiky crown of long, wide leaves that resemble the top of a pineapple. Found throughout New Zealand, the tree can grow up to 12m tall. It can exist quite comfortably in swamps, forests and on barren, windswept hillsides. The Maori call it *ti kouka* and used to eat the inner root and young leaf buds. The leaves were stripped and used for weaving and plaiting. The **mountain cabbage tree** is similar in many respects to the standard version except it doesn't produce a branched crown. Rather it produces a much larger, single head of broad, fibrous leaves. Particularly common in wetter regions, it thrives at higher altitudes than the ordinary cabbage tree.

The **kamahi** is a common forest tree that can be seen across the whole of New Zealand in lowland and montane forests. It is especially prevalent in areas of regenerating forest, where it can grow to around 25m tall. When it flowers it produces vast quantities of small white flowers that completely engulf the tree and produce a highly distinctive flavoured nectar, particularly popular with apiarists for the production of honey.

**Lancewood**, which the Maori knew as *horoeka*, is another highly distinctive tree which changes appearance dramatically as it grows. As a young plant it develops long, thin, toothed leaves that jag downwards as a defence against being eaten. As the tree matures and grows taller (up to 15m) the leaves become progressively shorter and eventually the adult tree's foliage develops into rounded clusters.

The omnipresent **manuka** can be seen in all sorts of locations from sea level up to 1350m. Depending on the altitude and climate in which it grows, it can resemble anything from a stunted mountain shrub to a 4m tall tree. Its reddish wood is very durable and settlers used it to fashion tool handles and fence poles. It was also used to brew a tea-like drink which Captain Cook was to adopt as a remedy for scurvy. It was this practice that earned it the nickname 'tea-tree'. It is also used to make a strongly flavoured type of honey.

N E W   Z E A L A N D

**Miro** is another widespread tree often found in podocarp forests. It can reach 25m tall. Its dark-grey bark flakes off revealing a hard, straight-grained timber. Beautifully figured, it's used for flooring and the construction of houses.

New Zealand's only species of native palm, the **nikau** is instantly recognisable. Most easily seen on the north-west coast of South Island, this unlikely tree lends a tropical air to the coast. The ringed trunk gives way to a bulbous head that supports several long, vertically projecting fronds. These fronds used to be interwoven to cover Maori houses. Strips of frond could also be used to create baskets or other woven objects.

The **rata** is a massive tree. Beginning life as a climber, it perches on a host tree and sends down aerial roots that eventually reach the ground. It also grows roots around the host tree and strangles it. Found in coastal and lowland forests throughout North Island, it can also be seen around Nelson in South Island. Its brilliant red flowers grow in large clusters and are highly distinctive. The **southern rata** predominates in South Island, where its strapping trunks were used for boat building. It's likely that this is where it got its alternative name, 'ironwood'.

One of the most beautiful and graceful native podocarp trees is the **rimu**, which can be recognised by its spreading foliage and drooping collection of small, vibrant, prickly leaves. Rimu can grow up to 30m tall and live for a very long time – some trees are estimated to be over 800 years old. Rimu was the principal native timber tree and has been used in house construction and furniture manufacture, which has led to its drastic depletion.

The quick-growing, tall **tawa** is a graceful tree that can be found throughout North Island and as far south as Westport. Its fruits ripen to a dark purple colour. The kernels of these fruits were eaten by the Maori, who also used the tree's straight-grained timber to make their long bird spears.

One of the most significant trees in the forest is the **totara**. This giant tree is common in lowland and mountain forests and can live for over 1000 years. The Maori used to prize totara wood as the best for constructing their massive war canoes. Because of its softness it was also the preferred wood for carving.

There are more than 80 species of fern in New Zealand. The most common is the **bracken fern**, which is found all over hillsides and grows to a height of 3m. New Zealand's national emblem, the **silver tree fern** or ponga, is an attractive plant that is widespread and easily identified. A trunk up to 10m tall supports a horizontal spread of fronds that can be 4m long. The underside of the frond is silvery-white whilst the upper side is a dark green. Maori would use broken fronds to mark their path through the forest, as the vivid underside would be clearly visible in the gloom. The **black tree fern** or mamaku is the tallest tree fern, reaching 20m in height. The vast crown comprises fronds that can grow to 7m long. The thick trunk is marked by an horizontal pattern left by old, fallen fronds. The **wheki** is the most abundant of the tree ferns. By sending out underground rhizomes it is able to grow in clusters. This happens most often in areas of regenerating vegetation. Smaller than the other species of tree fern, its trunk is often cloaked in a skirt of dead fronds.

# Practical information for the visitor

## DOCUMENTS AND VISAS

### Passport

A passport is essential for all visitors to New Zealand. Technically, all passports except those from New Zealand and Australia must be valid for at least three months after your proposed departure from New Zealand although in practice if your home country has an embassy in New Zealand that can renew your passport you may be able to get away with only one month. For Australians and New Zealanders, their passports must merely be valid on entry to the country, as is the case with those foreign passports with an Australian or New Zealand residence visa in them.

### Visas

For the latest information relating to the entry requirements for New Zealand, try the **Immigration Service website**, 💻 www.immigration.govt.nz.

**Australian citizens** or holders of current Australian resident return visas do not need a visa or permit to enter New Zealand. Once in the country they are able to stay indefinitely, as long as they don't have any criminal convictions. Neither do they need a work permit. **UK citizens** and British passport holders with permanent UK residency do not need a visa either. Upon arrival in New Zealand they will automatically be issued with a six-month visitor permit.

The citizens of the following countries **do not require a visa** to enter New Zealand as their country has a visa-waiver agreement; they will be issued with a three-month visitor permit upon arrival provided they have an onward ticket to a country that they have permission to enter and sufficient funds (calculated to be approximately NZ$1000 per month) to support themselves whilst in New Zealand: Andorra, Argentina, Austria, Bahrain, Belgium, Brazil, Brunei, Canada, Chile, Denmark, Finland, France, Germany, Greece, Hong Kong,

---

### ❏ EMBASSIES AND CONSULATES

There is a full listing of New Zealand embassies and consulates around the world at 💻 www.nzembassy.com.

**Australia** (☎ 02-6270 4211, 💻 www.nzembassy.com), High Commission, Commonwealth Ave, Canberra, ACT 2600; **Canada** (☎ 613-238 5991, 💻 www.nzhc ottawa.org), High Commission, Suite 727 Metropolitan House, 99 Bank St, Ottawa, Ontario KIP 6G3; **Ireland** (☎ 01-660 4233, 💻 www.nzembassy.com), Consulate General, 37 Leeson Park, Dublin 6; **UK** (☎ 020-7973 8422, 💻 www.nzembassy .com), High Commission, New Zealand House, 80 Haymarket, London SW1Y 4TQ; **USA** (☎ 202-328 4800, 💻 www.nzemb.org), Embassy, 37 Observatory Circle NW, Washington, DC 20008.

NEW ZEALAND

Hungary, Iceland, Ireland, Israel, Italy, Japan, South Korea, Kiribati, Kuwait, Liechtenstein, Luxembourg, Malaysia, Malta, Mexico, Monaco, Nauru, Norway, Netherlands, Oman, Portugal, Qatar, San Marino, Saudi Arabia, Singapore, Slovenia, South Africa, Spain, Sweden, Switzerland, Tuvalu, UAE, Uruguay, USA, Vatican City, Zimbabwe.

Citizens of all other nationalities need to obtain a **visitor's visa** in order to be allowed to enter the country. Normally valid for up to three months, these can be obtained from any New Zealand embassy or consulate for a fee roughly equivalent to NZ$130.

It is illegal to work in New Zealand on a visitor's visa. Non-residents, with the exception of those from Australia, must apply for a work visa and then a work permit. There are a small number of **working holiday visas** made available to citizens between the age of 18 and 30 from a number of countries including the UK, Ireland, Canada, Chile, Denmark, France, Germany, Hong Kong, Italy, Japan, South Korea, Malaysia, Netherlands and Sweden. This 12-month visa entitles you to undertake temporary work, thus enabling you to supplement your travel with a small income. There are limited numbers available and a variety of restrictions and rules for different nationalities, which are explained on the Immigration Service website.

**Visa and permit extensions**  Should you wish to stay longer than your allotted time you may apply for an extension to your visitor permit or visa. This can be done at any New Zealand Immigration Service office, the largest of which is in Auckland (☎ 09-914 4100, 450 Queen St); others are in Christchurch (☎ 03-365 2520, Carter House, 81 Lichfield St) and Wellington (☎ 0508-558 855; Level 7, Regional Council Centre, 142-146 Wakefield St).

## MONEY

New Zealand's currency is the dollar. This is subdivided into 100 cents. Notes are available to the value of NZ$5, NZ$10, NZ$20, NZ$50 and NZ$100. Coins are worth 10c, 20c, 50c, NZ$1 and NZ$2. Prices on items or services are listed to the nearest cent. Once the final bill has been calculated it is rounded up or down to the nearest 10c. Currency can be exchanged at banks, foreign exchange offices and at the airport.

### Goods and services tax

All goods and services are subject to a 12.5 per cent goods and services tax (GST), similar to the UK's VAT. This is normally included in the

❏ **Exchange rates**
Exchange rates can fluctuate wildly, but at the time of writing the New Zealand dollar was more or less stable against the Australian dollar but less so against the North American and European currencies. For the latest rates visit ⊟ www.xe.com/ucc.

| | |
|---|---|
| US$1 | = NZ$1.59 |
| Australian$1 | = NZ$1.26 |
| £1 | = NZ$2.59 |
| €1 | = NZ$2.20 |
| Canadian$1 | = NZ$1.40 |
| NZ$1 | = US$0.63 |
| NZ$1 | = A$0.79 |
| NZ$1 | = £0.39 |
| NZ$1 | = €0.45 |
| NZ$1 | = C$0.71 |

NEW ZEALAND

advertised price of the item or service. Goods bought from a duty-free shop are exempt from GST as long as you provide proof that you are travelling.

## Tipping

Tipping is neither obligatory nor expected for normal service. However, tipping in appreciation of special service is welcome and should be done. Five to ten per cent of the total bill is usually appropriate.

## Banks

Banks are usually open from 9.30am to 4.30pm on weekdays. Banks such as Westpac, ANZ and Bank of New Zealand are the most widespread. ATMs are common. All major **credit cards** – Visa, Mastercard, American Express and Diners Club – are accepted in New Zealand. Generally, **travellers' cheques** can be cashed at any trading bank and most large hotels. If you intend to stay in New Zealand for an extended period of time you may wish to consider opening a bank account and getting a card for an ATM. ANZ bank will open accounts for you before your arrival in the country. For more information contact Migration Services, ANZ, 1st Floor, 20 Martin Place, Sydney.

## GETTING AROUND

### By air

New Zealand is fairly compact and quite easy to travel around. Should you wish to cover large distances quickly and don't mind paying a little extra, flying is a good bet. The major domestic carrier is **Air New Zealand** (NZ tollfree ☎ 0800-737 000, 🖳 www.airnz.co.nz), which serves all the main cities and a number of smaller airports as well. **Qantas** (☎ 0800-808 767, 🖳 www.qantas.co.nz) also connects most of the major tourist destinations and larger cities. If you buy tickets before you arrive in the country you even save yourself the 12.5% GST which is not charged on purchases outside of the country. Air New Zealand offers the South Pacific Air Pass for journeys within the country or to Australia and some South Pacific Islands when booked at the same time as an international flight; the pass offers discounted flights within several 'zones'.

Regional operators include **Soundsair** (☎ 0800-505 005, 🖳 www.sounds air.co.nz), an airline specialising in flying from Wellington to Picton and offering a very competitive alternative to the ferry, and **Stewart Island Flights** (☎ 03-218 9129, 🖳 www.stewartisland flights.com), who run scheduled services between Invercargill and Stewart Island.

### By coach

The most common way to travel around the country is by coach. The main operators are **InterCity** (🖳 www.intercitycoach.co.nz) and **Newmans** (🖳 www .newmanscoach.co.nz), who cover the entire country and ostensibly share a timetable. Services run several times a day on the main routes. Timetables and prices are available from information centres and coach stations. Book early or online for the best fares. Smaller competitors include **Atomic Shuttles** (☎ 03-349 0697, 🖳 www.atomictravel.co.nz) who operate extensively throughout

South Island, **Guthreys Express** (☎ 0800-732 528, 🖳 www.guthreys.co.nz) who cover the northern half of North Island, **Naked Bus** (☎ 0900-62533, 🖳 www .nakedbus.com) who offer basic no-frills services on both islands, and **Wanaka Connexions** (☎ 0800-244 844, 🖳 www.time2.co.nz) who link Dunedin, Queenstown and Wanaka on the South Island.

## By train

Trains are often more expensive than the equivalent bus service, and the destinations covered are far fewer as a result of a lack of investment, making the train a poor alternative to the coaches. The few long-distance services left in use are tourist scenic services. All long-distance trains are run by **Tranz Scenic** (🖳 www.tranzscenic.co.nz), the longest of which is The Overlander between Auckland and Wellington via the central plateau and the hamlet of National Park. However, the most stunning service is the TranzAlpine between Christchurch and Graymouth on the west coast.

## By ferry

There are regular ferry links between North and South Island. The sea crossing takes about three hours. The **Interislander Ferry** (☎ 0800-802 802, 🖳 www .interislandline.co.nz) operates between three and five services every day, taking three hours to cross the strait. Alternatively, it is sometimes cheaper to sail with **Bluebridge** (☎ 0800-844 844, 🖳 www.bluebridge.co.nz) who run three or four services daily and take just under three and half hours to make the crossing. **Stewart Island Experience** (🖳 www.stewartislandexperience.co.nz) operates a regular ferry service between bluff at the foot of the South Island and Oban on Stewart Island.

## ACCOMMODATION

Although not necessarily the cheapest accommodation in the world, the general standard of places to stay in New Zealand is very high. There is also a wide variety of choice, although during peak season you should still consider booking well in advance to secure your first choice.

The hostel is a New Zealand institution and fantastic examples can be found throughout the country. B&Bs, homestays and lodges offer a variety of alternatives, whilst Kiwis themselves tend to prefer the well-equipped motels lining the entrance roads to most towns rather than hotels in the centres. Nonetheless there are plenty of international standard top-end hotels across the country as well. For details of accommodation on the Great Walks see p283.

---

❏ **Accommodation abbreviations**
Throughout this book abbreviations have been used when detailing accommodation rates. They are as follows: **dorm** = dormitory bed; **sgl** = single room; **dbl** double room. So, for example, sgl/dbl NZ$45/60 means that a single room costs NZ$45 per night, a double NZ$60.

## Campsites

Traditionally found on the outskirts of towns, these are often well equipped and may even have a communal kitchen, TV room and laundry facility. Tent pitches cost around NZ$10-15 per person. DOC also operate several hundred campsites, typically in breathtaking locations. Cheap and cheerful with few facilities, the sites are graded informal (free), standard (NZ$5-10) and serviced (NZ$10-15).

## Hostels

Apart from campsites these tend to be the cheapest places to stay, with dorm or bunk beds costing around NZ$20-27. In addition double and twin rooms are usually available for a little bit extra. Frequently situated in stunning locations they are generally very accessible. They are also great places to meet other travellers and to pick up information from the enthusiastic staff. Most hostels have a fully equipped kitchen, washroom, TV room and a noticeboard dedicated to advertising travellers' needs, requests and tips.

There are approximately 60 YHA (🖳 www.yha.co.nz) or associated hostels. YHA/HI members pay fractionally less than non members; membership can be arranged in your home country or in New Zealand (NZ$40, including a NZ$14 phonecard). The majority of hostels though, some 370 in all, are affiliated to the Budget Backpacker Hostel group (BBH, 🖳 www.bbh.co.nz); their annual guide, readily available from hostels and visitor centres, gives details and lists current prices. Anyone can stay at a BBH hostel but discounts are available if you present a BBH card (NZ$45, includes NZ$20 phonecard). There is also a number of hostels connected to VIP Backpacker Resorts (🖳 www.vip.co.nz).

## B&Bs, homestays and lodges

These vary from basic, clean but functional suburban homes to more exclusive boutique retreats. As a result rates vary from below NZ$100 to more than NZ$350 per double room. Homestays tend to be guest rooms in the owners' house where you can overnight and join the hosts for breakfast. Rural versions tend to be farmstays, which involve just that: staying with a family on a farm. For listings consult 🖳 www.bnb.co.nz or 🖳 www.bnbnz.com.

## Hotels and motels

Hotels can be either rooms (NZ$80-120) above pubs, or more usually conventional types of accommodation designed for businessmen or people on organised tours that come complete with all mod-cons, which cost upwards of NZ$150. Often of variable quality, there are frequently good deals to be had during the low season. Motels (NZ$100-150) provide self-contained accommodation with their own kitchen and facilities. Although often ugly, unprepossessing places they represent good value for groups travelling together.

## LANGUAGE

English is the main language of New Zealand. Te Reo Maori is also an official language although you are unlikely to hear it spoken widely on the streets, except perhaps in rural communities in the north and east of North Island.

If you do get the opportunity to visit a *marae* (see p50), such as on the Whanganui River Journey, learn a handful of phrases to use with your hosts. Just being able to say *Kia ora* (hi, hello), *Kei te pehea koe* ('How are you?' Response *kei te pai*, meaning 'Very well, thanks') and *E noho ra* ('goodbye') shows that you are willing to make the effort and will be appreciated.

Knowing just a few Maori words can also help make sense of place names. For instance, Waikaremoana is the Sea (*moana*) of Rippling (*kare*) Waters (*wai*) and Whanganui is the Great (*nui*) Harbour (*whanga*). A hill in southern Hawke's Bay boasts what is usually considered the world's longest place name, Taumatawhakatangihangakoauauotamateaturipukakapikimaungahoronukupo kaiwhenuakitanatahu, the rough translation of which when broken down into its constituent parts is 'the summit where Tamatea, the man with the big knees, the conqueror of mountains, the land-swallower who circumnavigated the lands, played his nose flute for his lover'.

## TIME

New Zealand has only one time zone. This is 12 hours ahead of Greenwich Mean Time, so if it's 9am in the UK it is 9pm in New Zealand. During New Zealand's daylight saving time, from the first Sunday in October to the first Sunday after 15 March, New Zealand is 13 hours ahead of GMT.

❑ **Public holidays**

| | |
|---|---|
| New Year | 1 January |
| Waitangi Day | 6 February |
| Good Friday | late March/April |
| Easter Monday | late March/April |
| ANZAC Day | 25 April |
| Queen's birthday | 7 June |
| Labour Day | 25 October |
| Christmas Day | 25 December |
| Boxing Day | 26 December |

## ELECTRICITY

New Zealand uses a 230/24volt, 50Hz AC power supply. Plug sockets take a three prong, flat-pin plug. Adaptors are readily available in the airports and throughout New Zealand.

## POST AND TELECOMMUNICATIONS

There are **post offices** in most communities and towns. If there isn't a dedicated post office one of the other shops in the town will provide some of the services, such as selling stamps. Each major town centre has a CPO, Chief Post Office, with poste restante facilities where mail will be held for 30 days. Letters sent within New Zealand cost 50c and take around two days to arrive. Postcards to anywhere in the world cost NZ$1.50; international letters sent to Europe and the United States cost NZ$2 and take 6-10 days to arrive.

Public **telephones** can be found throughout most towns. Direct dialling is available from nearly all telephones. Most payphones are card operated. These phonecards (denominations NZ$5-50) can be bought from bookshops, newsagents, petrol stations and other retailers. There are also some coin-operated phones. Alternatively, you may charge national and international calls to your credit card. The international code for New Zealand is ☎ 64. Directory assistance can be contacted by ringing ☎ 018 and the emergency services can be reached on ☎ 111. Phone numbers starting 0800 are tollfree in New Zealand only.

The **internet** is well established in New Zealand. Internet cafés have flourished and you shouldn't have any trouble locating one unless you're really in the middle of nowhere. Service isn't particularly quick but reasonable value at NZ$6-10 per hour.

## TOURIST OFFICES

New Zealand has a highly developed tourist office infrastructure. Even the smallest towns have a dedicated visitor information centre. The larger centres are part of the **i-SITE** network which is affiliated with the national tourist body Tourism New Zealand (🖳 www.newzealand.com) and boast trained staff, copious information brochures and leaflets and mountains of material relating to local activities and attractions. Staff often also act as booking agents and can organise all manner of trips, tours and itineraries on your behalf, although only with companies registered with them. In addition, there is a network of **DOC visitor centres** to help organise tramping activities and excursions into the national parks. They are good sources of information relating to track conditions, weather and the local environment.

Overseas tourist offices can be found in Australia (☎ 02-8220 9000; 1 Alfred St, Sydney), the UK (☎ 020-7930 1662; New Zealand House, 80 Haymarket, London, SW1Y 4TQ) and the USA (☎ 310-395 7480; 501 Santa Monica Blvd, Santa Monica, California 90401).

## MEDIA

New Zealand doesn't have a national newspaper as such although the *New Zealand Herald* (based in Auckland, 🖳 www.nzherald.co.nz), *The Dominion Post* (based in Wellington, 🖳 www.dompost.co.nz), *The Press* (based in Christchurch, 🖳 www.stuff.co.nz) and the *Otago Daily Times* (based in Otago, 🖳 www.odt.co.nz) are all available throughout the country. Various international papers are available in the larger cities. *Wilderness* (🖳 www.wilderness mag.com) is a monthly magazine covering tramping, kayaking, climbing and mountain biking.

There are five main TV channels and a handful of subscriber services offering pay-per-view channels. There is also a Maori TV channel, launched in 2004, which broadcasts news, sport, sitcoms and cultural programmes in Maori and English.

## DRIVING

In New Zealand motorists drive on the left. Speeds and distances are metric so road signs will advise you of the distance to each destination in kilometres. The speed limit on an open road is 100km/h whilst in an urban or built-up area this drops to 70km/h or 50km/h. **Seat-belts** are compulsory for both drivers and passengers in the front *and back* of the car.

NEW ZEALAND

To rent a car you must be 25 or older and will have to present a current driver's licence from your home country. You may hire or drive only the same vehicles that you are legally entitled to drive in your own country. Most major international companies – Avis, Budget, Hertz, National, Thrifty – are represented in New Zealand's major cities. Whilst driving you must carry your licence with you at all times and if it isn't written in English you must be able to provide a written translation upon request.

**Drink driving** is an offence and the police have the right to stop and test the driver of any vehicle at any time.

## FOOD

The New Zealand food scene has taken off in the last ten to fifteen years. Chefs and restaurateurs have discovered the fabulous larder of fresh, native ingredients on their doorstep and embraced the diverse ethnic elements that comprise New Zealand society. The development of **Pacific Rim cuisine**, which draws its inspiration from Europe, Asia and Polynesia, and the subsequent innovation and a willingness to experiment have led to a dramatic upturn in the quality of food to be found in New Zealand restaurants. For reviews and recommendations by locals visit 🖥 www.dineout.co.nz, an impressive database boasting an ever-expanding list of places to try all around the country.

Much of the menu revolves around New Zealand staples. **Seafood** is prevalent and frequently sensational. New Zealand's legendary green-lipped mussels are exceptionally flavoursome and the local oysters are equally fabulous. Scallops, crayfish and paua are also worth seeking out. Of the salt-water fish, snapper is the most common, whilst blue cod is a regional speciality. You may also be tempted by hoki, groper, John Dory or kingfish. Fish and chips is a perennial favourite although you may wish to substitute kumara (sweet potato) chips for the traditional version. There are also numerous excellent recipes for trout, although an archaic law passed in the 19th century (when trout was introduced to New Zealand), designed to protect sport-fishing, prevents the commercial purchase or sale of the fish. You are, however, perfectly entitled to catch it yourself. Another fresh-water species that may appear on a menu is eel, which is often served smoked.

New Zealand is also famous for the quality of its **meats**. Lamb and beef are the traditional foodstuffs although farmed venison, known as *cervena*, is becoming more common. Meat pies are popular and can usually be relied upon to be packed with meat. New Zealand also produces a substantial range of **cheeses**, many of which are award winning. The ubiquitous hard cheddar is surpassed by the creamy Kikorangi blue and Legato goat's cheese.

A wide range of **fruit** flourishes in New Zealand. Apples, pears and citrus fruits are all common. The kiwi fruit is a popular alternative, as is the sweet, scented feijoa. Fresh **vegetables** are plentiful and readily available. Staples such as potatoes, carrots, peas, cabbage, pumpkin and squash can be found in all supermarkets and groceries. In restaurants you may also come across

> **Food and wine festivals**
> Hugely popular food and wine festivals are held up and down the country during February and March showcasing the different regions' fresh produce and vintages. One of the most popular is Toast Martinborough (🖥 www.toastmartinbor ough.co.nz) which actually takes place on the third Sunday in November, with Wellington locals decamping in droves to enjoy the food drink and music on offer – some 8500 litres of wine are consumed on the day!
>
> For something a little different attend the Hokitika Wildfoods Festival (🖥 www .wildfoods.co.nz). In early March 20,000 brave gourmands descend on Hokitika on the South Island's west coast, to munch on huhu bugs, smoked eel, possum and other unusual bush tucker delicacies (or, more sensibly, stick to the wild venison and other roast meats on offer) whilst downing home-brewed beer and South Island wines over the course of this gluttonous weekend.

aubergines and capsicums. Pacific specialities include kumara, taro and yam, though these last two are more unusual.

Traditionally, New Zealand is a carnivorous society. **Vegetarian** restaurants are much less widespread except in the larger urban centres or in the more alternative communities. For a full listing of vegetarian restaurants in New Zealand, visit 🖥 www.vegdining.com or 🖥 www.vegetarian.org.nz.

You are unlikely to encounter many Maori restaurants. In order to enjoy customary **Maori cooking** you are likely to have to attend a traditional *hangi*, where meat and vegetables are steamed in an earth oven for hours and then served to large gatherings, usually of family members. Sizeable river stones are placed in the embers of a fire whilst a large pit is dug. The hot stones are then laid at the bottom of the pit and covered in wet sacking. Baskets of prepared meat, fish and vegetables including kumara, all wrapped in leaves, are lowered into the pit and covered with earth so that the steam and the flavours are trapped. Several hours later the baskets are uncovered and the food parcels unwrapped to reveal a wonderfully tender, flavoursome feast. The result is more than just a meal, it's an event.

## DRINK

There are a variety of beverages available in New Zealand, the vast majority of them palatable. Details of the various drinks can be found online at 🖥 www .brewing.co.nz or 🖥 www.nzwine.com. The **legal drinking age** is 18. Alcohol is served in most restaurants and cafés. **Licensing hours** tend to vary but most pubs and bars are open from 11am to 1am and nightclubs generally stay open until 3am. In some of the smaller, more rural towns there may not be many venues open much after 11pm. On Sundays off-licences are obliged to remain closed and restaurants can serve alcohol only with food.

**Beer** is drunk everywhere and is readily available in pubs and restaurants. On the whole, it is reasonable quality and tends to be about four per cent proof. Stronger five per cent versions exist but are mostly labelled as 'export'. Much of the beer brewed in New Zealand is made by two large producers: New

NEW ZEALAND

Zealand Breweries and Dominion Breweries (DB). The most widespread brands of beer include the ubiquitous Steinlager and its 'no-additives' cousin Pure, DB Bitter and Export, Tui and Lion Red. On South Island you will also come across Speights and Monteiths.

A few smaller breweries and microbreweries also exist. These include Macs who produce the splendid, stout-like Black Mac, and Founders, who produce the award-winning Long Black. Some pubs, such as the Loaded Hog chain, have also taken to brewing their own beer.

The cheapest beer in a pub is served on tap. It is most frequently served as a '7' (7 fluid ounces, equivalent to 200ml), a '12' (350ml, roughly half a pint), a 'handle' (half litre, known as a pint) or a 'jug'. A pint will usually cost NZ$5-8. A pint is usually a little less than its imperial equivalent. A jug isn't necessarily a litre – it's just that, a jug of beer, frequently three pints. It is cheaper to buy beer in bulk from an off-licence, where it is sold in six packs or cartons of twelve. Foreign beers are usually also available but at a price. There are, of course, the ubiquitous Irish pubs too, which serve Guinness as well as New Zealand beer.

New Zealand has a thriving **wine** industry. Although its reputation barely took off 30 years ago, many of the country's vineyards are beginning to rival the old-world equivalents in terms of quality. The nation's reputation is gaining in stature and looks set to continue to do so. These highly distinctive, premium quality wines have evolved to complement the variety of food available on most menus. New Zealand tends to produce better white wines than reds, since the climate is more suited to these types of grapes. However, Pinot Noir looks set to be the country's next big thing.

There are also some excellent Champagne-style sparkling wines made here as well as some aromatic dessert wines. The colder climate of South Island largely prohibits the growth of grapes, and although wine is produced in Central Otago and around Christchurch, the best-known regions are further north. Marlborough is famed for its Sauvignon Blanc and Hawkes Bay is renowned for its Chardonnay. Elsewhere, the Henderson region, Waiheke Island and Kumea Valley, all near Auckland, produce good-quality wines, as do the regions of Martinborough, Gisborne and Blenheim. Wine menus in restaurants tend to focus on local wines although you will probably come across Australian reds as well. A glass of wine costs $6-10. In an off-licence, bottles of wine sell from $10 upwards, although it is worth paying a little extra (NZ$15-20) for the better quality.

Most international **spirits** are readily available alongside the New Zealand-made vodka 42 Below. In addition, you may find several sickly-sweet local spirits that include feijoa and kiwi-fruit liqueur. South Island also produces a couple of brands of whisky.

**Non-alcoholic drinks** are also readily available. Soft drinks, milkshakes and smoothies are all popular. Tea can be found in a variety of different flavours and scents, whilst coffee is taken very seriously: you should have no trouble finding a short black (espresso), long black (weaker espresso), flat white (latte/espresso with milk) or cappuccino in most towns.

## THINGS TO BUY

There are a host of arts and crafts to consider when searching for a souvenir of New Zealand. Traditional **Maori artworks**, carvings, wood panels, figures and bowls made from native woods such as rimu are popular. Bone carvings, traditionally made from whale but more commonly now created from cow bone, also sell well. A number of places around the country allow you to create your own piece based on classic Maori design. Pendants made from gorgeous **greenstone** or iridescent paua shell frequently depict sacred spirits or animals and are loaded with meaning and significance. The most common design is the *heitiki*, which is a small, stylised Maori grotesque, frequently depicted sticking its tongue out in an aggressive challenge. These figures have great *mana*, power, and also serve as fertility symbols. These are often created with the intention of being given as gifts, having first been worn, since every owner adds something to its value. Beware of cheap, tacky imitations that can be found for sale at street markets and the like and avoid inferior Chinese jade. For guaranteed quality pieces you should shop in specialist art and craft stores close to the source of the raw material near Greymouth and Hokitika.

New Zealand is renowned for the quality of its **woollen products**. Very high quality, hand-spun, hand-dyed and hand-knitted garments such as jumpers, hats, gloves, scarves and mufflers can be bought throughout the country. New Zealand fashion boasts a couple of top designers including Karen Walker, Kate Sylvester and Trelise Cooper, whose clothing can be picked up at relatively reasonable rates.

## SECURITY AND CRIME

Violent crime is by and large uncommon in New Zealand. That which does occur is often reported vividly because it is so unusual. The country as a whole is generally safe and as long as you abide by the usual precautions and keep your wits about you, you should be fine. **Theft** from parked cars is the most common crime affecting visitors to New Zealand. This can take place in cities, rural car parks and at trailheads. In order to minimise the likelihood of this occurrence make sure that you don't leave any valuables on display in the vehicle and lock all bags in the boot. **Women travellers**, even when on their own, ought to be perfectly safe in most places. As ever, you should avoid isolated spots late at night and remain vigilant if you find yourself in an unknown area.

In the main, the police are helpful, friendly and can be relied upon.

### Drugs

Most drugs are illegal in New Zealand and you should not try to buy or sell them. Marijuana is fairly widespread and can be very potent. Much of the supply of marijuana is handled by gangs such as the Mongrel Mob and Black Power. The police will demonstrate a degree of tolerance towards cases of personal use but are less lenient when it comes to the more serious issue of dealing. They are also much less tolerant of hard drugs, many of which carry long custodial sentences for possession.

**PART 4: GATEWAY CITIES**

## Auckland

*Last, loneliest, loveliest, exquisite, apart*
 **Rudyard Kipling**, The Song of the Cities

### INTRODUCTION

Auckland is the largest and most accessible city in New Zealand and this thriving cosmopolitan city is considered one of the most desirable locations in the world to live. Although the city has come a long away since Kipling (see above) penned his poem and can no longer reasonably be referred to as 'loneliest' or 'apart', the verse is still a fitting description of, and tribute to, the city.

Two beautiful harbours, Waitemata and Manukau, provide a scenic canvas for this diverse metropolitan area, which comprises 48 volcanic cones, 50 islands, 22 regional parks and more than 50 vineyards. Auckland stretches from the town of Wellsford in the north to the rolling Bombay Hills in the south, including within its administration four distinct cities (Auckland, North Shore, Manukau and Waitakere) and three districts (Rodney, Papakura and Franklin) in one substantial urban sprawl. Nevertheless, it is one of the least densely populated cities in the world.

Surrounded by water, the ocean inevitably plays a large part in the lives of locals. Nicknamed the 'City of Sails', Auckland has the highest number of boats per capita in the world. The entire waterfront area enjoys a convivial atmosphere. Safe swimming beaches are tucked within sheltered bays whilst exposed stretches of shoreline are pounded by wild surf breaks.

The climate encourages outdoor activities such as tramping, mountain-biking, kayaking and horse-riding. More leisurely pursuits are also accommodated. Cafés and restaurants offering fine food are spread throughout the city as are shops and boutiques.

Auckland has all the facilities and amenities you could possibly need. This is the place to switch flights, organise visas and find work. However, the city is not simply a gateway to the rest of New Zealand: its vibrant nightlife, wide proliferation of arts centres, beaches and other attractions demand a longer, more fulfilling stay.

### HISTORY

Archaeological evidence suggests that human settlement of this area dates back over 800 years. Legend records that the first human inhabitants were the magical Turehu people. All subsequent Maori tribes of the region claim descent from the Turehu. However, their tribal identities are generally linked to the individual ancestral *waka*, canoes, that sailed to New Zealand from Hawaiki, the legendary home of the clever, mischievous demi-god Maui (see box p50).

The region became highly prized for its unique natural position, excellent fishing opportunities, rich volcanic soils and readily defensible volcano-top fortified sites. The area became known as **Tamaki Makau Rau**, 'The Spouse Desired by a Hundred Lovers', as it was coveted by all the tribes in the area and in due course was conquered and claimed by many of them: down the years the ownership of the area changed hands some 18 times amongst Maori tribes.

During the 18th century invaders from the Ngati Whatua tribe conquered Auckland. Today the Ngati Whatua are acknowledged as *tangata whenua*, ('the people of the land') of the Tamaki isthmus. Their *marae* occupies Bastion Point, overlooking Waitemata Harbour, whose name translates as 'Sparkling Waters'. The most accessible remains of pre-European Maori occupation are etched into the slopes of One Tree Hill and Mt Eden, where defensive fortifications are still clearly visible along with rectangular pits dug to hold kumara harvests.

Captain James Cook sailed past the area whilst charting the New Zealand coastline on one of his voyages of discovery. He missed Waitemata Harbour but he did leave several place names including Great Barrier and Little Barrier islands. In 1820 Samuel Marsden became the first-known European to explore the Hauraki Gulf. Then in 1827 the French explorer Dumont D'Urville sailed into Waitemata Harbour. He scaled Mt Victoria and tried to climb Mt Eden but abandoned the attempt because of the impenetrable vegetation. He recorded very little human presence on Auckland isthmus, concluding that the residents must have abandoned the area as a result of persistent armed raids by other tribes and, in the wake of a devastating smallpox epidemic, retreated to the Waikato region.

Following these early forays, **whalers and early traders** arrived in search of new opportunities. Missionaries also travelled to the area. In 1833 the region's first European village was established around a spa and saw-milling operation on Mahurangi River, where Warkworth stands today.

The year 1840 was central to the development of Auckland. The Treaty of Waitangi was signed by local Maori chiefs at Karaka Bay, Mangere and Awhitu. Later in the year Captain William Hobson, the governor of New Zealand, was invited by Ngati Whatua chiefs to establish the new colony's capital in Auckland. Impressed by the quality of land surrounding it and pleased by the fact that it adjoined two harbours, Hobson agreed to make Auckland the capital. A **sailing regatta** was held to celebrate the raising of the Union Jack, a tradition that is still observed every year on Auckland Anniversary Day (end January). The new capital was named after Hobson's naval commander, Lord Auckland, and was to be the country's capital for 25 years before losing the privilege to Wellington in 1865.

In 1841 Auckland had only around 1500 residents, though this number was swelled by a wave of immigrants a year later when the ships *Jane Gifford* and the *Duchess of Argyle* dropped 500 Scottish settlers on the shores. Auckland endured periods of depression along with eras of great economic success. The population continued to grow steadily and the city acquired a cosmopolitan flavour, with dozens of languages spoken on the streets. This theme continued throughout the 20th century. In the 1950s the post-war 'baby boom' further boosted the population. European **immigrants** continued to be attracted from countries such as Hungary, Holland and Yugoslavia, whilst Asian immigrants also found their way to New Zealand. Rural inhabitants began to relocate to the city and a large number of Maori migrated there as well. By 1970 Auckland's population had grown to 650,000.

The city survived the economic downturn of the 1980s and early 1990s and has picked itself up once again. Now with over 1.3 million inhabitants, it is home to about a third of the national population and is flourishing as an international, modern city.

## ARRIVAL AND DEPARTURE
### By air
Auckland is by far the busiest of New Zealand's international airports. Located 21km south-west of the centre in the suburb of Mangere it consists of an international and a domestic terminal. There is a free shuttle-bus service (daily 6am-10.30pm) between the terminals and a well-signposted footpath that takes ten minutes to walk.

At the **international terminal** there is a very helpful i-SITE Visitor Centre

---

**Customs and quarantine regulations**
New Zealand has very strict customs and quarantine regulations designed to protect its flora and fauna. There are stiff penalties for failing to observe these regulations so you must take time to read and complete the relevant declaration forms. Expect a short delay as you enter the country whilst airport officials check your luggage.

(☎ 09-275 6467; daily 5am-midnight). Staff there can make hotel bookings or you can use the free courtesy phones. Elsewhere there's a bank and a selection of duty-free shops. Whilst in the airport, pick up free copies of the annual *Auckland A–Z* and Jason's *Auckland – What's On* guide, published monthly. You may also be able to find the *Official Guide to Auckland*.

In the **domestic terminal** there is a Air New Zealand Visitor Centre (☎ 09-256 8480; daily 7am-5pm). All the terminals have left-luggage facilities and car-rental desks.

The simplest, cheapest way of getting into the city centre is to catch the **Airbus** (NZ tollfree ☎ 0800-247 287, 🖳 www.air bus.co.nz; NZ$15/22 one way/return, 45-60 mins, daily 3/hr, 2/hr after 6pm). The Airbus follows a set route and passes through Newmarket and Parnell before calling at most major hotels and backpacker hostels, the Britomart Transport Centre and Ferry Terminal. The first service from the airport departs at 5.20am and the last at 10.15pm. From the city centre the bus runs from 4.30am to 10.15pm and starts opposite the ferry terminal.

Alternatively, a multitude of **taxis and minibuses** vie for your trade at each terminal. For pick-up and departure phone Super Shuttle (☎ 0800-748 8850).

### By land
Travelling by **bus** is efficient and cost-effective. The main bus company in Auckland is InterCity (☎ 09-913 6100, 🖳 www.inter citycoach.co.nz), which operates from the Sky City coach terminal at 102 Hobson St. Tickets and information are available from the Contact Centre (☎ 09-623 1503; Mon-Thur & Sat 7am-9pm, Fri & Sun 7am-10pm). InterCity also operates Newman's Coach Lines (tollfree ☎ 0800-777707, 🖳 www.newmanscoach.co.nz). Smaller operators, including the Airbus, stop outside the Scenic Tours and Travel office at 172 Quay St, opposite the Downtown Ferry Terminal.

The New Zealand **rail** network (see p72) now covers only a few routes and destinations. The Overlander (stops include Hamilton, Palmerston North, Wellington and National Park Village) departs from Britomart Transport Centre daily.

If you are **driving**, State Highway 1 heads north all the way to Cape Reinga and south towards Hamilton, from where it splits to provide access to the Coromandel Peninsula and central area of North Island. See pp89-90 for information about hiring or buying a car.

## ORIENTATION
The backbone of the city is **Queen St**, which runs from the scruffy, concrete Queen Elizabeth II Square (QEII Square) on the waterfront to Bohemian Karangahape Rd (K Rd); it is lined with shops, banks, offices and arcades. The Aotea Centre and Square are adjacent to the road and the distinctive Sky Tower and Sky City complex are a couple of blocks west. Attractive Albert Park is just to the east.

The **city centre** is lively and bustling during the day. However, after office hours it can seem a little quiet. Viaduct Harbour, Princes Wharf and surrounding streets or the ever-lively K Rd are better alternatives at this time.

Sprawling suburbs surround the city centre. **Parnell** to the east is a stylish residential area with desirable restored houses set alongside restaurants and boutiques. Further east is the equally fashionable shopping district of **Newmarket**. To the west are **Ponsonby** and **Jervois** roads lined with good quality eateries and watering holes. Further afield are yet more residential suburbs, including **Mt Eden** to the south, **Takapuna** to the north and the eastern beaches along **Tamaki Drive**. Across the harbour is the small waterside suburb of **Devonport**, which can be reached by a 15-minute ferry ride from the town centre.

## WHERE TO STAY                 [map p85]
There is plenty of accommodation for all budgets; most people opt to stay in the city centre for convenience, but there are plenty of attractive options in the inner suburbs too. **Hostels** are widespread. **Hotels** range in quality and consequently price but in general provide a high standard of accommodation. There is also a range of excellent

**B&B** and guesthouse-style lodgings in the inner suburbs, whilst **motels** and **campsites** tend to be restricted to less central areas.

## City-centre hostels

The city centre boasts the largest hostels with the most spaces. It is still advisable to book in advance during the busiest months (Dec-Feb) though. The vast majority of hostels are on or near Queen St.

The best-known hostel is the enormous *base Auckland Central Backpackers* (base ACB; ☎ 09-358 4877, 💻 www.stayatbase .com; 500 beds; dorm NZ$27-30, twin/dbl NZ$70/90, en suite NZ$95) at 229 Queen St. Open 24 hours a day, base ACB boasts everything you might need: a travel centre, internet café, call centre and recruitment agency. It also has two TV lounges, a huge, modern kitchen and a dining area. There is a terrace bar as well as the cavernous, legendary Globe Bar, in the basement, where you can mingle with other backpackers every night of the week from 4pm until very late. Part of the same stable is *base Auckland* (☎ 09-300 9999, 💻 www.stayat base.com; dorm NZ$26-28, dbl/twin NZ$80/90) at 16-20 Fort St. For a city-centre location it's quite relaxed and the converted seven-floor office building makes for an unusual hostel with plenty of character. In addition, it offers all the usual facilities including a rooftop kitchen, BBQ area, spa and sauna and travel desk. There's also a women-only 'Sanctuary' floor.

*The Fat Camel* (☎ 09-307 0181, 💻 www.fatcamel.co.nz; dorm NZ$20-30, dbl/ twin NZ$60-70), on Fort St, is a functional place with frequently small, windowless rooms but the location is good and the staff are very friendly and helpful. Better is *Aspen House* (☎ 09-379 6633, 💻 www .aspenhouse.co.nz; standard sgl/dbl NZ$69/ 84, en suite dbl NZ$129), a good-value B&B-style hostel at 62 Emily Place. The communal areas are welcoming and the location, on a steep street adjacent to a park, is very attractive and relatively quiet.

With shared rooms rather than dorms per se, *BK Hostel* (☎ 09-307 0052, 💻 www.bkhostel.co.nz; twin bed share NZ$25-27, sgl/dbl NZ$40/50), 3 Mercury

Lane, is clean and secure despite its proximity to K Rd.

The city has two YHAs (💻 www.yha .co.nz): *Auckland International YHA* (☎ 09-302 8200, 💻 yha.aucklandint@yha.co .nz; dorm NZ$22-26, dbl/twin NZ$55, en suite NZ$70), 5 Turner St, is a big, modern, purpose-built block with superb facilities, whilst the slightly smaller *Auckland City YHA* (☎ 09-309 2802, 💻 yha.aucklandcity @yha.co.nz; dorm NZ$22-24, dbl/twin NZ$50) on the corner of City Rd and Liverpool St, is one of Auckland's largest and most-established hostels and comes complete with cosy common areas, a restaurant and city-wide views from the upper floors.

## Suburban hostels

Should you wish to escape the throng in the city centre, your best bet is either Parnell or Mt Eden.

**Parnell** is half an hour east of downtown Auckland on foot but is well served by public transport and has some of the finest backpacker accommodation in the city. *International Backpackers* (☎ 09-358 4584, 💻 international.bp@xtra.co.nz; dorm NZ$17-22, dbl/twin NZ$45) is at 2 Churton St, a quiet residential area, in the spacious old Parnell YHA building. There are several hostels on St George's Bay Rd: try *City Garden Lodge* (☎ 09-302 0880, 💻 www .citygardenlodge.co.nz: dorm $28-30, dbl NZ$68, twin NZ$58-68), at No 25, a friendly, spacious place in good grounds originally built for the queen of Tonga, or *Lantana Lodge* (☎ 09-373 4546, 💻 www.lantanalod ge.co.nz; dorm NZ$23, dbl/twin NZ$45), a compact, homely place at No 60.

**Mt Eden** is 4km south of downtown Auckland but is again readily accessible by public transport. The excellent *Bamber House Hostel* (☎ 09-623 4267, 💻 www .hostelbackpacker.com; dorm NZ$22-25, dbl/twin NZ$54-60), 22 View Rd, is noteworthy for its colonial-era house dating from around 1910, with high ceilings, a grand staircase and large garden; or try the commendable *Oaklands Lodge* (☎ 09-638 6545, 💻 www.oaklands.co.nz; dorm NZ$20-22, sgl/dbl and twin NZ$40/54-60), set in a large Victorian house, at 5A Oaklands Rd, and run by the same people.

Elsewhere, in **Ponsonby**, there's the bright, well-appointed *Uenuku Lodge* (☎ 09-378 8990, 🖳 www.uenukulodge.co.nz; dorm NZ$25-29, sgl/dbl and twin NZ$47/62-82) at 217 Ponsonby Rd; the charming, laid-back *Brown Kiwi* (☎ 09-378 0191, 🖳 www.brownkiwi.co.nz; dorm NZ$22-24, dbl/twin NZ$60) at 7 Prosford St; and *Verandahs* (☎ 09-360 4180, 🖳 www.verandahs.co.nz; dorm NZ$25-27, sgl/dbl NZ$48/66), a spacious, well-positioned late Victorian villa in a tranquil spot at 6 Hopetoun St.

In **Grafton** there's *Georgia Parkside Backpackers* (☎ 09-309 8999 or 0508-436 744, 🖳 www.georgia.co.nz; dorm NZ$20,

sgl/dbl NZ$44/50), 189 Park Rd, a grand old house overlooking the Domain.

**Hotels**

The *Hilton Hotel* (☎ 09-978 2000, 🖳 www.hilton.com; dbl NZ$390), 147 Quay St, Princes Wharf, is an outstanding modern hotel set right on the harbour's edge. Modelled on a luxury liner, each of the smartly decorated rooms has a terrace or balcony with panoramic views. Room prices begin at around NZ$390 but increase rapidly if you want a sea view. *Heritage Hotel* (☎ 09-379 8553, 🖳 www.heritage hotels.co.nz; dbl NZ$300-350), 35 Hobson St, was converted from a department store to good-quality accommodation and also offers tennis courts, a health club, and

---

## AUCKLAND – MAP KEY

**Where to stay**
1 Hilton
14 Aspen House
15 The Fat Camel
16 base Auckland
20 Heritage Hotel
21 Shakespeare Hotel
29 Sky City Hotel (in Sky Tower)
32 base Auckland Central
    Backpackers
41 Auckland International YHA
42 Auckland City YHA
43 BK Hostel
44 International Backpackers
45 Lantana Lodge
46 City Garden Lodge

**Where to eat and drink**
2 Euro; Wildfire
4 Degree
5 Loaded Hog
6 Kermadec
7 Portofino
8 Minus 5°
9 Harbourside Seafood Bar; Cin Cin
12 Rose & Crown
18 Food Alley
19 Grand Harbour
21 Shakespeare Tavern
22 The Grove

**Where to eat and drink** (*cont'd*)
23 The Blue Stone Room
24 Occidental Belgian Beer Café
25 Raw Power
26 Merlot
27 Meze Bar
29 Fortuna; Tamarind; Orbit; The
    Observatory (in Sky Tower)
31 Atrium on Elliot Food Gallery
32 Globe Bar
33 Tony's; Middle East Café
36 Tony's
40 Tanuki

**Other**
3 New Zealand i-SITE Visitor Centre
10 Ferry Terminal & DOC Visitor
    Centre
11 Britomart Transport Centre &
    railway station
17 American Express
28 Whitcoulls Bookshop
29 Auckland i-SITE Info Centre
30 Sky City Coach Terminal
34 Post Office
35 Aotea Centre
37 Auckland Art Gallery
38 Public Library
39 Tourist Info
47 Auckland Museum

indoor and outdoor pools. *Sky City Hotel* (☎ 09-363 6000, 🖳 www.skycity.co.nz; dbl NZ$300-plus), on the corner of Victoria St and Federal St, is part of the casino complex here. The rooms are fairly standard but benefit from the array of other facilities available to guests.

*Shakespeare Brewery & Hotel* (☎ 09-373 5396, 🖳 www.shakespearehotel.co .nz; dbl NZ$99) is a decent boutique hotel at 61 Albert St. The 100-year-old English-style pub (see p86) has ten rooms, some

with a terrace and view of the harbour, which offer comfort and convenience in a central location.

Finally, the city's finest B&B is the elegantly and sensitively restored *Peace and Plenty* (☎ 09-445 2925, 🖳 www.peace andplenty.co.nz; sgl NZ$230-265, dbl NZ$295-350) in the heart of Devonport at 6 Flagstaff Terrace. Superbly located, packed with antiques and treasures and thoroughly luxurious, this Victorian villa, dating from 1880, is the best bet for escaping the city

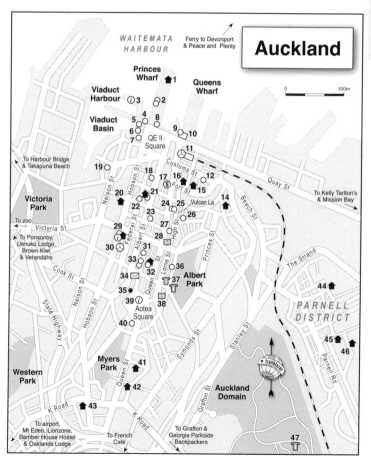

centre (see p89 for ferry services) and the more obvious brand-name hotels without sacrificing the highest levels of comfort.

## WHERE TO EAT AND DRINK

The Auckland restaurant scene has grown dramatically over the last decade or so and the food and wine on offer can be very sophisticated. Auckland has also perfected the style of cuisine known as **Pacific Rim**, drawing on its cosmopolitan heritage and ethnic diversity by blending Asian and Pacific flavours. Seafood features prominently on most menus; New Zealand green-lipped mussels and Clevedon coast oysters are particularly well known. There is also exceptional local lamb and venison on offer. Fine cheeses from the Puhoi Valley to the north of the city are also worth investigating.

Auckland has embraced café culture and there is a vast range of places to sit and leisurely sip a drink. The city-centre restaurants offer good food in pleasant settings while for somewhere with more atmosphere or character try a waterside restaurant in the Viaduct Harbour or Princes Wharf area. The inner-city suburbs of Parnell, Ponsonby and Herne Hill also offer countless, fashionable coffee shops and dozens of dining options.

To complement your meal there is a host of award-winning local **wines**. There are now more than 80 vineyards in the surrounding region. The oldest wine-producing area is Pleasant Valley, in west Auckland, which has been producing wine since 1902, whilst Clevedon to the south and Matakana to the north are much newer grape-growing districts. Look out for respected Auckland labels Kumeu River, Stonyridge and Matua Valley. Waiheke Island is famous for its red wines.

### City centre

Aside from the budget fast-food stands and takeaway options, the food halls often found in large shopping centres offer a wide range of cheap meals. **Atrium on Elliot Food Gallery**, on Elliot St, has counters offering South-East Asian, Chinese, Japanese and Italian food as well a bakery

selling reasonable coffee, and **Food Alley**, 9 Albert St, sells mostly Asian cuisine. Both are cheerful places and a meal at either will cost only about NZ$10.

Frequently the distinction between drinking and dining venues is blurred, with places serving both. Pubs such as the **Rose and Crown** (☎ 09-373 2071; NZ$10-15 for a meal) on Customs St, the historic **Occidental Belgian Beer Café** (☎ 09-300 6226; NZ$10-20) on Vulcan Lane, which specialises in *moules et frites*, and **The Shakespeare Tavern** (see p85; NZ$10-15) on the corner of Wyndham and Albert streets, is New Zealand's first brew pub (literally a pub that brews its own beer and keeps own-brand beers on tap); it also offers reasonably priced food and a good ambience. If you're just after a burger, salad or smoothie over lunchtime drop in on **Raw Power** (NZ$10-20 main course) on the first floor at 10 Vulcan Lane.

Restaurant-wise, Auckland has something to offer everyone. **French Café** (☎ 09-302 2770; NZ$35-45 main course, six courses NZ$100), at 210 Symonds St, is consistently voted one of the best restaurants in the city for its exquisite European-influenced food and slick service. **The Grove** (☎ 09-368 4129, ⌨ www.thegrove restaurant.co.nz; NZ$30-40 main course, tasting menus NZ$100) on St Patrick's square, Wyndham St, is a small, upmarket eatery offering superb contemporary fare and tasting menus in an atmospheric setting.

As its name suggests, **Merlot** (☎ 09-309 5456; NZ$26-30 main course), at 23 O'Connell St, specialises in wine and boasts more than 100 varieties to accompany its traditional French bistro-style dishes. **Tanuki** (☎ 09-379 5353) at 319B Queen St is a smart Japanese restaurant with a less formal saké bar offering cheaper snacks below it. For Chinese food try the bustling **Grand Harbour** (☎ 09-357 6889), at 18 Customs St West, whilst for Middle Eastern fare check out **Meze Bar** (☎ 09-300 7209; NZ$10-20 for tapas, NZ$30 main courses) at 1A Little High St or **Middle East Café** (NZ$7-10 for tapas) at 23A Wellesley St, something of a local institution. At 27 Wellesley St **Tony's** (☎ 09-373 2138;

NZ$30-35 main course) serves sumptuous steaks; there is a second branch at 32 Lorne St. *Harbourside Seafood Bar and Grill* (☎ 09-307 0486; NZ$50 main course), in the Ferry Terminal, has breathtaking sea views from its balcony and serves the freshest New Zealand seafood. *Cin Cin* (☎ 09-307 6966; NZ$20-35 main course) in the same building serves excellent seafood and oysters.

Sky Tower offers several dining options: *Fortuna* on Level 2 is the ultimate buffet restaurant, providing a spectacular variety of very reasonably priced foods (NZ$10-20 main course). The fusion of Eastern and Western flavours, incredible food presentation and the contemporary elegance of the interior make *Tamarind* (Level 3; NZ$25-40 main course) one of Auckland's premier dining experiences. *Orbit*, at 190m/623ft, is Auckland's only revolving restaurant and dishes up award-winning, New Zealand cuisine, whilst the *Observatory* (main course NZ$35-50) at the top of the Sky Tower is a brasserie-style buffet restaurant specialising in seafood.

### Viaduct Harbour and Princes Wharf

This is one of Auckland's most spectacular locations for dining out. Sprawling outdoor terraces adjacent to the harbour are often packed with people. Some of the restaurants here are the most acclaimed in New Zealand. *The Loaded Hog* (NZ$10-20 main course) in the Viaduct Basin is a noisy pub inspired by a rural New Zealand theme. Its own award-winning naturally brewed beers complement the unpretentious, robust menu.

*Euro* (☎ 09-309 9866; NZ$30-45 main course), Shed 22 on Princes Wharf, is one of the most stylish places to dine on modern New Zealand cuisine and makes for an exceptional treat. *Wildfire* (☎ 09-353 7595; NZ$35-45 main course), adjacent to Euro, is a Brazilian *churrascaria* (barbecue house) that specialises in meats and seafoods roasted over manuka coals, and rotisserie-style foods. *Kermadec* (☎ 09-309 0412; NZ$30-40 main course), on the first floor of the Viaduct Harbour, is a bustling brasserie. *Portofino* (☎ 09-356 7080;

NZ$30-40 main course), in Viaduct Harbour, is a chic Italian restaurant.

### Suburban dining

K Rd, Parnell and Ponsonby offer numerous places to eat. Open-fronted cafés, intimate bistros, quirky eateries and culturally diverse restaurants thrive here. Tranquil daytime cafés frequently metamorphose into much more rumbustious drinking dens later on. Your best bet is simply to wander the streets and see what takes your fancy. Be warned, though, these areas get busy at the weekend.

**K Rd** has interesting options although it is generally considered to be more of a late-night place. Check out the achingly hip café-bar *Alleluya* (☎ 09-377 8424; NZ$10-20 main course) in St Kevin Arcade at 179 K Rd, or visit the excellent-value and correspondingly popular *Satya* (☎ 09-377 0007; NZ$15-25 main course), at 271 K Rd, for South Indian themed food.

**Parnell** has some good-quality, medium-priced restaurants, many with outdoor seating. *Himalaya* (☎ 09-362 0215; NZ$15-25 main course), at 123 Parnell Rd, is a great Nepalese joint offering curries and vegetarian dishes, whilst *Di Mare* (☎ 09-300 3260; NZ$25-30 main course), set back from the road at No 259, is a great surf-and-turf option. *Iguacu* (☎ 09-358 4804; NZ$25-35 main course) at No 269 is a large, trendy venue popular with younger locals. For a change of pace visit *Chocolate Boutique* at No 323 for handmade chocolates and decent coffee or while away the time at *Rosehip Café*, set back from the main drag at 82 Gladstone, adjacent to the pretty rose gardens there.

**Ponsonby** is Auckland's busiest dining district (it even has its own website, 🖳 www .ponsonbyroad.co.nz) with several trendy places serving excellent cuisine. For breakfast head to *Dizengoff* (☎ 09-360 0108; NZ$15-20) for the perfect start to the day. Later in the day visit *Il Forno*, at 55 Mackelvie St, to pick up a pastry or snack. *SPQR* (☎ 09-360 1710; NZ$25-40 main course), at 150 Ponsonby Rd, is a fashionable Italian-style restaurant hangout that doubles as a bar. Over the road at No 127 is the ***Ponsonby Fish and Chip Co*** (☎ 09-378 7885) which sells superb, fresh take-away versions of exactly what you'd expect.

## NIGHTLIFE

Auckland has a variety of nightlife and entertainment options. Many of these are quite low-key during the week but come alive at the weekend; the best way to figure out what's on is to pick up a copy of the *New Zealand Herald* or one of the free guides to music, art, theatre and film available throughout the city (see p82).

The lively **pubs and bars** in the city centre attract large crowds. *Globe Bar* under base Auckland Central Backpackers (see p83) and *Embargo Bar*, at 26 Lorne St, are popular haunts. Elsewhere in the city are animated Irish-, English-, Belgian- and Russian-themed pubs and bars. *The Blue Stone Room*, at 9 Durham Lane, has good ales and local bands, whilst *Degree* is at 204 Quay St is a fairly standard harbour-basin boozer that's perennially popular.

For something a little different try *Minus 5°* (🖳 www.minus5experience.com) bar on Princes Wharf where you can spend half an hour sipping super-chilled vodka cocktails from an ice 'glass' in a bar sculpted entirely from ice.

The big **nightclubs** are generally located around the Viaduct, on K Rd and along Ponsonby Rd. These tend to charge an entrance fee. Most musical tastes are catered for and the energetic crowds carry on dancing until well into the following day. At weekends many venues are open 11pm-8am.

**Live music** and **theatre** is often staged in venues such as the purpose-built Aotea Centre at 50 Mayoral Drive, and Sky City Theatre (🖳 www.skycity.co.nz) on the corner of Victoria and Federal Sts. The Civic Theatre on Queen St has been restored to its art nouveau glory and is used by touring groups and international productions but also showcases dance, music and films. Smaller venues are scattered throughout the city. The Classic Comedy Club (☎ 09-373 4321, 🖳 www.comedy.co.nz; Mon-Sat) at 321 Queen St hosts local acts and touring performers.

The Force Entertainment Centre on Aotea Square is home to a giant IMAX and a monstrous 12-screen **cinema**. There's also a huge screen on the third level of the Sky City Metro, the mall standing at 291 Queen St. The Sky City complex also boasts two **casinos**.

## SERVICES

### Banks

There are plenty of banks, moneychangers and ATM machines on Queen St. It is always wise to check around before settling on an exchange rate, although in the main these are fairly consistent.

**American Express** (☎ 09-379 8286) at 105 Queen St, **Interforex** at 2 Queen St (☎ 09-302 3031) and 99 Quay St (☎ 09-302 3066) and **Thomas Cook** at both 159 Queen St (☎ 09-379 3924) and 34 Queen St (☎ 09-377 2666) all offer reliable exchange facilities. The **Bank of New Zealand** has a branch at the international terminal of the airport that is open to greet all incoming flights.

### Bookshops and map shops

There are several large **bookshops** in the centre of town. Whitcoulls, on the corner of Queen St and Victoria St, has a large range of New Zealand literature and illustrated books. It also has a very pleasant *café* on the first floor. Borders at 291 Queen St is another large store that stocks a vast range of material. The smaller but equally well-stocked Unity Books at 19 High St is a pleasure to visit. There are several second-hand bookstores, the best of which is probably Hard to Find (But Worth the Effort), which has branches at 238 K Rd and in Devonport at 81A Victoria St.

For a larger range of **maps** than is usually carried by standard bookshops, try Auckland Map Centre (🖳 www.auckland mapcentre.co.nz) in the National Bank Centre, Shop 3, 209 Queen St, or Speciality Maps at 46 Albert St.

### Information centres

In addition to the offices at the airport (see pp81-2), there are two visitor centres in downtown Auckland. **Auckland i-SITE**

Centre (☎ 09-363 7182, 💻 www.auckland nz.com; daily 8am-8pm) can be found in the atrium of the Sky City building. The **New Zealand i-SITE Centre** (☎ 09-307 0612; daily 9am-5pm) is at 137 Quay St.

The city is patrolled by **Auckland City Ambassadors** who are easily identifiable by their red and yellow uniforms. These individuals can answer queries and help to direct you should you get lost.

The **DOC Visitor Centre** (☎ 09-379 6476; Mon-Fri 9am-5pm) is in the Ferry Terminal on Quay St. From here you can book tramps or purchase maps and pamphlets for routes throughout New Zealand.

### Internet access
Places offering access to the internet have sprung up all over the city. Most of the backpacker hostels have some sort of connection. In general rates vary from NZ$2 to NZ$5 an hour. (See also below).

### Library
**Auckland Public Library** (☎ 09-377 0209; Mon-Fri 9.30am-8pm, Sat 10am-4pm, Sun noon-4pm), 44 Lorne St, includes a New Zealand room and a collection of rare books. Internet services are also available.

### Market
Victoria Park Market (daily 9am-6pm), within easy walking distance of Viaduct Harbour, has a food court, restaurants, stalls and several shops selling New Zealand-made goods. It's worth a visit to see if you can pick up a bargain.

### Medical treatment
**Auckland Hospital** (☎ 09-367 0000) on Park Rd, Grafton, and **North Shore Hospital** (☎ 09-486 1491) on Shakespeare Rd, Takapuna, are both public hospitals with accident and emergency clinics. Private clinics and registered medical practices are listed in the telephone directory under 'Hospitals'.

**Travelcare** (☎ 09-373 4621; Level 1, 125 Queen St) and the **Travellers' Medical and Vaccination Centre** (☎ 09-373 3531; Level 1, Canterbury Arcade, 170 Queen St) provide vaccinations and medical advice.

### Pharmacy
Auckland City Urgent Pharmacy at 60 Broadway, Newmarket, is open daily 9am-11pm. The alternative is to use the 24hr pharmacies in the hospital emergency departments.

### Post office
The main post office (Mon-Fri 7.30am-5.30pm), in the Bledisloe Building at 24 Wellesley St West, has poste restante facilities. There are several smaller post offices throughout the city.

### GETTING AROUND
To try and get to grips with Auckland's convoluted, busy public transport system visit the journey planner at 💻 www.maxx.co.nz, which covers buses, ferries and trains.

Most **buses** start or finish at the Britomart Transport Centre on Queen St. A quick and handy way to orientate yourself in central Auckland is to hop on the **Link bus** (daily 6am-11.30pm every 10-15 mins, NZ$1.60); it travels clockwise and anti-clockwise around a loop of the city, taking in the downtown area as well as the suburbs of Ponsonby, Parnell and Newmarket. The red **City Circuit buses** (daily 8am-6pm, free) run every 10 minutes and provide a hop-on-hop-off service around the inner city centre from Britomart Transport Centre, up Queen St to Auckland University and back via the Sky Tower. See also p90.

**Ferries** depart from the Ferry Terminal (☎ 09-424 5561) on Quay St. Fullers (💻 www.fullers.co.nz) runs ferries to Devonport daily 2-3/hr (journey time 10-15 mins). Information about timetables and routes is available from the terminal.

The majority of **car-hire** companies in Auckland have desks or offices at the airport but some are huddled together on Beach Rd. The big companies, such as Avis (☎ 09-526 2800), Budget (☎ 0800-652 227 or 09-375 2270), Hertz (☎ 0800-654 321 or ☎ 09-309 0989) and Thrifty (☎ 0800-737 070 or ☎ 09-309 0111), are the most reliable.

Cheaper deals can be organised through A 2 B Car Rentals (☎ 0800-616 111), Ace Tourist Rentals (☎ 0800-422 771), Backpacker Campervan and Car

Rentals (☎ 0800-422 2672 or ☎ 09-275 0200) and Rent-A-Dent (☎ 0800-736 823).

Many people who are staying for extended periods opt to **buy a car**. Dealers, newspaper advertisements and hostels are the best places to look. Backpackers Car Market (💻 www.backpackerscarmarket .co.nz), at 20 East St just off the K Rd, is a lively place with frequent deals to be had as backpackers sell directly to each other.

Car fairs at Manukau (☎ 09-358 5000) and Ellerslie Racecourse (☎ 09-529 2233, 💻 www.carfair.co.nz) are also popular. Arrive before 9.30am to get the best choice.

## WHAT TO SEE AND DO

There is a multitude of activities and distractions in Auckland: whether you're interested in history, culture, horticulture, wildlife, adrenaline sports or simply finding the perfect beach, Auckland has something for almost everyone.

To get around the main sights consider the hop-on-hop-off **Explorer Bus** (☎ 0800-439 756, 💻 www.explorerbus.co.nz) which runs every 30 minutes from the Ferry Terminal on Quay St and takes in Viaduct Harbour, Kelly Tarlton's Underwater World, Auckland Museum, Parnell, Sky City, Victoria Park Market and Auckland Zoo. An all-day pass costs NZ$30 and the tour includes full commentary.

Half-day **walking trips** presenting a Maori perspective can be booked with Tamaki Hikoi Tours (☎ 0800-282 5526)

and cost NZ$80. Alternatively, Potiki Adventures (☎ 0800-692 3836, 💻 www .potikiadventures.com) offer a full-day outing for NZ$145. See also box below.

## Auckland Art Gallery

Spread over two buildings this gallery (☎ 09-379 1349, 💻 www.aucklandartgallery .govt.nz; daily 10am-5pm) contains a wealth of important works. The main building (on the corner of Wellesley and Kitchener streets) has a permanent collection of New Zealand art including a number of Maori portraits but is undergoing an extensive and impressive restoration until 2010. The second building (on the corner of Wellesley and Lorne streets) houses contemporary art and other touring or temporary exhibitions. Admission is free though there may be charges for temporary exhibitions.

## Auckland Harbour Bridge climb and bungy jump

Organised trips up and over this iconic girder bridge offer a unique perspective of the city from 65m above Waitemata Harbour. To book a trip contact AJ Hackett (☎ 09-361 2000, 💻 www.aucklandbridge climb.co.nz) or visit their office at Westhaven Reserve, Curran St, Herne Bay. Trips run daily, last one and a half hours, cost NZ$120 and are open to those aged seven and over. For further thrills consider bungy jumping from the bridge. The

---

### 🕭 Walking in Auckland

Auckland's topography lends itself to walking. The finest track leads from coast to coast following a trail of yellow markers and milestones across a narrow neck of land between Waitemata and Manukau harbours. The 16km walk takes around four hours and takes in Albert Park, the adjacent historic buildings of Auckland University, Auckland Domain, the volcanic cones of Mt Eden and One Tree Hill and some of the leafier suburbs not usually visited. Buses run regularly in either direction so there's no need to retrace your footsteps. Maps and directions for this trail can be picked up from the city's visitor centres.

There are also plenty of hiking trails in the Waitakere and Hunua ranges to the west and south of the city respectively. Woodhill and Riverhead plantation forests attract mountain-bikers and motocross riders as well as walkers.

The DOC Centre (see p89) can sell you a series of pamphlets highlighting the best walks and trails in the Auckland area.

40m/131ft fall from a specially designed pod is the only harbour-bridge bungy in New Zealand; the experience costs NZ$120 and is open to those aged ten and over.

## Auckland Domain

This scenic 80ha public park to the east of the city centre is a very pleasant place for a stroll or picnic. This was the city's first park, established in the 1840s, and is replete with all the trappings of a mid-Victorian garden: formal flower-beds, spacious, landscaped lawns and a rotunda. The **Winter Garden** (admission free, Apr-Oct daily 9am-4.30pm, Nov-Mar Mon-Sat 9am-5.30pm, Sun 9am-7.30pm) is housed in two ornate greenhouses on either side of a shallow pond and has an extensive collection of temperate and tropical plants. Adjacent is the **Fernz Fernery**, an old scoria quarry that has been converted into a hollow that's now home to more than one hundred types of fern. There is a *café* here.

## Auckland Museum

Housed in a magnificent neoclassical building on top of Auckland Domain's hill, the three-storey museum (☎ 09-309 0443, 🖳 www.auck landmuseum.com; daily 10am-5pm, donation welcome, NZ$5 per adult suggested) houses a host of magnificent Maori treasures and South Pacific artefacts that are amongst the most important in New Zealand. The displays detailing Maori legends, culture and history are particularly interesting. This is also the only venue in Auckland that hosts Maori cultural performances (11am, noon, 1.30pm; NZ$20 adult, NZ$10 children). There is also an excellent collection of ethnology and natural history, military and social history and the decorative arts. Hands-on displays and interactive activities ensure that your interest never flags.

## Sky Tower

Auckland's Sky Tower (☎ 09-363 6000, 🖳 www.skycityauckland.co.nz), on the corner of Federal and Victoria streets, is the tallest structure in the Southern Hemisphere. At 328m/1076ft it is – just – taller than the Eiffel Tower, meaning that visitors to the city tend to take their bearings from the looming structure. Tickets to go up to the main observation lounge cost NZ$25/8 for an adult/child. It takes 40 seconds from pavement level to the main observation decks. From here the views are outstanding and you can get a true overview of the city.

For NZ$3 more, a special skylift takes you to the ultimate viewing platform, the **Skydeck** at 220m/722ft. The best time to go up the tower is at dusk as the sun sets and the city lights begin to come on. The worst time to go up is when there is low cloud or high winds, at which time the tower can sway up to 1m. It is possible to walk around the 192m-high outer halo of the tower with **Sky Walk** (☎ 0800-759 586, 🖳 www.sky walk.co.nz). The halo is 1.2m wide and has no safety rail or barrier, but you are roped to a rail above your head for safety. The breathtaking stroll costs NZ$135.

In true New Zealand style an outrageous activity has been organised whereby you fall at around 80km/h from 192m/630ft above the ground, secured by wire cables and reliant only on 'fan descenders', as used by stunt actors, to slow your descent: base jumping by wire! This is the highest **tower-based jump** in the world (aim for BNZ Bank Tower when leaping, ie jump up

In pursuit of the ultimate thrill: leaping from the 328-metre Sky Tower.

and out as if you are going to make the leap across to and land on it, so you achieve the best position/posture for the fall) and is symptomatic of New Zealand's obsession with adrenaline-based activities. To book a jump contact SkyJump (☎ 0800-759 586, ☐ www.skyjump.co.nz). The freefall lasts approximately 12 seconds and costs a cool NZ$195. Book both activities together and save NZ$60.

The **Sky Screamer** (☎ 09-377 1328, ☐ www.reversebungy.com), on the corner of Albert and Victoria streets, involves being shot 60m into the air in a sort of reverse bungy. Experience 5Gs as you accelerate to almost 200km/h in a stomach-clenching couple of seconds – all for NZ$40.

**Auckland Zoo**
The zoo (☎ 09-360 3819, ☐ www.auckland zoo.co.nz; daily 9.30am-5.30pm) is five minutes west of downtown Auckland on Motions Rd. Committed to the conservation and preservation of natural habitats, the zoo is home to over 900 animals including both foreign and native species. The nocturnal house represents many people's best chance of seeing a kiwi.

Entry costs NZ$19 for adults and NZ$9 for children aged up to 15.

**One Tree Hill**
This small **extinct volcano** (182m) in Cornwell Park, 6km south of the city, used to be the site of one of the largest Maori pa settlements (see p49) in the area. Terracing and kumara storage pits can still be seen on the slopes of the hill.

Known as Maungakiekie, 'The Mountain of the Kieke Tree', it used to have a single pine tree and an obelisk on its summit. The tree was attacked by a Maori activist who claimed that it stood as a reminder of European patriarchy; it was badly damaged in the attack and subsequently cut down in 2000. The obelisk remains. It is inscribed with text in Maori and English celebrating the friendship between the Maori and the Europeans. The 360° view from the top of this raised area is particularly good.

**Mt Eden**
Mt Eden (196m) is the highest point in the city. Named after the first Earl of Auckland, George Eden, it stands 4km south of the city centre. This prominent landmark, known as Maungawhau by the Maori, boasts a vast 50m-deep crater. The crater, known as Te Ipu a Mataaho, 'The Bowl of Mataaho', is named after the God of Volcanoes and is sacred to the Maori – so don't enter it. From the top there is a magnificent 360° view across to both the Pacific Ocean and the Tasman Sea. It is most easily reached by bus from Britomart.

**Kelly Tarlton's Underwater World**
This is a fantastic seawater **aquarium** (☎ 09-528 0603, ☐ www.kellytarltons.co.nz, 23 Tamaki Drive; daily 9am-6pm last entry at 5pm; NZ$30/14 adult/child, family discounts are available), built in old stormwater-holding tanks, conceived by the New Zealand diver and salvage expert Kelly Tarlton. A moving walkway carries you through a transparent underwater cavern allowing you to see New Zealand's marine life from the perspective of a scuba diver. You can step off the walkway at any time in order to get a better look at any of the fish around you. For a better view, you can swim with the fishes: a dive in the shark tank costs NZ$175 whilst the opportunity to swim with stingrays costs NZ$99. The Antarctic Encounter display is a unique look at this chilly environment, complete with king, emperor and gentoo penguin colonies and a replica of Scott's 1911 Antarctic base.

The Explorer bus calls here but Kelly's also operate a free shuttle bus hourly (45 mins journey time) from Sky City atrium.

**Devonport**
An inexpensive 12-minute crossing (see p89; NZ$9/4.40 adult/child) from the Ferry Terminal on Quay St brings you to the delightful suburb of Devonport. The charming, sleepy, historic town is full of cafés, art galleries and curio shops. Pretty parks and beaches are scattered along the shoreline. A short track leads up Mt Victoria, Taka a Ranga, and affords classic views of the Gulf

and back to Auckland Harbour and city centre. A further track skirts the strategic site of North Head, which protected the inner harbour, and offers you good views out over Hauraki Gulf. The **i-SITE information centre** (🖳 www.tourismnorthshore.org .nz; daily 8.30am-5pm) at 3 Victoria Rd has brochures on local sights and walks.

## Beaches

The sea and coastline form an intrinsic part of Auckland life and there are beaches everywhere: **Mission Bay**, which is only ten minutes from downtown Auckland, is a firm favourite with locals thanks largely to its proximity, sandy beaches, scenic esplanade and large number of cafés.

**Takapuna Beach** is ten minutes north of Auckland over the harbour bridge. Although it is only one of many calm northshore beaches, its long sandy stretches are comfortably close to the cafés and shops of Takapuna. **Long Bay** is a little further north where a coastal walkway leads north past grassy areas and safe swimming spots. Elsewhere, **Goat Island Marine Reserve**, to the east of Warkworth, has vast white-sand beaches adjacent to it. This is New Zealand's oldest marine reserve and the inshore waters teem with shoals of fish. In contrast, **Muriwai**, **Piha** and **Karekare beaches** on the spectacular west coast have black sand. The windswept beach is 48km long and is known for its good surfing. Over spring and summer it becomes home to thousands of Australian gannets that have spread from offshore islands to the mainland. The tracts of forest and sandy beaches here are best explored on horseback or by motorbike.

## Dolphin spotting

Take an organised trip into the Hauraki Gulf in search of common and bottlenose dolphins. Conservationists lead you in search of pods. You may also see orcas, whales and other marine animals.

**Dolphin Safari** (☎ 0800-383 940, 🖳 www.dolphinsafari.co.nz) run daily trips from the pier adjacent to the Ferry Terminal on Quay St. The five-hour trips cost around NZ$140. They enjoy around an 85% success rate in terms of dolphin sightings and

offer a subsequent trip for half the price should you fail to see any.

## Gulf islands

There are more than 50 islands in the gulf off Auckland. Some are no larger than a small atoll, but others are big enough and close enough to be regarded as commuter suburbs and day-trip destinations.

**Rangitoto** dominates the skyline of the inner harbour. Formed 600 years ago by a volcanic eruption, the entire island is coated in rugged black basalt lava. As well as a fascinating geology, there are spectacular panoramic views from the summit. Rangitoto is also home to the world's largest pohutakawa forest. Ferg's Kayaks (☎ 09-529 2230, 🖳 www.fergskayaks.co .nz) run guided kayak trips (departing daily at 9.30am and 5.30pm) across the 7km stretch of sea to the island lasting six hours and costing NZ$120. The later departure time means you have the opportunity to kayak by torch or moonlight.

**Tiritiri Matangi** is a conservation park further north. It has been cleared of predators and planted with more than three million native trees in a bid to create a haven for endangered birds including the kiwi and takahe.

**Waiheke Island** used to be covered in farmland before it became an artists' hideaway and a base for alternative lifestyles during the 1960s and '70s. It continues to be a laidback haunt for winemakers, olive growers and even commuters who are prepared to make the 55-minute trip to the mainland. **Kawau Island** is the location of the stately mansion that belonged to the first Governor General of New Zealand, Sir George Grey. Grey imported a variety of exotic plants and animals, of which peacocks and wallabies remain. Walking tracks lead through the regenerating native forest to beaches, Maori sites and old copper mines.

Further out, some 88km from the mainland, is **Great Barrier Island**. This large, craggy, sparsely populated island is laced with walking tracks. It is a haven for rare birds and also has sandy beaches that offer good-quality fishing.

# Wellington

*The swift winds of Wellington may swing
     into the west,
The clouds o'er Terawhiti may break
     within the south,
The rain-song of Wellington will linger
     in my breast,
For the moist kiss of Wellington is music
     in my mouth.*
**Boyce Bowden**, Wet Weather

## INTRODUCTION

Set in a natural amphitheatre south of the steep Rimutaka Ranges, perched on the edge of a spectacular harbour and encircled by steep-sided, verdant hills, Wellington is an attractive and compact city.

The clouds of Terawhiti that fill Boyce Bowden's poem provide a realistic flavour of Wellington and indeed the city is famed for its winds and weather, yet even the elements add to the thrill of being here: in the 1960s Jan Morris noted delightfully that the winter winds which 'sprang rasping out of the Antarctic, scurry and scour through the hilly streets of the capital, and so shake the frames of the wooden houses that you feel yourself to actually be at sea'.

Lively, youthful and full of history and culture, Wellington combines the edginess and modernity of a major city with the charming appeal of a small town. It is much smaller than Auckland, its population roughly only a third of the size, and the two have been embroiled in a friendly rivalry since the southern city inherited the mantle of New Zealand's capital. Long considered merely a gateway to South Island, Wellington is now a vibrant, cosmopolitan destination, known for its national treasures, cultural attractions, burgeoning restaurant scene and thriving café culture.

## HISTORY

Maori legend records that Wellington Harbour was once a giant lake inhabited by two *taniwha*, or mythical water monsters. One of them, Ngake, was desperate to roam the open sea and in a bid to escape the confines of the lake smashed through the land separating the lake and Cook Strait, in so doing creating the harbour entrance. The other taniwha, Whataitai, attempted to escape from the other side of Miramar Peninsula. Unfortunately the receding tide held him and he was turned to stone before he could reach the open sea. His body now forms the isthmus of Hataitai, upon which the airport has been built.

The legendary Polynesian explorer **Kupe** is believed to have been the first person to have arrived in Wellington Harbour, in around AD950, and his descendants, the Ngati Tara, became the first permanent settlers in the area. Kupe is credited with exploring and naming much of the coast and the islands found there. During the 1800s the Te Atiawa and Ngati Toa tribes migrated south from Taranaki and claimed the area for themselves. A complex mix of tribes now live in the region, although Te Atiawa are still recognised as *tangata whenua*, 'the people of the land'.

Neither Abel Tasman nor Captain Cook were able to enter Wellington Harbour as strong winds made it too tricky a proposition. Whalers landed on the Kapiti coast in the early 1800s but it wasn't until 1840 that **European settlers** arrived in the region to take advantage of a series of highly dubious land purchases organised by the New Zealand Company. Their ship, *Aurora*, brought a number of British settlers who established a settlement near Petone. However, this was abandoned when the Hutt River flooded and the settlers were forced to move south to a more sheltered area. They established Lambton Harbour and began to develop the area around Thorndon.

Initially there was very little flat land available to build on. Land reclamation began in 1952 and in 1955 a giant **earthquake** raised the land around the harbour by around 1m. This had the effect of draining the Te Aro swamp and creating additional land for development. Land reclamation has added around 150ha to the inner-city area and much of downtown Wellington actually sits on land that was at one time either underwater or part of a swamp.

The city expanded rapidly, becoming the hub of coastal shipping and the centre of a thriving import/export industry. As South Island was explored and opened up to habitation, so Wellington became more important as a link between the two islands. In recognition of this, the capital was moved from Auckland in 1865, making it the southernmost capital in the world. At this time, the city was christened Wellington in honour of the Iron Duke, Arthur Wellesley, the first Duke of Wellington.

The city has prospered ever since. It remains a busy port but a thriving tourist industry has sprung up. The building of the superb national museum, **Te Papa Tongawera** (see pp105-6), has further secured the city's place as New Zealand's political, cultural and commercial capital.

## ARRIVAL AND DEPARTURE
### By air
**Wellington International Airport** (🖵 www.wellington-airport.co.nz), around 5km south-east of the city centre, is a modern, efficient airport with a small visitor centre (☎ 04-385 5123; daily 7am-7pm) on the first floor of the main terminal. There is also a bureau de change, several shops, cafés and various car hire agencies.

The airport handles both international and domestic flights. The former dominate the schedule but there are daily departures to most of the major towns in New Zealand. Air New Zealand (☎ 0800-737 000, 🖵 www.airnz.co.nz) is the primary carrier. Qantas (☎ 0800-808 767, 🖵 www.qantas.co.nz) also operates several domestic flights as well as a series of trans-Tasman services. Soundsair (☎ 0800-505 005, 🖵 www.soundsair.co.nz) operate a regular service (6-8/day, about 25 mins, NZ$89/77 per adult/child aged up to 12, one way) between Wellington and Picton on South Island that is a good alternative to the ferry services (see By sea).

The cheapest way into the city is the **public bus** service, the Stagecoach Flyer, which runs every half hour between 7am and 8.20pm (NZ$5.50 airport to town centre). The Super Shuttle (🖵 www.supershuttle.co.nz) provides a 24hr door-to-door service from the airport to town centre that costs NZ$15-20 for the first person and then NZ$5 more for each additional person going to the same destination. There are also **taxis** (see also p105) outside the airport which can convey you into the heart of the city.

Leaving Wellington on an international flight there's a NZ$25 **departure tax**. See also box p13.

### By land
State highways 1 (SH1) and 2 (SH2) merge just to the north of the city and provide access to the rest of North Island. SH1 runs 658km north, through the Central Volcanic Plateau, to Auckland and beyond, whilst SH2 provides access to the East Cape region. Beware of Wellington's extensive one-way system whilst **driving** in the city centre.

Wellington is an important hub for **bus** transport. InterCity (☎ 04-385 0520, 🖵 www.intercity.co.nz) and Newmans Coach Lines (☎ 04-385 0521, 🖵 www.newmanscoach.co.nz) run regular services to key destinations. All of these depart from platform 9 at the railway station. Tickets can be bought in advance or at the reservation desk and ticket centre inside the station.

White Star (☎ 06-758 3338, 🖵 www.whitestarbus.co.nz) operates services along the west coast to Palmerston North, Wanganui and New Plymouth. These buses depart from opposite the train station on Bunny St. Kiwi Traveller (☎ 0800-500 100, 🖵 www.kiwitraveller.co.nz) covers the centre of North Island, with services to Palmerston North, Taupo and Rotorua. The memorably named Naked Bus (☎ 0900-625 33, 🖵 www.nakedbus.com) journeys to Palmerston North, Napier, Taupo and Auckland with plenty of stops en route, all departing from Bunny St.

Wellington's **railway** station (☎ 04-498 3000) is the final stop on the main north-south line from Auckland. The station is next to Lambton Quay on Bunny St.

### By sea
Two companies ply the route across Cook Strait between Wellington and Picton. The

journey is memorable and the approach to Picton through the fingers of the outer Marlborough Sounds, where the forested cliffs descend right to the water's edge and the hills disconnect from the mainland-like islands, is a spectacular way to arrive on South Island.

**Interislander's** (☎ 0800-802 802, 🖳 www.interislandline.co.nz) services take around three hours to make the crossing. The three large ferries, *Arahura*, *Aratere* and *Kaitaki*, offer a range of facilities including restaurants, cafés, bars and a cinema. They depart from Aotea Quay, 2km from the town centre, beside the motorway on SH1 at 1.55am, 8.25am, 2.15pm and 6.15pm. The return boat leaves Picton at 5.45am, 9.50am, 1.15pm and 6.05pm. Between mid November and April there is an additional service leaving Wellington at 10.35am and from Picton at 2.25pm. There is a complimentary shuttle-bus service from platform 9 of the railway station to the ferry terminal 35 minutes prior to each sailing. Passenger fares start at NZ$73/38 per adult/child. There is a NZ$15 surcharge per bike or surfboard. A motorbike costs NZ$78 and a car costs NZ$163-235. Discounts are usually available if you book your ticket in advance; only standard fares are available on the actual day of travel.

The alternative, frequently cheaper, service is with **Bluebridge Ferries** (☎ 0800-844 844, 🖳 www.bluebridge.co.nz) who are based at Waterloo Quay close to the train station. The ferries take roughly 3¹/₂ hours to make the crossing, departing Wellington at 3am (except Saturday), 8am, 1pm and 9pm (except Saturday) daily and returning from Picton at 2am (except Sunday), 8am (except Saturday), 2pm and 7pm daily. Fares start at NZ$55/25 per adult/child, with cars costing NZ$130, motorbikes NZ$60 and bikes NZ$15.

For up-to-date timetables and prices consult the companies' websites, since services and prices vary according to the season and the best deals are to be had online.

## ORIENTATION

Most of Wellington is built on the land adjacent to the harbour or the precipitous hills that rise all around the city. These hills have acted as a natural barrier and prevented the untidy sprawl associated with many cities.

The **city centre** is compact and easy to negotiate on foot. It is an engaging mix of old and new architecture. To the far north of the city is the oldest suburb, Thorndon, which is now the location of the parliament buildings and the distinctive Beehive. The heart of the city stretches from the railway station in the north to Cambridge and Kent terraces in the south-east. In between, the waterfront streets of Jervois Quay, Cable St and Oriental Parade are lively, revitalised areas and the setting for the giant Te Papa Museum.

The central business area is divided into four discernible districts, all within easy walking distance of each other. These diverse quarters reflect the city's distinct character. The **Lambton** quarter, to the north of the city, is a concentrated shopping experience. Leading retailers, cutting-edge fashion stores and an eclectic range of outlets stand comfortably side by side. There are seven shopping malls in the quarter, which is centred on Featherston St, Lambton Quay and Customhouse Quay. Adjacent to this is the **Willis** quarter, the setting for several 'lifestyle' shops. The Civic Square, City Gallery and City to Sea Bridge are all found here. Further south is the relaxed **Cuba** quarter. This innovative, alternative district plays host to restaurants and cafés as well as more unusual, up-and-coming shops and quirky secondhand stores. The **Courtenay** quarter, centred on Courtenay Place, is the entertainment district and Wellington's playground. There is a remarkable diversity of restaurants, cafés and bars situated here as well as cinemas and theatres. Behind the central business district the hillside rises up to the extensive Botanic Gardens and the suburb of **Kelburn**. East of the Courtenay quarter is the residential suburb of **Oriental Bay** and Mount Victoria, from where you can obtain excellent views of the city.

## WHERE TO STAY

Wellington offers several excellent accommodation options from backpacker hostels to motels, homestays to high-class hotels. Unusually, there is no campsite nearby though both Rosemere Backpackers and Rowena's Lodge, see Hostels, allow **camping** in their grounds.

Hotel tariffs vary considerably and they tend to be a little higher than in some other cities but there are often good deals to be had, particularly over the weekend. Although there are several places to stay, the most popular can get booked up during the busiest months (Dec-Mar) so booking ahead is necessary at these times.

### Hostels

Even though most of the hostels are very pleasant places to stay many have very poor parking facilities.

*Beethoven House* (☎ 04-939 4678; dorm NZ$24, dbl/twin NZ$60), 89 Brougham St, is something of an institution. The eccentric owner likes to call a spade a spade, occasionally to the shock of his guests, and wakes visitors in the morning by playing classical music before providing a complimentary breakfast.

*The Cambridge Backpackers* (☎ 0800-375 021, ☎ 04-385 8829, ☐ www .cambridgehotel.co.nz; dorm NZ$23-25, sgl/dbl NZ$59/75, en suite NZ$85/95), 28 Cambridge Terrace, is probably the most attractive hostel in the city centre and is part of a classically restored heritage hotel (see p100). Ideally situated, the Cambridge has a great atmosphere. There is a bar and restaurant in the same building and a well-equipped kitchen area although the communal room is small considering the potential number of users.

*Downtown Backpackers* (☎ 04-473 8482, ☐ www.downtownbackpackers.co .nz; dorm NZ$21-26, sgl/dbl NZ$58/75, en suite dbl NZ$85), 1 Bunny St, is a little further from the heart of the action, directly opposite the train station. The hostel is housed in a large 1930s' art deco building but lacks atmosphere. The rooms are reasonable enough though and there is a restaurant and very cheap bar on site too.

Both the hostels below offer a courtesy pick-up/drop off service from the bus/train stations and ferry terminal. *Rosemere Backpackers* (☎ 04-384 3041, ☐ www .backpackerswellington.co.nz; dorm NZ$27, sgl/twin/dbl NZ$50/62/66), 6 Macdonald Crescent, is in the centre of town up a short, steep street. Rooms are reasonably priced. *Rowena's Lodge* (☎ 04-385 7872 or 0800-801 414, ☐ rowenas@wellingtonback packers.co.nz; tent pitch NZ$10, dorm NZ$20, sgl/dbl NZ$30/45), 115 Brougham St, is set in a pleasant part of the city, a short walk from the centre. This friendly place is one of the few hostels to offer off-street car parking facilities.

The superb *Wellington City YHA* (☎ 04-801 7280, ☐ www.stayyha.com; dorm NZ$27-30, sgl/dbl and twin NZ$72/82, en suite dbl NZ$102), 292 Wakefield St, sleeps more than 300 people. Ideally located in the heart of Courtenay Place, its relaxed atmosphere and excellent amenities have ensured its perennial popularity. Many of the rooms even have harbour views.

The distinctive, zebra-striped *Wellywood Backpackers* (☎ 04-381 3899, ☐ www.wellywoodbackpackers.co.nz; dorm NZ$25-27, dbl/twin NZ$67, en suite NZ$75-85), 58 Tory St, is another well-appointed, centrally located hostel. Spacious rooms and comfortable communal areas, a spa pool and games area coupled with friendly staff and a laid-back atmosphere make this a pretty good bet.

*Worldwide Backpackers* (☎ 04-802 5590 or 0508-888 555 reservations only, ☐ www.worldwidenz.co.nz; dorm NZ$27, dbl/twin NZ$66), 291 The Terrace, is a smaller, homely venue that tempts guests by offering a complimentary breakfast and evening glass of wine.

The well-organised *base Wellington* (☎ 0800-227 369, ☐ www.basebackpack ers.com; dorm NZ$27-30, en suite dbl NZ$95) at 21-23 Cambridge Terrace is a large converted office block yards from Courtenay Place that now sleeps some 280

GATEWAY CITIES

people, has its own bar, small kitchen and lounge area. There's also a women-only 'Sanctuary' floor for those keen to escape the partying typical of the base buildings. The smaller, modern *Nomads Capital* (☎ 0508-666 237, 🖥 www.nomadscapital .com; dorm NZ$23-29, dbl and twin NZ$75-85) is at 118 Wakefield St and has a laid-back café-bar connected to it and a guest massage service, as well as a travel desk, fully equipped kitchen and BBQ area.

There are good discounts available for week-long stays.

## B&Bs and motels

The majority of B&Bs and motels are a little further out of town than the hostels and hotels, but most can readily be reached by a bus and many have better parking facilities.

*Booklovers Bed and Breakfast* (☎ 04- 384 2714, 🖥 www.booklovers.co.nz; en suite sgl/dbl NZ$180/220), 123 Pirie St,

---

### WELLINGTON – MAP KEY

**Where to stay**
2 Tinakori Lodge
6 Eight Parliament Street
8 Downtown Backpackers
9 Wellesley
15 Hotel Intercontinental
27 Rosemere Backpackers
29 Worldwide Backpackers
31 The Mermaid
34 Victoria Court Motor Lodge
40 Nomads Capital
41 Duxton Hotel
47 Museum Hotel
50 Kingsgate Hotel
52 Wellington City YHA
57 base Wellington
58 Halswell Lodge
59 The Cambridge Hotel & Backpackers
60 Wellywood Backpackers
61 The Marksman Motor Inn
62 Rowena's Lodge
63 Beethoven House
64 Booklovers B&B

**Where to eat and drink**
4 The Backbencher
17 Dockside
18 Shed 5
23 Lido
25 Tupelo
26 Studio Nine
30 Bodega
32 Fidel's
33 Logan-Brown
35 Midnight Espresso

**Where to eat and drink** *(cont'd)*
36 Floriditas
37 Ernesto
38 Matterhorn
42 Brewery Bar & Restaurant
44 Icon
45 Molly Malone's
46 Espressoholic
48 Martin Bosley's
49 Parade Café
51 Kai in the City
53 Wellington Sports Café
55 Motel; Chow
56 Hummingbird
57 Basement Bar (in base Wellington)

**Other**
1 Katherine Mansfield's birthplace
3 Westpac Stadium
5 The Beehive/Parliament buildings
7 Railway station
10 Carter Observatory
11 Cable car and museum
12 Thomas Cook
13 ANZ Bank
14 American Express International
16 Wellington City and Sea Museum
19 Ferg's Rock 'n' Kayak
20 BNZ Bank
21 Wellington Public Library
22 Wellington i-Site Visitors Centre
24 DOC Office
28 Victoria University
39 Post Office
43 Te Papa Museum
54 NBNZ

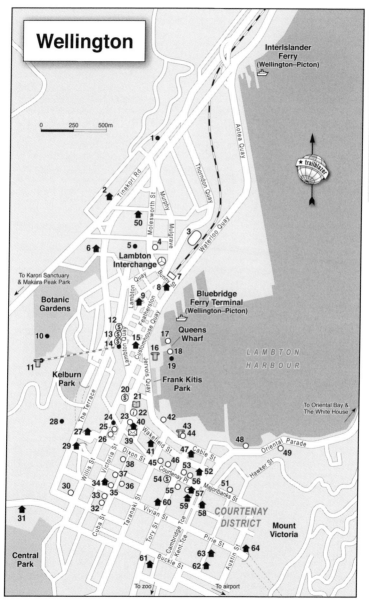

# Wellington

0    250    500m

InterIslander
Ferry
(Wellington–Picton)

Tinakori Rd

Molesworth St

Murphy St

Mulgrave St

Thorndon Quay

Aotea Quay

Waterloo Quay

1 ●

2

50

Lambton
Interchange

5 ●

4

3

7

8

9

Bluebridge
Ferry Terminal
(Wellington–Picton)

To Karori Sanctuary
& Makara Peak Park

6

Lambton Quay

Featherston St

Customhouse Quay

Jervois Quay

Botanic
Gardens

12

13

14

15

16

17

Queens
Wharf

18

19

LAMBTON
HARBOUR

10 ●

11

Kelburn
Park

Frank Kitis
Park

The Terrace

20

21

22

23

24

25

26

27

28 ●

29

39

40

41

42

43

44

To Oriental Bay &
The White House

48

49

Oriental Parade

Wakefield St

Cable St

Dixon St

Willis St

Victoria St

45

46

47

53

52

54

55

56

57

58

59

60

51

Majoribanks St

Hawker St

Courtenay Pl

38

37

36

35

34

33

32

30

COURTENAY
DISTRICT

Mount
Victoria

31

Cuba St

Taranaki St

Vivian St

Torry St

Cambridge Tce

Kent Tce

Pirie St

Austin St

Central
Park

61

62

63

64

Buckle St

To zoo

To airport

Mount Victoria, is an elegant place to stay. The house is poised between the delights of the city centre and the attractions of Oriental Bay. Large en suite rooms with panoramic views are filled with books that you can read or take away with you. A generous cooked breakfast is included in the price. *Eight Parliament Street* (☎ 04-499 0808, 🖳 www.boutique-bb.co.nz; room NZ$80-120) is a traditional Thorndon cottage in a quiet, charming setting. *The Mermaid* (☎ 04-384 4511, 🖳 www.mermaid.co.nz; sgl NZ$85-125, dbl NZ$95-140), 1 Epuni St, in the picturesque Aro Valley, a 10-minute walk from downtown, is a small, plush women-only guesthouse that has individually designed and themed bedrooms.

At 182 Tinakori Rd in Thorndon, *Tinakori Lodge* (☎ 04-939 3478, 🖳 www.tinakorilodge.co.nz; sgl/dbl NZ$99/140, en suite sgl/dbl NZ$120/170) is an old, surprisingly stylish, timber house in a quiet area. Tidy *Halswell Lodge* (☎ 04-385 0196, 🖳 www.halswell.co.nz; hotel room NZ$100, motel unit NZ$140-155, lodge rooms NZ$140-145, with spa NZ$155-170), 21 Kent Terrace, is a centrally located, reasonably priced venue with slightly plain hotel rooms and motel units, though this is made up for by the lavish de luxe lodge rooms, some with their own spa.

*The Marksman Motor Inn* (☎ 04-385 2499, or 0800-627 574 for reservations only, 🖳 www.marksmanmotel.co.nz; motel unit NZ$115-170), 42 Sussex St, is just south of Courtenay Place and offers clean, comfortable units that can get noisy. *Victoria Court Motor Lodge* (☎ 04-472 4297, 🖳 www.victoriacourt.co.nz; motel unit NZ$145-200), 201 Victoria St, is probably the pick of the motels with modern, spotless units, full facilities and plenty of parking.

### Hotels

*Cambridge Hotel* (see p97) is the best of the affordable central hotels. A renovated 1930s building, it is excellently situated and doesn't cost the earth. *Hotel Intercontinental* (☎ 0800-857 585, 🖳 www

.ichotelsgroup.com; room NZ$200-375), on the corner of Grey St and Featherston St, is a luxurious hotel that caters mainly for businessmen. It is priced accordingly but offers cheaper weekend deals. *Duxton Hotel* (☎ 0800-655 555, 🖳 www.duxton.com; room NZ$250-400), 148 Wakefield St, is another grand hotel that has all the requisite facilities, a brasserie and an à la carte restaurant. The stately *Wellesley* (☎ 04-474 1308, 🖳 www.thewellesley.co.nz; room from NZ$250), at 2-8 Maginnity St, used to be a gentleman's club and retains the original sense of charm, character and quality service. A handful of rooms decorated in Georgian period style, with art and antiques and a number of impeccable facilities including a billiard room and restaurant, are suitably first rate. Weekend deals make this all reasonable value.

*Museum Hotel* (☎ 0800-944 335, 🖳 www.museumhotel.co.nz; room NZ$200-325), at 90 Cable St, known locally as the 'Museum Hotel de Wheels' as it was rolled more than 100m from its original location to make room for Te Papa, is a blast of fresh air and boasts unusual décor, a bit of attitude and some surprisingly good deals for rooms with harbour views.

*Kingsgate Hotel* (☎ 04-473 2208, or ☎ 0800-805 205 for reservations, 🖳 www.portlandhotel.co.nz; room NZ$225), 24 Hawkestone St in Thorndon, is situated to the north of the city. The rooms are adequate and you can usually get substantial discounts on the rack rate, especially at weekends. Use of the hotel's gym is free.

### WHERE TO EAT AND DRINK

Wellington is a gastronomic delight. It is hugely cosmopolitan and offers a very wide range of restaurants (more than 400) catering for even the most exotic palette; many are amongst the country's finest. The city also benefits from having the award-winning vineyards of Wairarapa and Marlborough on its doorstep. There is also a thriving café culture.

In recent years there has been an explosion in the number of **fast-food and kebab restaurants** in the city centre, particularly in Courtenay Place. Other than these, **food courts** offer filling meals at cheap prices (around NZ$5-10); the best of these is on Jervois Quay. There are also **food markets** in the BNZ shopping centre on the corner of Willis and Williston streets and at the Asian Food Market on Cable St.

In a city that boasts more **cafés** per capita than New York, you are spoiled for choice for your caffeine fix. *Ernesto* (☎ 04-801 6878; dishes NZ$10-25) at 132 Cuba St has Caribbean-influenced bistro-style dishes. Less upmarket, *Fidel's* (☎ 04-801 6868; dishes NZ$10-20) at 234 Cuba St is a local institution plastered in images of Castro, which produces tasty breakfasts, snacks and main meals at all times of day. At *Midnight Espresso* (☎ 04-384 7014; dishes NZ$5-15), 178 Cuba St, you can grab vegetarian, vegan and the occasional meaty snack till 2am. *Espressoholic* (☎ 04-384 7790, dishes NZ$5-15) at 128 Courtenay Place may look like a bit of a dive but has a funky atmosphere and serves a mean coffee in its courtyard. *Lido* (☎ 04-499 6666; dishes NZ$10-30) on the corner of Wakefield St and Victoria St sits below an office block and offers respite for workers and visitors alike. Out of town head to the *Parade Café* (☎ 04-939 3935; dishes NZ$15-25) at 148 Oriental Parade which is laid-back and friendly with good food and attentive service – although sadly no sea-view as the deck area is set back from the water.

The best way to choose a **restaurant** is simply to amble around and pick whatever takes your fancy. *Chow* (☎ 04-382 8585; NZ$10-20 main course), 45 Tory St, is a stylish pan-Asian restaurant borrowing from half a dozen countries to bring you the best selection of tapas-style dishes. *Dockside* (☎ 04-499 9900; NZ$25-30 main course), on Queens Wharf, is set in a converted warehouse alongside the water's edge. It serves a wide array of superb seafood, but at a price. Book in advance to secure a table by the vast glass window overlooking the harbour. *Floriditas* (☎ 04-381 2212; mains NZ$20-30) at 161 Cuba St is an excellent bistro where fine food at reasonable rates is served in stylish surroundings. *Kai in the City* (☎ 04-801 5006; mains NZ$25-30) at 21 Marjoribanks St is a compact Maori eatery specialising in Maori-influenced food and is a great way to try some traditional dishes such as muttonbird or a hangi (see p77), whilst the owner leads a communal singalong.

*Icon* (☎ 04-801 5300; NZ$15-30 main course), on level 2 of Te Papa Museum (see pp105-6), is one of New Zealand's finest eateries. Lunch, brunch and dinner are served in this elegant venue but it's not particularly cheap. *Logan-Brown* (☎ 04-801 5114; NZ$40-45 main course), 192 Cuba St, is set in a vast renovated 1920s' banking chamber and enjoys a fabulous atmosphere. The Pacific Rim menu is innovative and full-flavoured and is complemented by an extensive list of local and imported wines. Set menus and pre-theatre deals are good ways to enjoy what's on offer without spending the earth. *Shed 5* (☎ 04-409 9069; NZ$35-75 main course) on Queens Wharf is another upmarket venue although there is also a good-value bar menu. Set in a converted 1888 woolshed it has a great harbourside setting and serves fabulous seafood. *Martin Bosley's* (☎ 04-920 8302; mains NZ$35-55) at 103 Oriental Parade is an innovative, excellent place specialising in seafood and views of the harbour that makes it one of the best places in the city to dine. *The White House* (☎ 04-385 8555; mains NZ$40), 232 Oriental Parade, is a little further out of town but well worth the trip. It has stunning harbour views and serves seafood and New Zealand dishes accompanied by organic vegetables.

## NIGHTLIFE

Wellington probably has New Zealand's liveliest nightlife. The atmosphere in the Courtenay quarter can be contagious as people spill out of one venue and roll into the next and the compact nature of the city allows people to explore a number of spots. As ever the distinction between bars and restaurants is blurred since most offer both food and drinks. However, there's a selection of very fine **pubs and bars** in the downtown area, centred on Courtenay

Place and the surrounding streets such as Cuba St, Blair St and Dixon St, extending as far as Willis St and Lambton Quay.

*The Backbencher*, on the corner of Molesworth St and Sydenham St East, is opposite the Beehive and the parliament buildings. The casual atmosphere is underlined by the spoof puppets of New Zealand's political figures that decorate the interior. The *Brewery Bar and Restaurant*, in a converted warehouse close to Te Papa Museum, has a great waterside location with outdoor seating and seriously good beer. The *Wellington Sports Café*, on the corner of Courtenay Place and Tory St, is a cavernous venue with giant-screen televisions showing various sports matches. It serves good-value food and can be pretty lively.

*Molly Malone's*, on the corner of Courtenay Place and Taranaki St, is a very popular, animated Irish theme pub. There is live music nightly and a list of around 100 whiskies to select from. *Bodega*, 286 Willis St, is another spot with live music; several local and touring bands have played here.

*Basement Bar*, below the base Backpacker building (see p98), is ideal for backpackers looking to kick-start an evening with cheap drinks, happy hours, live music and competitions designed to ramp up the atmosphere.

*Matterhorn*, 106 Cuba Mall, stands at the heart of Wellington's fashionable nightlife. Reached down a long tunnel, the garden bar serves good coffee, fine cocktails and wine. Contemporary Pacific Rim food is also available in its sophisticated restaurant section. The music continues until 3am throughout the week. *Tupelo*, 6 Edward St, and *Studio Nine*, 9 Edward St, are both popular late-night venues for mingling and dancing. *Motel*, 45 Tory St, is an exceptionally exclusive venue attached to Chow (see p101). A discreet location and stringent door policy ensure it's never overcrowded. *Hummingbird*, 22 Courtenay Place, is a small, French-influenced, art deco-inspired place with an extensive cocktail and wine list. It's ideal for people-watching while you tuck into French-Pacific fusion food.

Wellington is also home to the New Zealand Arts Festival and Fringe Festival (see opposite) and has a burgeoning professional **theatre** scene. The St James Theatre (💻 www.stjames.co.nz), 77-87 Courtenay Place, is a beautifully refurbished heritage venue. It hosts **opera**, **ballet** and **musical shows** and can comfortably seat 1500 people. It is also the home of the Royal New Zealand Ballet (💻 www.nzballet.org.nz). The BATS Theatre (💻 www.bats.co.nz), 1 Kent Terrace, is an intimate theatre that specialises in avant-garde, alternative shows, whilst Circa (💻 www.circa.co.nz) on the corner of Taranaki and Cable streets, is one of liveliest and most innovative theatres with a tradition of nurturing many of the country's up-and-coming directors and actors. The Opera House, 111-113 Manners St, is home to the New Zealand Opera (💻 www.nzopera.com) but also caters for touring productions and local shows.

**Cinema** is also very popular in the city. New Zealand director Peter Jackson is a local and much of the filming and production of the *Lord of the Rings* trilogy was done in the area. Film-screening details and timetables are available at 💻 www .film.wellington.net.nz. The Paramount Cinema complex on Courtenay Place and the Embassy (💻 www.deluxe.co.nz) at 10 Kent Terrace are the premier cinemas. The Rialto cinema on the corner of Cable St and Jervois Quay specialises in international independent films. Films and times are listed in the local newspapers.

**Westpac Stadium** to the north of the city is New Zealand's only purpose-built multi-functional stadium. Affectionately known as the Cake Tin, it is ostensibly a sports venue and hosts various big cricket and rugby matches. However, it also stages music concerts, cultural shows, exhibitions and other major functions.

### Festivals

For full details of Wellington's packed festival and events programme visit the i-SITE visitor centre (see opposite). The **International Rugby Sevens** tournament is hosted in Wellington during the first weekend of February. Later in February during odd-numbered years the **Cuba St Carnival** (🖳 www.cubacarnival.org.nz) attracts huge crowds.

The **New Zealand International Arts Festival** (🖳 www.nzfestival.nzpost.co.nz), held during March in even-numbered years, is the country's biggest cultural event with music, opera, theatre, poetry readings, dance and other shows all taking place across the city. **Wellington Fringe Festival** (🖳 www.fringe.org.nz) runs at more less the same time and celebrates more off-beat works. **Wellington Film Festival** (🖳 www.enzedff.co.nz) usually runs from mid-July to mid-August with screenings of indie flicks.

The bizarre **World of Wearable Art** (🖳 www.worldofwearableart.com) show descends on the city in the last two weeks of September.

## SERVICES
### Banks and exchange facilities
There are branches of most major **banks** (ANZ, BNZ and NBNZ) on Lambton Quay, as well as on Willis St and in Courtenay Place. American Express (☎ 04-473 7766) in the Books and More store, 280-292 Lambton Quay, and Thomas Cook at 358 Lambton Quay and 108 Lambton Quay, offer reliable **exchange facilities**.

### Bookshops and map shops
There are a fair number of large **bookshops** in Wellington.

Whitcoulls at 312 Lambton Quay and Dymocks at 366 Lambton Quay are also substantial and well-stocked. Unity Books at 57 Willis St is a good place to search for New Zealand literature. Bellamy's at 105 Cuba St and Arty Bees (🖳 www.artybees.co.nz) at 17 Courtenay Place have interesting secondhand selections.

The specialist **Map Shop** (🖳 www.mapshop.co.nz) on the corner of Vivian and Victoria streets, near Cuba St, stocks a wide range of regional and city maps as well as more detailed topographic maps that are ideal for trampers.

### Embassies and consulates
As you'd expect, most embassies and high commissions are located in the capital.

Among them are the **Australian High Commission** (☎ 04-473 6411, 🖳 www.australia.org.nz) at 72-78 Hobson St; the **Canadian High Commission** (☎ 04-473 9577) at 61 Molesworth St; the **British High Commission** (☎ 04-472 6049, 🖳 www.britain.org.nz) at 44 Hill St; and the **American Embassy** (☎ 04-472 2068, 🖳 www.usembassy.org.nz), which is at 29 Fitzherbert Terrace.

### Information centres
As well as the visitor centre at the airport (see p95), **Wellington i-SITE Visitor Centre** (☎ 0800-933 536, 🖳 www.wellington.nz.com; Dec-Mar Mon-Fri 8.30am-5.30pm, Sat & Sun 9.30am-5pm, closing slightly earlier the rest of the year) is in the city centre at 101 Wakefield St, on Civic Square. The staff will answer all queries and can make travel and accommodation bookings nationwide and book tickets for the ferry between Wellington and Picton. There is also a café and internet access is possible here. Look out, too, for the useful *Official Visitor Guide* to Wellington.

The **DOC** (☎ 04-472 5821, 🖳 www.doc.govt.nz; Mon-Fri 9am-5pm, Sat & Sun 10am-3.30pm) is at 18 Manners St. Staff can answer tramping enquiries and make the necessary bookings on your behalf. They also sell mapping and literature for each track.

### Internet access
Internet access is widespread in Wellington. Most hostels offer internet access and there are several dedicated cyber-cafés scattered throughout the city. The Public Library (see below) and i-SITE Centre (see above) also provide internet facilities.

### Libraries
**Wellington Public Library** (Mon-Thur 9.30am-8.30pm, Fri 9.30am-9pm, Sat 9.30am-5pm and Sun 1-4pm) is on Victoria St. The **National Library of New Zealand** (Te Puna Matauranga o Aotearoa; ☎ 04-474 3000, 🖳 www.natlib.govt.nz; Mon-Fri 9am-5pm, Sat 9am-1pm) is at 28-78 Molesworth St opposite the Beehive. It has the largest book collection in New Zealand.

The **National Archives** (☎ 04-499 5595, 🖳 www.archives.govt.nz), at 10 Mulgrave St, are home to several important constitutional documents including the remains of the original Treaty of Waitangi, on display in an environmentally controlled, sealed case. The archives are open to the public on weekdays 9am-5pm and Saturday 9am-1pm.

### Medical treatment
Wellington Hospital (☎ 04-385 5999) is on Riddiford St, Newtown. There are also hospitals on the High St in Lower Hutt (☎ 04-566 6999) and on Raiha St, Porirua (☎ 04-237 0179). In an **emergency** call the Free Ambulance (☎ 04-472 2999) to find out where the nearest on-call doctor is.

### Pharmacy
After-Hours Medical Centre and pharmacy (☎ 04-384 4944), 17 Adelaide Rd, Newtown, provides 24hr emergency treatment.

### Post office
The main post office is on Waterloo Quay. Poste restante mail can be collected between 8.30am and 5pm on weekdays. There are other post offices in the city.

### Shopping
Lambton Quay is the place to start looking for designer gear or quirky one-offs with the most concentrated selection of shopping in New Zealand. Kirkcaldie and Stains at 165-177 Lambton Quay is a giant emporium offering top-end clothes and other delights whilst the Old Bank Shopping Arcade nearby boasts cafés, boutiques and other places to spend your cash. Cuba St offers a more eclectic selection of funky secondhand clothes shops, record dealers and retro furniture outlets. Frutti and Ziggurat at Nos 176 and 144 respectively are good bets for outlandish, unusual outfits. Superb, authentic Maori pieces including carvings, sculptures, ceramics, greenstone and jewellery can be picked up at the Kura Gallery (🖳 www.kuragallery.co.nz) at 19 Allen St. Just up the road at No 23 is the ORA Design Gallery (🖳 www.ora.co.nz) where traditional and contemporary indigenous art can be bought.

Paua2thepeople (🖳 www.paua2the people.com) at 155 Marine Parade is a seaside gallery and workshop stocked with art and jewellery made from paua shell.

For tramping gear and other outdoor supplies try Mainly Tramping in the Grand Arcade on Willis St or one of the equipment stores lining Mercer St.

### GETTING AROUND
Wellington is compact: the city centre is approximately 2km in diameter. Consequently it is an ideal city to amble round (see box p106), soaking up the ambience and enjoying the sights.

However, if you are pressed for time or simply wish to rest your feet, take advantage of the capital's excellent public transport system. **Buses** operate from Lambton Interchange to the west of the train station. Fares are NZ$1.50 within the city centre and then increase according to a zone system. There is also an After Midnight service that runs hourly on the hour from Courtenay Place and Cuba St to destinations in the suburbs and costs NZ$3.50-7. The distinctive yellow Stagecoach circular buses take in the majority of the city-centre sights, making them ideal for those wishing to hop on and off as they see the city. The buses loop the city every 15 minutes and fares are NZ$3 for a complete circuit or any section of it. The Stagecoach Flyer runs from Queensgate in Lower Hutt through the city centre and out to the airport from 5.45am to 7.45pm during the week and 6.15am to 8.15pm at weekends. If you intend to use the bus a lot, buy a NZ$15 Metlink Explorer pass giving unlimited one day bus and train travel throughout the region. Alternatively the NZ$5 Daytripper pass covers central bus travel and the NZ$10 Star Pass includes the After Midnight services.

It is also possible to explore the Wellington region by **suburban train**. Tranz Metro (🖳 www.tranzmetro.co.nz) operates a range of services that depart the railway station on Bunny St regularly during peak hours and on the half-hour during off-peak times (9am-3pm). There are four lines that access the outer areas of the Wellington region, ending in Johnsonville and Paraparaumu on the Kapiti coast and Melling and Masterton in the Wairarapa region. This is a convenient way of exploring the Hutt Valley. For up-to-date information on times and fares collect a brochure from the railway station or from the i-SITE centre. Alternatively, for all bus or train information contact Metlink (☎ 0800-801 700), visit 🖳 www.metlink.org.nz or pick-up the free Metlink Network map.

There are several **car-hire** companies in Wellington. These are listed in the *Yellow Pages*. Prices tend to be higher than in Auckland due to a lack of competition. If you are thinking of heading south, it is cheaper and easier to hire a car in Picton and you will also save yourself the cost of transporting the car on the ferry.

If you're thinking of **buying/selling a car**, start by looking in newspapers or on hostel noticeboards for an idea of prices and what's available. Turners Auctions (☎ 04-587 1400, 🖳 www.turners.co.nz) at 120 Hutt Rd in Lower Hutt is a good bet.

It is also possible to hire **motor scooters**. Scooter Rental (☎ 04-384 7679), 70 Abel Smith St, rents out fully automatic scooters, though you must be 18 years or over and hold a current car driving licence. Contact the outfit directly for prices and further information.

**Bicycles** can be hired from Mud Cycles (☎ 04-476 4961, 🖳 www.mud cycles.co.nz) at 338 Karori Rd, who also lead guided trips and tours.

**Taxi ranks** are dotted about the city centre in popular areas. The largest taxi firm in the city is Wellington Combined Taxis (☎ 04-384 4444), though there are plenty of others including Green Cabs (☎ 0508-447 336) who use hybrid vehicles. A taxi to the airport costs around NZ$25.

## WHAT TO SEE AND DO
Wellington is renowned for its cultural and historic attractions as well as its adventurous outdoor activities. Museums and galleries are plentiful and there are numerous events and spectacles throughout the year. The surrounding countryside also provides ideal opportunities for more active pursuits. To get a grasp of the city layout and have its

best features pointed out, try a tour with Walk Wellington (🖳 www.walk.wellington .net.nz) who offers 90-minute strolls around the downtown area for NZ$20. See box p106 if you prefer to walk independently.

Hammonds Scenic Tours (☎ 04-472 0869, 🖳 www.wellingtonsightseeingtours .com) and 4WD Seal Coast Safari (☎ 0800-732 527, 🖳 www.sealcoast.com) offer a range of trips to see the seal colonies at Palliser Bay and Red Rocks respectively.

### Te Papa Tongarewa National Museum
Te Papa (☎ 04-381 7000, 🖳 www.tepapa .govt.nz; daily 10am-6pm, until 9pm on Thursday), on Cable St, is New Zealand's national museum and Wellington's biggest tourist attraction. Dominating the harbourside, the monolithic building cost around NZ$317 million to construct and was opened in 1998. The impressive, ground-breaking museum, whose name loosely translates as Our Place, traces New Zealand's history and development using sound, video and computerised displays. Exhibits introduce you to the landscape and wildlife of the country as well as tracing Maori culture and traditions, with the emphasis firmly on biculturalism. The museum's centerpiece, Te Marae, is a contemporary meeting house with carvings especially created for the museum. As well as ancient treasures there are sections devoted to contemporary art and culture and a host of interactive displays.

Entry is free although there may be charges for some of the short-term visiting

**Te Papa Tongarewa** – an outstanding celebration of the people, history, culture and art of New Zealand

exhibitions. Introductory tours of the museum cost NZ$10 and give you a good overview and layout of the huge site. You could take advantage of the lack of an entrance fee by exploring the museum for up to half a day before taking a break from the sensory overload and returning on a separate occasion to complete your visit. The museum also contains a gift shop, cafés, restaurant and an auditorium.

## Cable car

This is one of Wellington's most popular attractions. The distinctive red cable car (☎ 04-472 2199, ⌨ www.wellingtonnz.com/cablecar) runs from Cable Car Lane, 280 Lambton Quay in the heart of the city, under the corporate towers of The Terrace, past the university and Kelburn Park to the top of the Botanic Gardens, where the Lookout, Carter Observatory, Planetarium and Cable Car Museum can be found. The view from this point is fantastic and takes in the whole harbour and central city area. There are several walking trails snaking down through the gardens to Lambton Quay.

In 1898 it was decided to convert the hills directly above the city into a new suburb. This new district would need easy access to ensure its success and a cable car was chosen as the most efficient link between city and suburb. Construction of the cable car began in 1901 and the tramway was opened in 1902. It proved to be a huge success. In 1933 electricity replaced steam as the driving power for the cars. In 1978 the original system was closed and replaced by a more modern version, which is still in place today. At the upper terminus there is a small **Cable Car Museum** (Mon-Fri 9.30am-5.30pm, Sat & Sun 9.30am-4.30pm; free) that houses some of the original equipment and a handful of hundred-year-old cars.

The cars run every 10 minutes between 7am and 10pm on weekdays, 8.30am-10pm on Saturdays and 9am-10pm on Sundays. Fares are NZ$2.50 for an adult single, NZ$4.50 return.

## Botanic Gardens

The 26ha Botanic Gardens (☎ 04-499 1903; open daily and free) were established in 1868. They are made up of protected native vegetation and lawn areas as well as rose gardens containing 106 formal beds and a glass house that contains tropical and tem-

---

### Walking in Wellington

One of the easiest and most comprehensive ways to explore the city centre is on foot. There are a few simple itineraries detailed in the *Wellington Walkway* brochure that can be obtained from the visitor centre. There are also heritage trails through some of Wellington's oldest and most interesting districts. A *Heritage Trail* booklet can be bought from the visitor centre.

The streetscape along Oriental Parade is one of the city's finest. The trail through the **Botanic Gardens** is also very attractive and conveniently joins the **Thorndon Heritage trail**, which takes two to three hours to complete, explores the area around the Parliament buildings and takes in Katherine Mansfield's birthplace, the Roman Catholic Basilica, the Anglican St Paul's Cathedral and the Old Government Buildings, which are the second largest all-wooden buildings in the world.

The **Southern Walkway** is a four- to five-hour stroll that takes in views of Wellington Harbour and the central city area from either Oriental Bay or Mount Victoria. The **Eastern Walkway** is a shorter one- to two-hour trail that follows the spectacular coastline past the Wahine Memorial at Palmer Head. The **City to Sea Walkway** takes around four hours to complete. It begins at one end of Wellington and passes through the city before heading into the surrounding hills and suburbs, emerging on the craggy South Coast to overlook Cook Strait.

perate displays. The gardens are at their best in spring and summer when massed flowerings can be seen.

Within the gardens are the **Carter Observatory** (🖳 www.carterobservatory.org) – which was undergoing extensive renovations at the time of writing so check the website for details of exhibitions, planetarium shows and opening hours – **Golden Bay Planetarium** and the **Sundial of Human Involvement**. It is also possible to visit **Bolton St Memorial Park**, where many of Wellington's pioneers are buried.

Leaflets and walking maps are available at the cable car station and from the various information centres in the city.

### Wellington Zoo
Founded in 1906, Wellington Zoo (☎ 04-381 6755, 🖳 www.wellingtonzoo.com; daily 9.30am-5pm, last entry 4.15pm, NZ$15/7.50 per adult/child), at 200 Daniell St, New Town, is New Zealand's oldest zoo, committed to preserving and breeding animals that are under threat of extinction. Cages are forsaken in favour of more natural habitats. It is home to both native and foreign animals. The zoo is 4km south of the city centre and can be reached by taking the No 10 or No 23 Stagecoach bus to Newtown Park.

### Wellington City and Sea Museum
This interesting museum (☎ 04-472 8904, 🖳 www.museumofwellington.co.nz; Mon-Fri 10am-5pm, Sat & Sun 10am-5.30pm, free) is housed in a restored 1892 bond store, or customs house, on Queens Wharf, beside Jervois Quay. The traditional museum records the maritime and social history of the capital. It has a special section and photographic display devoted to the sinking of the car ferry *Wahine*, which was blown onto a reef just outside Wellington Harbour during a storm and later sank in the harbour in April 1968 with the loss of 51 lives.

### Katherine Mansfield's birthplace
New Zealand's most celebrated author was born at 25 Tinakori Rd, Thorndon, in 1888. Katherine Mansfield lived in Wellington until she was 19 years old, when she left to travel and settle in Europe. During this time she spent her first five years at this address, although she didn't have particularly fond memories of the place, describing it as 'that dark little cubby hole'. The house does, however, feature regularly in stories such as *Prelude* and *A Birthday*.

The building (☎ 04-473 7268, 🖳 www.katherinemansfield.com; Tue-Sun 10am-4pm; NZ$5.50/2 per adult/child) has been restored to reflect a typical lower-middle-class family home in the late Victorian era and is now a memorial to her. With its dark-stained wood, heavy drapes and furniture, the house has a somewhat overbearing and melancholic feel, but then so does much of her writing. Photographs of the time are displayed alongside excerpts of her writing.

### The Beehive (Parliament buildings)
New Zealand's parliament (☎ 04-471 9999, 🖳 www.parliament.govt.nz), on Bowen St, is made up of three buildings. The most famous is the highly distinctive seven-stepped **Beehive** designed by the British architect Basil Spence. This controversial modernist building was opened in 1980, several years after its architect's death. Adjacent to this is the 1922 Edwardian Neoclassical **Parliament House** and the Victorian Gothic **Parliamentary Library**, which dates from 1899. Free one-hour tours run every hour on weekdays from 10am to 4pm, Saturdays 10am-3pm and Sundays midday-3pm. These depart from the ground-floor foyer of Parliament House.

The Beehive, the country's parliamentary building, was designed by Sir Basil Spence.

## Old St Pauls

This church on Mulgrave St, dating from 1866, is a unique example of colonial Gothic architecture. Built originally as the parish church for Thorndon it was then used for almost a century as Wellington Cathedral. Built out of native timber, the warm wooden interior is enhanced by the stained-glass windows filtering the light. Entry is by donation and the church is open daily from 10am-5pm.

## Mount Victoria

The best view of the entire city, harbour area and neighbouring countryside is from the summit of Mount Victoria (196m/543ft) to the south-east of the city centre. Numerous scenes from the *Lord of the Rings* film trilogy were shot in Mount Victoria's city belt, including Hobbiton Woods. Stagecoach bus No 20 departs from the city centre on weekdays for the foot of the climb. If you wish to drive there, take Majoribanks St at the bottom of Courtenay Place, turn left on to Hawker St then take Palliser Rd before turning into Thane Rd, which leads to the lookout point.

## Karori Wildlife Sanctuary

The Karori Wildlife Sanctuary (☎ 04-920 2222, ⌨ www.sanctuary.org.nz) at the end of Waiapu Rd, Karori, is a unique protected area for endangered native wildlife; there are more than 30 native bird species, tuatara and giant weta here. Around 252ha of regenerating forest are criss-crossed by more than 35km of tracks that offer people of all levels of fitness the chance to experience the countryside. The visitor centre is open midday-8pm on weekdays between November and February and 10am-8pm at the weekend. From March to October the visitor centre is open midday-5pm on weekdays and 10am-5pm at the weekend. Guided tours and nocturnal outings can be arranged in advance. Entry to the sanctuary costs NZ$12/5 per adult/child.

## Ferg's Rock 'n' Kayak

Ferg's (☎ 04-499 8898, ⌨ www.fergs kayaks.co.nz) at Shed 6 on Queens Wharf hires out and sells kayaks and inline skates as well as running training courses and lessons. Guided tours of the city and harbour area can also be arranged. Ferg's is home to New Zealand's largest indoor climbing wall. Experienced instructors are on hand to help you tackle this remarkable 13m wall that replicates overhangs, boulders and other obstacles. The venue is open for climbers of all abilities, 10am-8pm on weekdays and 9am-8pm at the weekend. Single kayaks cost NZ$12-15 per hour to hire, double kayaks cost NZ$25 per hour and inline skates NZ$15 for two hours. Access to the climbing wall is NZ$15/9 for adults/children. Equipment hire prices vary.

## Makara Peak mountain-bike park

This collection of purpose-built trails set in 250ha to the west of Wellington provides year-round off-road riding for people of all abilities. Short trips and whole-day expeditions (☎ 04-476 4961, ⌨ mudzy@mudcy cles.co.nz) can be undertaken in this suburban area that offers superb views over Wellington. The entrance is at 1 Allington Rd, Karori. Entry to the park is free. Bikes can be hired from NZ$25 for half a day. Guided rides can be pre-booked and cost NZ$65.

## Beaches

Wellington's waterfront is full of cafés, restaurants and bars. **Oriental Bay** is an attractive place to walk along the foreshore, but the water here is not particularly clean or ideal for swimming. **Scorching Bay**, 13km to the east of the city centre, is better although the best beaches in the region are found further up the coast towards Otaki.

## Harbour cruises

Wellington Harbour is best appreciated from the water. There are various ferry trips to outlying islands, including Somes Island to the north-east of the harbour, which used to be a quarantine station. Contact Dominion Post Ferry (☎ 04-494 3339, ⌨ www.eastbywest.co.nz), Harbour City Cruise (☎ 04-386 2740) or Dolphin Sailing Academy (☎ 025-421 194) for details of destinations and fares.

# Using this guide

*Above all do not lose your desire to walk. Everyday I walk myself into a state of well-being and walk away from every illness. I have walked myself into my best thoughts and I know of no thought so burdensome that one cannot walk away from it. But sitting still, and the more one sits still, the closer one comes to feeling ill ... thus if one just keeps walking, everything will be alright.* **Soren Kierkegaard**, quoting words attributed to Buddha, in a letter, 1847

## ROUTE MAPS

### Scales and walking times

For each Great Walk, there is an **overview map** that shows the whole route and puts all the huts into context. This is drawn at a larger scale (ie less detailed) than the **route maps** that correspond to each stage's tramping. The map scale of the route maps varies slightly (between 1:40,000 and 1:80,000) from one track to the next, depending upon the length and distance covered in the course of each tramp. However, the maps within each tramp are drawn at the same scale so as to provide a consistent level of detail; each map also represents one full day's tramping from hut to hut. However, you may choose to create your own itinerary.

Approximate **walking times** are also indicated on each map. There are too many factors that can affect walking speed, such as the size of the group, level of fitness and the state of the weather; as such, they should be used as a rough guide only. Note that they refer to **walking time only** and do not include any time for breaks or food. The arrows show to which direction the walking time refers. Finally, the **map keys** are on p281.

### Gradient arrows

The track is marked as a dotted line. An arrow across the trail indicates a slope and always points uphill. Two arrows placed close together means that the gradient is steep. Note that the arrow points towards the higher part of the trail. If, for example, you are walking from A (at 80m) to B (at 200m) and the trail between the two is short and steep, it would be shown thus: A - - - >> - - - B.

### Fees

In the following guide an adult is deemed to be 18 years and over. Youth groups are defined as those aged 11 to 17 and children are aged 5 to 10. Pre-school age is self-explanatory. Fees are charged per person, per night.

In 2008 the Department of Conservation decreed that child and youth groups could stay in DOC huts free of charge, although a booking is still required.

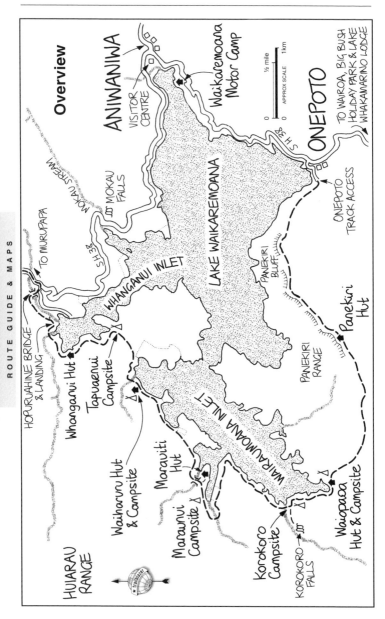

Overview

ANIWANIWA

Waikaremoana Motor Camp

VISITOR CENTRE

MOKAU FALLS

MOKAU STREAM

SH 38

TO MURUPARA

ONEPOTO

TO WAIROA, BIG BUSH HOLIDAY PARK & LAKE WHAKAMARINO LODGE

½ mile
APPROX SCALE
1km

LAKE WAIKAREMOANA

WHANGANUI INLET

ONEPOTO TRACK ACCESS

PANEKIRI BLUFF

PANEKIRI RANGE

Panekiri Hut

HOPURUAHINE BRIDGE & LANDING

Whanganui Hut

Tapuaenui Campsite

WAIKAREMOANA INLET

Waiharuru Hut & Campsite

Maraunui Hut

Marauiti Campsite

Korokoro Campsite

KOROKORO FALLS

Waipaoa Hut & Campsite

HUIARAU RANGE

# Lake Waikaremoana Track

*It's all so gigantic and tragic – even in the brightest sunlight it is so passionately secret.*
**Katherine Mansfield**, *Urewera Notebook*

## INTRODUCTION

This spectacular 46km walk circumnavigates most of Lake Waikaremoana in the centre of Te Urewera National Park. Located in the hinterland that separates central North Island and East Cape, the area is renowned for being a mysterious, emotive and spirit-filled landscape, full of spectacular, rugged terrain. The track edges the shimmering waters of the lake, meandering through ancient, remote forest. Te Urewera National Park and the Lake Waikaremoana catchment form part of the single largest block of native forest remaining on North Island. The walk itself is a moderately difficult three- to four-day tramp that includes one tough ascent.

The Tuhoe tribe, the 'Children of the Mist' (see p112), came to these forested hills long ago and made their home here. The area's isolation has for centuries shrouded and protected the Tuhoe and their spiritual and cultural traditions. As you walk around the lake, a sense of their history and presence pervades. Legends are rife and add a degree of intrigue and fascination to the land.

## HISTORY

Maori settlement of Te Urewera National Park stretches back probably to the 14th century. Maori history records that people settled in this area when Hine-Pukohu-Rangi, the 'Mist Maiden', came down from the sky, luring Te Maunga,

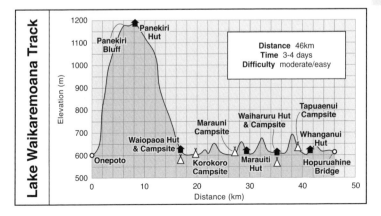

### The creation of Lake Waikaremoana

Maori legend relates the story of the creation of Lake Waikaremoana. Long ago, the great chief Maahu-tapoa-nui lived with his wife Kau-ariki at Waitokitoki. At that time there was no great lake; rather, below the Panekiri Bluff lay a deep river valley. One evening Maahu asked his daughter, Hau-mapuhia, to fetch some water from Te Puna a taupara, the sacred well. She refused to go and he subsequently flew into a terrible rage. Maahu had to go to the well himself and stayed there until his daughter came looking for him.

Overcome by anger, Maahu attacked his daughter, trying to drown her. In her distress, Hau-mapuhia called on the gods of the land for help and they transformed her into a *taniwha* (mythical water monster). As a taniwha, Hau-mapuhia knew that daylight was fatal to her. In a frenzied attempt to escape to the sea, she clawed at the earth. First she thrust northwards to form the Whanganui arm of the lake, but was barred by the Huiarau Mountain Range. She then turned eastwards and gouged the Whanganui-o-Parua arm, but once again she was blocked. In this way one by one the arms of the lake were formed until finally Hau-mapuhia attempted to escape at the lake's outlet near Onepoto. Unable to make good her escape, she was turned to stone by the dawn. She now lies in Waikaretaheke Stream, the only outlet of the lake, blocking the river's path to the sea. A lake duly formed behind the blockage and was christened 'Waikaremoana', which translates as 'The Sea of Rippling Waters'.

Still incensed, Maahu later threw his other children into the Wairaumoana arm of the lake, and they too turned to stone. Today they can be seen as the islands known as Te Whanau-a Maahu, 'The Offspring of Maahu'. Maahu then retreated to the coast, where he showed surprising affection for his murdered daughter, sending back gifts of shellfish, which account for all the shells found in the region today.

'The Mountain', to Earth with her. She married Te Maunga and their child was born mortal. Named Tuhoepotiki, his descendants were to become the Tuhoe people. Sons and daughters of the supernatural, the Tuhoe are still known as the 'Children of the Mist'.

In these pre-European times, life was disciplined and agricultural, determined by the practical demands of seasonal food gathering. These people developed a powerful bond with their land, resisting European invasion and influence which began with the arrival of the missionary Reverend William Williams in 1840.

During the 1860s, Te Urewera became caught up in conflicts between Maori and government troops. The Tuhoe sided with Waikato tribes against government forces at the Battle of Orakau in 1864. After this, the violence abated until the arrival of Te Kooti, one of the great Maori war leaders, following his escape from prison on Chatham Island. Attacking from the shelter of the hills and forests, he would stage swift assaults and promptly vanish before a counter-attack could be mounted. So successful was he that at one stage he and his followers held the entire Waikaremoana area.

The government began a sustained scorched-earth policy in an attempt to drive out Te Kooti. Several hundred died in battles at Ruatahuna and in 1870 the historic fortification at Onepoto was constructed. Sporadic guerrilla fighting continued until the Maori leaders agreed to pledge allegiance to the Crown in 1871. Te Kooti was still pursued by the armed constabulary but escaped into King Country (see box below), where he lived at large. Officially pardoned in 1883, he died at Ohiwa in 1893.

Years of hardship followed for the Tuhoe as much of their land was confiscated and that which was left to them remained under-developed. Disease and poor living conditions severely reduced their numbers. Out of this despair rose a charismatic leader, Rua Kenana, claiming to be Te Mihaia Hou, 'The New Messiah', as proclaimed by Te Kooti. Far-sighted and acutely aware of the problems facing his people, Rua Kenana inspired a Maori renaissance in Te Urewera. Placing heavy emphasis on customs, heritage, Maori language and oral tradition, he gave people hope at a time of deep depression. A powerful religious and secular leader, his teachings were considered highly influential. The government duly became suspicious of him, his philosophy and his stance on land issues. Arrested and tried for sedition, he was sentenced to one year's hard labour. He died in 1937 and is buried on one of the Waimana Valley *marae*. Nevertheless, his memory lives on amongst locals.

In 1925, the idea of preserving the region as a watershed was mooted. Support for the creation of a national park in the area grew and in 1954 the new park was officially declared. Although the first road into the park, between Murupara and Ruatahuna, was begun in 1895, it was not completed until 1930. State Highway 38, connecting Rotorua and Wairoa, cuts through the centre of the park but to this day remains a tortuous, winding, unsealed gravel track.

---

### King Country

King Country is a historic region that extends approximately from Hamilton in the north to Taumarunui in the south, and from Lake Taupo west to Kawhia on the coast. It is so-called because of the Maori King Movement, which developed in the Waikato region immediately to the north of this area in the late 1850s and early 1860s. The movement was a nationalistic uprising that culminated in the election of a Maori king. It stemmed from the realisation that, with the increase in European settlers and the subsequent pressure on Maori lands, the Maori needed a far greater degree of organisation and communication between tribes. The Maori also wished to have a leader equivalent to the British queen when dealing with the newly arrived settlers.

The election of Te Wherowhero as the Maori king in 1858 was seen by Europeans as an act of rebellion by the Maori. Tensions escalated and spilled over into violence and fighting. Armed conflict spread throughout North Island. Although the Maori recorded a historic victory in the Bay of Plenty, they were routed at Te Ranga. Te Wherowhero died in 1860 and was succeeded by his son, King Tawhiao. Fighting sputtered on all along the Waikato River until the Maori were overwhelmed at Orakau in April 1864. The king and his followers fled south into the area that has now become known as 'King Country'. The area developed a reputation as an inhospitable Maori stronghold, and indeed those Maori who lived here had almost no contact with European settlers for over a decade until King Tawhiao made peace in 1881.

The Lake Waikaremoana Track itself was constructed in 1962. Conducted as a volunteer project, it involved boys from fourteen secondary schools. Due to its isolation and the quality of the landscape, the track's popularity soared. This led to a dramatic increase in numbers tramping the track. In a bid to regulate the amount of trampers and minimise both overcrowding and environmental damage, DOC introduced a booking system in 2001.

## GEOLOGY

Te Urewera National Park is the largest wilderness in North Island. A jumble of forested ridges hiding steep-sided river gorges are the main features of the landscape. The heavily forested Huiarau and Ikawhenua ranges to the north and west of Lake Waikaremoana are comprised of greywacke – a rock made up of compressed layers of mud and sand originally deposited on the sea floor 120-160 million years ago. The eastern and southern sections of the park around Lake Waikaremoana consist of much younger rocks – predominantly alternating bands of mudstone and sandstone – laid down around 10-15 million years ago. Around two million years ago these softer sedimentary rocks were uplifted, emerging from the sea. Panekiri Bluff to the south and the Ngamoko Range to the east of the lake are spectacular features of the Wairoa Basin rim, where the uplifted sedimentary strata has broken, leaving a sandstone escarpment 500-600m high. Continuous erosion of the softer mudstone has resulted in the creation of major valleys such as the Aniwaniwa.

The lake itself is undoubtedly the focus of the park. It probably owes its origin to a large earthquake associated with the uplift of the landscape some 2200 years ago. As a result of the earthquake, a huge portion of the south-western end of the Ngamoko Range slid into the deep gorge of the Waikaretaheke River, forming a natural debris dam. Water backed up behind this slip to create a lake up to 248m/813ft deep. In 1946 the water level was lowered 5m as a result of a hydroelectric development. It now normally fluctuates within a 3m range, between 579 and 582m (1899 and 1909ft) above sea level.

## FLORA AND FAUNA

### Flora
The innumerable ridges of Te Urewera are blanketed in lush vegetation; even the tops are cloaked in a green mantle. Thick forest tumbles down to the water's edge, enhancing the lake's beauty. There are over 650 species of native plant in the park, including the rare and vulnerable. The vegetation is constantly evolving, courtesy of occasional disturbances by volcanic activity, storm and fire damage and as a result of the introduction of deer and possums to the area.

Where the lake level has been lowered as a result of the hydroelectric scheme, the vegetation is regenerating slowly. Pampas grass (toe toe) is particularly prevalent on the exposed lakeside.

At lower altitudes, the forest largely consists of rimu, rata, kamahi and tawa, whilst higher up red and silver beech trees predominate. At the highest points, around Panekiri Bluff, the silver beech trees are festooned with mosses and lichens.

## Fauna

Te Urewera is the largest forest reserve in North Island and consequently boasts a rich and varied collection of wildlife.

Although introduced animals have depleted bird numbers, some of New Zealand's rarer forest birds do survive here. Kaka, kakariki and kereru are all present and at night you still have a chance of hearing morepork and North Island brown kiwi. Of the more common forest birds, tui, bellbird, fantail and rifleman are widespread. On the lake you may also see mallard, paradise and grey duck as well as white-faced heron, kingfisher, New Zealand scaup and the introduced black swan.

Introduced predators, including stoats, possums and rats, have decimated kiwi numbers in New Zealand and now only a tiny percentage of the original population remains. In 1991 a joint Kiwi Recovery Programme was launched at Lake Waikaremoana focusing on predator control. Stoat and possum traps have been laid in a 1500ha block of forest in the Puketukutuku Peninsula and Pukehou areas to combat the largest threat to kiwi chicks. Kiwi numbers and movement are subsequently monitored. The result of this long-term project has been a successful increase in the kiwi population.

Both of New Zealand's rare indigenous mammal species, the long- and short-tailed bat, are found here, although you are extremely unlikely to see these elusive nocturnal creatures. Other animals present in the park include deer, feral pigs, hares, rabbits and possums. They compete with native wildlife for food and steps have been taken to curb their numbers. DOC encourages hunting these animals and permits are available from the Aniwaniwa Visitor Centre or any DOC office in the region.

A wide range of moths, butterflies, beetles, weta and stick insects can also be found in the bush, whilst the waterways support eels, inanga, torrentfish, bully and trout. Fishing licences are available from the shop at the Waikaremoana Motor Camp (see p117).

## PLANNING YOUR TRAMP

### When to go

The high altitude of this rugged, mountainous area ensures rainfall up to 2500mm per year. This is significantly higher than in the surrounding areas of Rotorua or Napier. Mist and fog are common early in the morning, but usually burn off quite quickly. Late summer and early autumn often enjoy protracted spells of warm weather. However, in winter it is possible to get snowfall at higher elevations. The track is open all year and most popular at Easter or during the school holidays from December to late January. The ideal time to tramp the track is between **February and March**, when the numbers of visitors are slightly lower but the weather remains excellent.

## Sources of information

The most useful places when it comes to organising or booking your tramp are the **DOC offices** in the area. They can advise you on all aspects of the track, weather conditions and what to take. They are also the best source of up-to-date information and can sell you all of the relevant pamphlets and maps.

The official **DOC office** for Lake Waikaremoana is in **Aniwaniwa Visitor Centre** (booking desk ☎ 06-837 3900, general ☎ 837 3803, 🖳 www.urewera info@doc.govt.nz or teurewcravc@doc.govt.nz, Te Urewcra National Park, Private Bag 2213, Wairoa), adjacent to the lake itself. It is open daily during the summer months, 8am-5pm. As well as organising Great Walk permits the staff here can also arrange boat hire and hunting permits and there is a small museum detailing the cultural and natural history of the region as well as running a short film about the park. There are also DOC offices in nearby **Murupara** (☎ 07-366 1080) and **Gisborne** (☎ 06-867 8531), which provide similar services.

Other than the DOC offices, tourist information centres are useful outlets when putting together an itinerary. They can also book hut accommodation and provide you with information relating to the trail. They also have timetables for public transport to and from the track.

The two most relevant **information centres** for this track are in Rotorua and Gisborne. Rotorua i-SITE Visitor Information Centre (☎ 0800-768 678 or 07-348 5179, 🖳 www.rotoruanz.com, Private Bag 3007), at 1167 Fenton St, has a dedicated DOC desk and is open daily 8am-5.30pm; Gisborne i-SITE Visitor Information Centre (☎ 06-868 6139, 🖳 www.gisbornenz.com, PO Box 170) is at 209 Grey St and is open daily 8.30am-5.30pm.

## Getting to the trailhead

Lake Waikaremoana can be approached from two directions. The main access road through the park, connecting Murupara and Wairoa, is **State Highway 38** (SH38). To the north-west this connects with **SH5**, about a twenty-minute drive south of Rotorua. Most of the 120km stretch of SH38 through the park is winding, unsealed gravel track. In fact it is the longest stretch of gravelled main road left in New Zealand. Long, dusty and incredibly scenic, it is a slow road to travel. Having wound through the forest, the road emerges by the lakeside, skirts its eastern side and meanders towards the **Aniwaniwa Visitor Centre**. Eleven kilometres north-west of the centre, you are afforded great views of **Mokau Falls**. These 34m/112ft falls are a spectacular introduction to the lake. The road runs in a loop towards, over and then away from the falls. There are a couple of excellent viewpoints on the approach to the falls.

Napier and Rotorua are served by InterCity bus services. There is a connecting service from Napier to Wairoa. Big Bush Holiday Park (see opposite), 4km from Onepoto, offers a collection service from Wairoa. The service operates daily on demand from Wairoa and costs NZ$30 one way. However, it is best to check in advance the latest timetable details with either DOC or the operators themselves.

Big Bush also serves both ends of the track, as does the Waikaremoana Motor Camp (see opposite) and Waikaremoana Guided Tours who operate from

Lake Whakamarino Lodge (see below). Big Bush Water Taxi can be contacted through the Holiday Park (see below); Waikaremoana Guided Tours can be reached on ☎ 06 837-3729; Home Bay Shuttles (☎ 06-837 3800, 💻 www.jeff @waikaremoana .com) operates out of the motor camp. Each operator will provide a water-taxi service from one end of the trail to the other. Fares to or from Onepoto or Hopuruahine Bridge at either end of the track start at NZ$25 per person. These services operate on demand during the quieter months, so you should check timetables well in advance. They will also organise a hut-to-hut luggage transfer for people who don't fancy lugging their packs from one to the other.

DOC will accept no responsibility for damage to vehicles left unattended in Te Urewera; thus it's best to leave your vehicle at a motor camp or holiday park.

### Local services

Lake Waikaremoana is remote. The nearest towns of note, Murupara and Wairoa, are 100km and 63km away respectively. It is therefore imperative to bring all the supplies you may need with you when you travel to the track. Both Murupara and Wairoa have food stores and tramping equipment shops.

At the lake itself, Waikaremoana Motor Camp offers some basic camping supplies in its general store but don't count on stocking up. There is also a petrol pump selling unleaded and diesel fuel here.

There are several accommodation options in the region: *Waikaremoana Motor Camp* (☎ 06-837 3826, 💻 www.lake.co.nz; chalet from NZ$78, family unit from NZ$88, bunkhouse NZ$140) has ten isolated chalets that sleep four or five nestling on the shore as well as two self-contained units for families and a bunkhouse that sleeps up to 10 people. Alternatively you can camp here, with pitches costing NZ$12/5 per adult/child. Some 4km from Onepoto is *Big Bush Holiday Park* (☎ 06-837 3777, 💻 www.lakewaikaremoana.co.nz; dorm NZ$25, dbl NZ$80), which has some bunks in a basic backpacker block and some more comfortable motel-style cabins. Tent pitches cost NZ$12 per person. There is also a café and bar. A little further away on the shores of the much smaller Lake Whakamarino is the slightly grander *Lake Whakamarino Lodge* (☎ 06-837 3876, 💻 www.lakelodge.co.nz; sgl NZ$57, dbl NZ$79, self-contained units NZ$100). Built in 1925 and once workers' quarters to support the nearby hydroelectric power station, the lodge is now an upmarket fishing retreat run by local Maori and offers reasonably priced accommodation and home-cooked meals in a superb setting. There is also some of the finest trout fishing in the area on the doorstep.

### Huts and campsites

There are five **huts** around the lake. Panekiri, Waiopaoa, Marauiti, Waiharuru and Whanganui huts all have bunks and mattresses, wood-burning fires or gas heaters and benches. There are no cooking facilities provided so you must carry portable stoves and sufficient fuel. Rainwater is collected and supplied. Toilet facilities are also provided on site.

**Camping** is possible only at the five designated campsites at Waiopaoa, Korokoro, Maraunui, Waiharuru and Tapuaenui. Rainwater supplies, toilets and sheltered areas are provided at campsites. There is no campsite at Panekiri Hut or anywhere on Panekiri Bluff. Several areas of the lake track have been damaged by irresponsible campers using unsuitable sites and cutting trees for firewood. Stick to the designated sites.

**Advance bookings** are obligatory if you wish to stay overnight on the track. A booking guarantees you a bunk/tent site for the particular date requested. The **nightly fee** for an adult in a hut/camping is NZ$25/12; children/youth are free. This booking system operates all year and there is no cheaper off-peak season for this tramp. From 1 October until 30 April you may stay a maximum of two nights at any one hut or campsite. Throughout the rest of the year you may stay a maximum of three nights in a hut or five nights at a campsite.

All bookings can be made at the Aniwaniwa Visitor Centre (see p116) at Lake Waikaremoana by telephone, fax, post or email. Various other information centres and DOC offices in North Island can also help you to secure bunks or tent sites. Alternatively book online at ⌨ www.doc.govt.nz. Payment must be made at the time of booking. You are strongly advised to book well in advance, particularly if planning to tramp during peak seasons.

## Maps
The best map available is the *Urewera Parkmap* (273–08) at 1:130,000 scale, which includes a 1:41,000 scale map of the track itself. Topomaps' *Waikaremoana* (W18) also covers the track, at 1:50,000 scale. Both can be purchased from DOC offices and information centres in and around the region. On some maps note that Panekiri Bluff, Range and Hut are shown as being spelt Panekire.

## Distances and times
The 46km track is largely in excellent condition and can be gently tramped in four days or fairly easily completed in only three. People tend to start from Onepoto, since they are usually based overnight nearby. This means that they have to scale Panekiri Bluff on the first day. However, this is by no means obligatory or entirely logical. It is possible to have a water-taxi drop you at the Hopuruahine Landing and then walk **anticlockwise** around the lake. This ensures that you tackle the hill climb on the penultimate day, after you have eaten your way through most of your food and stretched a few muscles into shape. Should you choose to tramp the track anticlockwise, allow extra time for the ascent from Waiopaoa Hut to Panekiri Bluff, whilst remembering that it will take you less time to descend from the bluff to Onepoto.

| | | |
|---|---|---|
| Onepoto to Panekiri Hut | 9km | 4-5 hours |
| Panekiri Hut to Waiopaoa Hut | 8km | 3-4 hours |
| Waiopaoa Hut to Marauiti Hut | 12km | 4-5 hours |
| Marauiti Hut to Waiharuru Hut | 6km | $1^{1}/_{2}$-$2^{1}/_{2}$ hours |
| Waiharuru Hut to Whanganui Hut | 6km | 2-$2^{1}/_{2}$ hours |
| Whanganui Hut to Hopuruahine Bridge | 5km | $1^{1}/_{2}$-2 hours |

ROUTE GUIDE & MAPS

## TRACK DESCRIPTION

### Onepoto to Panekiri Hut 9km/4-5 hours; Map 1

This first stage is the most strenuous part of the whole tramp. With little time to warm up, you have to climb steeply for several hours to reach the top of Panekiri Bluff, the highest point of the track, though the attractive forest and eventual glorious views are superb compensation for the effort expended. The initial section of this stage is dry, so make sure you have sufficient water.

Around 500m from SH38 is a **day shelter** with track information posted alongside a map of the track, including distances and a rough timescale that errs on the generous side. The beginning of the track is clearly signposted from here.

It begins by ascending steeply, climbing at a steady rate through red beech forest. Well maintained and graded (ie levelled for easier tramping), the track skirts **Sandy Bay** before leading through the former **Armed Constabulary Redoubt** on its way up **Panekiri Bluff**, the dramatic escarpment that dominates the landscape on the southern shores of the lake. The vegetation quickly becomes increasingly dense and verdant, with kamahi and rimu both widespread. Also common here is horopito, one of the earliest evolved and most primitive flowering shrubs. It grows in damp, shaded areas and is distinguishable by its beautifully coloured leaves which frequently overshadow its tiny flowers. When the leaves are chewed in their raw state, they have an almost spicy, peppery taste. Another common plant here is the rangiora, a relatively common shrub or small tree that grows in lowland forest. Its brittle branches support large, tough grey-green leaves. The Maori and early settlers used to bruise the leaves and apply them as a treatment to wounds or sores. However, the leaves are toxic and poisonous if chewed or swallowed. At ground level crown ferns dominate and are responsible for the high concentration of tannins in the soil and, consequently, the water system. Although often tea-coloured, the water is perfectly palatable but boil it to be absolutely safe.

Because of the dense vegetation, views of the lake are often only partial until, having climbed steeply to **Te Rahui** (964m/3162ft), you break out of the trees to enjoy a 360° panorama. Large sandstone rocks offer the chance to sit and stare at the lake or along the cliffs of the bluff. From here you continue the gentle ascent of **Panekiri Bluff**, passing, at least two and a half hours from Onepoto, **Pukenui Trig**, the highest point on the bluff and, at 1181m/3874ft, virtually the highest point on the tramp. Undulating along the ridge, the path then takes you to **Bald Knob** (1161m/3808ft), another great place to stop and admire the lake some 600m/1968ft below you. In the past the lake has been likened to a 'many faceted diamond', or an 'aquamarine starfish'; whatever shape, species or colour you perceive, there is no denying that it is a spectacularly beautiful view.

From the track's high point, the route continues along the ridge, undulating through mixed beech forest blanketed in mosses and lichens that give it an air of age and mystery, with exposed knobs and knolls providing walkers with views over the tree tops. After almost 4km from Pukenui Trig you reach a 10m sheer rock bluff with a **wire and timber staircase**, while a further 100m on the trees have been cleared and you come across **Puketapu Trig** (1180m/3870ft)

ROUTE GUIDE & MAPS

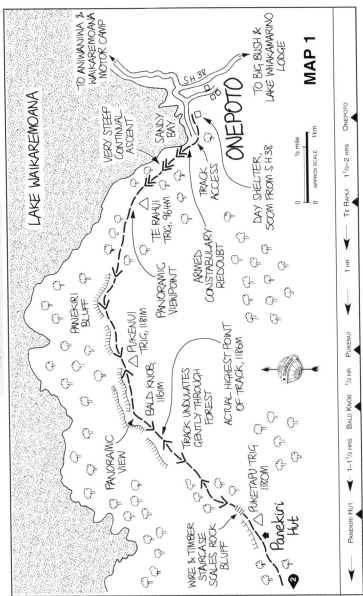

LAKE WAIKAREMOANA

MAP 1

TO ANIWANIWA & WAIKAREMOANA MOTOR CAMP

S H 38

ONEPOTO

TO BIG BUSH & LAKE WHAKAMARINO LODGE

VERY STEEP CONTINUAL ASCENT

SANDY BAY

TRACK ACCESS

DAY SHELTER, 500m FROM S H 38

ARMED CONSTABULARY REDOUBT

TE RAHUI TRIG, 964M

PANORAMIC VIEWPOINT

PANEKIRI BLUFF

PUKENUI TRIG, 1181M

BALD KNOB, 1161M

PANORAMIC VIEW

ACTUAL HIGHEST POINT OF TRACK, 1186M

TRACK UNDULATES GENTLY THROUGH FOREST

PUKETAPU TRIG 1181M

Panekiri Hut

WIRE & TIMBER STAIRCASE SCALES ROCK BLUFF

0   ½ mile
0   APPROX SCALE   1km

PANEKIRI HUT — 1–1½ HRS → BALD KNOB — ½ HR → PUKENUI — 1 HR → TE RAHUI — 1½–2 HRS → ONEPOTO

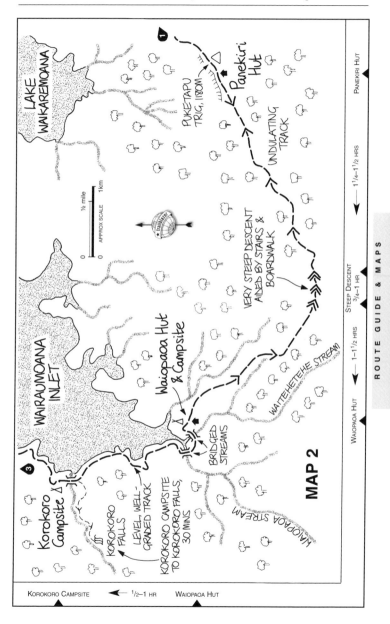

LAKE WAIKAREMOANA

PUKETAPU TRIG, 1180M

Panekiri Hut

UNDULATING TRACK

VERY STEEP DESCENT AIDED BY STAIRS & BOARDWALK

WAIRAUMOANA INLET

Waiopaoa Hut & Campsite

WAITEHETEHE STREAM

BRIDGED STREAMS

Korokoro Campsite

KOROKORO FALLS

LEVEL, WELL-GRADED TRACK

KOROKORO CAMPSITE TO KOROKORO FALLS, 30 MINS

WAIOPAOA STREAM

½ mile    1km
0         APPROX SCALE
trailblazer

MAP 2

ROUTE GUIDE & MAPS

PANEKIRI HUT ◄
◄── 1¼–1½ HRS
STEEP DESCENT ◄
¾–1 HR
◄── 1–1½ HRS
WAIOPAOA HUT ◄

KOROKORO CAMPSITE  ◄── ½–1 HR   WAIOPAOA HUT

and **Panekiri Hut**. The 36-bunk hut is supplied with rainwater from large collecting drums. The flat, grassy space next to the hut is a helicopter landing site used in emergencies and to airlift DOC staff and equipment into the area.

Perched right on the ridge, with vertiginous drops either side, the hut looks over the lake with the **Huiarau Range** to the north and endless countryside to the south. On a particularly clear day you may even be able to see the coastal town of **Wairoa**, over 60km to the south-east. It is well worth getting up early to catch the sunrise: often the lake is partially obscured by cloud and mist lying below the hut, creating a truly magical impression. As the sunlight catches the bluff and the shadows shorten, you will be privy to some outstanding views.

### Panekiri Hut to Waiopaoa Hut                    8km/3-4 hours; Map 2
This short, gentle stage is essentially a reverse of the previous one, the track continuing to undulate along the bluff before dropping steeply through the forest to the lake shortly before Waiopaoa Hut.

Beginning in primeval cloud forest, the track meanders south-west along the ridge for 3km, descending gently, negotiating a series of bluffs and rock gullies on the way, before veering gently to the west and north-west to drop swiftly down to the lake, plummeting 250m over 1km. Staircases and boardwalks help you to clamber to the base of a huge rock outcrop, though elsewhere the descent can be tricky, with roots and rocks making footing unstable. It can also be very slippery after rain, so take care. With the drop in altitude the vegetation changes dramatically. Mountain beech gives way to silver beech and podocarps, whilst mountain totara is replaced by tawa groves as the dominant understorey layer.

Towards the bottom the gradient lessens until you arrive at the lakeside and the **Waiopaoa Hut and Campsite**. The 30-bunk hut has a wood-burning stove and rainwater drums. There have been occasional rodent problems here so it is important to hang food out of reach of foraging pests on the hooks provided in the huts. The campsite lies adjacent to a sandy inlet, a gentle five-minute stroll through manuka glades from the hut. It is possible to swim here and, if the water level is low, to wander along the shoreline and explore the neighbouring bays. This is also a great spot for fishing.

Because this stage is short, you may wish to drop your packs at the hut and head to the Korokoro Falls side trip (see opposite), 3km further up the track. This will ensure you enjoy a full day's walk *and* you'll also have a shorter following day, as you will have already seen the falls. It may be possible to organise a water-taxi from the camp to the inlet adjacent to the Korokoro Falls junction, although it's pure chance as to whether a water-taxi will turn up while you're there.

### Waiopaoa Hut to Marauiti Hut                    12km/4-5 hours; Map 3
This is a fairly gentle day's tramp along the lake shore; it's worth starting early in the day so you can loiter at the many inlets and bays and fully enjoy the side trip to the attractive Korokoro Falls.

The track starts by turning inland from Waiopaoa Hut in order to cross both Waitehetehe and Waiopaoa streams over two consecutive footbridges. It then returns to the lake shore and follows the water's edge over a series of manuka

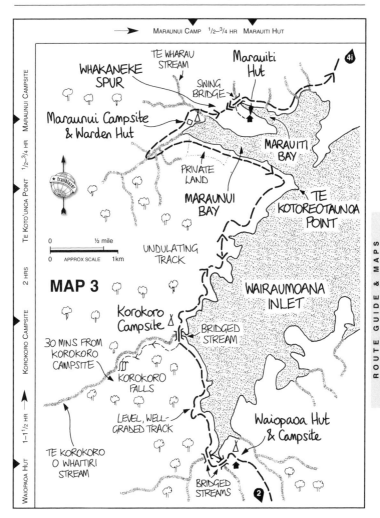

terraces and grassy flats, creeks and inlets. Around 3km from Waiopaoa Hut is the signposted junction to **Korokoro Falls**, a very scenic diversion from the track. Leave your rucksack by the junction and follow the enchanting, well-marked path for about 30 minutes alongside the smallish Te Korokoro o whaitiri stream, climbing through lush forest of tanekaha, stunted beech trees and tawa groves. The stream just doesn't prepare you for the size or splendour of the falls which are framed by ferns and beech trees. Dropping 22m over a sheer rock face beneath a dense bush canopy, after heavy rain the falls can become quite dramatic, covering the rock face and creating a shimmering rectangular curtain of water.

Having returned to the main track, continue around the lake for 200m and over a swing bridge to the **Korokoro Campsite**, a very pleasant, tranquil spot. The track then climbs about 40m above the shoreline, past a series of sheltered inlets; by pushing through the bush you can reach some of the more accessible beaches and swim or pause for lunch at your own private inlet.

The track now meanders for 3km until it reaches **Te Kotoreotaunoa Point**, where it turns north-west and descends into rock-strewn **Maraunui Bay**. From the bay's southern side you can see across to a hut adjacent to a campground. To reach it, continue on the path as it skirts the bay, passing several tracts of Maori reserve and privately owned land, each with its own private hut, including one that appears to have a TV aerial. The track then turns inland once more, following an unnamed stream that is said to be excellent for fishing. Having deviated inland for 1km, the track crosses the stream and doubles back on the far side to arrive at the official **Maraunui Campsite** by **Te Wharau Stream**. The hut is for park wardens only, not the public; the official DOC hut lies 1km further on over the beech-covered low saddle of **Whakaneke Spur**, visible across Maraunui Bay. Scrambling up between strongly buttressed trees, tawa and occasional rimu, you then descend steeply to Marauiti Bay from where a short sidetrack leads to the **Marauiti Hut**, situated on a grassy flat by the sheltered lakeside. With a faded red roof and cream exterior, this charming 26-bunk hut is set in an idyllic location that's perfect for swimming, fishing or simply relaxing on the large porch – assuming the sandflies aren't too persistent!

## Marauiti Hut to Hopuruahine Bridge      17km/5-7 hours; Map 4i & ii

From Marauiti Hut the track changes character, essentially following the contours around the lake. Aside from the occasional saddle to be crossed, there is little ascent/descent, so you should be able to maintain a steady pace.

Quite a lot of trampers walk out from Marauiti Hut, either to a pre-arranged water-taxi at Hopuruahine Landing or the road beyond Hopuruahine Bridge. For those with a bus connection early the next morning, Whanganui Hut (see p127) is a pleasant place to stay, leaving a simple 5km stroll for the next day.

Having back-tracked to the main trail, you cross the broad river flowing into the lake at Marauiti Bay on a large swing bridge. On the bay's north side, the track edges around rocky promontories before turning north-east into **Te Kopua Bay**, an isolated spot especially popular with anglers. The beautiful white-sand beaches are particularly well protected, ensuring smooth waters.

The track now briefly deviates inland, climbing about 60m over the saddle of a wide peninsula, dropping down from the headland to **Te Totara Bay** alongside an area of private land. Skirting this and **Ahimanu Bay**, you then cross a very slight headland joining Patekaha Island to the mainland. The track now sticks to the shoreline, passing several idyllic sandy beaches separated by rocky outcrops. Around 1500m from Patekaha you arrive at **Upokororo Bay**, the site of **Waiharuru Hut and Campsite**. This is the most modern hut on the walk, built in 1999 to replace Te Puna Hut which still features on some maps although

ROUTE GUIDE & MAPS

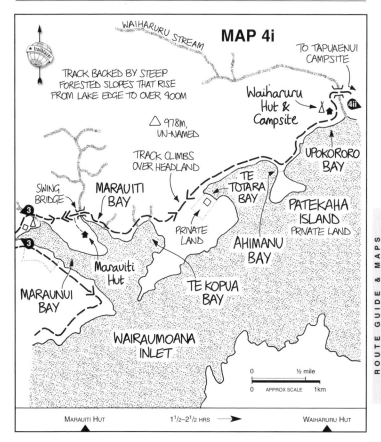

**MAP 4i**

WAIHARURU STREAM

TO TAPUAENUI CAMPSITE

TRACK BACKED BY STEEP FORESTED SLOPES THAT RISE FROM LAKE EDGE TO OVER 900M

Waiharuru Hut & Campsite

4ii

△ 978M, UN-NAMED

UPOKORORO BAY

TRACK CLIMBS OVER HEADLAND

TE TOTARA BAY

SWING BRIDGE

MARAUITI BAY

PATEKAHA ISLAND PRIVATE LAND

3

3

PRIVATE LAND

AHIMANU BAY

Marauiti Hut

TE KOPUA BAY

MARAUNUI BAY

WAIRAUMOANA INLET

0          ½ mile
0    APPROX SCALE    1km

ROUTE GUIDE & MAPS

MARAUITI HUT          1½–2½ HRS  ⟶          WAIHARURU HUT

it has now been pulled down. This new hut has 40 bunks, a sizeable kitchen and a large deck area that affords splendid views of the bay and lake. From the hut, the track heads inland to cross Waiharuru Stream, before returning to the lakeside. Crossing **Upokororo Stream** (see Map 4ii), you then climb 100m over a bush-covered saddle, part of the **Puketukutuku Range** and a designated site of the Kiwi Protection Programme. Consequently, you should see several stoat and possum traps, part of the intensive predator control initiative.

The track passes through some resplendent, mature rimu and tawa forest, winding between manuka and patches of tree fern. This wonderfully varied forest is rich in insects and birdlife making for a very pleasant stretch of tramping. You then drop off the headland to **Tapuaenui Bay** on the Whanganui Inlet. There is a day shelter and campsite here. The track negotiates a further series of

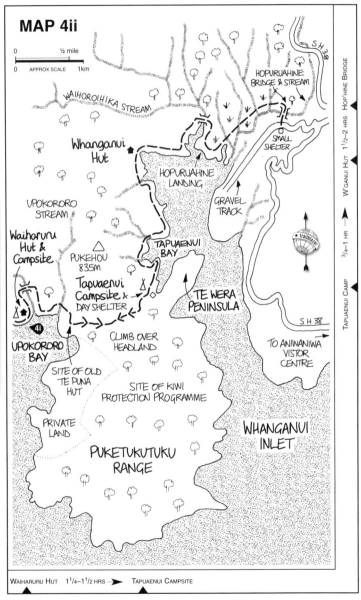

bays to arrive eventually at the **Whanganui Hut**. This lightly used 18-bunk hut stands on a grassy flat between two streams, with a small beach directly in front of the hut area and a better one five minutes further up the track.

The final section of the walk begins with a pleasant, gentle stroll through bush to the Waihoroihika Stream. Once across the bridge, you pass a spur before arriving at the signposted **Hopuruahine Landing**, a sandy bay offering great views back across the lake to Panekiri Bluff and a final place to swim.

You then turn into the wide, grassy **Hopuruahine Valley**, following the north-western side of the Hopuruahine Stream through two pleasant grassy meadows to arrive at a point opposite the access road. A final swing bridge crosses the broad river and deposits you at the roadside opposite a small shelter.

It's less than 1km along the gravel track to the junction with **SH38**, from where the majority of buses operate. From the junction it is a thirty-minute drive around the eastern side of the lake to Aniwaniwa Visitor Centre.

# Tongariro Northern Circuit

*Here you may see that heart bared, see the process of the making and moulding of the land by fire, ice and water. Mother Earth reveals her inmost secrets here, she pulses with never ceasing, sometimes fiery energy.*
**James Cowan**, as quoted in the DOC pamphlet *Tongariro Northern Circuit*

## INTRODUCTION

In the heart of North Island lies Tongariro National Park. This spectacular volcanic park is full of unique lunar landscapes, surrounded by the fragile debris of old craters, extraordinary coloured lakes and steaming hot pools.

The Northern Circuit comprises a 49km tramp beneath intimidating volcanic cones amidst captivating lunar landscapes where you are afforded a glimpse of the earth at its creation. Tramping between strange rock forms and

> **The legend of Ngatoro-i-rangi**
> The Ngati Tuwharetoa and the Ngati Rangi, the two major tribes that live in the shadow of Tongariro's volcanoes, believe them to be *tapu*, sacred. They believe that Ngatoro-i-rangi, ancestor of the Ngati Tuwharetoa (and the navigator of *Te Arawa*, one of the first canoes to reach New Zealand from Hawaiki; see p49), arrived in the Bay of Plenty and journeyed south looking for land for his people. In a bid to survey the surrounding land he scaled Mount Ngauruhoe. However, upon reaching the summit of the mountain, he became caught in a blizzard. Trapped in the snowstorm he called to the gods to send warmth. They responded by sending fire from within the earth. It issued forth from the ground, creating the craters of Ngauruhoe and Tongariro. Saved by this heat, he gave thanks and sacrificed a female slave, Auruhoe, whose body was cast into a crater. He then laid claim to the surrounding land for his people.

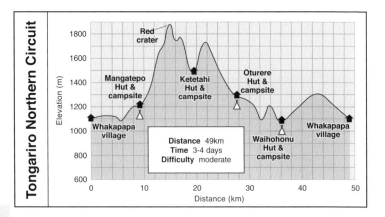

**Tongariro Northern Circuit**

Red crater

Mangatepo Hut & campsite

Ketetahi Hut & campsite

Oturere Hut & campsite

Whakapapa village

Waihohonu Hut & campsite

Whakapapa village

**Distance** 49km
**Time** 3-4 days
**Difficulty** moderate

around unusually coloured, striking landmarks, you are constantly surrounded by places where the Earth's energy steams and issues from vents and cracks – a place the photographer Craig Potton suggests TS Eliot might have described as a 'still turning point'. Youthful, temporary and ever-changing, this landscape reminds you of nature's unpredictability and potential power.

The tramp is centred on three large active volcanoes, Mount Ruapehu and Mount Tongariro with the high-tented cone of Mount Ngauruhoe forming part of the latter's volcanic massif. This stunning triumvirate forms the roof of New Zealand's North Island. Mount Ruapehu (2797m/9174ft) is the highest peak on North Island. Mount Ngauruhoe (2291m/7515ft) is the most active volcano on the mainland. Mount Tongariro (1967m/6452ft) gave its name to the national park due to its special cultural significance to local Maori tribes.

### HISTORY

Maori history and legend has always been intricately linked to Tongariro (see box p127). Many early chiefs were buried on its slopes and the land came to be considered *tapu*, sacred. Maori traditions dictated that no man could enter the region, in the belief that the mountain spirits would destroy him. They therefore actively sought to prevent anyone from ascending its slopes. They themselves would travel only as far as Ketetahi hot springs in order to bathe, but would venture no further. In some circumstances the Tuwharetoa would refuse to even look at the mountain for fear of breaking its tapu.

Early European explorers were dissuaded from travelling in the area and risked the wrath of the Maori if they did so. However, in 1839 the botanist and explorer John Bidwell made the first European ascent of Mount Ngauruhoe. Though rewarded with the knowledge that he stood where no other European had been, his insensitive actions greatly offended and angered the Tuwharetoa chief, Te Heuheu Mananui.

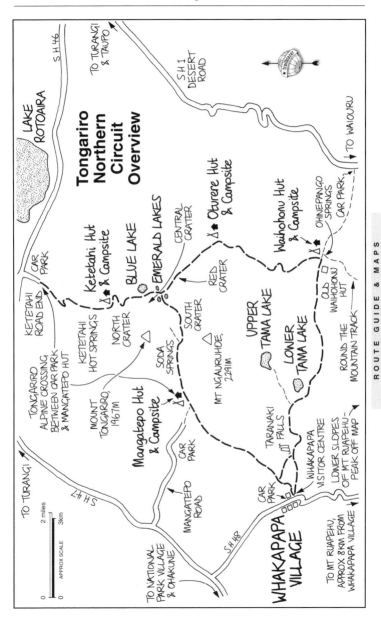

For the next twelve years, European explorers were kept away, until in 1851 the mountaineer Sir George Grey conquered one of Mount Ruapehu's lesser peaks, again without permission from the Maori guardians of the land. However, it wasn't until 1879 that George Beetham reached the actual highest point of the mountain and in so doing saw Crater Lake for the first time.

By the 1880s a steady stream of explorers and geologists were descending on the region. As well as a fascination with the mountains themselves, Europeans were also interested in using the surrounding countryside for practical purposes. In the late 1800s sheep were farmed in and around the Mangatepo Valley. However, inaccessibility, poor grazing and the difficulties of shipping wool out of the region all contributed to the demise of sheep farming in this area by the 1920s.

As well as pressure from Europeans, there were rival tribal claims to the land. Conflict was inevitable. After the New Zealand Land Wars, during which the Tuwharetoa sided with the rebel Te Kooti Rikirangi (see p55), rival tribes demanded the redistribution of the land by the Crown. Te Heuheu Tukino IV, paramount chief of the Tuwharetoa, feared that this division of the land would result in the loss of their sacred volcanoes and a loss of mana for the tribe. In 1885 he declared:

*'If our mountains of Tongariro are included in the blocks passed through the court in the ordinary way, what will become of them? They will be cut up and sold, a piece going to one Pakeha and a piece to another. They will become of no account, for the tapu will be gone. Tongariro is my ancestor, my tapuna, it is my head; my mana centres around Tongariro... I cannot consent to the court passing these mountains through in the ordinary way.'*

In 1887, in a final bid to avoid the division of the land, Te Heuheu Tukino took the unprecedented step of giving the sacred volcanoes to the Crown and the people of New Zealand, to be turned into a national park in memory of his tribe, declaring 'The mountains of the south wind have spoken to us for centuries. Now we wish them to speak to all who come in peace and in respect of their tapu.' His foresight and selfless action ensured that the land became New Zealand's first national park and only the fourth in the world, guaranteeing the preservation of the land and its heritage.

An act of parliament formally established Tongariro National Park in 1894. Use of the land has evolved considerably over the intervening years but even now 'Tongariro still smokes ... the ancestral fires still burn and the land lives on for all ...' (Te Heuheu Tukino IV, 1887).

As the number of people using the park grew, so better access and accommodation was required. Between 1901 and 1903 huts were built at Ketetahi and Waihohonu. The original 'Grand Tour' took people by paddle steamer up the Whanganui River to Pipiriki. Here they were collected by horse-drawn coaches and delivered to Waihohonu. Railway services further opened up the region. The main trunk line was completed in 1908. This led to the development of the western side of the park and soon a road to the village of Whakapapa was built.

The interest in skiing led to further developments. Numerous huts were built in and around Whakapapa, including the grand four-storey Chateau Hotel which opened in 1929. Visitor numbers rocketed in the 1950s and '60s as roads were sealed, tracks cut and the area's reputation spread.

The original area gifted to the country amounted to 2630ha. This has been steadily increased by government purchase of surrounding land and the national park now covers almost 78,000ha. The unusual features and extraordinary beauty of the region led to it being awarded World Heritage status by UNESCO in 1990. Following this, the criteria for cultural sites was reconsidered. Consequently, recognition was extended to areas that had spiritual and cultural value as well as to buildings or structures and thus, in 1993, Tongariro National Park was designated a Cultural World Heritage site as well, making it one of only a handful of places in the world to achieve dual status.

## GEOLOGY

The andesitic volcanoes of Tongariro National Park lie at the southern end of the Taupo Volcanic Zone, the region of volcanic activity stretching from Mount Ruapehu through the Rotorua lakes to the continuously active volcano of White Island in the Bay of Plenty. A tectonic plate boundary can be found just east of North Island, where the Pacific plate dips beneath the Indian-Australian plate, creating a line of volcanoes that extends from Tonga to Mount Ruapehu.

In geological terms, the Tongariro volcanoes are relatively young. They do, however, offer a graphic illustration of the phenomenal power generated by tectonic plate subduction.

**Mount Ruapehu** (2797m/9174ft) is a large, complex volcano that has developed from successive eruptions over the last 200,000 years or so. It is the highest point on North Island and still boasts the remnants of eight glaciers. Although much diminished, particularly in the last 40 years, these glaciers once extended below 1300m and are the only glaciers left on North Island. Mount Ruapehu also boasts one of the world's few hot crater lakes that exists surrounded by permanent glaciers and snowfields. It is certainly one of the world's most accessible hot crater lakes.

A huge eruption in 1945 sent ash clouds as far as Wellington. On Christmas Eve, 1953, an ice wall holding back Crater Lake gave way and an enormous flood of mud, volcanic debris and water, known as a lahar, swept down the Whangehu River devastating everything in its path. It destroyed the Tangirai rail bridge moments before a crowded passenger train was due to cross, causing it to plunge into the valley below. One hundred and fifty-one people died in what remains one of New Zealand's worst ever disasters. Almost fifty years to the day since the 1945 eruption, Mount Ruapehu burst into life again on 23 September 1995. Thousands of skiers witnessed a spectacular eruption as rock and ash sprayed from the crater. Luckily the ski fields escaped damage, but lahars flowed down Whangehu, Mangaturuturu and Whakapapanui valleys, emptying Crater Lake completely. The volcanic activity lasted for three and a half weeks. The lake began to refill until a large eruption on 17 June 1996 emptied it again. Ash, fire fountains and sonic booms all formed part of this dramatic eruption. Crater Lake has since refilled once more, although it may take up to twelve years to reach its previous level, future volcanic activity allowing.

**Mount Tongariro** (1967m/6452ft) is a very complex volcano. It is possible to determine eight craters in the massif, which measures 8km by 13km in total.

**Mount Ngauruhoe** (2291m/7515ft) is the youngest volcano of the three, probably about 5000 years old. Because of its young age, it has largely escaped the weathering effects of erosion and retains its perfect conical shape. Both Maori and geologists consider Mount Ngauruhoe to be part of the old Tongariro volcano. Traditionally it has erupted at least every nine years, although it hasn't exploded since 1975. The most spectacular lava flows occurred in 1949 and 1954. The active Red Crater last emitted ash in 1926.

## FLORA AND FAUNA

### Flora

The vegetation in Tongariro National Park has evolved to survive in a wide spectrum of frequently harsh weather conditions. Temperatures range from mild to freezing; icy winds sweep the area's exposed sections and the vegetation must cope with extremes of rainfall, snow and in some areas even a *lack* of moisture. Over 550 species of native plants are found in the park, around 80 per cent of which are endemic to New Zealand. Amongst them are 12 types of native conifer, 36 varieties of orchid and over 60 species of fern.

Vegetation in the exposed Rangipo Desert has evolved to exist under rocks or in cracks and crevasses. These areas offer some shelter from the battering effects of the wind. The plants have also developed long roots that search out water amidst the gravel.

Elsewhere, in moister sites, mountain shrubland dominates. Most of the plants here tend to be herbaceous. Tussock shrublands are populated by daisies, mosses, red tussocks and other species. Introduced heather is also taking a hold.

The forest sections are dominated by mountain beech. Forming a wide belt along the western and southern slopes of Mount Ruapehu, it's markedly absent from mounts Tongariro and Ngauruhoe. Silver and red beech are here, primarily on the eastern slopes of Tongariro and the southern slopes of Mount Ruapehu. Unfortunately, their rigidity makes them prone to damage by heavy snowfall.

Rimu, kamahi and rata are also found scattered throughout the park, usually at elevations of between 600 and 900m (1960 and 2950ft). They support much of the insect- and bird-life found in the park.

### Fauna

Despite its largely barren appearance, Tongariro is home to a deceptively wide variety of fauna. A broad range of birds, in particular, flourishes here, especially in the forested areas: North Island robin, whitehead, kereru, fantail, chaffinch, tui, tomtit, blackbird, yellow-crowned parakeet and kaka are all present. There are even a few North Island brown kiwi.

New Zealand's only native mammals, the short- and long-tailed bats, reside here, as do skinks and geckos, which are most likely to be visible during the warmer summer months. Cicadas, weta, huhu and caterpillars inhabit the forests. Introduced species including hares, possums and red deer have made Tongariro their home too. They are responsible for damaging the alpine and forest vegetation and for modifying the native forest understorey through browsing.

## PLANNING YOUR TRAMP

### When to go

The climate in this region is strongly influenced by the prevailing westerly winds. It can be highly temperamental. As the moisture-laden clouds from the Pacific Ocean reach the mountainous volcanic plateau, they are forced to rise. This results in large quantities of rain. Around 190 days a year are rain-affected, bringing up to 2500mm per annum. By the time the clouds reach the eastern side of the region, the Rangipo Desert, they have largely deposited the moisture they were carrying as rain or snow. Consequently, the eastern region is a barren landscape of dark-reddish ash, largely devoid of vegetation.

Even though the prevailing winds are westerly, Tongariro is subject to all winds and conditions. There is no definite wet or dry season. Heavy snows accompanied by dramatic drops in temperature may occur at any time of the year. The ideal time to tramp the circuit is between **December and March** when the circuit is usually clear of snow and the weather is less likely to be as severe. However, the weather pattern remains highly unpredictable and you must be prepared for all conditions, no matter what the initial outlook.

In winter, snow and ice make the circuit a difficult proposition, not to be undertaken lightly. However, with adequate clothing, the correct equipment and a degree of experience it is possible to visit and enjoy Tongariro at this time.

### Sources of information

There's a **DOC office** at Whakapapa Visitor Centre (Private Bag, Mount Ruapehu; ☎ 07-892 3729, 🖥 whakapapavc@doc.govt.nz) that is ideally placed to offer advice and help you to prepare for your tramp. Open 8.30am-5pm on weekdays and 8am-5pm at weekends, they can book all accommodation and huts and supply detailed maps and pamphlets of the track. They also have a fascinating exhibition here recording the history and background of the area. There is also a DOC office in Turangi (Tongariro Taupo Conservancy, Private Bag; ☎ 07-386 8607, 🖥 ttcinfo@doc.govt.nz), which opens weekdays 8am-5pm and offers similar services. There's no i-SITE or visitor centre in National Park although there is a website, 🖥 www.nationalpark.co.nz, covering most aspects of the town and the activities available around it.

**Information centres** in the main towns nearby can book huts and answer questions. Some may also be able to sell you the requisite mapping. Turangi i-SITE Visitor Information Centre (☎ 07-386 8999, 🖥 www.laketauponz.com, PO Box 34), at Ngawaka Place, is open daily 9am-5pm; Ruapehu i-SITE Visitor Information Centre (☎ 06-385 8427, 🖥 www.visitruapehu.com, PO Box

36) at 54 Clyde St, Ohakune, is open 9am-5pm on weekdays and 9am-3pm at weekends, whilst Taupo i-SITE (☎ 07-376 0027, 💻 www.laketauponz.com, PO Box 865) on Tongariro St, is open daily 8.30am-5pm.

## Getting to the trailhead

The nearest reasonably-sized towns are Turangi to the north-east and Ohakune to the south-west. Tongariro National Park is well served by state highways. The famously scenic SH1 (the Desert Rd) on the eastern side of the park links Turangi and Waiouru. SH4 and SH47 on the western side of the park run from Taupo to National Park Village, via Turangi. There is also a regular passenger rail link, the Tranz Scenic Overlander (💻 www.tranzscenic.co.nz), between Auckland and Wellington that stops in National Park Village.

Although the Tongariro Circuit can be accessed from a variety of points, it is usually started from Whakapapa village or the Mangatepo road end.

Whakapapa village can be reached from Taupo or Turangi by catching the daily shuttle service operated by Alpine Scenic Tours or Intercity. If you are staying in National Park Village you will have access to several bus services that can shuttle you to Whakapapa or the Mangatepo or Ketetahi road ends. This service is primarily aimed at people attempting the Tongariro Alpine Crossing. Companies include Adrift Guided Outdoor Adventures (☎ 0800-462 374, 💻 www .adriftnz.co.nz), Adventure Headquarters (☎ 07-386 0969, 💻 www.adventure headquarters.co.nz), Howard's Lodge (see opposite), Plateau Shuttle (see Plateau Lodge p136), Tongariro Expeditions (☎ 0800-828 763, 💻 www.ton gariroexpeditions.com), Tongariro Track Transport (☎ 07-892 3716) and Tongariro Volcanic Adventures (☎ 07-892 2870, 💻 www.npbp.co.nz) who operate out of the National Park Backpackers (see opposite).

> ### It's not just about the tramping – other activities in the region
> Although the focus in the region is the Tongariro Northern Circuit and the shorter Tongariro Alpine Crossing, there are other attractions and activities. Probably the most famous is the renowned 42 Traverse, a 4- to 6-hour **mountain bike** ride along 45km of old logging tracks that weave through Tongariro Forest. The going is rutted but pretty good although the gradients in both directions can be steep. The trail starts 18km north-east of National Park on SH47 and finishes in Owhango, 24km north of National Park. For those still in search of a two-wheel adrenaline fix try the gruelling 50km Fishers Track that starts and finishes in National Park, although there is a half-length version that's almost all downhill, after which you can arrange to be collected and chauffeured home rather than face cycling uphill for a further 25km. Bikes can be hired from Howard's Lodge (see opposite) or Kiwi Mountain Bikes (☎ 0800-562 4537, 💻 www.kiwimountainbikes.co.nz).
>
> Alternatively, hire a **quad bike** (💻 www.bushbuggies.com) from Ward St in National Park and join them for a guided off-road tour of the surrounding native forests. Trips can be tailor-made to suit experience and budget.
>
> More relaxing than these activities are the short **flights** available from Mountain Air (💻 www.mountainair.co.nz/) who will take you up in a Cessna to see the Tongariro Alpine Crossing and Northern Circuit from the air.

There are several car parks in Whakapapa. From the village it is a three- to four-hour walk to Mangatepo Hut. By starting at the Mangatepo road end, it is only a thirty-minute walk to Mangatepo Hut. Should you wish to access the circuit from another area, your options are twofold. Either begin from the Ketetahi road end car park, which is a two- to three-hour walk from Ketetahi Hut, or from the car park just off SH1, a 60- to 90-minute walk from Waihohonu Hut.

Hitching throughout the park is difficult as traffic on the roads is fairly light.

Visitors are advised not to leave valuables in parked cars and to make all transport arrangements before setting off. For a full list of current operators, times and routes contact the DOC office in Whakapapa.

## Local services

The small hamlets and towns in the Tongariro area are scattered and fairly remote. You are best off staying in either Whakapapa or National Park Village.

**Whakapapa** boasts a small food store, a petrol station, a café, pub, the visitor centre (see p133) and several places to stay. Try the *Holiday Park* (☎ 07-892 3897, 💻 www.whakapapa.net.nz; tent pitch NZ$17/10 per adult/child, dorm NZ$25, cabin from NZ$60-70, self-contained units from NZ$84-99), *Skotel Alpine Resort* (☎ 07-892 3719, 💻 www.skotel.co.nz; backpacker wing dorm NZ$30, sgl/twin/dbl with facilities or tpl NZ$40/55/80, hotel dbl from NZ$130), a wooden complex with sauna, spa, gym, restaurant and bar, or the stately *Bayview Chateau Tongariro* (☎ 07-892 3809, 💻 www.chateau.co.nz; dbl from NZ$190, suite NZ$250-1000); opened in 1929 this grand neo-Georgian mansion is spectacular to see and offers the lavish facilities and classy service you'd expect to find in one of New Zealand's most renowned hotels.

Around 15km from Whakapapa, the small community of **National Park Village** (see map p136) spreads out from a crossroad junction linking SH4 and SH47. It has a petrol station and small shop, some very congenial bars, a railway station and a selection of hostel-style accommodation.

The friendly *National Park Backpackers* (☎ 07-892 2870, 💻 www.np bp.co.nz; tent pitch NZ$14 per person, dorm NZ$26-31, twin/dbl NZ$67-86), on Finlay St, has a well-equipped kitchen, spa pool and its own 8m-high indoor climbing wall boasting more than 50 different routes; the comfortable *Ski Haus* (☎ 07-892 2854, 💻 www.skihaus.co.nz/; tent pitch NZ$12 per person, dorm NZ$19-21, dbl/twin NZ$58), on Carroll St, has a spa and 'conversation pit' for guests to hang out in when not at the bar or in the sociable restaurant. The excellent *Howard's Lodge* (☎ 07-892 2827, 💻 www.howardslodge.co.nz; dorm NZ$26-27, dbl or twin NZ$68, en suite NZ$85, suites from NZ$140), on the same road, has accommodation for all budgets, two spacious lounges with log fires, a pool table and free spa as well as a decent outdoor shop and info service where you can book onward buses. On Millar St is the spacious *Pukenui Lodge* (☎ 07-892 2882, 💻 www.tongariro.cc; dorm NZ$20-26, dbl/twin NZ$65, en suite NZ$75, chalet from NZ$180). There's also the cosy, well-equipped *Adventure Lodge* (☎ 07-892 2991, 💻 www.adventurenationalpark .co.nz; dorm NZ$25, dbl/twin NZ$65, motel unit from NZ$130), on Carroll St, with rooms to suit most budgets, two hot spa pools, an open log fire and a large

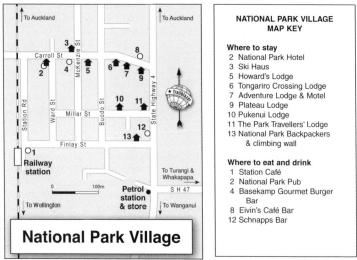

National Park Village

**NATIONAL PARK VILLAGE
MAP KEY**

**Where to stay**
2 National Park Hotel
3 Ski Haus
5 Howard's Lodge
6 Tongariro Crossing Lodge
7 Adventure Lodge & Motel
9 Plateau Lodge
10 Pukenui Lodge
11 The Park Travellers' Lodge
13 National Park Backpackers
   & climbing wall

**Where to eat and drink**
1 Station Café
2 National Park Pub
4 Basekamp Gourmet Burger
   Bar
8 Eivin's Café Bar
12 Schnapps Bar

covered BBQ area. They offer a number of good value deals on accommodation, meals and transport to and from the Tongariro Crossing.

Slightly more salubrious accommodation can be found at the *National Park Hotel* (☎ 07-892 2805, 🖳 nationalparkhotel@xtra.co.nz) connected to the red-roofed pub at the end of Carroll St; it offers clean, compact rooms in a building full of genuine character and ambience dating from 1913. *The Park Travellers' Lodge* (☎ 07-892 2748, 🖳 www.the-park.co.nz; dorm NZ$30, dbl NZ$95-115, loft apartment NZ$105-140) on the corner of Millar St and SH4 is a giant, sprawling place with heated spa pool, house bar and its own reasonably priced café-restaurant. All rooms are en suite and tastefully kitted out with mod-cons and their own fridge-freezers. *Plateau Lodge* (☎ 07-892 2993, 🖳 www .plateaulodge.co.nz; standard quad NZ$30, dbl NZ$70, en suite dbl NZ$90, apartment NZ$155 for two, NZ$20 per additional person up to a maximum of six) on Carroll St has spotless two-bedroom apartments capable of sleeping up to six as well as en suite lodge rooms. The attractive, peaceful, white-panelled *Tongariro Crossing Lodge* (☎ 07-892 2688, 🖳 www.tongarirocrossing lodge.com; dbl suite NZ$139, four-bed suite NZ$298), 37 Carroll St, has spacious suites with their own lounge areas, over-sized beds and en suite facilities.

For **food**, you could try the old-fashioned *National Park Pub* connected to the hotel (see above), which also has a takeaway service, or the lively *Schnapps Bar* on SH4 which serves hearty pub fare for NZ$10-25. Bar snacks and generous portions of filling local fare such as lamb shank and great steaks are available throughout the day although you may find you have to fight for a space around the large open fire, particularly if the pub is showing the rugby on its giant screens or hosting a live music act. Alternatively the *Basekamp Gourmet*

*Burger Bar* on Carroll St has around 20 varieties of burger including lamb, venison and veggie falafel versions as well as wood-fired pizza. Check out the array of climbing kit and memorabilia on the walls including items signed by Sir Edmund Hillary. *Eivin's Café Bar* on Carroll St is ideal during the day for hearty breakfasts and decent brunch snacks but also serves evening meals and has a range of wines and cocktails. The *Station Café* is situated within the historic railway station; the small garden is ideal for sumptuous breakfasts whilst the main evening à la carte menu is popular enough to require booking ahead.

Despite the presence of these settlements and the basic shop in the petrol station opposite the junction with SH47, it is still advisable to bring food and equipment for the tramp before you arrive in the region.

## Huts and campsites

There are four **huts** on the circuit. Bookings are not required but you must secure a **Great Walks hut pass** in advance if you intend to stay at Mangatepo, Ketetahi, Oturere or Waihohonu huts. A pass entitles you to spend a given number of nights in the DOC facilities on the track from the date of issue. You can buy your hut pass from local visitor centres or DOC offices, in order to avoid the higher premiums charged by the wardens. The huts are supplied with bunks, mattresses, toilets, rainwater, gas heating and gas stoves (stoves are available only during the summer months so you must carry portable cooking gear at all other times of the year). There is usually a warden on duty in each hut during the peak summer season (October to June) providing information and regular weather updates as well as to check hut passes. Outside the summer season, the huts are not serviced and off-season rates apply.

**Campsites** have been established near each of the huts. A Great Walks pass is still required for camping. The **adult hut fee** for the summer season is NZ$25 and NZ$15 for the rest of the year; the **camping fee** is NZ$20 and NZ$5 for the same periods. There is no charge for children or youths.

## Maps

The best maps for this area are the 1:80,000 scale *Tongariro Parkmap* (273–04) or the 1:50,000 scale *Tongariro* (T19) by Topomaps. These can be purchased at DOC offices and information centres around the region.

## Distances and times

The three- to four-day circuit follows a well-marked route. Although not unduly taxing, it can become difficult if weather conditions deteriorate. However, even in poorer conditions the track is still visually stunning. Take your time on each section in order to better appreciate the land's power, its rugged terrain and stark, desolate beauty.

| | | |
|---|---|---|
| Whakapapa village to Mangatepo Hut | 9km | 3-4 hours |
| Mangatepo Hut to Ketetahi Hut | 10km | 4-5 hours |
| Ketetahi Hut to Oturere Hut | 8km | 3-4 hours |
| Oturere Hut to Waihohonu Hut | 8km | $2^1/_2$-$3^1/_2$ hours |
| Waihohonu Hut to Whakapapa village | 14km | 5-6 hours |

ROUTE GUIDE & MAPS

## TRACK DESCRIPTION

### Whakapapa village to Mangatepo Hut          9km/3-4 hours; Map 1

This short section is often overlooked by trampers who can drive to the Mangatepo car park shortly before Mangatepo Hut. It is a gentle tramp which in the past had a tendency to become muddy and unpleasant after heavy rains. Since being improved, the track is much better but it still essentially acts only as a means of accessing the more substantial highlights to come.

From the **Whakapapa Visitor Centre** head up **Ngauruhoe Place** and along the Lower Taranaki Falls track. The path begins by meandering through open grasslands and the occasional patch of beech forest. Just over 1km from the start, the track forks. Take the left branch and cross the footbridge over **Wairere Stream** (the right-hand fork leads to Taranaki Falls and the Tama Lakes; see p146 and Map 4, p147).

The undulating path crosses areas of grass and tussock as well as several streams, mostly now bridged, although in the past they had to be tramped through. During heavy rain this section would become muddy and the streams would erode the track. This in turn led most trampers to skip this section entirely and begin at Mangatepo car park.

The track maintains its course with views of Mount Ngauruhoe to the east as well as, in the foreground, Mount Pukekaikiore (1692m/5550ft), one of the older vents of the Tongariro complex. To the north is Mount Pukeonake (1225m/4018ft), a low scoria cone (ie one made of solidified lava) with a rough and pitted surface. Both Pukekaikiore and Pukeonake were in existence at the time of the last ice age, when the glaciers carving down from Mount Tongariro created the Mangatepo Valley.

Breaching a couple more streams you climb to a small ridge and complete this preliminary walk by skirting around Mount Pukekaikiore into the Mangatepo Valley and the **Mangatepo Hut and Campsite**, five minutes away. The 24-bunk hut has good views of the following day's walk up the valley to the South Crater. Close to the hut is the track leading to the car park and day shelter at the Mangatepo road end, the drop-off point for the majority of trampers undertaking the Tongariro Crossing.

### Mangatepo Hut to Ketetahi Hut          10km/4-5 hours; Map 2

The track from Mangatepo Hut to Ketetahi Hut is part of the renowned Tongariro Alpine Crossing (see box p143). Termed the 'finest one-day walk in New Zealand', it's a spectacular day's tramp through some truly unusual volcanic scenery. Fairly strenuous and exposed throughout, it demands good weather to enjoy its many features. In very low or dense cloud it can become a tedious, difficult slog.

Because of the large numbers of people undertaking the Crossing, if you're staying at Mangatepo Hut make an early start to avoid the massive surge of people streaming up the valley later on. The streams in the area are unsuitable for drinking due to the large quantities of volcanic chemicals leaching into them, so make sure that you carry sufficient water with you.

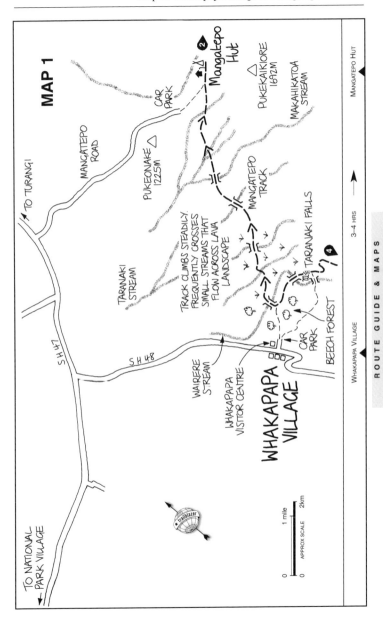

MAP 1

TO TURANGI

MANGATEPO ROAD

PUKEONAKE 1225M

MANGATEPO Hut

CAR PARK

PUKEKAIKIORE 1692M

MAKAHIKATOA STREAM

MANGATEPO TRACK

TARANAKI STREAM

Track climbs steadily, frequently crosses small streams that flow across lava landscape

TARANAKI FALLS

SH 47

SH 48

WAIRERE STREAM

WHAKAPAPA VISITOR CENTRE

WHAKAPAPA VILLAGE

CAR PARK

BEECH FOREST

TO NATIONAL PARK VILLAGE

trailblazer

0     1 mile     2km
APPROX SCALE

WHAKAPAPA VILLAGE        3-4 HRS        MANGATEPO HUT

The track begins by following the Mangatepo Stream up the valley, scrambling over a series of lava flows from Mount Ngauruhoe. Flows of older, grey lava are partially covered by the tracks of lumpy black lava from later eruptions, the most recent just fifty years ago. There has been some debate as to the origin of the Mangatepo Valley, but the easily discernible moraine and scree ridge on the north-west side of the valley suggests that it is glacial.

After an hour you reach the head of the valley and a junction with a five-minute spur track to **Soda Springs**. Full of bubbles of dissolved gases, the spring emerges from under an old lava flow, the strong smell of sulphur informing you when you are close. The surrounding area is often boggy, the extra moisture supporting mosses and plants that give the area colour and vibrancy in summer.

Having returned to the main track, continue up the valley, ascending steeply to reach, after 45 minutes, the **Mangatepo Saddle** between Mount Tongariro and the base of Mount Ngauruhoe. Although the route is steep, the track is clearly marked amidst the lava rubble. The views from the saddle are superb, both of the ascending, endless lines and ridges of Mount Ngauruhoe in front of you and the countryside stretching to the west. If it is particularly clear, you may even be able to make out the perfect cone of Mount Taranaki, some 140km away on the west coast.

There is a signpost indicating the route to follow for an **ascent of Mount Ngauruhoe**. This is a very tempting side trip which in fine weather is a very achievable proposition, time allowing. However, because there is so much else to see on this stage of the track you may wish to omit the ascent so you can fully appreciate the other features to come. If you do decide to climb Ngauruhoe, the return trip takes around three hours. It is a 600m climb on deep, strength-sapping scree. This ascent should not be attempted in bad weather or during winter without both mountaineering experience *and* the correct equipment. Poles mark the early stages of the ascent but soon stop. Follow the rock ridge at the base of the volcano directly uphill. Beyond the ridge you can access the outer crater gully, where you have a choice: turn left and climb to the highest point on the outer crater or right to the top of the inner crater. Do not, however, enter the inner crater, which often has strong, overpowering gases inside. Watch out, too, for falling rocks and be aware of the danger of dislodging a small avalanche of scree onto other climbers below you. The panoramic views from the top are exemplary. The route for the next couple of days can be clearly seen and the particularly eagle-eyed should be able to determine the various huts on the track.

Back on the main track, continue from the Mangatepo Saddle across the **South Crater**, which isn't actually a true crater but a drainage basin for the surrounding volcanoes. Nevertheless it is an impressive feature, looking like a vast natural amphitheatre. The track across is flat and peculiarly lunar, marked by tall poles. Large rocks ejected from the volcanoes lie scattered on the orange-yellow clay soil, which may be dusty or muddy underfoot depending on the weather.

At the far side of the crater, the track climbs steeply 200m along a sharp spur. At the top of the ridge you look out over Oturere Valley and the Kaimanawa Mountain Range to the east. Swinging north you proceed along the ridge past some large, prominent boulders. The track peaks at the day's highest point, the strangely beautiful **Red Crater** (1886m/6186ft), shortly after. The crater is so named because of the implausible colour of its sheer sides.

A poled route now branches off to the summit of **Mount Tongariro**. This two-hour return track is fairly easy and passes through an interesting volcanic area. The summit is marked by two trig points. The true summit is the second of the two trigs, concealed by a rocky prow.

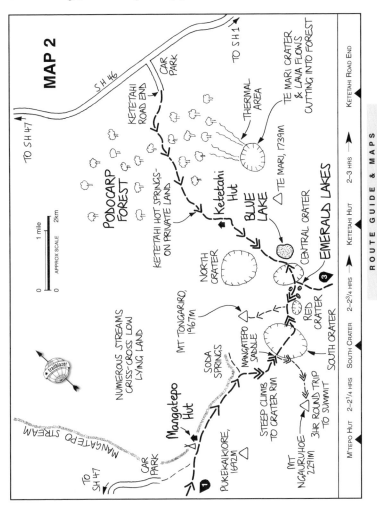

Back on the main trail, the track skirts the edge of Red Crater. The route is high and exposed and you must be well equipped, even if undertaking only the Crossing, since it can be a hostile place in bad weather. As you traverse the crater rim, peer into its fuming interior. The odd feature on the far side of the crater is a dyke, an old magma feeding pipe that leads into the vent of the volcano. More durable than the surrounding ash and scoria, it has become exposed as softer rock is eroded from around it.

You now descend steeply on the far side of the crater, dropping 200m past a series of steaming, hissing vents. The soft, shifting red-black scree is unstable underfoot and you quickly slip-slide to the bottom, arriving at the vibrant **Emerald Lakes**. These impossibly turquoise lakes owe their colouring to minerals washed out of the Red Crater. They fill old explosion pits and make for arresting features in an otherwise barren landscape of rock and scoria.

The track passes between the lakes and then divides: the right-hand fork heads south-east towards Oturere Hut, whilst the left fork continues north, descending sharply into the **Central Crater**. Like South Crater, this is actually a drainage basin. Having crossed Central Crater on a level surface amidst pock-marked boulders and lava bombs left from previous eruptions, you now climb 30m to a ridge adjacent to **Blue Lake**. As you cross Central Crater look back to see Red Crater, Mount Ngauruhoe and Mount Ruapehu aligned behind you. There is also a good view of a large black lava flow that cooled on the crater floor. Blue Lake has formed where cold freshwater has filled an old vent. It used to be called Te Waiwhaakatao-te-Rangihiroa, 'Rangihiroa's Mirror', after the Maori Te Rangihiroa who explored the volcanic plateau around 1750.

The track skirts the lake then begins to descend Mount Tongariro's northern flank beneath North Crater. This large flat-topped crater once contained a lava lake that cooled and infilled the vent. Now zigzagging on long switchbacks, you pass through a fragile alpine area of red tussock; it is vital you stay on the track, resisting the temptation to descend in a straighter, faster line.

The path descends 300m before you arrive at the well-positioned **Ketetahi Hut**. This 26-bunk hut is a pleasant spot to stay: although overrun by day-trippers, by late afternoon they will have left in order to meet their buses, allowing you to enjoy in peace the excellent views of lakes Rotoaira and Taupo and Mount Pihanga to the north-east.

### Ketetahi Hut to Waihohonu Hut                    16km/5$^1$/$_2$-7$^1$/$_2$ hours; Map 3

This outstanding stretch offers a sharp contrast to the previous day, showcasing an entirely different aspect of the region. Following an initial climb it is predominantly downhill, and free from the crowds of the Crossing.

The initial part of the day is spent retracing your steps. The path climbs 200m steeply, zigzagging to the top, where it eases along the gully that leads to the saddle between Blue Lake and North Crater. The ascent is a steady slog, although the views offer a heady distraction.

Dropping into Central Crater, follow the poles and cairns across the level surface to the junction for Oturere Hut just before the Emerald Lakes. You should be here ahead of the crowds arriving from Mangatepo and can thus enjoy the eerie stillness of the area, punctuated only by the hissing of the steaming vents nearby. Taking the left-hand path, head south-east around one of the lakes. Turning your back on the majestic bulk of Mount Tongariro you drop steeply down a narrow spur into the **Oturere Valley**, with views of the valley itself, the Kaimanawa Range and the Rangipo Desert. This section is one of the track's best-kept secrets and will seem positively serene in comparison to the previous day.

### The Tongariro Alpine Crossing

The world-famous Tongariro Alpine Crossing, between the Mangatepo road end and the Ketetahi road end, is 17km and takes six to eight hours to complete. If you are planning to do this, follow the path as it descends through tussock scrubland and passes the Ketetahi Hot Springs. These are on private land and there is no access to them. Historically the 40 fumaroles, boiling springs and mud pools were well known by Maori and Europeans alike for their health-giving and recuperative properties. They were held to be particularly good at easing rheumatism and clearing up skin diseases. The local Maori afford the springs the same sense of veneration as the volcanic peaks. Consequently, it is essential you respect the spring's *tapu*, or sacredness, by not visiting them. A stepped track descends through sub-alpine shrubs, offering good views of a 450-year-old lava flow from the Te Maari Crater that cuts through the forest below. The vegetation that grows on the flow is mainly youthful shrubs that will develop in size as the flow ages.

For its final section, the track descends into light podocarp forest. Totara trees shelter mapou and koromiko whilst crown ferns and mosses line the track edge. Lower down you pass through an area of regenerating forest. Once heavily logged, this section is now incorporated into the Tongariro National Park. This means a pleasant change in scenery and temperature. Following a small stream for most of the way you emerge at the Ketetahi road end. The water from this stream is unsuitable for drinking because of the chemicals washed out of the hot springs.

At the road end is a **shelter** and car park from where buses collect trampers returning to Whakapapa or National Park Village.

ROUTE GUIDE & MAPS

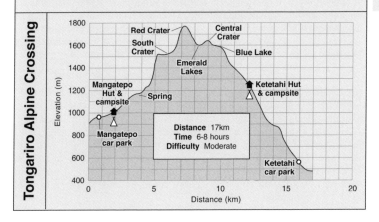

Tongariro Alpine Crossing

Red Crater
Central Crater
South Crater
Blue Lake
Emerald Lakes
Mangatepo Hut & campsite
Spring
Ketetahi Hut & campsite
Mangatepo car park

Distance 17km
Time 6-8 hours
Difficulty Moderate

Ketetahi car park

Elevation (m)
Distance (km)

It is about an hour to the valley floor where the track meanders alongside Oturere Stream amidst clumps of tussock grass, passing large lava formations and piles of rock up to 10m high in a haunting lunar landscape. The unusual jagged lava forms are the remnants of early eruptions from Red Crater where the lava cooled so quickly that it became 'frozen' into these shapes. From afar they resemble termite mounds. This is a superb section of tramping which complements and contrasts with the previous day. The Crossing showcases the volcanoes' violent potential, but the Oturere Valley reveals their long-term legacy and the two should be seen together in order to garner a complete impression.

After a period of level tramping, descend briefly to the lightly used 26-bunk **Oturere Hut**, nestled alongside an old lava flow. The hut is well-sited with views of Ngauruhoe through the windows. Set just to the west of a small gorge, there is an attractive waterfall cascading down a small cliff about 5 minutes' walk away. Peaceful and much less visited, Oturere makes a great overnight stop.

Heading south and passing alongside the eastern flank of Mount Ngauruhoe, the track undulates over open gravel fields across stream valleys. Vegetation here is engaged in a constant struggle to survive volcanic eruptions, altitude and climate. The open landscape and loose scoria make recolonisation and regeneration very difficult. Weave between sculpted pillars of lava and follow four-foot tall wooden poles and orange arrows daubed on rocks in places where the path becomes indistinct.

Still going south towards Mount Ruapehu, the track now drops into a valley to cross an upper branch of the Waihohonu Stream, continues through a forested valley, winds between beech trees in stark contrast to the surrounding lunar landscape, then climbs 80m to top a small knoll. Here it breaks out onto a clear ridge with good views before descending about 50m through forest to arrive at the new **Waihohonu Hut and Campsite** set just above a river. There's a small shingle shoreline just below the hut and several spots that make good bathing pools although the water tends to be icy cold. Over a further rise about 40 minutes south from Waihohonu Hut is the **Rangipo Desert** proper, with its ash gullies and high pumice ridges. High winds and frequent dust storms plague these badlands and the vegetation becomes increasingly sparse and hardy.

From the 28-bunk Waihohonu Hut there are a couple of short **side trips**. A 30-minute return trip takes you to the historic **Old Waihohonu Hut** (see Map 4, p147). You will actually be visiting this on the next stage, but if you decide to visit now cross the wooden bridge over the river and head west towards Whakapapa village for a short distance before encountering a signposted junction which leads to the site of the old hut. Built in 1903 this hut, the oldest recreational mountain hut in New Zealand and the first in Tongariro National Park, was used as a stopover for stagecoaches travelling to Tokaanu, a thermal area on the shores of Lake Taupo, as part of the 'Grand Tour'. The hut is no longer used for accommodation but is preserved as a historical building in a bid to show trampers what conditions used to be like on the track. The walls are a double layer of corrugated iron supported by cut totara, sandwiching a layer of pumice for insulation.

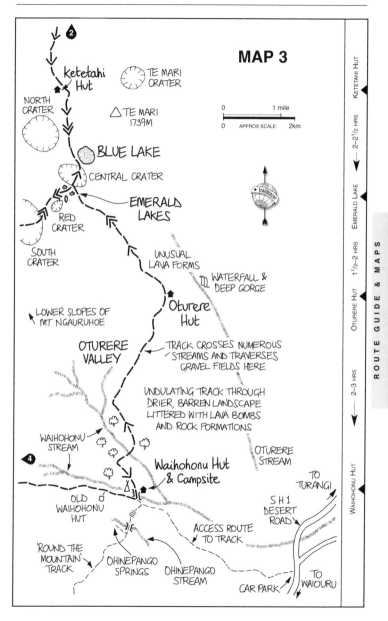

**MAP 3**

Ketetahi Hut

TE MARI CRATER

NORTH CRATER

△ TE MARI 1739M

0 _____ 1 mile
0 ___ APPROX SCALE ___ 2km

BLUE LAKE

CENTRAL CRATER

EMERALD LAKES

RED CRATER

SOUTH CRATER

UNUSUAL LAVA FORMS

WATERFALL & DEEP GORGE

LOWER SLOPES OF MT NGAURUHOE

Oturere Hut

OTURERE VALLEY

TRACK CROSSES NUMEROUS STREAMS AND TRAVERSES GRAVEL FIELDS HERE

UNDULATING TRACK THROUGH DRIER, BARREN LANDSCAPE LITTERED WITH LAVA BOMBS AND ROCK FORMATIONS

OTURERE STREAM

WAIHOHONU STREAM

Waihohonu Hut & Campsite

OLD WAIHOHONU HUT

ACCESS ROUTE TO TRACK

SH1 DESERT ROAD

TO TURANGI

'ROUND THE MOUNTAIN' TRACK

OHINEPANGO SPRINGS

OHINEPANGO STREAM

CAR PARK

TO WAIOURU

KETETAHI HUT

2–2½ HRS

EMERALD LAKE

1½–2 HRS

OTURERE HUT

2–3 HRS

WAIHOHONU HUT

ROUTE GUIDE & MAPS

An alternative side trip is the 50-minute return walk to **Ohinepango Springs**. On the far side of the wooden bridge head south, joining the 'Round the Mountain' track. Cross a section of heath-like tundra and several river beds before descending a set of wooden steps to stand on the bottom of a dry stream. Follow the gently undulating path along the stream bed until you reach a wooden bridge across the Ohinepango Stream. Here a signpost indicates where to find the cold, crystal-clear springs as they bubble up from beneath an old lava flow and discharge into the Ohinepango Stream.

## Waihohonu Hut to Whakapapa village          14km/5-6 hours; Map 4

This attractive final section is a reasonably gentle affair that allows you to once again marvel at the incredible forces that have created the tortured landscape through which you are tramping.

From the hut the track descends to the Waihohonu Stream, which it crosses on a wooden bridge, before arriving at a junction. The track left heads east to the Desert Rd, whilst straight ahead is the 'Round the Mountain' track which skirts the eastern slopes of Mount Ruapehu.

You, however, should turn right and head west along the broad, eroded Waihohonu track, passing the **Old Waihohonu Hut** (see p144) after 1km. The track undulates gently as it crosses several streams that have worn away the tussocks and soil. The views are amazing as long as the weather is clear since you pass beneath Mount Ngauruhoe's cone to the north and Mount Ruapehu's snow-capped peak to the south.

The track climbs gently to the **Tama Saddle** between these two volcanoes where it branches, a side path heading north-east for ten minutes to the viewpoint overlooking the **Lower Tama Lake**. Continuing on the same path takes you on a 70-minute return trip along a steep, exposed ridge to the **Upper Tama Lake** (1314m/4310ft), which has impressive views of Mount Ngauruhoe beyond. Both lakes are infilled explosion craters.

Beyond the junction, the main track continues west, traversing six streams before reaching Wairere Stream where it meets the Taranaki Falls loop. The right-hand track here passes the falls where the Wairere Stream plunges 20m down an old lava flow into a boulder-ringed pool that makes a perfect final plunge pool; to view the falls drop down the steep flight of steps and look back up at the cascade. The track then continues beside the stream through mountain beech forest. At a junction take the left hand fork for Whakapapa Village: the right hand fork here crosses the stream and returns to Mangatepo Hut.

Alternatively, the left-hand track from the Taranaki Falls junction descends gently but steadily through tussock and scrubland. Either route takes 45-60 minutes to work its way back to Whakapapa village.

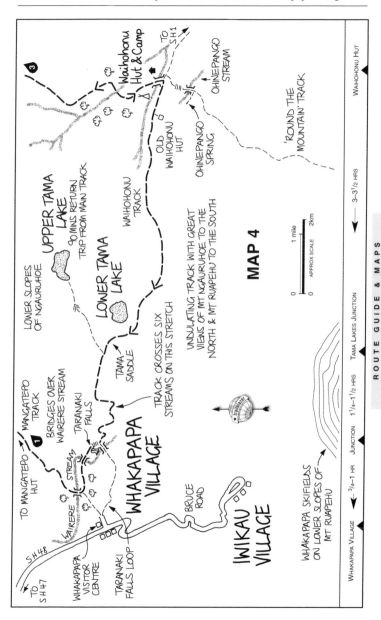

MAP 4

# Whanganui River Journey

*'Ko au te awa, ko te awa ko au' – I am the river, the river is me*  Maori proverb

## INTRODUCTION

Although most definitely not a tramp, the Whanganui River Journey is part of New Zealand's Great Walks network. This 145km 'Great Walk on water' begins in Taumarunui and finishes in Pipiriki, in the south-west of North Island. The whole trip usually takes five days to complete although it is possible to organise a shorter three-day itinerary.

| Whanganui River Journey |
| :---: |
| **Distance**  145km |
| **Time**  3-5 days |
| **Difficulty**  moderate/easy |

The timeless Whanganui River has its source high on Mt Tongariro in the centre of North Island. Beginning as an alpine stream it gathers waters from Mt Ngauruhoe and Mt Ruapehu, descending through the Central Volcanic Plateau towards Taumarunui. From here it sweeps south-west towards the town of Wanganui and the Tasman Sea. Along its course it collects water from 7382 sq km of watershed, becoming a mighty waterway. Although not the longest river in New Zealand, it is by far the longest continually navigable one in the country. Maori canoes, Victorian paddlewheelers, steamers and more recently kayaks and jet boats have plied these waters. Along its banks flourished some of New Zealand's earliest settlements, both Maori and European. The result is a fascinating and exciting history. Despite changes to the river and the people who lived here, the Whanganui remains a waterway of great beauty and mystery. The 145km section that comprises the River Journey takes in remote stretches of outstanding scenery, important Maori sites and areas of colonial history.

### The creation of the Whanganui River

Four mighty mountains once stood at the centre of Te Ika a Maui, North Island; Tongariro, Ruapehu, Ngauruhoe and Taranaki. Each of them loved a beautiful bush-clad mountain, Pihanga, who stood close by. Pihanga chose the venerable Tongariro from amongst her suitors and they were married.

For hundreds of years the mountains lived in harmony until Tongariro caught Taranaki making improper advances to Pihanga. A great fight between the two ensued that shook the earth to its core. Fire erupted from the mountains and dust and ash clouds darkened the skies as they battled. Eventually, Tongariro triumphed and Taranaki was forced to flee. Wild with grief and anger, tearing himself from his roots. Wild with grief and anger he rushed recklessly towards the setting sun, gouging a deep furrow in the earth as he went. Upon reaching the coast he settled and still sits in grand isolation there today.

From the side of Tongariro a spring of clear water issued forth to fill and heal the wound Taranaki had made in the earth. The river it formed became the Whanganui.

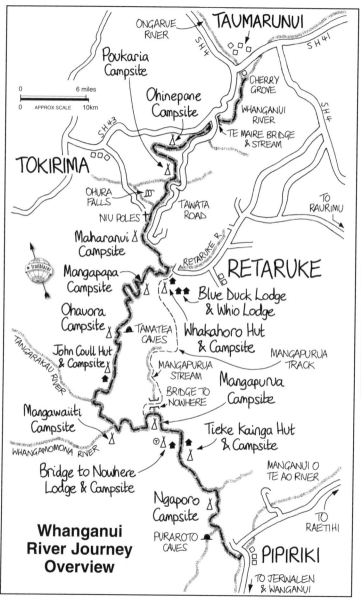

Whanganui
River Journey
Overview

Although the river is justly famous for its rapids – there are 239 named rapids in the stretch from Taumarunui to Wanganui – they are not regarded as difficult. Taumarunui is only 195m above sea level and the resulting gentle gradient of the river ensures that the rapids rarely exceed a 1m drop, allowing canoeists of all abilities the chance to travel through this scenic wilderness.

This is considered to be one of the finest multi-day canoe trips in the world, so trade in Shank's pony for a canoe and paddle and exchange your pack for a set of water-tight barrels in order to enjoy some of North Island's most eye-catching and inaccessible countryside.

## HISTORY

The earliest occupation of the Whanganui River dates from 1350 when the people of the Te Atihau Nui a Papa Rangi settled into the valley. The Maori quickly realised the value of the sheltered valley and the gentle gradient of the river encouraged its use as a major access route from the coast into the interior of North Island. These early inhabitants cultivated the protected terraces and built complex eel weirs along river channels precisely where currents converged to trap eel and lamprey as they migrated upstream. The river was considered a highly spiritual place (see box p148). Every significant bend had a *kaitiaki*, guardian, governing the *mauri*, life-force, of that area. All the rapids were named.

As more people settled in the area, so the river became linked by a series of *hapu*, sub-tribes, which came to be known as 'the plaited braids of Hinengakau'. The *mana*, prestige, of each settlement was dependent on the way in which the living areas around it were maintained. Standards of sustenance, defence and hospitality also reflected on the standing of the tribe.

ROUTE GUIDE & MAPS

### The legend of Tama-tuna

The legendary chief Tama-tuna lived on the banks of the Whanganui. He had aspirations to build the fastest canoe on the river. A huge totara tree grew just above his kainga at a place called Kohutu, upstream from Pipiriki. It was from this tree that he sought to hollow his canoe. He began to cut it down with a stone axe, but the tree toppled over the bank into the river, where it lay submerged in a deep hole from which it was impossible to drag it. Unwilling to give up such valuable timber, Tama-tuna resolved to hollow out the tree whilst it lay underwater. He spent several days at the *tuahu*, sacred altar, reciting his *karakaria*, prayers, to give himself power over the river waters.

One morning, unnoticed by his friends, he dived down to the log and began to work. His tribe didn't know what had become of him until they spied a continuous stream of wood chips rising to the surface above the totara trunk. They watched and waited for their chief. At dusk he re-emerged from the water, having been alerted that the sun was setting by the eels that emerged from their holes to wind around his legs.

After this he dived down daily to work on the log until the eels, his great friends, foretold the end of the day. After several months the canoe was finished and it rose to the surface. It proved to be sleek and beautiful and as expected was the fastest canoe to travel the river. With great pomp and ceremony it was christened *Tahuri-to-aro-rangi* and Tama-tuna's fame and mana grew and spread.

European missionaries arrived in the 1840s and began to have a major impact on the region. Maori occupation patterns began to evolve too. Previously war, peace, destruction and regeneration had been the recurring themes of Maori life. With the arrival of Europeans, villages moved from fortified pa sites to unfortified kainga settlements where adjacent land was more suitable for farming.

During the 1860s the steamer *Moutoa* reached Pipiriki from Wanganui. This led to increased interest in the scenic attractions of the area. The Hatrick and Co Riverboat Service began operating regular trips, initiating a remarkable era on the river. By 1891 a regular ferry service was operating alongside the Maori canoes, carrying people, mail and goods to the European settlements north of Wanganui. As a direct consequence, a burgeoning tourist trail developed between Wanganui and Mt Ruapehu.

At the same time, concerns were voiced regarding the clearance of land on the river banks. The Whanganui River Trust was established in 1891 and gradually more and more tracts of land were set aside for scenic purposes. This forethought has resulted in the preservation of one of the largest areas of unmodified lowland forest in North Island. At its peak the riverboat tourist service had 12 boats and an international reputation. In the early 1900s the river became known as the 'Rhine of New Zealand'.

Following World War I, the government actively sought to relocate servicemen to the area, offering incentives to them to take holdings adjacent to the river. However, the land proved difficult to clear or farm. The isolated plots could not support these new landowners, who relied almost exclusively on the riverboats for contact with the outside world.

The main riverboat traffic faltered during the 1920s as roads improved and a rail link was established between the coast and the interior. This, coupled with poor productivity, decreasing product prices and regenerating forest, forced most farmers off their plots. The only legacies of this period of settlement are a handful of dilapidated ruins and the aptly named Bridge to Nowhere, which stands as a testament to these inhabitants' failure to tame nature. By 1942 the valleys around the river had been abandoned or closed to farming. Nonetheless, riverboats still plied their trade on the Whanganui until the late 1950s. In 1986, 74,231ha of scenic reserves, Crown land and state forest were gazetted New Zealand's eleventh national park. Since then, Maori have returned to lay claim to the guardianship of the land and, having fought for recognition and inclusion in a co-management scheme with the DOC, the two have agreed to jointly ensure the continued preservation of the land.

## GEOLOGY

Whanganui National Park is set in a comparatively youthful landscape. This area was a seafloor basin in the mid-Tertiary period, which over the intervening 25 million years was gradually infilled with enormous amounts of sediment and occasional layers of gravel and shells. Several million years ago the area was uplifted as the sea retreated to the south-west. The layers of seafloor sediment, now compacted into sandstone and mudstone, *papa*, gently tilted south and became exposed. The softness of the mudstone ensured that a random pattern of gullies and streams developed. The result is the heavily dissected landscape characterised by an intricate pattern of steep-sided ridges and valleys. The Whanganui River easily cut through the soft papa, creating a series of lazy bends that coil across the landscape. In some places these meanders are so accentuated that the river has virtually doubled back on itself. Further erosion will in time result in the river cutting through the narrowing necks of these loops to shorten its course and create stranded ox-bow lakes. The sharp ridges, vertical bluffs and deep gorges are ideal conditions for spectacular waterfalls, which frequently spring from the looming walls and plunge into the river.

Erosion is still very much a force at work today as shown by the muddy, sediment-laden waters of the Whanganui and the sections of forest that are undercut, sheer off and tumble into the river leaving exposed papa cliffs.

## FLORA AND FAUNA

### Flora

The Whanganui River flows through the largest remaining area of untouched lowland forest in North Island. Present vegetation patterns have been brought about by a combination of climate, altitude, soil and rock type and gradient. Fertile lowland flats coated in ash from nearby volcanoes support a wide range of plants. Substantial areas are clothed in broadleaf podocarp forest. These are dominated by kamahi and tawa, with scattered groves of rimu, miro and northern rata. Other species to be found include pukatea, rawarewa, five-finger, rangiora, coprosma, cabbage tree and tree ferns. Stands of black beech can be seen on ridge crests. The sheer walls that rise from the river are blanketed in ferns. Communities of sedge and herbaceous plants cling to these cliffs as do mosses, liverworts, lichens and fungi, to form stunning vertical gardens.

### Fauna

The extensive forests provide a habitat for a variety of different **bird** species. Those most frequently seen include kereru, fantail, tui, North Island robin, warbler and tomtit. Swallows and kingfishers can often be seen swooping above the river water, catching insects on the wing, whilst falcons hover overhead on warm thermals. Kaka and yellow-crowned parakeet are also present but are much rarer and in decline. Brown kiwi and morepork inhabit the park but you are more likely to simply hear them calling at night rather than see them.

The river is rich in **aquatic life**. Eels, lamprey, several species of native fish including the endangered kokopu, freshwater crayfish and black flounder are all plentiful. However, it is worth bearing in mind that eel numbers have decreased to such an extent that where the early Maori used to set 380 eel traps on the river, up until recently the current *iwi* (tribe) maintained only four.

There are several introduced **mammals** in the park. Wild goats and deer can be seen on the gentler cliff sides. The hunting of pigs, goats and deer is encouraged and permits can be obtained from the DOC at Taumarunui, Pipiriki and Wanganui. Feral cats, stoats and possums are also present.

The controversial use of 10:80 poison to kill possums still continues. The counter-argument states that the 10:80 is retained in the fatty tissue of the dead animal, which if eaten means that the poison enters other animals or birds and passes up the food chain. Maori are especially concerned that this is not the best way to deal with the possum problem but until an alternative method is sanctioned the practice persists.

## PLANNING YOUR RIVER TRAMP

### When to go
The region is generally temperate although the weather is still unpredictable and can change quickly. It is affected by varying degrees of rainfall. In the southern section of the river this amounts to 900-1250mm of rain per year, whilst in the northern section this increases to 1200-2000mm per year. Don't attempt to canoe the river when the water levels are rising or it is in flood. Although it may not actually be raining on the river, the catchment area is so vast that run-off from the surrounding mountains can cause the river volume to increase dramatically in a very short space of time. In particular, after heavy storms the river has been known to rise 20m overnight.

The temperature remains relatively stable, with summer being pleasantly warm and winter fractionally cooler. The summer season for canoeing the river is October to the end of April. The most popular times are Christmas and the school summer holidays in January. The ideal time to undertake the journey is probably late in the summer season, in either **February or March**. During winter the river is mostly deserted as the cooler weather, shorter days and stronger currents are less conducive for paddling in.

### Itinerary options
There are several options available to canoeists depending on how much time you have available. The ultimate is the **five-day** paddle from Cherry Grove to Pipiriki that takes in all the rapids and historical sites along the river. The upper two days offer a contrasting experience to the lower three and are well worth doing if you can make the time. If time is short, the **three-day** trip from Whakahoro to Pipiriki on the lower section of the river makes for a popular alternative. The first night is spent in John Coull Hut and you have the option of camping or staying at Tieke Kainga or the Bridge to Nowhere Lodge on the second evening. This way you are able to visit the Bridge to Nowhere and tackle the three biggest rapids on the river. The **two-day** stretch from Cherry Grove to Whakahoro includes a number of rapids but also the Ohura Falls and the historic Niu Poles. If you've just got **one day** spare, the stretch from Cherry Grove to Ohinepane still features 42 named rapids and makes for an exhilarating day-trip.

Alternatively, if you are looking to tramp a section of this wilderness and explore some of its hidden historical corners, you should consider tackling the three-day **Mangapurua Track** that links Whakahoro to the Mangapurua landing on the Whanganui River. The track can be walked in either direction and then combined with a jet boat ride to complete the circuit. Most people opt to take a jet boat to Mangapurua and then tramp to Whakahoro, where there is road access. For details of the walk see pp169-71.

## Sources of information

There are several **DOC offices** in the vicinity of the Whanganui River. The largest is in Wanganui (☎ 06-349 2100, 🖳 wanganuiconservancy@doc.govt.nz, Private Bag 3016), on the corner of Ingestre and St Hill streets. There are also offices at both the start of the River Journey in Taumarunui (☎ 07-895 8201, PO Box 50), at Cherry Grove, and at the end, in Pipiriki (☎ 06-385 5022), on Rd 6, although both of these smaller offices are occasionally unmanned.

Outfitters and organisations renting canoes and equipment can also sell you the requisite hut passes. They also stock leaflets and pamphlets relating to the river and the section that includes the River Journey.

**Information centres** in the surrounding area are good sources of material and can recommend an outfitter or group who can equip you for the journey. Wanganui i-SITE Visitor Information Centre (☎ 06-349 0508, 🖳 www.wanga nui.com) at 101 Guyton St is quite useful. Taumarunui i-SITE Visitor Information Centre (☎ 07-895 7494, 🖳 www.visitruapehu.com, taumaranui.vic @xtra.co.nz), in the railway station on Hakiaha St, open 9am-4.30pm during the week and 10am-4pm at the weekend, is also a handy place from which to glean information. There are also i-SITE offices at 38 Seddon St, Raetihi (☎ 06-385 4805) and 54 Clyde St, Ohakune (☎ 06-385 8427, 🖳 www.visitruapehu.com, PO Box 36) that can provide you with inspiration and practical material.

## Outfitters and agencies

Canoes and kayaks can be hired from several outfitters who operate close to the river. These organisations can also provide other gear, including the use of waterproof storage barrels and life-jackets; drop you off at the river and collect you once your trip is completed; look after your vehicle; and provide you with insurance against any breakages. Some of them may also run guided trips, though the river is not particularly difficult to navigate and as long as you are fairly independent and confident of being able to manage in the wilderness there is no real need for a guide. They can, however, bring the river to life for you by recounting its history and pointing out its interesting features.

● **Blazing Paddles** (☎ 07-895 5261 or 0800-252 946, 📄 07-895 5263, 🖳 www .blazingpaddles.co.nz, 1033, SH4, Taumarunui)  A well-established organisa-tion with headquarters some 10km south of Taumarunui that provides an excel-lent service. Independent trips cost NZ$220 for three days and NZ$250 for the full five days. They also provide detailed maps and good quality background material. You can stay in bunkrooms on site before starting your trip for NZ$25 per person.

● **Bridge to Nowhere Tours** (☎ 0800-480 308, 🖳 www.bridgetonowhere tours.co.nz)  Operating from the Bridge to Nowhere Lodge (see p158) and with an office in Wanganui, this classy outfitter offers canoes for hire and also leads guided trips on the river. They also offer a combination half- or full-day outing whereby you take a jet boat upstream and paddle back down.

● **Canoe Safaris** (☎ 06-385 9237 or 0800-272 335, 🖳 www.canoesafaris.co.nz, 5 Miro St, Ohakune) Runs upmarket all-inclusive guided trips (three days NZ$595, five days NZ$840) down the river. They can also organise self-guided trips for NZ$165/190 for three/five days.

● **Taumarunui Canoe Hire** (☎ 0800-226 6348 or 07-896 6507, 🖳 www.taumarunuicanoehire.co.nz) Located 12km north of Taumarunui, this outfit offers canoes for hire (NZ$245/260 for three/five days).

● **Wade's Landing Outdoors** (☎ 07-895 5995, 🖳 www.whanganui.co.nz, Rd 2, Owhango) Adjacent to Whakahoro, at the start of the third day of the River Journey, this company organises self-guided canoe trips and will transport you to the launch site at Taumarunui should you wish to undertake the five-day trip. Prices start at NZ$150 for three days and rise to NZ$180 for five. Guided trips with one guide per five boats are also available on request. They have a second base in Raurimu, close to National Park Village.

● **Whanganui Tours** (☎ 06-347 7534, 🖳 www.whanganuitours.co.nz, 10 Porritt St, Wanganui) Small outfit hiring out canoes by the day. Three-day trips start at NZ$210 and five days cost NZ$350. A guide to accompany you will cost NZ$120 per day.

● **Yeti Tours** (☎ 06-385 8197 or 0800-322 388, 🖳 www.canoe.co.nz, PO Box 140, Ohakune) Large professional operator with good equipment and lots of knowledge leading two- to six-day guided trips down the river; the three-day trip begins at NZ$575 and the six-day trip costs NZ$850. There are supplements for hiring camping equipment or tents too. Canoes can be hired for independent outings; a three-day trip costs NZ$165, the five-day trip NZ$215.

● For a different introduction to the Whanganui, consider joining an expedition led by the Maori who live along the river. **Waka Tours** (☎/🖳 06-385 4811, 🖳 www.wakatours.com, 19 George St, Raetihi) provide a Maori cultural experience for those who are keen to connect with the spiritual side of the river as well as feel the essence of the *mauri*, life-force, which the river possesses for the traditional inhabitants of the Whanganui. Travelling in a six-man canoe, you are taken through an 87km section of the river known as the 'middle reaches', starting in Whakahoro. The three-day trip costs NZ$650. **Whanganui River Guides** (☎ 07-896 6727, 🖳 www.whanganuiriverguides.co.nz, 32 Miriama St, Taumarunui) employs local Maori as guides on its multi-day guided excursions. Trips are quite expensive, costing NZ$540 for three days and NZ$900 for five days. Self-guided trips cost NZ$255/425 for three/five days. **Wairua Hikoi Tours** (☎ 06-345 3485 or 06-342 8190, 🖳 tourism@wanganui.govt.nz), Jerusalem, on Whanganui River Rd, is another Maori operator emphasising the cultural aspects of the Whanganui River Journey.

Other than canoeing the river, you can take a **jet boat** trip with most operators offering four- to six-hour trips to the Bridge to Nowhere. Bridge to Nowhere Tours (lodge ☎ 025-480 308, home ☎ 06-348 7122, 🖳 www.bridgetonowheretours.co.nz), which operates from the Bridge to Nowhere Lodge on the Whanganui River, and Whanganui River Adventures (☎ 0800-862 743, 🖳 www.whanganuiriveradventures.co.nz) both run jet boat trips upstream from

ROUTE GUIDE & MAPS

Pipiriki. Whanganui Jet (☎ 0800-538 8687, 💻 www.whanganuijet.co.nz) and Whanganui Scenic Experience (☎ 0800-945 335, 💻 www.whanganuiscenicjet .com) also organise jet-boat excursions, this time from Wanganui, while Wade's Landing Outdoors (see p155) operate out of Whakahoro.

## Getting to the trailhead

If you are hiring equipment or canoes, your hire operator ought to collect you from a pre-arranged pick-up point and return you to an agreed destination for a fee. Quite often operators include the cost of transport with the hire fee of canoes on multi-day trips. This ensures that you don't need to stay adjacent to the start of the River Journey, but can travel to it from National Park Village (see pp135-7) or other surrounding towns.

Owing to its inaccessible nature it requires a modicum of effort to reach the river – especially if using public transport. In theory you should be able to take canoes on public transport, though it will be awkward, inconvenient and guaranteed to irritate the driver. If you are considering the five-day trip down the river you'll begin in Taumarunui and finish in Pipiriki. There are other entry and exit points along the river at Ohinepane and Whakahoro. Between Whakahoro and Pipiriki there is no road access whatsoever, so once past Whakahoro you must be prepared to push right on to Pipiriki.

The traditional launch site at Taumarunui, Cherry Grove, is situated just off SH4, which links Auckland, Hamilton and Wanganui. There are several public transport options that connect Taumarunui: both buses and taxis operate regular services. Around 21km to the south from here there is a road that connects SH4 to Ohinepane Campsite on the banks of the Whanganui River. The last road access point at Whakahoro is connected to SH4 by roads from Owhango and Raurimu. This long, winding road is largely unsealed and twists through some fabulous, remote scenery. At the far end of the River Journey, Pipiriki can be accessed by road from Raetihi, 27km to the east, or via the scenic Whanganui River Rd that branches off SH4 15km north of Wanganui and follows the river for 64km to Pipiriki. There's a mail-run service operating from Wanganui to Pipiriki (☎ 06-344 2554) from Monday to Friday that will shuttle you between the two towns. This is an organised tour, as well as an actual mail run, which stops at historic sites including the Kawana Flour Mill, Jerusalem Church and the marae at Koriniti.

## Local services

At the start of the River Journey, at the confluence of the Whanganui and Ongarue rivers, stands **Taumarunui**. This small town was an important settlement in pre-European times and acted as the meeting place for three important Maori tribes, the Whanganui, Tuwharetoa and Maniapoto. European influence in the area remained minimal until the development of communication links in the early 1900s saw the town become an important staging point on the trip from Wanganui to Auckland. Nowadays it feels a little run-down and there is little to delay the visitor other than the river. There are a selection of cafés and takeaways as well as a small food store. Accommodation options include the

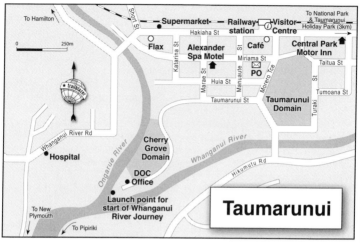

Taumarunui

decent **Taumarunui Holiday Park** (☎ 07-895 9345, 🖥 www.taumarunuiholi daypark.co.nz; tent pitch NZ$13 per person, cabin sgl/dbl NZ$40-45, cottage NZ$65) on the banks of the Whanganui on SH4, which offers powered and unpowered sites and cabins. Alternatively try **Central Park Motor Inn** (☎ 07-895 7132, 🖥 www.central-park.co.nz; units NZ$65-120) on the corner of Maata and Hakiaha St, which has a variety of units and suites available as well as its own bar and restaurant, spa, sauna and pool, or **Alexander Spa Motel** (☎ 07-895 8501, 🖥 www.alexandermotel.co.nz; units sgl/dbl NZ$70/85) at 6 Marae St, which has clean comfortable units and a spa pool.

For **food**, there are several places where you can dine for around NZ$15-25; the best is **Flax** at 1 Hakiaha St, which boasts the most diverse menu and does a decent brunch for NZ$10-15. Evening meals cost NZ$25-30.

At the southern end of the River Journey is **Pipiriki**. Whilst this is the most important community on the River Rd and a major gateway to the national park, it is little more than a collection of houses. There's also a free campsite with toilets and water supply.

### Huts and campsites

There's a combination of huts and campsites along the Whanganui River. In the course of your journey you will probably use both so make sure you take a tent. Hire operators can often arrange for you to borrow or **hire a tent**. You may use the huts at Whakahoro, John Coull or Tieke Kainga or camp at Ohinepane, Poukaria, Maharanui, Whakahoro, Mangapapa, Ohauora, John Coull, Mangawaiiti, Mangapurua, Tieke Kainga or Ngaporo. Regardless of your choice, from October to April you must buy a **hut and campsite pass** before beginning your journey, even though you do not need to book hut or campsite spaces in advance. There are three grades of pass available depending on how long you plan to be on the river and where you intend to stay. The 'Full Journey' pass is valid for five days on the river and costs NZ$45. There is a slightly cheaper version, the 'Journey excluding Tieke Kainga' pass aimed at those staying in the Bridge to Nowhere Lodge (see below), that costs NZ$35. Canoeists spending two days and one night on the river between Taumarunui and Whakahoro can buy a 'Taumarunui to Whakahoro only' pass for NZ$10. All of the passes can be bought from DOC offices, information centres and tour operators. If bought on the river there is a NZ$15 surcharge payable on the spot. Children under the age of 17 do not need a pass.

**Huts** are provided with bunks, mattresses, heating stoves, toilets and cooking facilities. Bottled gas is supplied at John Coull and Tieke Kainga, whilst Whakahoro has a wood stove and electric cooking elements, and wardens are stationed at John Coull Hut. At the **campsites** there are shelters, toilets and a water supply.

During the rest of the year the fee for using the facilities along the river is NZ$15.

There is one **lodge** along the river: *Bridge to Nowhere Lodge* (☎ 0800-480 308, 💻 www.bridgetonowheretours.co.nz; see p154 for jet boat tour and canoe trip details) situated opposite Tieke Kainga, between John Coull Hut and Pipiriki. It has various standards of accommodation from campsites to comfortable double/twin rooms and bunkrooms. The rooms have magnificent forest and river views and you can often hear kiwi calling at night and sometimes see fallow deer in the grounds. You can self-cater (NZ$45 per person) or opt for a fullboard deal (NZ$125 per person). There's also a licensed bar and restaurant and a 24-hour emergency phone. These facilities are often used by guided groups so if you intend to stay here you must book in advance to be sure of securing one of the handful of rooms.

Set a little further back from the river, above Whakahoro are two other up-market accommodation options that make a change from camping on the river banks. Blue Duck Lodge and Whio Lodge (☎ 07-895 6276, 💻 www.blueduck lodge.co.nz) offer a high standard of accommodation in secluded surroundings. They are named after the endangered Blue Duck, or Whio, that can be seen on the Retaruke River, and the owner, who is committed to conservation and the protection of these native birds, runs a predator-trapping and habitat-enhancing programme here. *Blue Duck Lodge* (from NZ$120 for two people, plus NZ$30 per additional adult, up to a maximum of eight people for NZ$300 per night) has space for up to eight people to stay on a self-catering basis, with a fully equipped kitchen, large dining room, lounge and panoramic windows looking out over the river. *Whio Lodge* (dorm NZ$30, dbl, NZ$70) is a converted shearer's quarters that has now been renovated and turned into dormitory-style rooms and a separate double room. There is also an open-plan kitchen, dining and lounge area.

Tieke Kainga is an unusual DOC hut. Originally one of many old fortified pa sites on the river, it has been revived as a marae and is occasionally occupied by Maori. You are welcome to stay on the marae but must abide by the code of behaviour; see p169 for details.

## Maps

Due to its length, this is a difficult Great Walk to cover simply on a single map of any reasonable detail. Topomaps' *Taumarunui* (S18), *Raurimu* (S19), *Whangamomona* (R19), *Matemateaonga* (R20) and *Ngamatapouri* (R21) cover the entire length of the River Journey between them.

## Distances and times

The Whanganui River Journey is a relatively easy canoe trip. Although the distances involved each day are reasonably long, they are by no means difficult or technically hard. The river flows steadily, helping your progress. The average speed of the river is around 5km/h. Gentle paddling will ensure that you travel at around 6km/h whilst more vigorous strokes are likely to take your speed up to around 8km/h. You can undertake day trips at the start of the river or canoe from Cherry Grove to Whakahoro. Once past Whakahoro there is no exit from the river and you will not be able to turn back. The usual journey time from Whakahoro to Pipiriki is three days.

The rapids that you encounter are generally small and easily negotiated though on some of the larger ones you do run the risk of being overturned or swamped. Depending on how often this happens will affect how quickly you complete each section.

| | | |
|---|---|---|
| Cherry Grove to Poukaria | 36km | 5-6 hours |
| Poukaria to Whakahoro | 21km | 4-5 hours |
| Whakahoro to John Coull | 37.5km | 5-6 hours |
| John Coull to Tieke Kainga | 29km | 5-6 hours |
| Tieke Kainga to Pipiriki | 21.5km | 4-5 hours |

## River safety

There are several basic rules that you must abide by whilst on the river. You must **wear a life jacket** at all times for your own safety. Whilst you are on the river show consideration for other canoeists and make sure you are aware of other river users, including jet boats. Craft travelling upriver must give way to those travelling downstream. Canoeists must allow jet boats to overtake and move clear of them by slowing down or even stopping.

Should you be overtaken by a jet boat whilst paddling on the river, paddle to the right, unless this means that you paddle across the path of an oncoming jet boat, in which case you should stay to the left. As the jet boat passes, turn the canoe at right angles to the boat's wake in order to minimise the unsettling impact of the waves.

If you are passed by a jet boat travelling in the opposite direction, ease gently forward until the boat is past you. You should bear in mind that jet boats are much less manoeuvrable when they are travelling slowly and cannot be relied on to make sharp adjustments to avoid you. Once they have entered a stretch of rapids, jet boats can't slow down or stop.

When approaching a rapid, head for the centre of the 'V' that forms in the water. Aim through this and keep paddling smoothly. Watch out for choppy water or 'pillows' when approaching the rapids in order to select the best path through them. If you are not confident of the way through, paddle to the shore and take a moment to think through your approach before tackling the rapid. If you do come out of the canoe, let yourself float to the surface and then try to catch hold of your boat or its tow rope. The rapids are all quite brief and once you are in the calm water beyond them you can attempt to climb back into your canoe.

## JOURNEY DESCRIPTION

### Cherry Grove to Poukaria Campsite        36km/5-6 hours; Map 1

This first day is a thrilling introduction to the river. Departing from Taumarunui you pass through rolling hills and farmland typical of New Zealand. There are a great number of recognised rapids in quick succession along this stage, ensuring that you quickly learn to master your canoe. The water on this section is generally shallow so be careful when judging the main stream of the river.

Beginning from **Cherry Grove** you launch into **Ongarue River**. To avoid being swept into the snags on either side of the river here, launch facing upstream and paddle out into the centre of the river before turning round. A few strong strokes bring you to the confluence with the Whanganui. Turn right and join the broad **Whanganui** as it flows south-west. Immediately after the confluence of the two rivers is the first, small rapid.

The river flows through a pleasant area of rolling farmland with a series of small rapids jumbling past in quick succession. Although there is plenty of chop and foam none of these is particularly difficult to negotiate. The rapid that is most likely to cause problems is **Whakatarino**, as you approach Herlihy's Bluff. Here the river surges into a mudstone wall and creates a pressure wave. By keeping this wave on your right you ought to be able to avoid the churning water. Watch out for the shingle beach and small whirlpool to your left though. The river then meanders lazily in large sweeping bends, shadowed by the road hidden above it.

After about two hours the river passes under the **Te Maire Bridge**, a rickety-looking, single-track bridge teetering on spindly supports. This is one of only two bridges to cross the river between Taumarunui and Wanganui. Beyond the bridge the river eases between the Whanganui River road and the Paparoa road, past the Te Maire tributary stream. There are a number of kainga (Maori villages) in this area but you cannot stay at them.

An hour after the bridge the river approaches the signposted **Ohinepane Campsite**, just below a pair of rapids and easily spotted by the jet-boat ramp on the right-hand bank. There are 12 tent pitches here and a basic shelter for cooking under. Beyond Ohinepane the river banks become steeper and the valley more gorge-like. The river rounds a broad bend and doubles back on itself, leaving the road. Turning south it straightens until it abuts the Paparoa road and swings south-west again. Five kilometres further on, the river passes **Poukaria Campsite**. A wide shingle beach of perfectly smooth and river-rounded pebbles

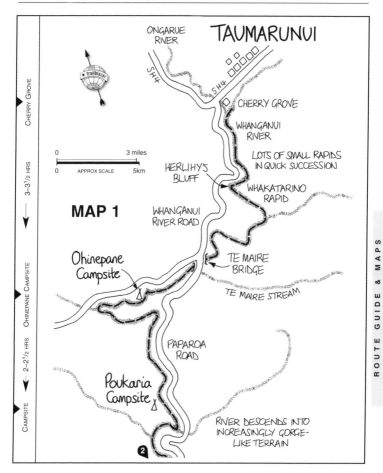

MAP 1

on your right backs onto a gentle slope, on top of which sits a shelter and camp-site. Make sure that you haul your canoe far enough up the beach and tie it firm-ly to something secure to prevent it being washed away should the river rise during the night.

## Poukaria Campsite to Whakahoro Hut          21km/4-5 hours; Map 2

This shorter day includes some superb scenery and important historical sites. It is worth making a reasonably early start so as to leave yourself sufficient time to explore the Ohura Falls and Niu Poles. There is also a relatively lengthy off-river journey to the DOC hut and campsite at Whakahoro.

Beyond Poukaria the Whanganui River continues to wind south-west. Hidden high above is the Tawata road. The early sections involve several small rapids interspersed with slower stretches of water. The major obstacle on this section of river is the **Paparoa Rapid**. As you approach the rapid the river is split by an untidy heap of boulders in the middle. Take the right-hand channel, even though it looks less like the correct option, since the left-hand channel takes the river over a boulder barrier that is impassable safely in a canoe.

The Whanganui is joined by several smaller tributaries. These can make interesting diversions and usually reward closer investigation with the discovery of a small waterfall or tranquil pool. The most significant river to join the Whanganui along this stretch is the **Ohura**, 11km downstream from Poukaria. Their confluence is marked by a wide **three-tiered waterfall** that drops about 3m over the last step into the Whanganui. Only this final step is visible from canoe level. At certain times of year hordes of elvers (young eels) can be seen inching up the margins beside the falls.

Also here is the important Maori settlement of Maraekowhai, the site of the Niu Poles. Just beyond the mouth of the Ohura there is a small landing point. This has become tricky to use as erosion has worn away the bank. Having moored your canoe securely here, scramble up the poorly defined track and past a picnic table to the top of the cliff. Standing here are the **Niu Poles**. These ceremonial crosses were built during the mid-1800s at a time when Maraekowhai was a stronghold for rebellious Maori looking to combat the further encroachment of Europeans onto their land. In 1862 a religion based upon a combination of Old Testament doctrine and traditional Maori beliefs was founded in Taranaki by Te Ua Haumene. Born out of a disaffection with the Crown and the recently imposed Christian religion, the followers of this new Pai marire religion, known as the Hau Hau, became synonymous with the movement to repel the Europeans. In 1864 the Hau Hau built a war pole, *rongo niu*, which has two crossed arms that point to the four points of the compass. A spirit was put into the pole by a *tohunga*, priest, and radiated out through the arms of the cross, summoning warriors from all over to gather and fight the Europeans. The Hau Hau used to fly flags from the poles and chant prayers and incantations.

The movement flourished between 1862 and 1865. Te Ua Haumene was captured in 1866 and without its leader the movement began to falter. Once the fighting along the Whanganui River had come to a halt, a peace pole, *rere kore*, was built to combat the influence of rongo niu and preserve harmony.

The poles are not the only interesting things about Maraekowhai. During the mid-1800s a flour mill was constructed here by missionaries. Designed to mill the wheat that was grown extensively by local Maori, it probably never actually functioned and has long since been torn down; no visible remains are evident today. Then in the early 1900s a 36-bed hotel ship, the *Haselbad*, was floated down from Taumarunui to Maraekowhai. It operated here until 1927 when it was towed to Retaruke River, where it was eventually destroyed by fire.

About 3km beyond the Ohura River junction the Whanganui takes a right-angled turn to the left and 1km after that it passes **Maharanui Campsite**,

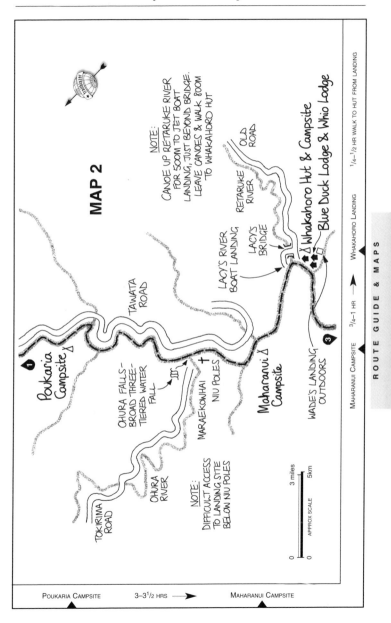

MAP 2

NOTE:
CANOE UP RETARUKE RIVER FOR 500m TO JET BOAT LANDING, JUST BEYOND BRIDGE. LEAVE CANOES & WALK 800m TO WHAKAHORO HUT

OLD ROAD

RETARUKE RIVER

LACY'S RIVER BOAT LANDING

LACY'S BRIDGE

TAWATA ROAD

Poukaria Campsite

OHURA FALLS– BROAD THREE-TIERED WATER FALL

MARAEKOWHAI NIU POLES

Maharanui Campsite

WADE'S LANDING OUTDOORS

TOKIRIMA ROAD

OHURA RIVER

NOTE:
DIFFICULT ACCESS TO LANDING SITE BELOW NIU POLES

Whakahoro Hut & Campsite
Blue Duck Lodge & Whio Lodge

APPROX SCALE

0   3 miles
0   5km

POUKARIA CAMPSITE   3–3½ HRS →   MAHARANUI CAMPSITE

MAHARANUI CAMPSITE   ¾–1 HR →   WHAKAHORO LANDING   ¼–½ HR WALK TO HUT FROM LANDING

ROUTE GUIDE & MAPS

indicated by a name board. A large grassy meadow above the river makes for a pleasant campsite.

Four kilometres after Maharanui, at the end of a gentle stretch of slow water, is the junction with the **Retaruke River**. Immediately before the confluence is the historic Lacy's River Boat landing, which is also the takeout point should the Retaruke River be in flood. Five-hundred metres along the Retaruke, through several small rapids and under a metal single-track bridge, Lacy's Bridge, is a jet-boat landing site. Leave the river at this point and securely fasten your canoe to the bank. (By the way, note the dent in the upstream side of the bridge. This was caused by a large tree that had been washed downstream in particularly heavy rains and which slammed violently into the flooded bridge. The fact that the bridge is usually a clear 15m above the water is a chilling indication of just how swollen and powerful the river can become in flood.) Above the jet boat ramp is a gravel track which you should follow as it climbs away from the river to an area of farmland. Some 400m from the landing point is **Whakahoro Hut and Campsite** set in a farmer's field overlooking the river. There are 12 beds in the hut and around 70 tent pitches available. Slightly further up the track, set on a small rise overlooking the DOC hut, are **Blue Duck Lodge** and **Whio Lodge** (see p158) as well as the office of the river outfitter Wade's Landing Outdoors.

### Whakahoro Hut to John Coull Hut                37.5km/5-6 hours; Map 3

Whakahoro is the last entry/exit point before Pipiriki, 88km further downstream. Beyond this point you will not be able to turn back or leave the river. The long section of river to John Coull Hut is stunningly attractive and slips past in a relaxed, easy fashion.

Paddling back down the Retaruke River, rejoin the Whanganui River. Gentle farmland quickly gives way to steep-sided cliffs that will remain with you for the next couple of days. As you progress these cliffs become steeper and taller, rising up to 60m from the river, and overgrown with ferns and other precariously perched plants forming beautiful vertical gardens.

Throughout the day you must cross several small rapids. When the river is low there may be exposed boulders or partially submerged tree trunks that need to be avoided or scraped over.

Almost immediately upon rejoining the Whanganui River you pass several old concrete slabs and iron stanchions that were used to berth the riverboats that plied their trade on the river. The river narrows as it plunges between the cliffs and, following a series of dramatic twists and turns, at the head of a pronounced meander is **Mangapapa Campsite**. Beyond is the striking, sculpted **Man O'War Bluff** that has been eroded to resemble an old battleship.

Sixteen kilometres beyond the campsite is an obvious, rounded hollow in the left bank. This is **Tamatea Cave**, the legendary home of a *taniwha*, a mythical water monster. The cave is just above a pair of rapids, and between admiring the cave and negotiating the rapids you are likely to miss the signpost for **Ohauora Campsite**, set between the rapids on the right-hand bank. Beyond the campsite is a further 10km of relatively flat water that flows through some highly scenic

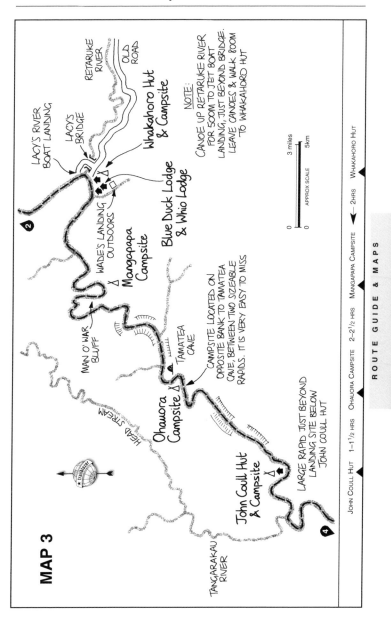

MAP 3

TANGARAKAU RIVER

RETARUKE RIVER

OLD ROAD

LACY'S RIVER BOAT LANDING

LACY'S BRIDGE

Whakahoro Hut & Campsite

**NOTE:**

CANOE UP RETARUKE RIVER FOR 500m TO JET BOAT LANDING, JUST BEYOND BRIDGE. LEAVE CANOES & WALK 100m TO WHAKAHORO HUT

0    3 miles
0    5km
APPROX SCALE

WADE'S LANDING OUTDOORS

Blue Duck Lodge & Whio Lodge

Mangapapa Campsite

MAN O' WAR BLUFF

Tamatea Cave

CAMPSITE LOCATED ON OPPOSITE BANK TO TAMATEA CAVE, BETWEEN TWO SIZEABLE RAPIDS. IT IS VERY EASY TO MISS

Ohauora Campsite

HEAD STREAM

John Coull Hut & Campsite

LARGE RAPID JUST BEYOND LANDING SITE BELOW JOHN COULL HUT

JOHN COULL HUT   1–1½ HRS   OHAUORA CAMPSITE   2–2½ HRS   MANGAPAPA CAMPSITE   2HRS   WHAKAHORO HUT

ROUTE GUIDE & MAPS

country. Waterfalls tumble down the sheer cliffs, streaking the mudstone and providing moisture for the host of plants clinging to the cliffs. Take time to examine the ghostly, skeletal tree trunks visible underwater as you slide past.

Rounding a large bend you come across the flotsam-littered shingle beach and sandy banks below **John Coull Hut**. There is a reasonably sized rapid just beyond the landing point so take care when beaching your canoe. This attractively situated 24-bunk hut and campsite is set on the edge of the forest. Glow-worms can be seen at night above the boardwalk joining the hut and camping area. During the summer season there are usually wardens based here who will happily discuss the river's history and answer any questions that you might have.

### John Coull Hut to Tieke Kainga Hut                29km/5-6 hours; Map 4
This is a historically rich stretch of the river, reflecting both the Maori and colonial past of the Whanganui. It is worth making an early start from John Coull Hut in order to be able to fully enjoy all the sights and complete the side trip to the Bridge to Nowhere.

As soon as you launch your canoe from the beach below John Coull Hut the river carries you into a large rapid. The area of land immediately beyond John Coull Hut is known as **Puketapu** and there is evidence of Maori occupation in this area. A series of trenches are the last remains of battles that took place here between Topine te Mamaku and members of the Ngati Tu during the mid-1800s. In the 1890s a Maori kainga was established here although it has now vanished beneath a veil of regenerating vegetation.

Two kilometres downstream from the hut the **Tangarakau River** joins the Whanganui. In 1901 this major tributary was cleared for steamer navigation for a distance of 18km. Ferries transported mail and supplies to the settlers of the Tangarakau and Whangamomona districts until a heavy flood in 1904 refilled the gorge with logs and debris causing the service to be abandoned. It is possible to canoe about 1km up the river to explore.

The Whanganui twists and turns in a southerly direction past the junction with the **Whanagamomona River** which, with its shallow waters and pronounced rapids, is navigable only for a couple of hundred metres. Two kilometres beyond here is the more impressive **Mangawaiiti Stream**, which joins the Whanganui on the right-hand side from a deep ravine that makes for an interesting and impressive detour. Just downstream of the ravine is a landing area of shingle, log and mud from which a track heads up the cliff to a small grassy flat. This is the attractive **Mangawaiiti Campsite**. If you choose to stop here overnight make sure you pull your canoe right up to the grassy flat because, in the case of heavy rain, your canoe will be washed away if left on the shingle beach.

The stretch of Whanganui beyond here has a history of failed European settlement. **Otumangu Landing** is a reminder of the returning WWI servicemen who were sent to develop and farm this valley. There is a small rock platform here with an iron stanchion embedded in it. A partially eroded track scales the cliff above the platform. Just beyond the landing the Otumangu Stream enters the Whanganui River via a narrow, steep-sided gorge.

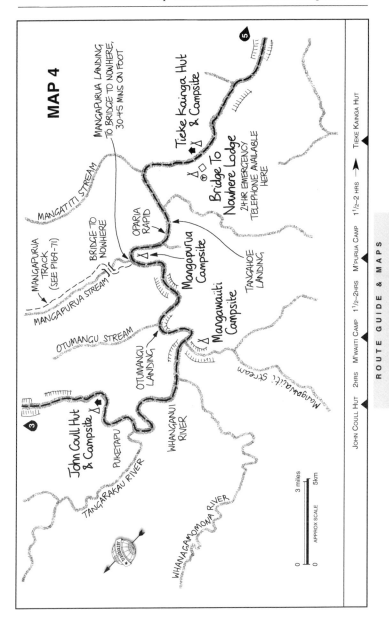

**MAP 4**

MANGAPURUA LANDING, TO BRIDGE TO NOWHERE, 30-45 MINS ON FOOT

MANGATITI STREAM

MANGAPURUA TRACK (SEE P164-71)

BRIDGE TO NOWHERE

MANGAPURUA STREAM

OTUMANGU STREAM

Tieke Kainga Hut & Campsite

Bridge To Nowhere Lodge
24HR EMERGENCY TELEPHONE AVAILABLE HERE

OPARIA RAPID

Mangapurua Campsite

TANGAHOE LANDING

Mangawaiiti Campsite

OTUMANGU LANDING

Mangaparareke Stream

WHANGANUI RIVER

PUKETAPU

John Coull Hut & Campsite

TANGARAKAU RIVER

WHANGAMOMONA RIVER

APPROX SCALE

0 — 3 miles

0 — 5km

**ROUTE GUIDE & MAPS**

JOHN COULL HUT — 2HRS — M'WAIITI CAMP — 1½-2HRS — M'PURUA CAMP — 1½-2 HRS — TIEKE KAINGA HUT

Six kilometres further downstream a line of palm trees on the left-hand bank indicates the approach of the **Mangapurua Landing** and, on the right-hand bank, the **campsite** of the same name. An iron mooring post juts out of the steep left-hand bank here. A track leads upstream then climbs steeply up the cliff. This is the start of the track to the **Bridge to Nowhere** and also the beginning of the Mangapurua Track (see pp169-71) that tramps north to Whakahoro. The gentle 1-1¹/₂ hour return trip to the Bridge to Nowhere is well worth the time and effort. The track follows the awesome chasm of the Mangapurua Stream inland. Huge tree ferns overhang the narrow gorge and thick native forest reaches to the interior. The track is well-graded although frequently narrow. Just before the bridge is a cliff known as Morgan's Bluff that has occasionally been the scene of landslips, the latest of which closed the track temporarily in late 2008 and damaged the bridge. Before setting off, check with your outfitter that the trail is open and in a good state of repair.

The Mangapurua Stream and valley acted as a barrier, the high, steep-sided cliffs a virtually impassable obstacle to the land beyond. Towards the end of the war this valley was opened for settlement by returning soldiers on rehabilitation farms. There were some 35 holdings in the valley and, initially at least, the pioneer settlers were able to clear the land of its virgin native forest and transform it into farmland. In the late 1920s and early 1930s Mangapurua even boasted a school. Settlers relied exclusively on river steamers for contact with the outside world, while a swing bridge provided the only crossing point on the Mangapurua Stream. A more substantial concrete bridge was built in 1935 and officially opened in 1936 to facilitate easier access to the remote valley. The bridge was supposed to be part of a link road between Raetihi and Taranaki.

Unfortunately, it was hardly ever used since most farms had already failed by this time. The problems of poor access, regenerating forest, river erosion and a slump in product prices eventually forced the majority of settlers to abandon their land. By 1942 only three families remained in Mangapurua. A severe flood later that year further damaged the valley and the government advised them to leave. The Mangapurua Valley was officially closed in May of that year.

Wide grassy clearings, fence-posts, road lines and building materials are the only remnants of these farms. The most substantial legacy is the solid concrete bridge that still spans the Mangapurua Stream. Now known as the **Bridge to Nowhere**, it stands as a testament to the failed hopes and aspirations of the early settlers. Hanging across the water immediately upstream of the bridge are the last vestiges of the ancient swing bridge.

Poignant though it may be, don't spend too much time loitering at the bridge since it marks only the halfway point on the day's paddle. The Whanganui continues to flow steadily south, crossing the **Oparia Rapid**. This marks the point at which the largest canoe ever built on the river, *Tauwharepuru*, was lowered from the cliff top on ropes made from supplejack vines. It is alleged to have been large enough and sufficiently stable to carry 100 warriors. A little way below the rapid is an underwater mineral spring in the bank and just downstream is the private **Tangahoe Landing** that provides access to Tangahoe farm. This point was served by ferry steamers as recently as 1957. Beyond the landing the river continues through an area of outstanding scenery.

Five kilometres on, **Tieke Kainga** lies on the left-hand bank and the **Bridge to Nowhere Lodge** (see p158) is on the opposite side. Tieke is a 20-bed DOC hut built on the site of an old Maori pa that has been revived as a marae (see p282). As such, you must adhere to marae protocol if you stay here, though the site is not permanently occupied by Maori. In front of the marae stands an impressively carved pole, sculpted in traditional fashion. Made from a giant totora tree it features the faces of symbolic ancestors and a series of elaborate swirls and curves said to represent the rapids and currents of the Whanganui. These poles are traditionally placed in strategic points throughout the landscape to signify the relationship between the people and the land.

If the marae is occupied when you arrive you must announce yourself from the river bank and then be invited onto the site where you will be expected to participate in a *powhiri* ('welcome') ceremony before entering the marae. Having been greeted by the Maori in the traditional manner, one of you will be required to respond. You then join in the traditional *hongi* by pressing noses.

Having arrived as strangers, you are now part of the *whanau*, the extended family group, and may come and go as you please. Cooking and dining is done in a communal fashion and the Maori will be glad to tell you about their background and culture. The Maori do not tend to provide written accounts of the history of their *awa*, river, or *whenua*, land, but pass it on as *korero*, speech. This is a rare chance to hear their story, a fascinating insight and the opportunity to experience it ought to be grasped. If the marae is not occupied when you arrive, you are still free to use the dining area, bunk rooms and campsite. Some of the facilities may be locked though. Please respect this.

You must not smoke in the bunkhouse or bring alcohol onto the marae.

*(cont'd on p172)*

## MANGAPURUA TRACK (40km/14-16hrs; overview map p171)

The Mangapurua Track links the Mangapurua Landing on the Whanganui River to Whakahoro. Although you can tramp the trail in either direction, most people opt to take a jet boat to Mangapurua and then hike to the road at Whakahoro so the route description is laid out in this direction here. It takes three days to traverse the wilderness, following first the Mangapurua Stream and then the Kaiwhakauka Stream through two different, contrasting valleys. The route follows old pioneer trails and is gentle and well-graded. At the height of settlement, the Mangapurua Valley was home to some 35 families and the Kaiwhakauka Valley to another 16. Today there are no people living in the valleys but a handful of fractured chimneys, broken hedges, rows of exotic trees and the smothered outlines of houses remain as testament to these settlements. Aside from the DOC hut at Whakahoro (see p164) there are no huts along the route and you will have to camp at one of the designated sites. There are, however, toilet facilities provided at these locations.

### Mangapurua Landing to Bettjeman's, 5hrs

From the landing on the Whanganui River pick up the trail that follows the Mangapurua Stream towards the **Bridge to Nowhere** (see opposite). The concrete bridge reached after 40 minutes is an impressive monument to those who tried to eke out a living in these valleys after being relocated here post-WWI. Cross the bridge and continue on the true left bank of the **Mangapurua Stream** towards the head of the valley. Occasional grassy clearings amidst the thick vegetation are the remnants of old pastures cut to provide crops and feed for livestock. Regenerating vegetation has slowly reclaimed the cleared land, however. There is a sequence of plaques along the trail identifying the families that lived in the area. **Bennett's farm**, one of the first in the lower valley, stands just before **Battleship Bluff**, a giant rock wall that looks like the prow of a ship, which you reach 1¹/₂hrs after leaving the Bridge to Nowhere.

An hour upstream from the Bluff is another farm site, **Hellawell's**, close to Waterfall Creek. This point stands about halfway down the valley and was a useful meeting point for those living in the area. **Waterfall Creek** issues into the Mangapurua Stream from the east. For an interesting diversion follow the creek upstream for twenty minutes to reach the foot of the falls. Return to the main path by retracing your footsteps.

Beyond the creek the Mangapurua Valley narrows and deepens. The path contours along the rim of the gorge below, edging around a series of bluffs. The most striking, just after **Cody's farm**, is known as **Currant Bun Bluff** because of the dark, rounded rocks sticking out of the paler mud. Three hours after leaving Battleship Bluff you arrive at **Bettjeman's**. The farm here was the last to be abandoned, in 1942. Once a reasonably sized homestead, all that remains are a couple of damaged chimney stacks and a row of poplars that line the old road. This makes a good campsite, as there is a reliable water supply from a nearby stream and toilet facilities are provided.

### Bettjeman's to Mangapurua Trig, 3-4hrs

This short section sees you head roughly east for the day as the valley flattens and widens once again. Some 20-30 minutes after setting out you will come to Tester's, which was the site of the first school in the valley. The school ran for 13 years from 1926 to 1939, although its pupils frequently numbered less than ten. An hour from Bettjeman's is another farm, **Johnson's**. This is another pleasant spot to camp, with water available from the tributary flowing into the Mangapurua Stream nearby. Next up is **Walsh's farm**. From here the path begins to climb. It crosses **Slippery Creek** on a swing bridge and ascends gently through thick, uncut forest to arrive at the **Mangapurua Trig** 2-3hrs after leaving Johnson's. The track actually goes around the hill whilst a short side path climbs to the trig itself, at 663m/2175ft the highest point on the tramp. There are panoramic views from the top and on a clear day you can see the volcanoes of Tongariro and Egmont national parks. There is also a decent campsite with water and toilets nearby.

### Mangapurua Trig to Whakahoro, 6-7hrs

Descend from the trig and after a quarter of an hour take a sharp left-hand turn to start bearing northwards again as you enter the Kaiwhakauka Valley. Ignore the Raetihi-Ohura Road that continues straight on. The broad, easy path now follows the **Kaiwhakauka stream**. This valley is very different to the Mangapurua Valley and large sections of attractive tawa and podocarp forest remain undisturbed, with far fewer of the grassy clearings and homesteads that characterise the previous days' walking. In places the trail crosses small tributaries on swing bridges, but remains on the westerly bank of the stream for around 4-5hrs before crossing the more substantial **Depot Bridge**, a swing bridge across the stream used for moving livestock, and continuing on the easterly side of the Kaiwhakauka Stream. The path then joins a disused road and meanders towards **Whakahoro Hut and Campsite** where you once again are treated to views of the Whanganui River.

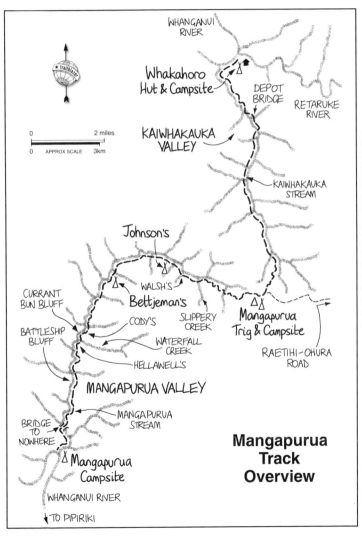

ROUTE GUIDE & MAPS

## Tieke Kainga Hut to Pipiriki          21.5km/4-5 hours; Map 5

The final section of the River Journey is shorter in comparison to the preceding days. The sheer-sided gorges gradually give way to gentler landscapes again as the river widens. Longer stretches of flat water are broken by the two largest rapids that you will have to negotiate on the trip and which will almost certainly test your ability to stay afloat.

If present, the Maori at Tieke Kainga will probably congregate to wave you off as you launch your canoe from the badly eroded banks below the marae. The river quickly pulls you downstream, ushering you onwards. After 10km of steady paddling the Whanganui is joined by the large **Manganui o te Ao River**, which drains the western slopes of Mt Ruapehu. The crystal-clear waters support trout and the rare blue duck and once provided a major transport route to the Central Plateau area. The river was vital to this region's development and can be readily explored by canoe.

Two kilometres downstream on the Whanganui is the first of the big rapids, **Ngaporo**, with pressure waves up to 1m high that can tumble a canoe quite easily. By aiming for the centre of the 'V' and paddling hard and straight you should be able to stay upright. On the far side of the rapid is the **Ngaporo Campsite**, set above a large shingle landing. It's an ideal spot to hang out and watch other canoeists tackle the Ngaporo.

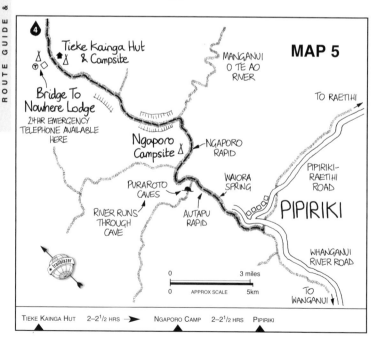

The river curves past the **Puraroto Caves**, with a lively stream running through them, before straightening for the final run to Pipiriki. A kilometre further on is the final obstacle, the **Autapu Rapid**, generating yet more sizeable pressure waves that boil and churn beneath a sheer cliff. A long eddy at the end will catch your canoe and spin you around if you don't paddle through the rapid and beyond it. A rocky shore on the left-hand side of the river will provide some sanctuary and enable you to haul your canoe back upstream for a second run, should you so choose. Beyond the rapid is a final stretch of flat water that allows you to relax and absorb the views that become apparent as the fern-clad cliffs recede and are replaced by gentler hills.

Rounding a final right-hand bend the **Pipiriki Landing** hoves into view, where your hire operator should, hopefully, be waiting to collect you.

# Abel Tasman Coast Track

*'... clear waters, unspoilt environment and idyllic golden sand bays ... It's easy to understand why New Zealand's Conservation Department considers this one of the country's world ranking great walks'*
**Sir Edmund Hillary**, quoted in the *Abel Tasman National Park Experience* brochure

## INTRODUCTION

This is not your typical New Zealand tramp in so far as there are no peaks to climb or high passes to cross. It is by far the easiest of the Great Walks. However, the 51km track is coastal walking at its very finest. The track is blissfully simple and its beauty self-evident. Golden crescent beaches lapped by the clear Tasman Sea back onto sections of verdant forest. Miles of extraordinary, striking coastline demand your time and attention.

The well-cut, graded track is impossible to lose and is therefore ideal for trampers of all abilities. Consequently this means that there are large numbers of people on the track and indeed it is the most popular Great Walk. However, should you wish to escape the majority of trampers, day-trippers and sea kayakers, focus on the top section of the track, from Awaroa to Whariwharangi. This section includes many of the track's best features but is largely free of the congestion that can blight the earlier sections.

## HISTORY

Traditions and recorded history relating to the lands of Abel Tasman National Park indicate that the area was occupied or affected by human activity up to 800 years ago. Forty years of archaeological surveys here have uncovered more than 120 sites of occupation. Middens, storage pits, terraces and defensive structures suggest that the sites were once established settlements inhabited by the Maori for many years.

ROUTE GUIDE & MAPS

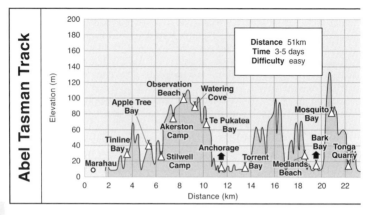

**Abel Tasman Track**

Distance 51km
Time 3-5 days
Difficulty easy

The mild climate and protected coastline lured a succession of Maori tribes to the area, although much of the land usage was seasonal, based around hunting, fishing and horticulture, including the cultivation of kumara, sweet potato. As Awaroa is the largest estuary, it probably supported the most established settlement. The first named resident at the top of South Island was Pohea, who arrived from the Whanganui district around 1450. Having established a pa at Auckland Point, he and his followers explored the region widely.

The Ngai Tara tribe occupied much of the area from 1550, before the Ngati Tumatakokiri expelled them in the early 1600s and became dominant over a large tract of land in the region. The Tumatakokiri were in occupation at the time when the Dutchman Abel Tasman arrived. In December 1642 seafarer Tasman, leading an expedition initiated by the Dutch East India Company to discover land rumoured to lie in the southern seas, made landfall off the west coast of New Zealand's South Island. His two ships sailed north from the vicinity of Punakaiki, rounding Farewell Spit and entering the large, open bay that it protected. Contact was made with the local Maori, the Ngati Tumatakokiri, although neither side fully appreciated or understood the greetings or challenges issued. On 19 December 1642 further confusion led to conflict. It is believed that Abel Tasman fired a cannon to announce his intention of going ashore. The Maori interpreted this as a sign of war and launched their waka. In the ensuing engagement four Dutch sailors were killed. Abel Tasman responded by weighing anchor and sailing out to sea. He bestowed on the area the name Moordenaers Bay, 'Murderers' Bay', to commemorate the incident. The name has since wisely been changed to Golden Bay.

Captain Cook arrived in 1770 and charted Cook Strait as well as naming several inlets and bays. The Frenchman Dumont D'Urville was the next European explorer to scour the coastline. Rounding Farewell Spit on 14 January 1827, he observed and named Separation Point. He proceeded to sail down the east coast, anchoring in an area of sheltered water in the lee of an island, which

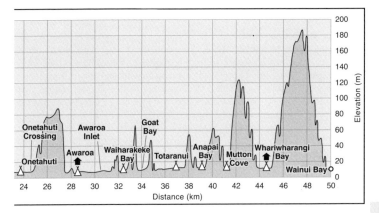

he christened Adele after his wife. In the course of investigating the coast he also named Observation Beach, where an observatory was set up to monitor stars and plot his location, and Watering Cove, where freshwater supplies were taken on board. The coastline and its picturesque appearance hugely impressed D'Urville. He gathered a variety of flora and fauna specimens as well as establishing cordial relations with the local Maori.

Meanwhile, the Tumatakokiri were finally displaced in the late 1790s by an alliance of Maori tribes. The new rulers were in turn conquered by a massive conglomeration of tribes from Taranaki and Tainui, who swept through the region in 1828. The modern *tangata whenua*, people of the land, the Ngati Rarua, Ngati Tama and Te Ati Awa, trace their ancestry back to these last invaders.

European settlers arrived in the mid-1850s. Relying on logging and ship-building to sustain them, the settlements failed once all the easily accessible

### The tale of the Canaan *taipo*

In 1843, the explorer Charles Heaphy crossed the Takaka Hill in the Canaan area whilst travelling from the west to east coast. Upon his arrival at the coast, the local Maori asked him if he had encountered the *taipo*, goblin, which lived in the mountains. When pressed further, some of the Maori refused to speak further about the Canaan area for fear of offending the taipo. Eventually one of the Maori explained that, once upon a time, their seasonal pa had been attacked by a collection of rival Maori tribes. Escaping from their enemy they fled into the surrounding countryside, taking refuge in the hills of the Canaan area. Upon arriving there a fearful rumbling noise was heard issuing from underground. Terrified by what they believed to be the voice of a taipo, the Maori retreated back down the hill.

The explanation for these rumblings lies in the limestone features in the area. Loud rumbles are often still heard after heavy rain in the Canaan area. The underground drainage system through which fresh rainfall rushes is thought to be responsible for the unusual noises.

timber had been felled. Farms and homesteads also foundered as the granite-based soils are largely infertile, suited only to supporting gorse and bracken.

Concerned at the exploitation of the natural resources and the damage that was being done to the coastline, local conservationist Perrine Moncrieff launched a vigorous campaign to have 15,000ha of Crown land made into a national park. The campaign gained momentum with the suggestion of using Abel Tasman's name for the park in conjunction with the approaching 300th anniversary of his arrival in Golden Bay. In November 1942 Prime Minister Peter Fraser duly announced the government decision to set aside an area of land for use as a national park. Since then further acquisitions, purchases and land donations have swelled the size of the Abel Tasman National Park, although it still remains the smallest in New Zealand.

## GEOLOGY

Abel Tasman National Park comprises two very different rock types. Inland the Canaan area is situated at the northern end of a band of marble (see box p175). This pressure-cooked limestone is prone to erosion by water and this has resulted in several visually striking land-forms, sinkholes, underground waterways and cave systems, including the deepest vertical shaft in the Southern Hemisphere, Harwood's Hole, which penetrates 900m into the Earth's interior.

In sharp contrast, the hinterland and coastal areas are made up of granite. This has weathered to produce the coarse golden sands of outstanding beaches such as those around Totaranui and Torrent Bay. The texture and colour of the beaches is directly linked to the characteristics of the local granite. The granite frequently splits vertically along joins to leave columns. Huge rounded boulders are produced by exfoliation, whereby flakes of granite are eroded until the surface becomes smooth and polished.

The coastline has become heavily indented where the large tidal range and action of the sea has eroded the softer stone from between the ridges of more resistant rock.

## FLORA AND FAUNA

### Flora

The vegetation in this park has been affected and modified by human action more than anywhere else. The scars of fires and tree clearing are still evident.

The flora in the region reflects the infertile nature of the soils that traditionally develop on granite. However, damp gullies above sea level support thick forest. Little, though, has survived in its original state due to the exploitation of natural resources and widespread felling of trees for the fledgling timber industry. The gullies provide a starting point for regenerating vegetation such as tree ferns, shrubs and supplejack vines to take hold.

Beech is the dominant larger tree; indeed, all five species of beech are found in the region. Mountain beech exists on the highest reaches of the park around rocky outcrops. Silver beech can be seen growing in the colder, wetter, sourer

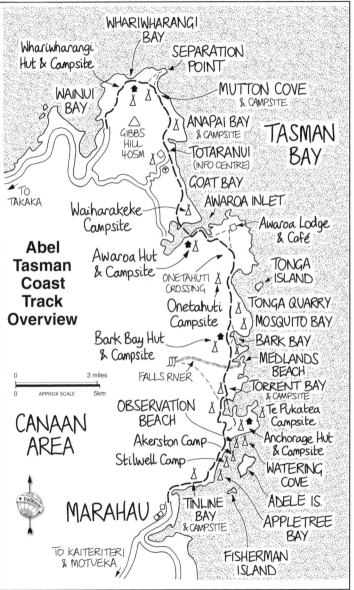

WHARIWHARANGI BAY

Whariwharangi Hut & Campsite

SEPARATION POINT

WAINUI BAY

MUTTON COVE & CAMPSITE

GIBBS HILL 405M

ANAPAI BAY & CAMPSITE

TASMAN BAY

TOTARANUI (INFO CENTRE)

TO TAKAKA

GOAT BAY

AWAROA INLET

Waiharakeke Campsite

Awaroa Lodge & Café

**Abel Tasman Coast Track Overview**

Awaroa Hut & Campsite

ONETAHUTI CROSSING

TONGA ISLAND

Onetahuti Campsite

TONGA QUARRY

MOSQUITO BAY

Bark Bay Hut & Campsite

BARK BAY

MEDLANDS BEACH

0 ___ 3 miles
0 ___ APPROX SCALE ___ 5km

FALLS RIVER

TORRENT BAY & CAMPSITE

CANAAN AREA

OBSERVATION BEACH

Te Pukatea Campsite

Akerston Camp

Anchorage Hut & Campsite

Stilwell Camp

WATERING COVE

★ trailblazer

ADELE IS.

MARAHAU

TINLINE BAY & CAMPSITE

APPLETREE BAY

TO KAITERITERI & MOTUEKA

FISHERMAN ISLAND

ROUTE GUIDE & MAPS

upland soils, often in association with kamahi, rata and the outrageously pineapple-topped mountain neinei. Hard beech prefers the better quality, moister inland soils; on droughty soils it develops a stunted, broken appearance. Red beech is a close relative of hard beech and grows across much of the inland sections of the park. Black beech can tolerate very poor and dry soils and as a consequence it is found on the dry ridge tops, cliffs and headlands close to the sea.

Where fire has been used to clear the land, the soils have degraded. In the most affected areas, south of Torrent Bay, these soils can now support only manuka and various lichens. The park's sandy estuaries are protected by barrier sand spits and in the main are affected only by the highest tides. They often support salt marsh vegetation such as sea primrose, glasswort and assorted rushes.

### Fauna
Many of the native **bird** species documented by D'Urville in the early 1800s have vanished from the region. However, a wide variety does still flourish here. Bellbird, fantail, kereru and tui are the main forest species, whilst pukeko and weka can be found around the estuaries and wetlands. Wading birds including white-faced heron and oystercatchers stalk the estuaries and shoreline, whilst gannets, shags and terns fish offshore. Little blue penguins take to the sea to feed during the day but return to the islands off the coast to sleep in burrows.

The tidal inlets support a diverse range of **fish**, worms and crabs which are preyed on by coastal birds.

**Fur seals** are found in two areas along the track. In 1993 a marine reserve was established around Tonga Island. Seal numbers have increased significantly thanks to new arrivals from elsewhere and the seals have subsequently begun to breed in the reserve now too. They can also be found off the remote granite headland at Separation Point.

## PLANNING YOUR TRAMP

### When to go
The Abel Tasman Coast Track is blessed with some of the finest weather in New Zealand. The mild climate and high number of sunshine hours make it an attractive destination at almost any time of year. Mountains to the west and south protect and shelter the coastline from the harsher winds. Although 1800mm of rain per year falls on the coast, it does so only in a few separate days, ensuring lengthy dry spells throughout summer and autumn.

Because of the stable, mild climate, the track can be tramped at any time of year. The official peak season runs from the start of October to the end of April. The track is at its busiest in summer, when the beaches can become overrun with day-trippers and sea kayakers. Many people now choose to avoid the crowds and tramp at other times of year. However, don't be fooled by the tropical appearance in winter because it can get cold at night and the sea temperature drops dramatically. It's only the very hardy that choose to swim at this time.

The months of **February and April** are slightly quieter than the busiest periods, yet they still offer an ideal temperature to be on the coast.

In summer the scrub on the edge of the forests becomes tinder dry. Fires are a very real risk in the park. Use only purpose-built fireplaces and be sure to extinguish the fire after use. If dry weather persists for long periods a fire ban may be introduced.

## Sources of information

The official **Abel Tasman Park Headquarters and DOC office** (☎ 03-525 8026, 🖳 goldenbayao@doc.govt.nz, PO Box 166), in Takaka at 62 Commercial St, is open 8am-4.30pm on weekdays. Between Christmas and late January the office is also open on weekends. This is a good place to book your accommodation and transport for the track. **Kahurangi National Park Visitor Centre** (☎ 03-528 1810, 🖳 motuekaao@doc.govt.nz, PO Box 97), on the corner of King Edward and High streets in nearby Motueka, also handles information and sells passes and mapping for the track. It is open 8am-4.30pm on weekdays.

However, the handiest place to book your tramp is Nelson (see p181). The DOC counter in the **Nelson i-SITE Visitor Information Centre** (☎ 03-548 2304, 🖳 www.nelsonnz.com, 🖳 nelsonvc@doc.govt.nz, PO Box 194), at 77 Trafalgar Street, on the corner of Trafalgar and Halifax St, open daily 8.30am-noon and 1-4.30pm, is ideally placed to help you organise all aspects of your tramp. The friendly staff will advise you as to your options. They also sell the relevant maps and pamphlets for the track.

Other than the DOC offices, the **information centres** in the same towns can help you with all aspects of your pre-planning. The Golden Bay i-Site Visitor

---

### Alternative activities

The stretch of coast along which the Abel Tasman track runs is not just a treat for trampers. There are plenty of other ways to enjoy the white sands and warm water. One of the most popular is **sea kayaking**, with an increasing number of people opting to paddle the length of the track, stopping at the secluded bays and camping on the beaches overnight. There are a multitude of options open involving part or all of the track and it's possible to go it alone or as part of a guided group. Instruction is usually given and most companies will start you out in a double kayak unless you can demonstrate sufficient competence in a single kayak. Tents can also be hired from most outfitters: **Abel Tasman Kayaks** (☎ 0800-732 529 or 03-527 8022, 🖳 www .abeltasmankayaks.co.nz), Main Rd, Marahau; **Kaiteriteri Kayaks** (☎ 0800-252 925 or 03-527 8383, 🖳 www.seakayak.co.nz), Kaiteriteri Beach, Kaiteriteri; **Kiwi Kayaks** (☎ 0800-695 494 or 03-528 7705, 🖳 www.kiwikayaks.co.nz), Main Rd, Marahau; **Marahau Sea Kayaks** (☎ 0800-529 257 or 03-527 8176, 🖳 www.msk.net.nz), Franklin St, Marahau; **Ocean River** (☎ 0800-732 529 or 03-527 8022, 🖳 www.seakay aking.co.nz), Main Rd, Marahau; **The Sea Kayak Company** (☎ 0508-252 925 or 03-528 7251, 🖳 www.seakayaknz.co.nz), 506 High St, Motueka; **Wilson's Abel Tasman** (☎ 0800-223 582 or 03-528 2027, 🖳 www.abeltasman.co.nz), 265 High St, Motueka.

Other options include **yacht rental** and private charters with Abel Tasman Sailing Adventures (☎ 0800-467 245 or 03-527 8375, 🖳 www.sailingadventures.co.nz) or **swimming with seals** in the seal colony, which can be organised by Abel Tasman Seal Swim (☎ 0800-252 925 or 03-527 8383, 🖳 www.sealswim.com) or Maori Uncut (☎ 0800-252 925, 🖳 www.maoriuncut.co.nz); both are based on Kaiteriteri Beach.

Centre (☎ 03-525 9136, 💻 www.goldenbay.net.nz), at 1 Willow St, Takaka, is open daily. The equivalent Motueka i-Site Visitor Centre (☎ 03-528 6543, 💻 www.motuekaisite.co.nz), on Wallace St, has a dedicated Great Walks booking desk that can be contacted on ☎ 03-528 0005. It is open 8.30am-5pm on weekdays and 10am-5pm at the weekend during the summer.

## Getting to the trailhead

The track is readily accessible at several points, much more so than most other Great Walks. At the southern end, Marahau is 18km from Motueka and 67km from Nelson. Totaranui, mid-way up the track, can be reached by a twisty gravel track from Takaka, 32km away. At the northern end of the track, Wainui can be accessed from Takaka too.

A large number of **bus operators** provide regular services to the various start and finish points on the track. Buses leave Nelson and Motueka for Kaiteriteri, Marahau, Totaranui and Wainui. For up-to-date timetable information and fare prices contact: Abel Tasman Coachlines (☎ 03-548 0285, 💻 www .abeltasmantravel.co.nz, 27 Bridge St, Nelson), Golden Bay Coachlines (☎ 03-525 8352, 💻 www.gbcoachlines.co.nz), Nelson Bays Shuttles (☎ 03-540 3852, 💻 www.nnbays.co.nz), Nelson Lakes Shuttles (☎ 03-521 1900, 💻 www.nelson lakesshuttles.co.nz), Trek Express Track Shuttle (☎ 0800-128 735 or 03-540 2042, 💻 www.trekexpress.co.nz). Local taxis can also run you to and from the track.

**Boat services** and **water-taxis** operate out of Kaiteriteri and Marahau, stopping at several spots along the track. Due to the impressive nature of the coastline, this has become a preferred way to begin or finish the track. It enables you to access an area or walk out one way and return by boat, thereby preventing you from having to retrace your steps. The contrasting view of the track from on the water completes your impression of this area. Most operators also include a trip to the Tonga Island Marine Reserve on the way up and down the coast.

For full itineraries, timetables and additional information contact Abel Tasman Aquataxi (☎ 03-527 8003 or 0800-278 282, 💻 www.info@aqua taxi.co.nz), Abel Tasman Sea Shuttle (☎ 03-528 9759, 💻 www.abeltasmansea shuttles.co.nz, Kiwi Water Taxis (☎ 03-528 7705, 💻 www.adventureabeltasman .com), Marahau Water Taxis (☎ 03-527 8176 or 0800-808 018, 💻 www.abeltas mancentre.co.nz) or Wilsons Abel Tasman (☎ 0800-223 582 or 03-528 2027, 💻 www.abeltasman.co.nz).

All of the information centres and DOC offices will be able to advise you on itineraries, access and timetables for both bus and water-taxi operators.

## Local services

The closest towns to the track are Marahau and Takaka. **Marahau** is close enough to walk to the southern end of the track. About 18km north of Motueka, it is a small hamlet with a handful of accommodation options and a café. The following provide a variety of tent sites, dorms and rooms at reasonable rates: well-established and ideally situated ***Beach Camp*** (☎ 0800-808 018, 💻 www .abeltasmanmarahaucamp.co.nz; tent pitch NZ$20 for one person NZ$30 for two, dorm bed NZ$20, dbl NZ$45, cabin NZ$60) on Franklin St; modern, spotless *Marahau Lodge* (☎ 03-527 8250, 🖳 www.abeltasmanmarahaulodge.co.nz; dbl NZ$130-230) on Marahau Beach Rd; Alpine-esque *Ocean View Chalets* (☎ 03-527 8232, 🖳 www.accommodationabeltasman.co.nz; dbl NZ$110); and homely and spacious *The Barn* (☎ 03-527 8043; tent pitch NZ$13, dorm NZ$25-26, dbl NZ$62) on Harvey Rd. Note there are no food stores in Marahau, although there is a basic camp shop at the Beach Camp, so stock up before you arrive.

At the northern end of the track, albeit 21km from the trail end, is **Takaka**. Boasting a café, restaurant, supermarket, information centre and a couple of accommodation options, Takaka is a pleasant, sunny, slow town. Offering tent sites and beds is the small and peaceful *Annie's Nirvana Lodge* (☎ 03-525 8766, 🖳 www.nirvanalodge.co.nz; dorm NZ$25-28, sgl/dbl NZ$40/60) on Motupipi St, which is now actually run by the YHA; the homely *Barefoot Backpackers* (☎ 03-525 7005, 🖳 www.bare-foot.co.nz; dorm NZ$22-23, sgl/dbl NZ$40/50) at 114 Comercial St; the quirky, cosy *Kiwiana* (☎ 0800-805 494) at 73 Motupipi St and the larger *Golden Bay Motel* (☎ 0800-401 212, 🖳 www.goldenbaymotel.co.nz; dbl NZ$95-130) at 132 Commercial St.

The best place to arrange your trip and rest before or recover after your tramping exertions is **Nelson** (see map p183). This idyllic town is an attractive, thriving place that benefits from more sunshine than anywhere else in New Zealand. Replete with all the amenities and services you might need, it is the best equipped base in the region.

The rambling *Club Nelson* (☎ 03-548 3466, 🖳 clubnelson@xtra.co.nz; tent pitch NZ$15, dorm NZ$23, sgl/dbl NZ$40/50-56), at 18 Mount St, and well-equipped, purpose-built *Nelson Central YHA* (☎ 03-545 9988, 🖳 www.yha .co.nz; dorm NZ$26, sgl NZ$41, dbl/twin NZ$64, en suite NZ$80), at 59 Rutherford St, are both good choices while at 42 Weka St stands the popular and even cheaper *Paradiso Backpackers* (☎ 03-546 6703, 🖳 www.backpackernel son.co.nz; dorm NZ$22-25, dbl NZ$56), which has its own volleyball court and pool as well as the more standard facilities. *The Palace Backpackers* (☎ 03-548 4691, 🖳 www.thepalace.co.nz; dorm NZ$23, sgl/dbl NZ$45/56) at 114 Rutherford St has plenty of atmosphere and character. Although not particularly central, *Tasman Bay Backpackers* (☎ 0800-222 572, 🖳 www.tasmanbayback packers.co.nz; dorm NZ$24, dbl NZ$60) at 10 Weka St has great value rooms and a really friendly atmosphere, whilst *Trampers Rest* (☎ 03-545 7477) at 31 Alton St offers compact, cosy rooms and a plethora of useful insights into the region.

At 335 Trafalgar Square the slightly more upmarket *Accents on the Park* (☎ 03-548 4335, 🖳 www.accentsonthepark.com; dorm NZ$20-28, dbl NZ$56-89) is set in a grand Victorian house but boasts soundproofed rooms, a spa pool, bar and bistro, and additional modern facilities. Other quality options in this bracket include the highly sociable *The Bug* (☎ 03-539 4227, 🖳 www.the bug.co.nz; NZ$23-25, dbl/twin NZ$60-70) at 226 Vineyard St which is adorned with VW Beetle paraphernalia, and the compact *The Green Monkey* (☎ 03-545 7421, 🖳 www.thegreenmonkey.co.nz; dorm NZ$24, dbl NZ$58) at 129 Milton St, set in a converted villa that retains plenty of charm, comfort and ambience.

Of the plentiful **motels** and **B&B** accommodation, there's superb, tranquil *Cambria House* (☎ 03-548 4681, 🖳 www.cambria.co.nz; sgl/dbl from NZ$230/275), a beautifully restored late 19th-century homestead at 7 Cambria St, while *Riverlodge Motel* (☎ 03-548 3094, 🖳 www.riverlodgenelson.co.nz), at 31 Collingwood St, has smart, well-appointed and reasonably priced units (NZ$95-180). Just out of town but worth the short journey are *Wheelhouse Inn* (☎ 03-546 8391, 🖳 www.wheelhouse.nelson.co.nz; NZ$130-190 for two people sharing, NZ$15 per additional person per night), 2km west of town at 41 Whitby Rd, which has attractive apartments set on a wonderfully landscaped hillside overlooking the bay; and *Nelson Beach Hostel* (☎ 03-548 6817, 🖳 www.nelsonbeachhostel.co.nz; dorm NZ$25, dbl or twin NZ$56), 4km west at 25 Muiritai St, just back from Tahunanui Beach, where there are good-value rooms in a very laid-back and friendly environment.

Nelson has a number of great little places to grab a flat white (NZ equivalent of a latte, made with espresso and milk, although generally slightly stronger than your average European latte) and a snack: try *Morrison St Café* at 244 Hardy St for good breakfasts and snacks in an arty environment; *Stingray Café* at 8 Church St for a pizza on their outdoor terrace or a decent cocktail in the evening; the licensed *Yaza Café* on Montgomery Square for free-range, organic fare and *Zippy's* at 276 Hardy St for vegetarian dishes and seriously good coffee. If you're after a quick and tasty snack or looking for something to soak up the alcohol late at night grab a kebab or salad from *Akbabas* at 130 Bridge St. For **dining**, try the quality Indian-influenced dishes at *Indian Café*, 94 Collingwood St, Thai noodle and wok dishes at *Poppy Thai*, 142 Hardy St, or the Italian cuisine of *Lambretta's* at 204 Hardy St. Along the seafront there are more options including the *Boatshed Café* on Wakefield Quay at the end of Haven Rd, a converted boat shed perched on stilts over the bay that specialises in seafood and boasts peerless views. For Nelson's best food book in advance to secure a table at the elegant, European-influenced *Hopgoods*, at 284 Trafalgar St, which sources local produce and serves a range of superb seasonal dishes. Good pubs include the English-style *Victorian Rose* at 281 Trafalgar St, the Irish-themed *Maen Fiddler* at 145 Bridge St and *Grumpy Mole*, at No 141 Bridge St. There's live music and DJ sets most nights at *Phat Club* at 137 Bridge St whilst many of the pubs have live music come the weekends.

## Huts and campsites

Because of the high visitor numbers to the Abel Tasman Track during the summer, between early October and the end of April you must pre-book your bunk space at the huts by purchasing a **Great Walks pass**. This entitles you to stay in the designated accommodation on the designated day. The requisite passes can be bought from DOC offices, visitor centres, some hotels and tour operators.

The **adult hut fee** in the summer season is NZ$30 and NZ$12 for the rest of the year; the **camping fee** for the equivalent periods is NZ$12/8. Children and youth are free for both huts and camping.

Each of the **huts** at Anchorage, Bark Bay, Awaroa and Whariwharangi has bunks, mattresses, heating, toilets and water supply. There are no cooking

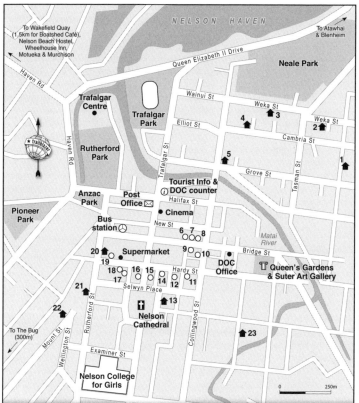

# Nelson

## Where to stay
1 The Green Monkey
2 Paradiso Backpackers
3 Tasman Bay Backpackers
4 Cambria House
5 Riverlodge Motel
13 Accents on the Park
20 Nelson Central YH
21 Palace Backpackers
22 Club Nelson
23 Trampers Rest

## Where to eat and drink
6 The Grumpy Mole Bar
7 Phat Club
8 Maen Fiddler
9 Akbabas
10 Indian Café
11 Zippy's
12 Morrison St Café
14 Lambretta's
15 Victorian Rose Pub
16 Hopgoods
17 Stingray Café
18 Poppy Thai
19 Yaza Café

facilities, so portable stoves and fuel must be carried at all times. There will most likely be a warden on duty at each hut, too, to check hut passes and impose a fine if they have not been prepaid.

Almost every accessible beach has a **campsite** located on it. There are 21 campsites along the length of the track, each equipped with basic facilities. Open fires are permitted only where designated fireplaces have been constructed, so it is necessary to carry portable stoves at all times. It is also possible to camp at Totaranui, which is equipped with a shelter, cold shower and toilets. In order to use the campsites you must purchase a **camp pass** in advance of your trip. A camping pass can be upgraded to a hut pass after 6pm as long as there is space in the hut and the difference in price is paid. You can stay in any hut or campsite for a maximum of two consecutive nights throughout the year except for Totaranui where you are entitled to stay for just one night.

There is an attractive, expensive ecolodge at *Awaroa* (☎ 03-528 8758, 🖥 www .awaroalodge.co.nz; dbl NZ$350-450) that has lavish double rooms, a comfortable lounge and library and most modern facilities. There is also a fine café and bar here that is open to everyone, not just guests of the lodge.

## Maps

The Abel Tasman Coast Track is featured clearly on the *Abel Tasman Parkmap* (237–07), at 1:50,000 scale. Topomaps' *Tarakohe* (N25) and *Takaka* (N26) also cover the track. All of these can be bought from DOC offices or information centres near to the track.

## Distances and times

This is an easy, gentle track that can be tramped in either direction. The highest point is just 150m above sea level and much of the route follows the beaches along the shoreline. Most people tramp the track one way in three to five days, dawdling on the golden sands, paddling in the sea and enjoying the cooler forested sections. Although quality footwear is necessary, it isn't even essential to have proper walking boots for this track. Having reached the end, people usually catch a water-taxi back. Buses can also be pre-arranged to meet you.

The only real considerations are the three tidal estuaries that can each be crossed only two to three hours either side of low tide (plus a fourth, Onetahuti, which can be crossed three to four hours either side of low tide). True, there are high-tide routes around Torrent Bay and Bark Bay but these are quite tortuous and less fun than the low-tide alternatives, while at Awaroa Inlet there is simply no alternative to wading across the estuary. Thus a degree of forethought is required to ensure that you are in the correct place at the appropriate time and tide level. DOC offices and information centres can advise you in advance of tide times and instruct you as to when it is safe to cross the estuaries.

| | | |
|---|---|---|
| Marahau to Anchorage Hut | 11.5km | $3^1/_2$-$4^1/_2$ hours |
| Anchorage Hut to Bark Bay Hut | 9.5km | $2^1/_2$-$3^1/_2$ hours |
| Bark Bay Hut to Awaroa Hut | 11.5km | $3^1/_2$-$4^1/_2$ hours |
| Awaroa Hut to Whariwharangi Hut | 13.0km | 4-5 hours |
| Whariwharangi Hut to Wainui Bay | 5.5km | $1^1/_2$-$2^1/_2$ hours |

## TRACK DESCRIPTION

### Marahau to Anchorage Hut     11.5km/3$^1$/$_2$-4$^1$/$_2$ hours; Map 1

This short, easy day gently introduces you to the track. By passing through some attractive areas with historical resonance, it allows you to unwind and begin to absorb your surroundings.

From the shelter and car park 1km north of Marahau, the track crosses the **Marahau River estuary** and mud-flats on a causeway. It then climbs slightly through bracken and gorse as it meanders 2.5km to **Tinline Bay** and its **campsite**. There is a signpost at this sheltered clearing indicating the Tinline Nature Walk, a 30-minute loop that passes through an area of native forest. This is the sort of vegetation that once covered the entire southern section of the track before logging and burning altered its character permanently.

From Tinline Bay the main track heads east, passing after 500m the junction with the inland track. Sticking with the coast track, it continues north-east, skirting **Coquille Bay** and rounding **Guilbert Point**. The French names on this section are the legacy of D'Urville's early exploration. Passing an area of private land you gain great views of **Apple Tree Bay** ahead and the Astrolabe Roadstead between the shore and Adele Island, where D'Urville anchored his ships in 1827.

The track hugs the coastline 20m above the shore with several paths leading down onto the beaches below. There are campsites at **Apple Tree Bay** and **Stilwell Bay**, both with fine swimming, though sea-kayakers frequently swamp these areas.

Beyond Stilwell Bay the track passes through kanuka groves. After **Yellow Point**, next to which is **Akerston Bay and Campsite**, the track heads inland and through gullies filled with ferns, climbing for 1km to a clearing and crossroads. A history of continuous burning and clearing has resulted in a barren landscape here. Stunted groves of manuka are evident, struggling to survive in the hostile soils. There are good views north from here of Torrent Bay and the series of repeating beaches, coves and headlands that stretch ahead.

The track to Anchorage Hut is well signposted. Turn right and head east, ignoring the junction left as the track starts to descend. Quickly dropping to the sweeping sands of Anchorage Beach, you turn right to **Anchorage Hut**. This 24-bunk hut is adjacent to a campground with more than 50 sites. This can result in a large, noisy gathering of people.

However, nearby there are smaller, quieter campsites by two attractive little beaches – beaches which also make pleasant side-trips for those staying at the hut. A one-hour loop heads east then north through scrublands and passes the site of a small pa on **Pitt Head**, before circling round to an idyllic beach at **Te Pukatea Bay**, while **Watering Cove** can be reached via a 45-minute track that heads south across a dry ridge.

### Anchorage Hut to Bark Bay Hut     9.5km/2$^1$/$_2$-3$^1$/$_2$ hours; Map 2

This is a very short day which could easily be combined with the following one to create a comfortable seven-hour tramp to Awaroa. However, stopping at Bark Bay enables you to enjoy the beach and the surf for an entire afternoon.

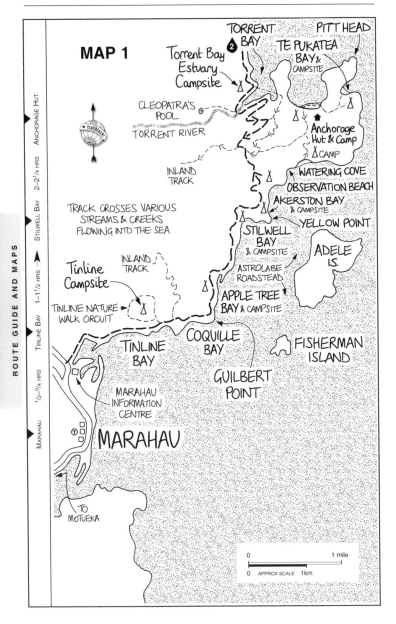

ROUTE GUIDE AND MAPS

MARAHAU — 1/2–3/4 HRS — TINLINE BAY — 1–1½ HRS — STILWELL BAY — 2–2¼ HRS — ANCHORAGE HUT

MAP 1

TORRENT BAY

PITT HEAD

TE PUKATEA BAY & CAMPSITE

Torrent Bay Estuary Campsite

CLEOPATRA'S POOL

TORRENT RIVER

Anchorage Hut & Camp

△ CAMP

INLAND TRACK

WATERING COVE

OBSERVATION BEACH

AKERSTON BAY & CAMPSITE

YELLOW POINT

TRACK CROSSES VARIOUS STREAMS & CREEKS FLOWING INTO THE SEA

STILWELL BAY & CAMPSITE

ADELE IS.

Tinline Campsite

INLAND TRACK

ASTROLABE ROADSTEAD

APPLE TREE BAY & CAMPSITE

TINLINE NATURE WALK CIRCUIT

COQUILLE BAY

FISHERMAN ISLAND

TINLINE BAY

GUILBERT POINT

MARAHAU INFORMATION CENTRE

MARAHAU

TO MOTUEKA

0          1 mile

0    APPROX SCALE   1km

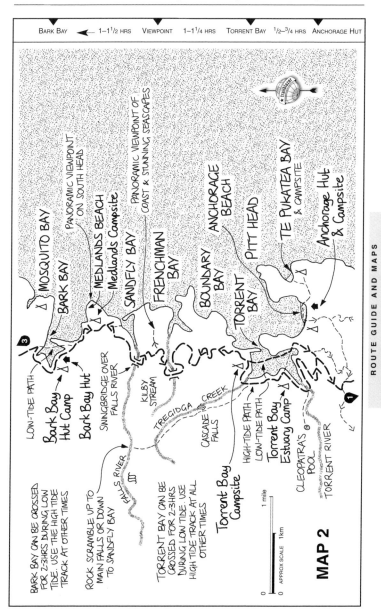

BARK BAY ◄— 1–1½ HRS  VIEWPOINT  1–1¼ HRS  TORRENT BAY  ½–¾ HRS  ANCHORAGE HUT

MOSQUITO BAY

BARK BAY

PANORAMIC VIEWPOINT ON SOUTH HEAD

MEDLANDS BEACH
Medlands Campsite

SANDFLY BAY

PANORAMIC VIEWPOINT OF COAST & STUNNING SEASCAPES

FRENCHMAN BAY

BOUNDARY BAY

ANCHORAGE BEACH

TORRENT BAY

PITT HEAD

TE PUKATEA BAY & Campsite

Anchorage Hut & Campsite

LOW-TIDE PATH

Bark Bay Hut Camp

Bark Bay Hut

SWINGBRIDGE OVER FALLS RIVER

KILBY STREAM

TRECIDGA CREEK

CASCADE CREEK

HIGH-TIDE PATH
LOW-TIDE PATH

Torrent Bay Estuary Camp

BARK BAY CAN BE CROSSED FOR 2–3HRS DURING LOW TIDE. USE THE HIGH TIDE TRACK AT OTHER TIMES

ROCK SCRAMBLE UP TO MAIN FALLS OR DOWN TO SANDFLY BAY

FALLS RIVER

TORRENT BAY CAN BE CROSSED FOR 2–3HRS DURING LOW TIDE. USE HIGH TIDE TRACK AT ALL OTHER TIMES

Torrent Bay Campsite

CLEOPATRA'S POOL

TORRENT RIVER

1 mile

1km

APPROX SCALE

0

MAP 2

ROUTE GUIDE AND MAPS

From the hut, tramp west to the far end of Anchorage Beach, where the track climbs over a small headland and drops into **Torrent Bay**. Two to three hours either side of low tide it is possible to head north across the sand and firm mud-flats. However, if you missed the low tide slot, double back to the junction above Anchorage Hut and follow the signposted all-tidal track which circles Torrent Bay in the bush before dropping down to the shoreline and **campsite** at the north-ern end of the bay. From Torrent Bay Estuary Campsite, a side path leads south for 20 minutes along the Torrent River to a deepish pool of clear water carved out of a massive chunk of bedrock. **Cleopatra's Pool** is a great swimming hole and a good way to escape the crowds on the beach. A second well-graded path heads north from the Torrent Bay Campsite on a one-hour detour following Tregidga Stream to **Cascade Falls**, which are pleasant if not totally spectacular. Return the same way or stay on this track and walk to the Falls River. It is then possible to scramble and rock-hop your way down to the falls on this section of the river to a reunion with the main path at the swing bridge.

The main track passes through a cluster of private holiday homes, then climbs inland. Rising 100m it edges around Kilby Stream to arrive at a low sad-dle from where two good vantage points can be reached. You then descend to the Falls River outlet, crossing the stream on a large swing bridge. By scram-bling upstream for 20 minutes you get to view the falls themselves – an extremely impressive sight.

Beyond the river the track sidles over another headland, past a junction with a path branching off right to the attractive **Sandfly Bay**, before bringing you to a second panoramic viewpoint above **South Head**. It then tumbles downhill for almost 20 minutes, past **Medlands Beach** and **campsite**, to Bark Bay. Turning left, you follow the beach round, past a sandy spit upon which **Bark Bay Campsite** is located, to the **Bark Bay Hut**. Although very busy, this 34-bunk hut is situated in a beautiful spot edged by calm, sheltered waters.

### Bark Bay Hut to Awaroa Hut          11.5km/3¹/₂-4¹/₂ hours; Map 3

This is an excellent day's tramp through Tonga Island Marine Reserve, along some particularly lovely beaches, through some superb forest and via interest-ing historical sites. It is possible to cross Bark Bay two to three hours either side of low tide by walking 10 minutes along the spit and across the exposed flats. At high tide, however, it is necessary to spend half an hour following the inland all-tidal path that rounds the bay. On the far side of the bay, the track heads well inland and climbs 100m to a low saddle through regenerating manuka forest. Climbing over several ridges you lose the sensation of being by the sea.

The track then descends over 1.5km to the disused **Tonga Quarry**. Building-grade granite was cut and quarried from the beach here in the early 1900s and was used in the construction of several prominent buildings in Nelson and Wellington. A plaque describes the operation. A winch base, some abandoned square blocks and the vestiges of a jetty remain at the abandoned site, along with the small **Tonga Quarry Campsite**. At low tide it is possible to scramble back south along the rocks towards **Arch Point**, smooth, sea-sculpted arches formed by the repeated pounding of the waves.

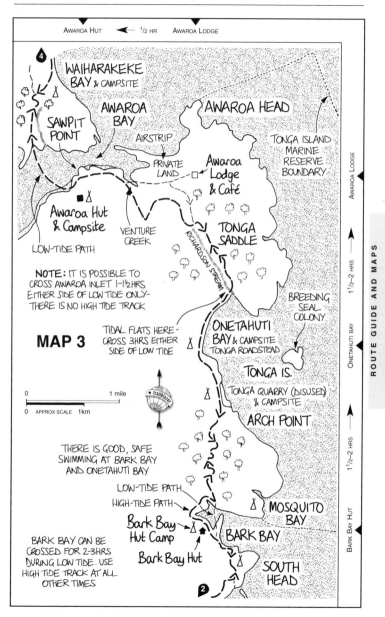

AWAROA HUT  ←  ½ HR  AWAROA LODGE

**4**

WAIHARAKEKE BAY & CAMPSITE

AWAROA BAY

AWAROA HEAD

SAWPIT POINT

AIRSTRIP

PRIVATE LAND

Awaroa Lodge & Café

TONGA ISLAND MARINE RESERVE BOUNDARY

Awaroa Hut & Campsite

VENTURE CREEK

TONGA SADDLE

LOW-TIDE PATH

RICHARDSON STREAM

**NOTE:** IT IS POSSIBLE TO CROSS AWAROA INLET 1-1½HRS EITHER SIDE OF LOW TIDE ONLY - THERE IS NO HIGH TIDE TRACK

BREEDING SEAL COLONY

**MAP 3**

TIDAL FLATS HERE - CROSS 3HRS EITHER SIDE OF LOW TIDE

ONETAHUTI BAY & CAMPSITE
TONGA ROADSTEAD

0 _____ 1 mile
0  APPROX SCALE  1km

★ trailblazer

**TONGA IS.**

TONGA QUARRY (DISUSED) & CAMPSITE

**ARCH POINT**

THERE IS GOOD, SAFE SWIMMING AT BARK BAY AND ONETAHUTI BAY

LOW-TIDE PATH

HIGH-TIDE PATH

Bark Bay Hut Camp

Bark Bay Hut

BARK BAY CAN BE CROSSED FOR 2-3HRS DURING LOW TIDE. USE HIGH TIDE TRACK AT ALL OTHER TIMES

MOSQUITO BAY

**BARK BAY**

**SOUTH HEAD**

**2**

ROUTE GUIDE AND MAPS

AWAROA LODGE

1½-2 HRS

ONETAHUTI BAY

1½-2 HRS

BARK BAY HUT

The main track scuttles up an incline from the quarry and drops immediately onto **Onetahuti Beach**. The graceful curve of the beach is best viewed from the clearing just above it. There is a good, protected **campsite** and perfect swimming spots at the southern end of the beach.

At the beach's northern end you turn inland to a small tidal flat that must be crossed within three hours of low tide. The track then climbs past the swampy estuary of Richardson Stream and climbs to **Tonga Saddle**. Looking back you get grand views of the Tonga Roadstead and Tonga Island.

As the path begins its descent, it forks, the left-hand path ambling to Awaroa Inlet while the right descends steeply to **Awaroa Lodge and Café** (see p184). This attractive spot makes for a very relaxing diversion, allowing you to treat yourself in a way that just isn't possible on other Great Walks: with bacon and mussel fritters, chilli and lime fishcakes or pan-fried catch of the day. Washed down with beer or wine, this makes for a fine reward after a day's tramping.

From the lodge the track heads west across an area of scrubland, cuts through some private residences and passes a grass airstrip to arrive at **Venture Creek**. Orange discs mark the way across the creek, which should be forded at low tide. They then lead you around **Sawpit Point** and into the broad Awaroa Inlet and its namesake the **Awaroa Hut** huddled on the shoreline.

The 22-bunk hut looks out over the enormous inlet and provides great views of the sunset. Because the beach is oriented east–west, the departing sunlight bathes the whole estuary, highlighting the tidal sand patterns and shell banks in strong golden light.

### Awaroa Hut to Whariwharangi Hut                13km/4-5 hours; Map 4

This is a dramatic stretch of coastline. After Totaranui the track becomes noticeably quieter and emptier since many people do not appreciate that the Coast Track actually extends to Wainui Bay. The final section is wild and rugged, epitomised by the barren Separation Point. The beautiful coastline and established seal colonies make this a highlight of the track.

Careful consideration needs to be given to the tide times, since Awaroa Inlet can be crossed only $1^{1}/_{2}$-2hrs either side of low tide and there is no high-tide alternative. Follow the orange discs across the shell-littered tidal flats towards **Pound Creek**. The crossing will take about half an hour and requires some wading even at the lowest tide.

From the northern side of the inlet the track climbs over a low saddle and drops to the exquisite **Waiharakeke Bay** and its **campsite** where a timber mill once operated. Leading back into the forest and passing above rocky **Ratakura Point**, the path emerges at **Goat Bay** where large rata trees decorate the shoreline and drop vibrant red flowers in summer. Passing along the beach you then ascend **Skinner Point** to a fabulous look-out point that has views north to Totaranui and south back towards Awaroa Head, before climbing off the viewpoint to emerge on the stunning crescent of sand previously seen from above. The path then leads to the **information centre** and vast, sprawling **campsite** at **Totaranui**, which you reach $1^{1}/_{2}$-2hrs after leaving Awaroa. Water taxis are able to access the beach here and pick up or drop off trampers on request.

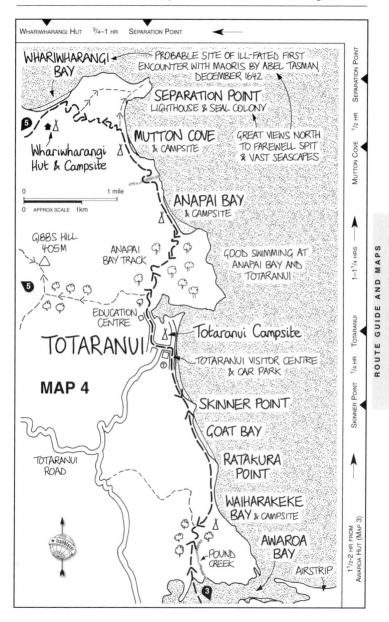

WHARIWHARANGI BAY

PROBABLE SITE OF ILL-FATED FIRST ENCOUNTER WITH MAORIS BY ABEL TASMAN DECEMBER 1642

SEPARATION POINT
LIGHTHOUSE & SEAL COLONY

5

Whariwharangi Hut & Campsite

MUTTON COVE
& CAMPSITE

GREAT VIEWS NORTH TO FAREWELL SPIT & VAST SEASCAPES

0          1 mile
0   APPROX SCALE   1km

ANAPAI BAY
& CAMPSITE

GIBBS HILL
405M

ANAPAI
BAY TRACK

GOOD SWIMMING AT ANAPAI BAY AND TOTARANUI

5

EDUCATION CENTRE

TOTARANUI

Totaranui Campsite

MAP 4

TOTARANUI VISITOR CENTRE & CAR PARK

SKINNER POINT

GOAT BAY

RATAKURA POINT

TOTARANUI ROAD

WAIHARAKEKE BAY & CAMPSITE

AWAROA BAY

POUND CREEK

AIRSTRIP

3

★ trailblazer

Right margin labels:
SEPARATION POINT
1/2 HR
MUTTON COVE
1–1¼ HRS →
TOTARANUI
1/4 HR
SKINNER POINT
↑
1½–2 HR FROM AWAROA HUT (MAP 3)

The avenue of plane and macrocarpa trees in front of the information centre was planted by the settler William Gibbs in 1855 at the time when he built a model farm in the area. Pukeko are frequently seen pecking in the long grass at the base of the trees. The track turns right and follows the gravel road past an education centre to the start of the Anapai Bay Track. Follow it as it crests a low saddle before descending through lush forest to **Anapai Bay** and a **campsite**. At the northern end of the bay, striking sea-washed granite columns stand proud. Crossing sandy beaches alternated with rocky headlands covered in regenerating kanuka, the path sticks mostly to the shore, deviating inland briefly before reaching the double bay of **Mutton Cove** and its **campsite**.

Midway along the beach the track divides. While the left-hand track climbs inland, rising above the coast and following an old farm track before dropping down to **Whariwharangi Bay**, the right-hand path continues north along the beach, negotiating the headland that divides Mutton Cove. Following this path to the right, there's a second junction at the far end of the beach. Taking the right-hand fork that breaks out of the forest, edge along a ridge towards the exposed granite headland of **Separation Point**. A steep, crumbling track then drops to a flat area upon which a lighthouse has been built. **Farewell Spit**, the longest sand-spit in New Zealand, extending nearly 30km across Golden Bay in an arc, is visible to the north. Maori myths record that one of the ancient names for New Zealand's South Island was Te Waka o Aoraki, 'Aoraki's Canoe', which is derived from the story of the voyage of Aoraki in which he was caught in a violent storm. His waka, crew and cargo were all turned to stone, in the process creating South Island. The *tau ihu* (prow) of the waka formed Farewell Spit, Golden Bay and Tasman Bay.

Fur seals often congregate here on the warm flat rocks or play exuberantly in the sea just offshore. Most of the seals here are males or juveniles who migrate from breeding colonies further south to spend the winter here. Dolphins and orcas have also been spotted. Gannets fish in the waters off the Point, diving and plunging magnificently. This is a splendid spot to just loiter and gaze at the seascape.

Sidling back along the ridge to the junction, now take the other path and head west for about 30 minutes. The track loops round to rejoin the main Coast Track on the saddle midway between Mutton Cove and Whariwharangi Bay. Descending through regenerating scrubland, follow the track as it zigzags leisurely down to another glorious beach, this one backed by a gentle curve of old macrocarpa trees. It is believed that it was here, or at least in this vicinity, that Abel Tasman (see pp50-1) had his unfortunate, ill-fated encounter with the local Maori in 1642.

At the western end of the beach, a small track leads 500m inland to **Whariwharangi Hut and Campsite**. This unique 20-bunk hut was originally a farmhouse built in 1897 by John Handcock. Later used as a stockman's hut, it eventually fell into disrepair. It was restored from this derelict state and converted into a DOC hut in 1980. It is a superb building with a unique atmosphere, set in a tremendous location. Whariwharangi Beach makes an ideal place to watch the sun set and rise whilst gentle waves proceed in a stately fashion to the golden sands. At night the lighthouse on the end of Farewell Spit can be seen winking in the distant darkness.

## Whariwharangi Hut to Wainui Bay        5.5km/1¹/₂-2¹/₂ hours; Map 5

This final section is a very simple walk out to the car park at Wainui from where connecting shuttle bus services depart.

The track heads into the forest behind Whariwharangi Hut, follows a small stream and climbs inland, out of the bay, to a saddle overlooking Wainui Inlet. This substantial tidal inlet features in Maori mythology. Te Komakahua, the leader of the *kahui tipua*, ogres with magical powers, was forced to separate warring factions within his group. He chose to isolate one of these giant beasts in an east-facing cave in Wainui Inlet. Ngara Huarau became the bane of passing travellers, ambushing and attacking them until finally tricked by a young girl into attending a feast supposedly in his honour. Whilst he slept, the building he rested in was set ablaze and he perished.

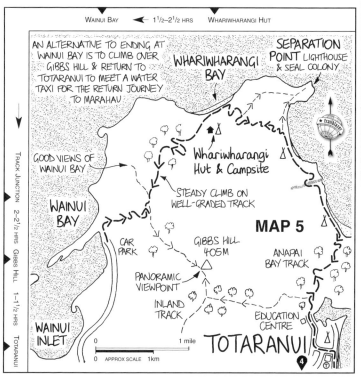

ROUTE GUIDE AND MAPS

There is a junction on the saddle, the left-hand fork of which leads up **Gibbs Hill** (405m/1328ft) and connects with Totaranui. Although this is not part of the Great Walk, it makes for a very satisfying, straightforward loop, allowing you to reach a substantially higher viewpoint before dropping down to the **information centre** at Totaranui, from where it is easy to connect with a water-taxi returning south to Marahau or Kaiteriteri. The trip over the hill takes three or four hours. The Coast Track itself winds down from the saddle, passing over and around gorse-covered ridges that are slowly regenerating from a bushfire in 1978. Arriving at the shoreline, the track bears left along the estuary edge to emerge at the car park 500m later.

# Heaphy Track

*Kia Hora Te Marino, Whakapapa-pounamu Te Moana, Kia Tere Te Karohirohi I mua I Tou huarahi* – 'May the calm be widespread, May the sea glisten like greenstone, May the shimmer of light dance before your path.'  **Maori blessing**

ROUTE GUIDE AND MAPS

## INTRODUCTION

The Heaphy Track is an exceptional 82km tramp in the north-west of South Island. It is the longest Great Walk and probably the most diverse, encompassing the widest range of scenery.

The four- to five-day track follows a historic, scenic highway from the inland forests across a high rolling plateau of alpine scrub to the west coast. The contrast between the luxuriance of the forests and the emptiness of the plateau is striking. Furthermore, the chance to experience the noise and power of the west coast ocean should not be passed up since it is very unusual to be able to walk alongside this stretch of sea. Well-graded and benched, the track is not

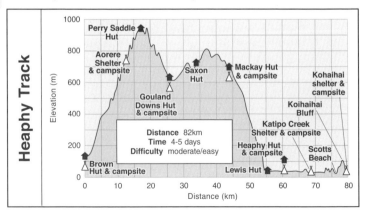

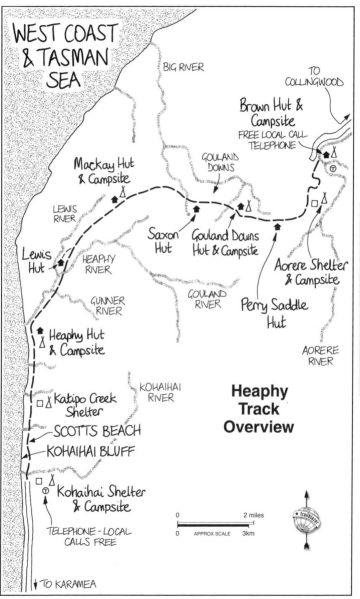

WEST COAST & TASMAN SEA

BIG RIVER

TO COLLINGWOOD

Brown Hut & Campsite
FREE LOCAL CALL TELEPHONE

GOULAND DOWNS

Mackay Hut & Campsite

LEWIS RIVER

Saxon Hut

Gouland Downs Hut & Campsite

Aorere Shelter & Campsite

Lewis Hut

HEAPHY RIVER

GUNNER RIVER

GOULAND RIVER

Perry Saddle Hut

AORERE RIVER

Heaphy Hut & Campsite

KOHAIHAI RIVER

Heaphy Track Overview

Katipo Creek Shelter

SCOTTS BEACH

KOHAIHAI BLUFF

Kohaihai Shelter & Campsite

TELEPHONE - LOCAL CALLS FREE

0        2 miles
0   APPROX SCALE   3km

TO KARAMEA

ROUTE GUIDE AND MAPS

unduly arduous, which means that you are free to focus on your surroundings. It is also varied, inspiring a host of emotions that are likely to linger in the memory, along with the sensation of tramping on sand to the unceasing sound of the surf, long after you have walked off the track.

## HISTORY

Maori occupation of this north-western area of South Island stems from the 16th century, when they arrived in search of food. Moa thrived in the region and formed a significant part of the staple diet for hunter-gatherer tribes. Settlements were established along the coast, usually around river mouths and estuaries. Maori from Golden Bay, to the east, travelled across the central section of South Island to reach the coast in search of *pounamu*, or greenstone, which was highly prized for tools, weapons and jewellery. A second track traversed the empty Gouland Downs from Aorere to the Whakapoai (Heaphy) River, and the Maori also travelled north of the Heaphy River mouth, up the rugged coastline, using flax ladders to negotiate the huge bluffs and cliff faces they encountered.

Early expeditions by European explorers gave way to visits by sealers and prospectors in the early 1800s. The draughtsman Charles Heaphy and a surveyor, Thomas Brunner, explored the west coast as far as the Heaphy River in 1846. Their Maori guide, Kehu, told them of the existence of an inland track. However, Europeans did not traverse this route until 1859 when the gold miner Aldridge crossed it, followed by prospectors James Mackay and John Clark the next year.

The discovery of gold around Karamea inspired a small rush and led to the track across the downs being upgraded to pack-animal standard. John Saxon surveyed the track in 1888 and made further improvements but the failure to uncover large quantities of gold meant that the rush was unsustainable. By 1900 the track had fallen into disrepair and become wildly overgrown. Nevertheless, huts were built at the Heaphy River mouth, Lewis and Gouland Downs in the early part of the 20th century.

The North-West Nelson Forest Park was established in 1965 and the old tracks and trails, the early visitors' only legacy, were uncovered once more. Improvements were made to huts and many of the rivers were bridged in order to increase the track's popularity. The countryside that surrounds the track was listed as a wilderness area in 1989 and in 1995 the Kahurangi National Park was created, incorporating the former North-West Nelson Forest Park. This new protected area is the second largest park in New Zealand after Fiordland.

## GEOLOGY

Kahurangi National Park, which includes the Heaphy Track, is a geologically complex area. Some of New Zealand's oldest rocks can be found here, many of which have been subjected to the shaping processes that moulded the country.

Sedimentary rocks comprise the majority of the park. Formed inside the earth's crust these became exposed after sustained periods of uplift. Glacial erosion shaped most of the mountains in the region and left a series of small hollows, many of which have been filled by lakes. Alongside this belt of rock is a band of igneous material. Pink granite can be seen along the Heaphy Track amidst the usual red-brown soils.

The region is renowned for its unusual downs country. These large rolling downs are remnants of a geological period between two eras of uplift. Unbuckled and still with the original sediment layer on top, these areas provide a distinctly different landscape to those usually experienced on the other Great Walks. Dissected by deep gorges cut by slow meandering streams, they support a host of native vegetation. The powerful ocean off the west coast of South Island has fashioned the rugged shoreline. The spectacular cliffs, rock stacks and exposed bluffs are constantly pounded by these large sculpting waves.

## FLORA AND FAUNA

### Flora

Because of the diverse range of landscapes that the Heaphy Track negotiates, the flora here is very varied. Over half of New Zealand's native plant species live in the region and the remote sections of the track provide refuge for many vulnerable plants that have vanished from more accessible areas.

The steep hill country is covered in soil of low fertility and dominated by beech forest, with red beech giving way to silver and hard beech on the dry, infertile ridges. At the highest points the trees are stunted and blanketed in moss. The soils of the rolling downs country have been steadily leached of nutrients and support only tussock grasses, small shrubs and herb fields. Heather and gorse manage to thrive in the exposed areas. The stunted, sun-bleached skeletons of silver beech trees and manuka dot the landscape. However, some rare and endemic plants do grow here. Beyond the downs, soil fertility improves and a greater variety of vegetation can be seen. Lush podocarp forests thrive where rimu, miro and matai jostle with broadleaf species including rata and kamahi. Supplejack vines straggle earthwards from their high perches whilst smaller shrubs strain towards the light.

As you near the western coast, the climate becomes milder and wetter. Consequently the forests become almost sub-tropical in appearance. Glorious nikau palms make their first appearance here and continue to line the track as it passes along the coast, lending the area a tropical feel. Beneath them a variety of large-leaved plants clump together in order to brace themselves against the relentless wind gusting off the sea.

### Fauna

The remoteness of the region has ensured that a host of wildlife has survived here undisturbed. A wide variety of **birds** thrive here because of the unmodified nature of the forests. Bellbird, tui, weka, fantail, pipit, riflemen, kereru and robin are all widespread. The waterways support most of New Zealand's native freshwater birds and grey and paradise ducks can be found in the larger river valleys while the least accessible streams still support a handful of rare blue ducks. It is also possible, though it's unlikely, that you'll come across morepork, falcon, great-spotted kiwi and rock wren. The coastal area is home to a variety of seabirds. Gulls, terns, oystercatchers, shags, herons and kingfishers can all be found exploiting the rich food resources. The long- and short-tailed bat are both present; the short-tailed species was, for over 30 years, thought to have vanished from here until sightings in 1996 proved otherwise.

**Geckos** and skinks sun themselves on exposed rocks that also support a host of insect and invertebrate fauna. The spectacular carnivorous **land snail**, genus *Powelliphanta*, is here too. Unique to New Zealand, these large colourful snails shelter during the day and emerge at night, usually after rain, to hunt the native giant worms found in the park. Some 20 different species of giant snail are found here, the largest being *Powelliphanta superba prouseorum*, which can be found in the national park, usually in the vicinity of limestone outcrops where they can obtain sufficient calcium to nourish their shells. You are not permitted to remove snails or even their empty shells from the track.

**Introduced animal species** such as red deer, chamois, feral pigs and goats have begun to alter the ecosystem although their numbers are still relatively low. Possums are the worst threat, impacting severely on the growth of rata trees and reducing the numbers of *Powelliphanta* by eating them. The streams and waterways that criss-cross the track are clean and clear, although frequently tea-coloured due to the tannins washed out of the forest soils. Free from the predatory, introduced trout, they are a haven for **eels** and **native fish species**.

## PLANNING YOUR TRAMP

### When to go

The west coast of New Zealand is prone to heavy rainfall, which can occur at short notice and with devastating effect. The predominantly westerly winds bring heavy rain off the sea. Up to 5000mm per year falls on the western reaches of the track and all the rivers are fed by the run-off from the higher ground. These small streams can easily flood during periods of prolonged rainfall. Likewise, Gouland Downs can become boggy and marshy after sustained rain.

The downs are highly exposed areas and are frequently subjected to cold winds and thick fog, making them a treacherous proposition. It is relatively easy to get lost here in adverse conditions since there are no obvious landmarks by which to navigate. Snow and frost can linger in the river gorges for long periods. Snow may fall across the track, even at lower altitudes. Nonetheless, the track can be walked at any time of year. Numbers are heaviest from Christmas to late January, so the ideal time to come is **mid-February through March**, when the weather ought to be a little more stable and the track slightly quieter.

Make sure that you are properly equipped with warm and waterproof clothing. Except during the summer, it may be wise to carry a tent as a back-up.

### Sources of information

As for all Great Walks, the relevant **DOC offices** are armed with the most up-to-date information and staffed by genuine enthusiasts who can help to advise, plan and book. They will also be able to sell you the appropriate maps and pamphlets. There is a DOC office in the official Kahurangi National Park Visitor Centre in Motueka (see p179). However, it is probably more convenient for most people to book through the DOC counter in Nelson i-SITE Visitor Information Centre (see p179) or at the i-SITE Centre in Takaka (see p179). The DOC office (☎ 03-782 6852) in Karamea at 82 Waverley St is not always staffed.

On the western side of the track the **information centres** in Karamea and Westport can also book all huts or campsites and supply mapping. Karamea Visitor Information Centre (☎/🖹 03-782 6652, 🖳 www.karameainfo.co.nz, PO Box 94) is on Market Cross. Westport i-SITE (☎ 03-789 6658, 🖳 www.west port.org.nz) can be found at 1 Brougham St.

## Getting to the trailhead

The Heaphy Track is remote. Because of the rugged terrain and the fact that the track is a long line rather than a circuit, reaching the trail is slightly problematic. The start and finish of the track are in fact more than 460km apart by road. The eastern end of the track is 35km from Collingwood (see p200), the western end 16km from Karamea (see p200). Although there are car parks at either end at which you can leave your vehicle, you still have the problem of collecting it at the end of the tramp. However, should you wish to take your own transport and leave it at one of the car parks, it is possible to fly from one end of the track to the other. There are airstrips at Karamea and Takaka, from where it is easy to connect with the car parks at the track's ends. The flight above Kahurangi National Park is an exciting hop over some outstanding landscapes and a memorable way to start or conclude your tramp. Check out Remote Adventures Air Transport (☎ 03-525 6167, 🖳 www.remoteadventures.co.nz) or Abel Tasman Air (☎ 03-528 8290, 🖳 info@abeltasmanair.co.nz) for further details.

Public transport options are available at both ends of the track. The **eastern end** is best accessed either from Collingwood or from Nelson via Motueka and Takaka. The Original Farewell Spit Safari outfit (☎ 0800-802 257) has a regular morning shuttle service from Collingwood to the start of the track. Abel Tasman Coachlines (☎ 03-548 0285) and Golden Bay Coachlines (☎ 03-525 8352, 🖳 www .gbcoachlines.co.nz) operate daily services from Nelson, which stop in Motueka, Takaka and Collingwood before arriving at the trailhead. The Heaphy Bus Co Ltd (☎ 03-540 2042, 🖳 www.theheaphybus.co.nz) operates an on-demand service to either end of the track. Note that the approach road to the eastern end of the track fords three small creeks just before the car park. After heavy or prolonged periods of rain these creeks swell considerably and may become impassable, preventing access. Adjacent to the trailhead there is a DOC hut, Brown Hut, which has a telephone (local calls are free) if you want to ring for a shuttle or taxi.

The **western end** of the track also has a shelter and telephone from which you can summon a shuttle bus or taxi at the end of your tramp. Local calls are again free. Karamea Express (☎ 03-782 6757, 🖳 info@karamea-express.co.nz) operates a daily pick-up service between the track end and Karamea. There are regular buses from Karamea to Westport, from where connecting services run to Nelson and other larger towns.

ROUTE GUIDE AND MAPS

## Local services

The best place to organise your tramp in advance is **Nelson** (see pp181-2). The closest towns to either end of the track are Collingwood to the north-east and Karamea to the south. **Collingwood** is a scenic town perched on its own peninsula. It is the access point to Farewell Spit and is used to trampers passing through. There are food stores, a petrol station and medical facilities and some accommodation. *Motor Camp* (☎ 03-524 8149; tent pitch NZ$16, hut NZ$28, cabin NZ$60) on William St is friendly enough, while the tidy *Beachcomber Motel* (☎ 03-524 8499, 🖳 goldenbaybeds@xtra.co.nz; dbl NZ$100-150) on Tasman St and the compact, under-stated *Somerset House* (☎ 03-524 8624, 🖳 www.backpackerscollingwood.co.nz; dorm NZ$29, sgl/dbl NZ$45/70) at 10 Gibbs Rd are good alternatives. For **food**, *Collingwood Café* has snacks and other simple meals for NZ$10-20, *Collingwood Tavern and Bistro* is also reasonable, while *Courthouse Café* in the town's 1901 court building has an imaginative and good-value menu serving up mainly organic staples.

**Karamea** is the northernmost town on the west coast, set on the narrow floodplain of the Karamea River. Originally a campsite for miners and prospectors searching for gold, it is now a quiet, end-of-the-road town. There is a small food store and a petrol station. *The Last Resort* (☎ 03-782 6617, 🖳 www.last resort.co.nz; tent pitch NZ$24, dorm NZ$28, dbl NZ$75-105, studio NZ$125, cottage NZ$150) on Waverley St/SH67 is an attractive, sprawling hotel that includes a large restaurant and bar. Dorms and shared rooms are fairly priced. On the same road, *Rongo Backpackers* (☎ 03-782 6667, 🖳 www.rongoback packers.com; tent pitch NZ$25, dorm NZ$27-30, dbl or twin NZ$76) is a very laid-back, easy-going place with green credentials, an artistic bent, attractive gardens and its own community radio station.

A little south of the centre are the *Bridge Farm Motel* units (☎ 0800-527 263, 🖳 www.karameamotels.co.nz; dbl NZ$100-140), set on an alpaca farm. *Karamea Village Hotel* (☎ 03-782 6800, 🖳 karameahotel@xtra.co.nz; motel unit NZ$95-105), on the corner of Waverly St and Wharf Rd, is reasonable and has most mod-cons, while *Karamea Memorial Domain* (☎ 03-782 6719; tent pitch NZ$14, dorm NZ$10) has a basic campsite. Around 15 minutes' drive south of Karamea is the *Wangapeka Backpackers Retreat and Farmstay* (☎ 03-782 6663, 🖳 www.wangapeka.co.nz; tent pitch NZ$8 per person, dorm NZ$20, sgl/dbl NZ$40/65) on the Atawhai Farm, set in 30 acres of bush adjacent to the Little Wanganui River, which makes for a relaxing place to recharge after the tramp. Aside from self-catering you can sign up for breakfast and dinner for a further NZ$15.

For **food** in Karamea, try *Saracens Café* opposite the visitor centre for snacks, pies and sandwiches; otherwise a good bet is the cheap bar menu at *Karamea Village Hotel*, whilst for slightly more formal fare drop in on the restaurant at the *Last Resort*.

## Huts and campsites

Those wishing to stay in one of the track's seven **huts** will require a **Great Walks pass**, which can be purchased from DOC offices and information centres in the north-west of South Island. The summer season runs from early October to the end of April and is marginally more expensive than at other times of the year. Failure to pre-purchase a pass will result in you being charged a higher premium on the spot.

The **adult hut fee** in the summer season is NZ$25 and for the rest of the year NZ$15. The **camping fees** are NZ$12.50 and NZ$8 respectively. Children and youth are free.

Brown Hut is located right at the start of the track. Perry Saddle, Gouland Downs, Saxon, Mackay, Lewis and Heaphy huts are stretched out along the track. All are equipped with bunks and mattresses, toilet facilities, wood stoves for heating and a water supply. The majority also have gas-cooking stoves, the exceptions being the Brown and Gouland Downs huts. Consequently, it is best to carry a portable stove to ensure that you have the maximum flexibility in terms of where you choose to stay. There may be a warden on duty at some of the huts during the summer season to check hut passes and advise you as to the following day's weather conditions. There is a two-night maximum stay in each hut.

**Camping** is allowed at designated sites along the track. There are campsites by Brown Hut, Aorere Shelter, Gouland Downs, Mackay, Heaphy, Katipo Creek Shelter and Kohaihai Shelter. A camp pass can be upgraded to a hut pass after 6pm if space is available in the relevant hut and the price difference is paid.

## Maps

Unfortunately the best map, the *Heaphy Trackmap* (245) that showed the route at 1:63,360 scale, is out of print and you will be very lucky indeed to find it. Fortunately, *Kahurangi Parkmap* (274–13) is more than adequate. It covers the area that includes the track at 1:150,000 scale and is available at DOC offices and information centres in the region. Topomaps' *Cobb* (M26) and *Heaphy* (L26) also provide coverage of the track and can be purchased in the same places.

## Distances and times

The well-graded track is usually walked from east to west, although it's possible to do it in reverse. Relatively easy, it is a little longer than the other Great Walks which may come as a slightly unpleasant surprise to inexperienced trampers. By walking east to west you enjoy the forested sections first whilst climbing to Perry Saddle. With the majority of climbing behind you, you can then truly savour the unusual landscapes of the expansive downs and the rugged coastline. Walking along these magnificent beaches and watching the vibrant sunsets at the mouth of the broad Heaphy River make for a stunning conclusion.

If you do walk from west to east, allow extra time for the ascent from Lewis to Mackay huts and less for the descent from Perry Saddle to Brown huts.

| | | |
|---|---|---|
| Brown Hut to Perry Saddle Hut | 17km | 5-6 hours |
| Perry Saddle Hut to Saxon Hut | 13km | 3-4 hours |
| Saxon Hut to Mackay Hut | 14km | 3-4 hours |
| Mackay Hut to Lewis Hut | 13.5km | 3-4 hours |
| Lewis Hut to Heaphy Hut | 8km | 2-3 hours |
| Heaphy Hut to Kohaihai Shelter | 16.5km | $4^1/_2$-$5^1/_2$ hours |

ROUTE GUIDE AND MAPS

## TRACK DESCRIPTION

### Brown Hut to Perry Saddle Hut                    17km/5-6 hours; Map 1

The first stage begins with an ascent to Perry Saddle and includes the highest point on the track. It is a steady but not especially steep climb through lush forest that occasionally gives way to offer you excellent views.

Adjacent to the car park at the trailhead is **Brown Hut**. This 16-bunk hut was built for people who have travelled a long distance, allowing them to rest overnight before setting off early the following day. By staying here you also make sure that you are on the track before the hordes on the shuttle buses from Nelson and Collingwood arrive.

The track passes alongside the hut and follows **Brown River** upstream for almost 200m before crossing it via a footbridge. Marker poles indicate the direction across a grass flat before the track dives into the forest and begins the slow slog up to **Perry Saddle**. A series of switchbacks lifts you rapidly into the mountains. Originally constructed as a packhorse track in 1893, the trail is broad and level. Climbing over a small spur, there are views down to the Aorere Valley.

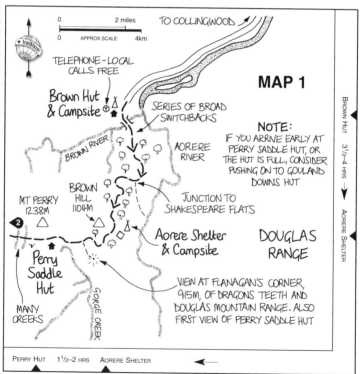

**ROUTE GUIDE AND MAPS**

★ trailblazer

0 ____ 2 miles
0 ____ APPROX SCALE ____ 4km

TO COLLINGWOOD ↗

TELEPHONE – LOCAL CALLS FREE

Brown Hut & Campsite ☎ ⌂ ▲

SERIES OF BROAD SWITCHBACKS

**MAP 1**

BROWN RIVER

AORERE RIVER

**NOTE:**
IF YOU ARRIVE EARLY AT PERRY SADDLE HUT, OR THE HUT IS FULL, CONSIDER PUSHING ON TO GOULAND DOWNS HUT

BROWN HILL 1104M

MT PERRY 1238M ▲

JUNCTION TO SHAKESPEARE FLATS

Aorere Shelter & Campsite

**2**

Perry Saddle Hut

DOUGLAS RANGE

MANY CREEKS

GORGE CREEK

VIEW AT FLANAGAN'S CORNER, 915M, OF DRAGONS TEETH AND DOUGLAS MOUNTAIN RANGE. ALSO FIRST VIEW OF PERRY SADDLE HUT

BROWN HUT  3½-4 HRS →  AORERE SHELTER

PERRY HUT  1½-2 HRS  AORERE SHELTER  ←

The track continues evenly, arriving after 1¹/₂ hours at a signposted junction. The left fork descends to the Shakespeare Flats, but take the right fork and continue to climb through the rich forest of rimu, miro and beech trees. After a further two hours or more you'll reach **Aorere Shelter and Campsite**, set in a clearing surrounded by cabbage trees. This emergency shelter has a benched sleeping area and water supply and views of the Aorere Valley stretching north. Beyond the shelter, the track continues to climb but now at a gentler gradient.

Three kilometres later it forks again. A short scramble up to the left takes you to the rocky promontory of **Flanagan's Corner** (915m/3001ft), the highest point on the track from where you can see the jagged Douglas Range and Mt Olympus (1519m/4982ft). It is also possible to see Perry Saddle Hut, your next destination, to the west, perched on the grassy saddle several kilometres away.

The right fork, meanwhile, descends slightly for the next 2km before emerging on a grassy, tussock-clad saddle. The 24-bunk **Perry Saddle Hut** is here, with glorious views of the Dragon's Teeth on the Douglas Range. Nearby is the deep, clear **Gorge Creek** which, though cold, is a popular place for swimming. If you arrive early at the hut you may fancy pushing on to the much quieter, atmospheric Gouland Downs Hut, 1¹/₂-2 hours beyond Perry Saddle.

### Perry Saddle Hut to Saxon Hut          13km/3-4 hours; Map 2

The landscape changes entirely on this stage. Leaving the forest, the track ambles across a series of vast rolling downs, circumnavigating deep stream-gouged trenches. It is an attractive, exposed area that can be quite eerie at times but which provides a fascinating contrast to the track's other landscapes.

Cutting across Perry Saddle and along **Perry Creek** through beech dominated forest, you climb a slight rise and, cresting this ridge, the whole character of the track changes. The forest gives way to the vast alpine basin of **Gouland Downs** stretching away to the west. The track coils through grasses, gorse, herb fields and the skeletal remains of weather-worn stunted beech trees. If you arrive here sufficiently early, a discernible blue haze and low mist often cloak the downs, exaggerating their 'otherworldliness'. The track crosses Fawn, Quintina and then Sheep creeks as it winds across Gouland Downs. You get your first tantalising glimpse of Gouland Downs Hut, almost invisible in this vast emptiness, after an hour. Having passed the famed pole to which trampers tie old boots, the track doubles back on itself and approaches the hut.

The track descends and crosses the gorge created by **Cave Brook** before climbing to 10-bunk **Gouland Downs Hut**, built in 1936 and retaining much of its venerable character, with a large open fireplace making it particularly cosy. Just beyond the hut is an area of limestone karst landscape that has been eroded by rain into caves. If exploring the area, watch out for hidden potholes. The quiet downs come alive at night, when morepork and kiwi calls can be heard and weka are frequently spotted.

The track beyond the hut continues west through a small patch of beech forest, emerging once more into the open to traverse the northern section of the downs. It descends gently as it crosses Shiner Brook, Big River and Weka Creek as they curl aimlessly across the landscape before plunging to the Tasman Sea.

It is possible to ford these streams but should they be swollen after heavy rainfall, swing bridges are provided. The downs have the potential to become marshy after protracted rains and low cloud or mist makes them treacherous as there are no obvious landmarks by which to navigate.

After **Weka Creek**, the track climbs slightly and there are good views back across the downs to Perry Saddle. Skirting along and occasionally beyond the treeline, the track climbs gently before arriving at **Saxon Hut**, nestling on the edge of the downs. This 16-bunk hut is the newest on the track. Named after the surveyor John Saxon, it is a hospitable place to stay.

## Saxon Hut to Mackay Hut                    14km/3-4 hours; Map 2

This short, easy day's tramp acts as a transition from the inland section of the trail to the west coast. Crossing the last of the downs you finish poised above the descent to the coast, with outstanding views beyond to the broad Heaphy River mouth and raging Tasman Sea.

The track starts by heading west, dropping slightly to the **Saxon River flats**. In wet weather this section can become very boggy and difficult and you should wait for the high waters to recede. Beyond, the track crosses **Blue Duck Creek** before climbing 100m on a broad ridge. The trail passes beneath Mt Teddy (870m/2854ft) and at the top of the ridge passes into **Mackay Downs**.

Crossing first **Blue Shirt Creek** then **Monument Creek**, you hug the edge of the downs amongst patches of scrub. Short sections of boardwalk lead you across the potentially muddy southern end of the downs until shortly afterwards the geology of the region changes and the soil underfoot becomes firmer, granite-based bedrock. Crossing **Deception Creek** you climb slightly to arrive at **Mackay Hut**, perched on a knoll above the track. From the 26-bunk hut you can look down on the descent that follows and can see the Tasman Sea for the first time, 15km to the south-west and 750m below you. Named after the explorer James Mackay, who first pushed for the creation of a bridle track linking Collingwood and the coast, this is a lovely hut. Lounging on the deck area you can watch the sunset slip into the sea before the night time calls of morepork and kiwi begin to reverberate across the nearby downs.

## Mackay Hut to Heaphy Hut                  21.5km/5-7 hours; Map 3

This is a longish day, although much of it is downhill. The landscape changes once again as you turn your back on the downs, descend through thick forest and emerge on the rugged west coast where nikau palms and white-sand beaches give the area a tropical feel.

From the hut, the track turns south-west and begins its gradual descent to the coast. Beech forest gives way to a denser, more verdant version, full of large-leaved plants. The track edges along the hillside with steep drops tumbling to one side, forested slopes looming on the other and frequent, tantalising glimpses of the increasingly broad **Heaphy River** through the trees. The track drops more than 600m over 12km before it levels out at the confluence of the Heaphy and smaller Lewis rivers. The 20-bunk **Lewis Hut** is located down a side trail adjacent to the two rivers. Named after the surveyor Charles Lewis, it is a pleasant spot although plagued by sandflies.

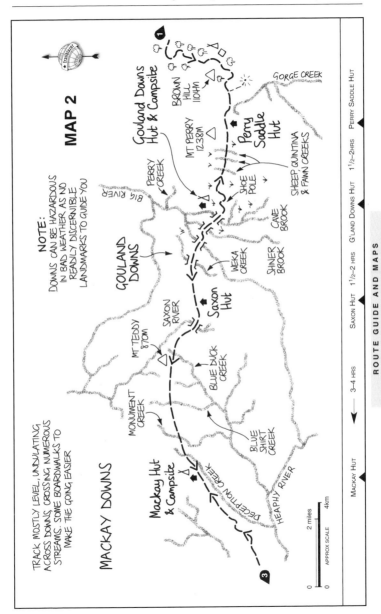

MAP 2

NOTE:

DOWNS CAN BE HAZARDOUS IN BAD WEATHER AS NO READILY DISCERNIBLE LANDMARKS TO GUIDE YOU

TRACK MOSTLY LEVEL, UNDULATING ACROSS DOWNS, CROSSING NUMEROUS STREAMS. SOME BOARDWALKS TO MAKE THE GOING EASIER.

MACKAY DOWNS

GOULAND DOWNS

Gouland Downs Hut & Campsite

Mackay Hut & Campsite

Monument Creek

Mt Teddy 870M

Blue Duck Creek

Blue Shirt Creek

Heaphy River

Deception Creek

Saxon Hut

Saxon River

Weka Creek

Shiner Brook

Cave Brook

Perry Creek

Big River

Mt Perry 1238M

Brown Hill 1104M

Gorge Creek

Perry Saddle Hut

Shoe Pole

Sheep Quintia & Fawn Creeks

① ③

2 miles

4km

APPROX SCALE

ROUTE GUIDE AND MAPS

| MACKAY HUT | 3-4 HRS | SAXON HUT | 1½-2 HRS | G'LAND DOWNS HUT | 1½-2HRS | PERRY SADDLE HUT |

The track climbs beyond the hut over a forested ridge above the Lewis River. Crossing on a large swing bridge, shortly afterwards the track arrives at a second large swing bridge spanning the Heaphy. Immediately on the other side, the flora changes noticeably. Nikau palms, New Zealand's only palm tree and a distinctive feature of the west coast, make their first appearance. The vegetation in general becomes denser and more lush with climbing and perching plants sitting high on the trunks of taller trees, straining for the sunlight and benefitting from the nutrients in the leaf litter collected in the branches.

The river itself is usually sluggish, particularly as it nears the sea and widens further. The track sticks to the river's edge, sidling along it through delightful avenues of nikau palms and tree ferns. After 3km it crosses **Gunner River** and then a short while later **Murray Creek**, both by swing bridge. Continuing south-west, boarded on the one side by the river and on the other by the forested limestone cliffs, you pass a sandy flat and approach the **Heaphy Lagoon**, skirting a steep outcrop to emerge at an open grassy area alongside the **Heaphy Hut**. This magnificent 30-bunk hut is perfectly located: back from the shore, adjacent to the Heaphy River mouth and surrounded by nikau palms and forest. Ahead is a curved sandy spit that forms the sheltered lagoon, beyond which the waves of the Tasman Sea rush the beach in a mad babble. The frequently strong winds whip the wave tops into a veil of spray and the crashing of the waves creates a continuous roar. The beach is littered with flotsam and jetsam as well as wave-stripped driftwood and makes for an interesting stroll. Mussels abound on the rocky headlands and can easily be gathered to supplement a final supper. Swimming in the sea, however, is neither wise nor recommended since it is powerful and there is a very strong undertow. Instead, the sheltered lagoon and Heaphy River, though cold, make ideal swimming spots.

Sandflies can be a problem here, particularly in the early evening, but shouldn't distract you from watching the sunset or strolling aimlessly along the vast empty beach at dusk. The hut is in fact situated adjacent to the remains of one of New Zealand's oldest archaeological sites: the nearby bank of the Heaphy River was once a 13th- or 14th-century village. Unfortunately two thirds of the site has now eroded and been reclaimed by the river.

### Heaphy Hut to Kohaihai Shelter 16.5km/4¹/₂-5¹/₂ hours; Map 4

This final section is one of the most stunning sections of tramping on the Heaphy Track, no matter what the weather. The track hugs the shore, frequently deviating onto the beach. Mostly level, it provides little physical challenge, thus allowing you to fully immerse yourself in the raw beauty of the coast as it is pounded and shaped by the waves. When the weather is bad or stormy, the beaches become covered in a frothy foam and the waves align in huge sets before rushing the beach. In warmer, sunnier conditions it feels akin to a tropical island. Before setting out from Heaphy Hut, take note of the high-tide times posted in the hut by the warden, since the sea level will determine which track you take when crossing Crayfish Point later in the day.

The track begins by heading south from the hut. The river mouth here is at the junction of two ancient greenstone trails. The site has been variously

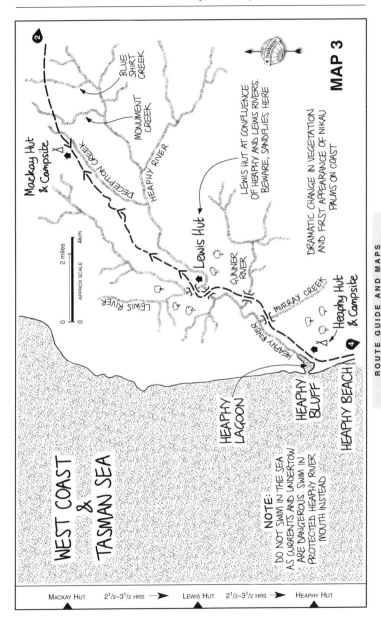

MAP 3

BLUE SHIRT CREEK

MONUMENT CREEK

HEAPHY RIVER

DECEPTION CREEK

Mackay Hut & Campsite

APPROX SCALE
0 — 2 miles
0 — 4km

LEWIS RIVER

Lewis Hut

GUNNER RIVER

LEWIS HUT AT CONFLUENCE OF HEAPHY AND LEWIS RIVERS. BEWARE, SANDFLIES HERE

DRAMATIC CHANGE IN VEGETATION AND FIRST APPEARANCE OF NIKAU PALMS ON COAST

MURRAY CREEK

HEAPHY RIVER

Heaphy Hut & Campsite

HEAPHY LAGOON

HEAPHY BLUFF

HEAPHY BEACH

WEST COAST & TASMAN SEA

NOTE:
DO NOT SWIM IN THE SEA AS CURRENTS AND UNDERTOW ARE DANGEROUS. SWIM IN PROTECTED HEAPHY RIVER MOUTH INSTEAD

MACKAY HUT  2½–3½ HRS →  LEWIS HUT  2½–3½ HRS →  HEAPHY HUT

occupied for more than 500 years and is still considered sacred by local Maori. Ahead of the hut, the track passes into the forest for 1km before crossing **Cold Creek** and regaining the shoreline. The track runs alongside the beach beneath a series of hills that sweep down to the shore. Most people opt to walk on the beach, fringed by hardy, salt-tolerant plants, and there are several access points readily visible.

You now pass along **Twenty Minute Beach** before re-entering the bush, only to emerge shortly after on **Nettle Beach**. From here the track cuts inland slightly to round **Mid Point**. It then crosses **Katipo Creek**, named after New Zealand's only poisonous insect, the extremely rare katipo spider, on a long swing bridge and passes **Katipo Creek Shelter and Campsite**. This basic

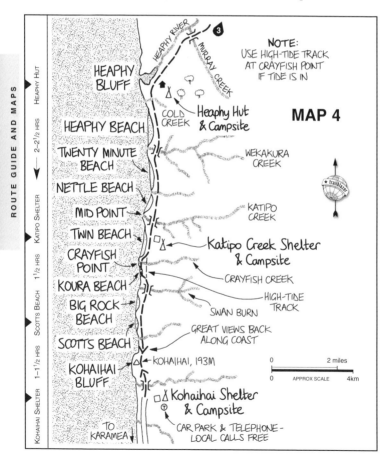

ROUTE GUIDE AND MAPS

HEAPHY HUT — 2-2½ HRS — KATIPO SHELTER — 1½ HRS — SCOTTS BEACH — 1-1½ HRS — KOHAIHAI SHELTER

HEAPHY BLUFF

HEAPHY BEACH

TWENTY MINUTE BEACH

NETTLE BEACH

MID POINT

TWIN BEACH

CRAYFISH POINT

KOURA BEACH

BIG ROCK BEACH

SCOTTS BEACH

KOHAIHAI BLUFF

HEAPHY RIVER
MURRAY CREEK

NOTE:
USE HIGH-TIDE TRACK
AT CRAYFISH POINT
IF TIDE IS IN

COLD CREEK
Heaphy Hut & Campsite

MAP 4

WEKAKURA CREEK

★ trailblazer

KATIPO CREEK

Katipo Creek Shelter & Campsite

CRAYFISH CREEK

HIGH-TIDE TRACK

SWAN BURN

GREAT VIEWS BACK ALONG COAST

KOHAIHAI, 193M

0        2 miles
0   APPROX SCALE   4km

Kohaihai Shelter & Campsite

CAR PARK & TELEPHONE - LOCAL CALLS FREE

TO KARAMEA

structure marks the halfway point between Heaphy Hut and Kohaihai Shelter. The track returns to the shore at **Twin Beach**, which is actually two beaches separated by a rocky headland.

At the far end of the second one you cross Crayfish Creek and arrive at **Crayfish Point**. At high tide it is essential that you use the safe high-water track to cross the Point. This had become overgrown and virtually impassable but should be cleared and in use again by the time you read this. The sea here is particularly dangerous and the rocky scramble around the Point should be undertaken only two hours either side of low tide.

Beyond Crayfish Point the track leaves the shore briefly, climbing above **Koura Beach**, over **Swan Burn** and past **Big Rock Beach**, dropping once more to the sea and **Scotts Beach** after 3km. There is a picnic area and campsite here and it makes a pleasant place to loiter if you are ahead of schedule to meet your shuttle bus.

The final section of the tramp begins with a steady climb, rising 100m over the low **Kohaihai Saddle**. At the top of the saddle a side path scrambles to a superb lookout point with views back along the beaches and headlands. Ahead, the track descends from Kohaihai Bluff, winding down to the walk's end. A final swing bridge over Kohaihai River deposits you at the **Kohaihai Shelter** and car park where a public phone can be used to summon an on-demand shuttle bus, in case you did not book one or have been so distracted by the highlights of the track that you missed your pre-arranged rendezvous.

❖

# Routeburn Track

*The Harris Saddle was worth the long climb for the sight of the panorama of summits to the west, a succession of mile-high mountains – Christina, Sabre, Gifford, Te Wera, and Madeline. I could not imagine mountains packed more tightly than this – a whole ocean of whitened peaks, like an arctic sea.*          **Paul Theroux**, *The Happy Isles of Oceania*

## INTRODUCTION

New Zealand's second most popular Great Walk, the Routeburn Track is for many people the country's finest multi-day tramp. South-west New Zealand is one of the great remaining wildernesses of the Southern Hemisphere. The Maori referred to it as Te Wahipounamu, 'The Place of Greenstone'.

The track comprises a moderately difficult 33km high-mountain traverse that links Fiordland and Mount Aspiring national parks, two of New Zealand's largest, least altered natural places. It is usually tramped in two to three days. Popular in summer, in winter it becomes hazardous and impassable. Full of magnificent walking country on tracks that combine dense forest, grassy river flats and vast exposed mountain slopes, the Routeburn epitomises the region's tranquility and grandeur.

## HISTORY

Before the arrival of European explorers, the Routeburn Track was used by the southern Maori as a link to the sources of *pounamu*, or greenstone, which was highly valued for its beauty and as a raw material for tools, weapons and ornaments. Since the most greenstone was to be found on the west coast, this track became a link between the inland settlements by Lake Whakatipu and the Hollyford Valley to the west.

European explorers also came to recognise the importance of this track as an access route. In 1860 the explorers Cameron, McGregor and Foote reached the headwaters of the North Branch of the Routeburn whilst searching for a passage to the coast. The prospector Patrick Caples later reached and christened Lake Harris and the Harris Saddle, both named after the then Superintendent of Otago, John Hyde Harris. In 1861 runholders David McKellar and George Gunn travelled up the Greenstone Valley and climbed Key Summit, in so doing becoming the first Europeans to see the Hollyford Valley. Other surveyors, prospectors and explorers followed using this route.

These explorations led to the proposal of a track linking Queenstown and the west coast as early as 1863. However, it was deemed too difficult and the project was abandoned. The lack of any real funds stymied any attempts to breach the Harris Saddle by more than the lightest trail.

During the 1870s work began to cut a track from the new pioneering settlement at Martin's Bay to Lake Whakatipu. However, poor funding, incorrect routing and other delays led to the demise of this venture. The small, isolated settlement at Martin's Bay subsequently faltered and was abandoned.

Ironically, during the 1880s the Routeburn became fêted for its tourist potential. Visitors were carried on horseback to the Routeburn Flats and then guided on foot onto Harris Saddle. In 1909 the tourist department allocated funds for the development of the track and the creation of two bridges. Four years later the Public Works Department began construction on the track,

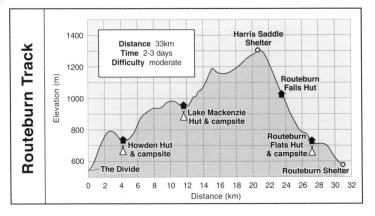

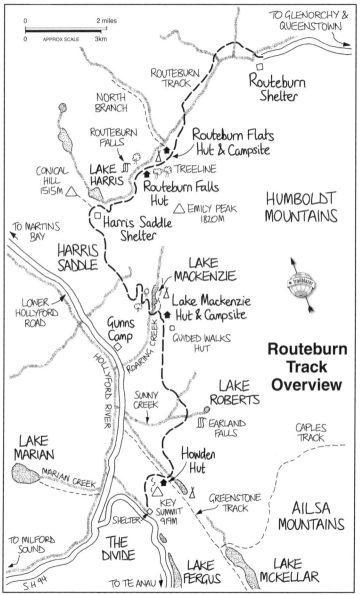

TO GLENORCHY &
QUEENSTOWN

0   2 miles
0   APPROX SCALE   3km

ROUTEBURN
TRACK

Routeburn
Shelter

NORTH
BRANCH

ROUTEBURN
FALLS

Routeburn Flats
Hut & Campsite

CONICAL
HILL
1515M

LAKE
HARRIS

TREELINE

Routeburn Falls
Hut

EMILY PEAK
1820M

HUMBOLDT
MOUNTAINS

Harris Saddle
Shelter

TO MARTINS
BAY

HARRIS
SADDLE

LAKE
MACKENZIE

LOWER
HOLLYFORD
ROAD

Gunns
Camp

Lake Mackenzie
Hut & Campsite

GUIDED WALKS
HUT

ROARING CREEK

HOLLYFORD RIVER

SUNNY
CREEK

LAKE
ROBERTS

Routeburn
Track
Overview

CAPLES
TRACK

LAKE
MARIAN

MARIAN CREEK

EARLAND
FALLS

Howden
Hut

GREENSTONE
TRACK

AILSA
MOUNTAINS

TO MILFORD
SOUND

SHELTER

THE
DIVIDE

KEY
SUMMIT
919M

SH 94

TO TE ANAU

LAKE
FERGUS

LAKE
MCKELLAR

trailblazer

ROUTE GUIDE AND MAPS

employing two gangs to work from either end simultaneously, using wheelbarrows, picks and shovels. World War I interrupted the programme; work was not resumed until the 1960s with the manufacture of several huts, all since replaced. In 1992 the new Harris Saddle Shelter was built and work was done to realign the tracks over Harris Saddle in order to minimise environmental damage.

In January 1994 massive floods destroyed all the river bridges between the Routeburn Falls Hut and the Glenorchy road end. Huge landslips caused by the sustained wet weather destroyed hundreds of metres of track. These scars on the landscape are still visible although the path has since been repaired.

## GEOLOGY

The Routeburn Track offers you a chance to witness a landscape in the aftermath of an ice age. Traversing two spectacular glacier-sculpted sandstone mountain ranges, it winds between the formidable granite peaks of Fiordland's Darran Mountains and the crumbling schist ranges of Mount Aspiring National Park. The narrow valley of the Hollyford River is a major topographic boundary and one of the most dramatic in New Zealand. The fault separates the hard igneous rocks of Fiordland from the schist and sandstone of north-west Otago.

The features in the region are predominantly of glacial origin. During the last ice age, which ended some 10,000 years ago, huge glaciers carved out the metamorphic and sedimentary rocks. The vast Hollyford Glacier covered the main divide at Key Summit, so named because it stands at the apex of three rivers, the Hollyford, Eglinton and Greenstone. The glacier stretched from Martin's Bay 50km south around the southern Darran Mountains into the Greenstone and Eglinton valleys. When the glaciers retreated they left their distinctive imprint on the landscape: deep U-shaped valleys, smaller hanging valleys, lake-filled cirque basins and sharp ridges, all easily distinguishable along the track.

Although there are no longer any glaciers left in this part of the Humboldt Mountains, they can still be seen from the track. The Donne Glacier high on the slopes of Mt Tutoko and others on Mt Madeline are visible on the adjacent Darran Mountains. These are the southernmost glaciers in New Zealand.

The legacy of the glaciers is apparent in the smooth rock faces and stripped surfaces of the mountains, most evident near to the sandstone outcrops around the Routeburn Falls Hut. The parallel striations scratched into the surface by harder rock being dragged over them by the moving ice are clearly visible.

## FLORA AND FAUNA

### Flora
The track is highly forested. Red beech is evident at lower altitudes in the Routeburn Valley. Mountain beech occurs everywhere, particularly at higher altitudes around Routeburn Falls and Lake Mackenzie, whilst silver beech is more common on the wetter, Hollyford Valley side of the track. The understorey of the forest is made up of broadleaf, fuchsia, coprosma and flax. The ubiquitous mosses and lichens also prevail here.

Above the treeline, between Lake Mackenzie and Routeburn Falls Hut, the vegetation switches to a colourful and contrasting array of sub-alpine shrublands, meadows and herb fields. The Harris Basin is home to a variety of flowering plants including daisies and buttercups, which in summer are wonderfully vibrant and scented. The white and yellow flowers of tree daisies form a spectacular display. Various buttercup species also have bright yellow or white flowers. The flowering occurs between November and February. In contrast the 'pineapple' shrub has drooping red fronds. In the Harris Basin, where the soils are deeper, the ground is densely packed with plants that include shrubs and ground-hugging species. Mountain ribbonwood, one of New Zealand's few deciduous trees, can be found in the gulleys. It is also evident in natural clearings such as The Orchard and amongst regenerating vegetation re-colonising avalanche paths.

In the bog areas and wet hollows, particularly around Key Summit, the plants tend to be smaller but no less colourful. Sundew, bladderworts, orchids and daisies all thrive around the tarns. White caltha, a creeping herb with star-shaped, strongly scented flowers, comes into bloom just as the snow melts. The native forget-me-not is one of the most attractive plants of the sub-alpine zone, its flowers ranging in colour from chocolate to lemon.

Ground-hugging cushion plants, adapted for cold, wet and windy conditions, inhabit higher or less-favourable sites.

### Fauna

The varied flora and different habitats allow for a wide range of **bird species**. The most common birds are the native grey warbler, chaffinch and riflemen. Sparrows, thrush, tui, fantail and bellbird are also evident throughout the forest. Small flocks of brown creeper and tomtit may make excursions above the treeline into the sub-alpine shrubland, where pipits are also fairly common.

In the sub-alpine zone, kea inhabit the headwaters of the valleys in order to take advantage of the berries and invertebrate fauna that make up their diet. Their abrasive, almost callous call echoing around bluffs and cirques is a feature of this section of the track. New Zealand falcons often hunt here too. The only true alpine species is the rock wren, found on bluffs and boulder-strewn slopes above 1200m. You may be lucky enough to spot the rare blue duck alongside the fast-flowing upper reaches of the Routeburn.

**Red deer** and **chamois**, introduced as sporting game, live throughout the mountains. The goat-sized chamois, from Austria, was introduced in 1907, whilst red deer from British stock were released between 1851 and 1914. Their browsing has had a negative impact on the forest. Hunting and recreational deer stalking is allowed but a permit must be secured before entering the park.

The region supports a rich diversity of **insects** including moths, grasshoppers and crickets. These alpine insects tend to be darker and larger than their lowland counterparts.

Introduced brown and rainbow **trout** can be found in the lower sections of the Routeburn. Brown trout are also present in Lake Howden. Fishing is permitted in the rivers but not in Lakes Howden and Mackenzie and anglers must acquire a licence.

## PLANNING YOUR TRAMP

### When to go

The Routeburn Track spans a high rainfall area. The Darran Mountains act as a barrier for the prevailing north-west winds that must rise to cross them, depositing their rain on the western slopes. However, the rain-shadow is dramatic and pronounced. Whilst Fiordland receives around 7000mm of rain per year, the Routeburn enjoys 5000mm and Glenorchy, to the east, only receives 1200mm.

The weather is highly unpredictable and changeable. Cold snaps, snow, heavy rain and strong winds may occur at any time of year. Adequate preparations and appropriate clothing are essential. The exposed section over Harris Pass is vulnerable to particularly cold winds and driving rain, which can adversely affect your chances of making the crossing.

The weather tends to be most settled from **December to March**. Autumn and spring bring changeable weather.

During the winter months much of the land above the treeline may be coated in snow, which can make the track impassable. Deep snowdrifts and steep icy sections become substantial obstacles. Thirty-two avalanche paths cross the Routeburn Track, with the most dangerous areas being located north of Earland Falls, the slopes above Lake Mackenzie and the area above Lake Harris. Spring and late winter are the seasons most prone to avalanches, although any heavy rain or snowfall could trigger a collapse. A winter crossing of the Routeburn Track is a serious proposition that requires a lot of skill and proper equipment. Early snows effectively close the track to all but the most experienced trampers.

### Sources of information

The Routeburn Track can be accessed from either end. This means that you can choose where you would like to book your tramp. Should you choose to start from **The Divide**, to the south-west, you are most likely to arrange your tramp in **Te Anau**. The **DOC office** (☎ 03-249 7924, 🖳 fiordlandvc@doc.govt.nz, PO Box 29) in the Fiordland Visitor Centre on Lake Front Drive is open daily 8.30am-6pm during summer and 8.30am-4.30pm during the rest of the year. A dedicated **Great Walks booking desk** (☎ 03-249 8514, 🖳 www.doc.govt.nz), which deals with all the hut bookings and answers questions, is open daily 8.30am-4.30pm from November to April and weekdays only outside this period. **Fiordland i-SITE office** (☎ 03-249 8900, 🖳 fiordland-isite@realjourneys.co.nz) can be found in the Real Journeys building at 85 Lakefront Drive and is open daily from 8.30am-5.30pm.

Should you choose to tramp from the Glenorchy road end, to the east, you will probably want to arrange your tramp in **Queenstown**. There is a well-equipped **i-SITE Visitor Information Centre** (☎ 03-442 4100 or 0800-668 888, 🖳 www.queenstown-nz.com, PO Box 230) on the corner of Camp and Shotover streets, open daily 7.30am-7pm. Both this and the **Information and Track Centre** (☎ 03-442 9708, 🖳 www.infotrack.co.nz, PO Box 681) at 37 Shotover St can arrange transport to both ends of the track, sort out hut bookings and offer sound advice on what to expect on the walk itself. Next door at

38 Shotover St in Outside Sports shop is the **Queenstown DOC office** (☎ 03-442 7935, 🖳 queenstownvc@doc.govt.nz), which is open 8.30am-5.30pm and has a Great Walks desk that can arrange hut tickets and bookings.

**Glenorchy Visitor Information Centre** (☎ 03-441 0303, 🖳 www.glenorchy-nz.co.nz) at 2 Oban St also has lots of useful information and can help with accommodation bookings, track enquiries and transport issues.

### Getting to the trailhead

The track is not a circuit and can be walked in either direction. Both ends are relatively remote and some 325km apart by road, but they are well served by public transport during the peak season.

The Divide car park and shelter are adjacent to SH94, 28km east of Milford Sound and 84km north of Te Anau. At the other end of the track, the Routeburn Shelter and car park are located at the end of the Glenorchy–Routeburn road. Glenorchy is 28km and Queenstown 75km away from the track's eastern end.

Travelling from either Te Anau or Queenstown, you can organise reasonable transport packages that will drop you off at one end, collect you at the other and deliver you to a variety of final destinations. All details and schedules are available from information centres and DOC offices in the area.

Both Tracknet (☎ 03-249 7777, 🖳 www.greatwalksnz.com) and Kiwi Discovery (☎ 0800-505 504, 🖳 www.kiwidiscovery.com/tracks) provide transport from Te Anau or Milford Sound to the Divide. Backpacker Express (☎ 03-442 9939, 🖳 www.backpackerexpress.co.nz), Buckley Transport (☎ 03-442 8215, 🖳 www.buckleytransport.co.nz), Info & Track Centre (☎ 03-442 9708, 🖳 www.infotrack.co.nz) and Kiwi Discovery (☎ 0800-505 504, 🖳 tracks @kiwidiscovery.com) all serve the Routeburn Shelter end of the track.

You should consult timetables ahead of your trip and book your transport in advance in order to avoid disappointment or the chance of being stranded.

Whilst it is possible to hitch to The Divide, the road is not particularly heavily travelled. There is no through traffic at the Routeburn Shelter and it is unlikely that you will encounter a car with spaces.

### Local services

Although Milford Sound and Glenorchy are closer to the track, Te Anau or Queenstown are far larger and better equipped for preparing for your tramp.

There is some accommodation close to **Milford Sound** at the well-run, rustic *Milford Sound Lodge* (☎ 03-249 8071, 🖳 www.milfordlodge.com; unpowered/powered sites NZ$16/20, dorm NZ$30, dbl/twin NZ$85, chalet NZ$225), 2km from Milford Wharf on the approach road, adjacent to the Cleddau River. The restaurant here does reasonable pizza but there's also a well-stocked public kitchen and a large communal area, complete with piano, in which to hang out. In the town itself there's a café-cum-bar, the *Blue Duck*, which serves up an extensive buffet during the day and hearty pub grub in the evenings, but no real food stores or equipment shops.

At the other end of the track, **Glenorchy** has a small selection of places to stay including a spacious *Holiday Park* (☎ 03-441 0303, 🖳 www.glenorchy-nz.

ROUTE GUIDE AND MAPS

co.nz; unpowered/powered pitch NZ$15/20 per person, dorm NZ$25, cabin 1 person/2 people NZ$50/58), behind the central store and information centre at 2 Oban St; the slightly plain but welcoming *Glenorchy Hotel* (☎ 03-442 9902, 🖳 www.glenorchynz.com; dorm NZ$30, sgl/dbl NZ$70/100, en suite dbl NZ$120-130), at the corner of Mull and Argyll streets; and, adjacent to it, *Glenorchy Lodge* (☎ 03-442 9968, 🖳 wakatipu@xtra.co.nz; room NZ$100-125). For **food**, you can eat in the café connected to Glenorchy Lodge for around NZ$20-25, or at the atmospheric *Glenorchy Café*, which can rustle up scrambled eggs, cakes and decent coffee. There is also a pub, garage and a small local store selling possum fur products. If you're after somewhere a bit different to spend a couple of days, 26km from Glenorchy on the far side of Lake Wakatipu but close to the start of the Routeburn Track, is *Kinloch Lodge* (☎ 03-442 4900, 🖳 www.kinlochlodge.co.nz; dorm NZ$30, dbl NZ$80-120, heritage dbl NZ$175-195). This superb retreat has an outdoor hot tub with lake views, bright, comfortable rooms in a modern block and some cosier 'heritage' ones in the 19th-century homestead as well as a decent café-restaurant on site. They can arrange the five-minute boat trip from Glenorchy (NZ$10) and also organise transport to the trailhead.

**Te Anau** is a much larger settlement sprawled attractively alongside the lake of the same name. The Maori originally christened Te Anau 'Marakura', meaning Red Earth because of the prolific red lichen that grows on rocks throughout the region. Following further exploration of the area they re-named it 'Te Ana-Au', meaning Cave of Rushing Water, presumably in reference to the Glowworm Caves (see box p220) on the western shore. The town has several supermarkets and supply stores that can provide everything you may need. It is a very pleasant place to stay with plenty of attractions and things to see or do. To get a real feel for Fiordland visit **Fiordland Cinema** (☎ 03-249 8844) on The Lane to watch the half-hour screening of *Ata Whenua: Shadowlands*, a fantastic feature, shot mostly from a helicopter, that explores the region and showcases its finest scenery. If you're after any bits of kit stop by **Outside Sports** (🖳 www.teanausports.co.nz) on Town Centre. A range of accommodation is on offer to cater for all budgets. Hostels include homely *Rosie's Backpacker Homestay* (☎ 03-249 8431, 🖳 backpack@paradise.net.nz; dorm NZ$32, dbl NZ$74) at 23 Tom Plato Drive; the large, friendly and shabby *Te Anau Lakefront Backpackers* (☎ 03-249 7713, 🖳 www.teanaubackpackers.co.nz; tent pitch NZ$18 per person, dorm NZ$26-28, dbl NZ$72-92) at 48 Lake Front Drive; and the very decent, modern *Te Anau YHA* (☎ 03-249 7847, 🖳 www.yha.co.nz, 🖳 yha.teanau@yha.co.nz; tent pitch NZ$10, dorm NZ$28, sgl/dbl NZ$45/72) on Mokonui St. The well-equipped, popular *Te Anau Top 10 Holiday Park* (☎ 0800-249 746, 🖳 www.teanautop10.co.nz; tent pitches NZ$32-44, dbl NZ$73-170) is at 128 Te Anau Terrace. Around 1km south of central Te Anau on the road to Manapouri, just beyond the visitor centre, there is also the spacious and attractive *Lakeview Holiday Park* complex (☎ 03-249 7457, 🖳 www.teanau.info) comprising a *Campsite* (unpowered/powered NZ$15/17.50), *West Arm Lodge* (sgl/dbl NZ$32/90, cabin NZ$65-75, motel

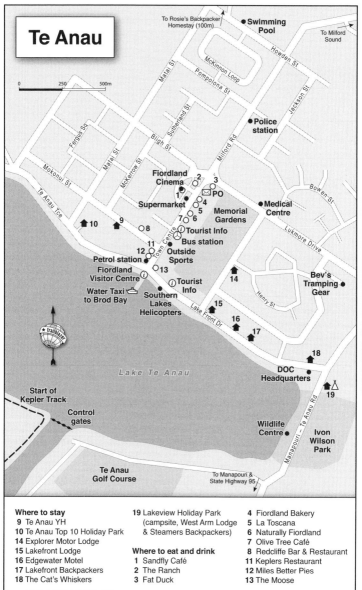

# Te Anau

**Where to stay**
9 Te Anau YH
10 Te Anau Top 10 Holiday Park
14 Explorer Motor Lodge
15 Lakefront Lodge
16 Edgewater Motel
17 Lakefront Backpackers
18 The Cat's Whiskers

19 Lakeview Holiday Park
  (campsite, West Arm Lodge
  & Steamers Backpackers)

**Where to eat and drink**
1 Sandfly Café
2 The Ranch
3 Fat Duck

4 Fiordland Bakery
5 La Toscana
6 Naturally Fiordland
7 Olive Tree Café
8 Redcliffe Bar & Restaurant
11 Keplers Restaurant
12 Miles Better Pies
13 The Moose

unit NZ$120-130) and **Steamers Backpackers** (dorm NZ$26, dbl NZ$65), which is a little soulless but nonetheless comfortable and well-appointed.

Lining the lakefront, or just back from it, are several hotels and motels. The comfortable **Edgewater Motel** (☎ 03-249 7258, ⌨ www.edgewater.net.nz; dbl/twin NZ$95-130) at 52 Lake Front Drive; the immaculate **Lakefront Lodge** (☎ 03-249 7728, ⌨ www.lakefrontlodgeteanau.com; unit NZ$160-240) at No 58; quirky **Explorer Motor Lodge** (☎ 03-249 7156; unit NZ$90-150) at 6 Cleddau St; and pretty, family-run **Cat's Whiskers** (☎ 03-249 8112, ⌨ www .catswhiskers.co.nz; B&B from NZ$130-195) at 2 Lake Front Drive all provide motel units and facilities.

For **food**, **Fiordland Bakery** and **Keplers**, which does mainly local fare, are both on Town Centre. Adjacent to Kepler's stands **Miles Better Pies**, where for around NZ$5-10 you can snack on wild venison or lamb and mint pies, pasties or raisin toast and coffee. There's also **La Toscana** at 108 Town Centre for pizza and pasta and the stylish, funky **Olive Tree** at No 52, which serves big break-fasts, oriental dishes and old-fashioned roasts, and **Naturally Fiordland** at No 62 that serves decent pizza. Furthest from the lake on Town Centre stands the **Fat Duck** where you can get generous portions of wholesome local food done well. **Sandfly Café** at 9 The Lane is a laid-back locals hangout where you can grab a tasty snack and good coffee. Some of the best food can be found at **Redcliffe Bar and Restaurant** at 12 Mokonui St, which serves manuka-smoked salmon, lamb rump, hare or wild venison in an atmospheric settler's cottage-style pub built from recycled materials and decked out with black and white photos depicting life on a farming station. Occasionally there is also live music in the charming, rustic bar. For pubs, try **The Ranch** on Milford Rd which has a huge selection of food on offer, or **The Moose** on Lake Front Drive.

**Queenstown** is New Zealand's premier tourist destination. This excellent-ly situated, lively focal point for the area has everything you might want or need. Food stores and equipment shops, including **Alpine Sports** (⌨ www .alpinesports.co.nz) at 4 Brecon St, are numerous, as are cafés, bars and restau-rants. There is a wide range of accommodation too. Of the hostels, compact, friendly **Alpine Lodge** (☎ 03-442 7220, ⌨ www.alpinelodgebackpackers.co.nz; dorm NZ$24-26, dbl NZ$60) at 13 Gorge St is well located. **Base Discovery Lodge** (☎ 03-441 1185, ⌨ www.stayatbase.com; dorm NZ$26) at 49 Shotover St is a giant, raucous place ideal for people intent on partying and has its own venue, the Altitude Bar for just such evenings. **Black Sheep Backpackers** (☎ 03-442 7289, ⌨ www.blacksheepbackpackers.co.nz; dorm NZ$27, dbl/twin NZ$65) at 13 Frankton Rd is convenient and atmospheric and also a mine of useful information and advice. **Bumbles** (☎ 03-442 6298, ⌨ www.bumbles backpackers.co.nz; dorm NZ$28, dbl NZ$60) at 2 Brunswick St is busy and bustling yet remains homely. **Bungi Backpackers** (☎ 03-442 8725, ⌨ www .bungibackpackers.co.nz; dorm NZ$21-24, dbl/twin NZ$51) at 15 Sydney St is a comfortable, ramshackle old place. Contemporary but fairly characterless **Butterfli Lodge** (☎ 03-442 6367, ⌨ www.butterfli.co.nz; dorm NZ$24, dbl NZ$58) at 62 Thompson St is nonetheless clean and quiet. **Hippo Lodge** (☎ 03-

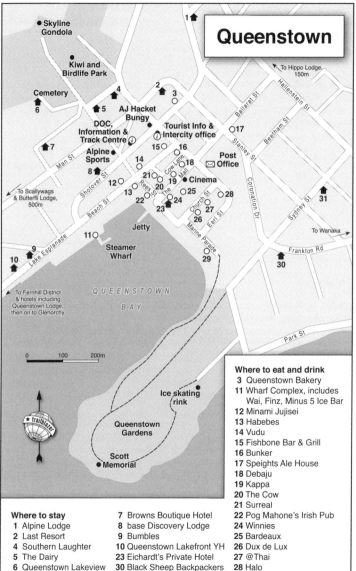

# Queenstown

**To Hippo Lodge, 150m**

**To Scallywags & Butterfli Lodge, 500m**

**To Wanaka**

**To Fernhill District & hotels including Queenstown Lodge, then on to Glenorchy**

Skyline Gondola

Kiwi and Birdlife Park

Cemetery

AJ Hacket Bungy

DOC, Information & Track Centre

Tourist Info & Intercity office

Alpine Sports

Post Office

Cinema

Jetty

Steamer Wharf

Lake Esplanade

*QUEENSTOWN BAY*

Ice skating rink

Queenstown Gardens

Scott Memorial

Ballarat St · Hallenstein St · Beetham St · Stanley St · Coronation Dr · Sydney St · Man St · Shotover St · Rees St · Beach St · Cow Lane · The Mall · Church St · Earl St · Marine Parade · Frankton Rd · Park St

★ trailblazer

0    100    200m

## Where to eat and drink

**3** Queenstown Bakery
**11** Wharf Complex, includes Wai, Finz, Minus 5 Ice Bar
**12** Minami Jujisei
**13** Habebes
**14** Vudu
**15** Fishbone Bar & Grill
**16** Bunker
**17** Speights Ale House
**18** Debaju
**19** Kappa
**20** The Cow
**21** Surreal
**22** Pog Mahone's Irish Pub
**24** Winnies
**25** Bardeaux
**26** Dux de Lux
**27** @Thai
**28** Halo
**29** Coronation Bathhouse

## Where to stay

**1** Alpine Lodge
**2** Last Resort
**4** Southern Laughter
**5** The Dairy
**6** Queenstown Lakeview Holiday Park
**7** Browns Boutique Hotel
**8** base Discovery Lodge
**9** Bumbles
**10** Queenstown Lakefront YH
**23** Eichardt's Private Hotel
**30** Black Sheep Backpackers
**31** Bungi Backpackers

442 5785, 💻 www.hippolodge.co.nz; tent pitch NZ$16, dorm NZ$27-28, sgl/dbl NZ$40/65) at 4 Anderson Heights is a converted suburban house boasting some great views over the lake. *Last Resort* (☎ 03-442 4320; dorm NZ$25-27) on Memorial St is a small, scruffy yet friendly and justifiably popular hostel. *Queenstown Lakefront YHA* (☎ 03-442 8413, 💻 www.yha.co.nz; dorm NZ$25-29, sgl NZ$56, dbl/twin NZ$72) is a large, sprawling, basic but busy establishment at 88-90 Lake Esplanade. A little more upmarket is *Scallywags* (☎ 03-442 7083, dorm NZ$26, dbl NZ$64) a 10-minute steep climb to 27 Lomond Crescent, which has a very inclusive familial atmosphere and great views. *Southern Laughter* (☎ 03-442 8828, 💻 www.southernlaughter.co.nz; dorm NZ$25-26, dbl/twin NZ$56-68), 4 Isle St, is friendly, funky and good-value.

In addition to the above there are also plenty of motels (units NZ$100-150) and hotels (rooms NZ$150-200). Near the centre there's small, intimate *Browns Boutique Hotel* (☎ 03-441 2050, 💻 www.brownshotel.co.nz; sgl/dbl NZ$275/295) at 26 Isle St. *The Dairy* (☎ 0800-333 393 or 03-442 5164, 💻 www.thedairy.co.nz; sgl/dbl from NZ$400/430) on the same street at No 10, is a centrally located, converted corner shop that now offers top-end luxury accommodation with quality touches, at a price. At the very top-end, *Eichardt's Private*

---

### OTHER ACTIVITIES

**Te Anau** Surprisingly, there aren't many adrenaline-fuelled adventures around Te Anau. The most popular trip is to explore the 200m long **Glowworm Caves** on Lake Te Anau's western shore. Real Journeys (☎ 0800-656 503, 💻 www.realjourneys.co.nz) run two-hour guided tours of the cave system by boat and on foot. A little south of the DOC Visitor Centre is **Te Anau Wildlife Centre**, which is home to a number of endemic species and one of just a few places where you can see the rare takahe. For a change of pace try **kayaking** with Fiordland Wilderness Experience (💻 www.fiordlandseakayak.co.nz).

**Glenorchy** Burgeoning tourist numbers mean that alternative activities have begun to take off in Glenorchy. Try **jet boating** on the Dart River with Dart River Safaris (☎ 0800-327 853, 💻 www.dartriver.co.nz) or **kayaking** with Kayak Kinloch (☎ 03-442 4900, 💻 www.kayakkinloch.co.nz). Alternatively whilst **canyoning** tackle the waterfall jumps, abseils and pool dives in a nearby canyon with Routeburn Canyoning (☎ 03-441 4386). Dart Stables (☎ 0800-474 3464, 💻 www.dartstables.com) run a range of **horse rides** lasting from several hours to several days. The best of the local **walks** are the Glenorchy Walkway through the wetlands alongside the Rees River (1hr) and the ascent of Mt Alfred (5-6hrs).

**Queenstown** In comparison, Queenstown is spoiled for adventure. Ride the **Skyline Gondola** (💻 www.skyline.co.nz) at Brecon St for superb scenic views of the lake and surrounding mountains. The Skyline **Luge** (☎ 03-441 0101) allows you to cruise or race back down the hill on a purpose-built track. Leap off the 47m/154ft high **Ledge Bungee** (☎ 03-442 4007) at the top of the gondola or tackle the 43m/142ft **Kawarau Bridge Bungy** (☎ 03-442 1177) 23km from the town or the simply awesome 134m/440ft **Nevis Highwire Bungy** (☎ 03-442 4007) above the Nevis River. All three are operated by AJ Hackett (💻 www.bungy.co.nz), who has an office on the corner of Camp and Shotover streets.

*Hotel* (☎ 03-441 0450, www.eichardtshotel.co.nz; suites NZ$1425-1645) on the corner of Marine Parade and Searle Lane is a fabulous, renovated icon dating from the 1860s when Queenstown was a booming gold-mining town. Each of the five opulent suites is luxurious and well-appointed, with superb lakeside views. The house bar with its comfortable sofas and log fire is a chic, sophisticated place to while away an evening.

One kilometre out of town *Queenstown Lakeview Holiday Park* (☎ 03-442 7252, 🖳 www.holidaypark.net.nz; tent pitch NZ$32, cabin NZ$40, motel unit NZ$100-120) is a sprawling open space with various types of accommodation, all at affordable rates. There's more upmarket accommodation at Fernhill, 2km to the west, including *Queenstown Lodge* (☎ 03-442 7107, 🖳 www.qlodge .co.nz; dorm NZ$34-39, sgl/dbl NZ$114/228) on Sainsbury Rd.

For **food**, *Queenstown Bakery* on Shotover St is open 24hrs and serves decent cakes, pies and snacks. Of the cafés, *Vudu* on Beach St and *Halo* on Camp St are the best, serving an inexpensive, eclectic mix of foods. The latter is also licensed. For quick snacks try the falafel wraps and salads from *Habebes* in Wakatipu Arcade or the fresh sushi and Japanese-influenced bento boxes at *Kappa* on Level 1 The Mall. Pizza and pasta can be found at *The Cow* on Cow

If bungy's not your thing, try one of the World's highest **rope swings** at the 109m/ 360ft Shotover Canyon Swing (☎ 03-442 6990, 🖳 www.canyonswing.co.nz) or the smaller but no less scary Ledge Sky Swing at the Ledge Bungy site (☎ 03-442 4007). There's **jet boating** on the Shotover and Kawarau Rivers with Shotover Jet (☎ 0800-746 868, 🖳 www.shotoverjet.co.nz) or Kawarau Jet (☎ 0800-529 272, 🖳 www.kjet .co.nz). Both rivers are also ideal for **whitewater rafting** in the company of Queenstown Rafting (☎ 03-442 9792, 🖳 www.rafting.co.nz) or Extreme Green Rafting (☎ 03-4428517, 🖳 www.nzraft.com).

If you think boats are too easy, try **river surfing**, where you float downstream with just a boogie board for company operated by Serious Fun (☎ 0800-737 468, 🖳 www.riversurfing.co.nz) or Mad Dog River Boarding (☎ 03-442 7797, 🖳 www .riverboarding.co.nz).

Back on land (barely) there's half-day trips to nearby 12-Mile Delta Canyon for **canyoning** expeditions with Routeburn Canyoning (☎ 03-441 3003, 🖳 www.canyon ing.co.nz). There are twelve via ferrata style routes featuring fixed rungs, rails and cables for **climbing** on Queenstown Hill. Rungway (☎ 0800-786 492, 🖳 www.rung way.co.nz) and Alpine Climb (🖳 www.independentmountainguides.co.nz) offer instruction, kit hire and expeditions. **Mountain bike** trails criss-cross the hillsides around Queenstown and guided trips are run by Fat Tyre Adventure (☎ 0800-328 897, 🖳 www.fat-tyre.co.nz) and Vertigo (☎ 0800-837 844, 🖳 www.vertigobikes.co.nz).

Get above it all and try **paragliding** with Tandem Paragliding (☎ 0800-759 688, 🖳 www.paraglide.net.nz), based at the top of the gondola. Marginally more low key but no less competitive is **Frisbee Golf** (🖳 www.discgolf.co.nz), played out on a course in the Queenstown Gardens. If you're just after a **walk**, stroll round the attractive Queenstown Gardens (30mins-1hr), yomp up Bob's Peak or 900m high Queenstown Hill (2-3hrs), or tackle the rather tougher 1746m Ben Lomond (7-8hrs) for panoramic views.

Lane or *Winnies* at 7 The Mall, which offers rather more gourmet toppings such as spinach, roasted pumpkin and Kapiti feta cheese or smoked chicken, cranberry and Kapiti brie.

*Finz* on the ground floor of Steamers Wharf does affordable seafood, great fish'n'chips and generous portions of spit-roasted chicken or lamb whilst *Surreal* at 7 Rees St serves a decent all-day breakfast and good-value mains. For more salubrious dining, try *@thai* at 8 Church St for authentic South-East Asian flavours, Thai curries and tasty Tom Yum soup, or *Minami Jujisei* at 45 Beach St for award-winning Japanese cuisine. *Wai* on Steamer Wharf boasts a stunning outdoor location and outstanding seafood, or try the exceptional *Fishbone Bar and Grill* at 7 Beach St which probably has the largest array of seafood in town and some of the best chowder. For a treat there's the historic *Coronation Bathhouse* on Marine Parade, a spectacular spot from which to enjoy the sunset while tucking into splendid, albeit pricy, regional fare and well-matched wine.

Queenstown's **nightlife** revolves around its pubs, all of which also serve up hearty pub grub, including the popular *Winnies* at 7 The Mall, the heaving Irish bar *Pog Mahone's* at 14 Rees St, *Speights Ale House* on the corner of Stanley St and Ballarat, *Dux de Lux* at 14 Church St, which also hosts live music, and the more refined *Bunker* on Cow Lane. There are good cocktails and hip DJs at *Bardeaux* in Eureka Arcade and *Debajo* on Cow Lane or for novelty try the vodka-based drinks in the *Minus 5 Ice Bar*, where everything is carved from ice, on Steamer Wharf.

## Huts and campsites

During the peak season, from November to April, it is compulsory to book your Routeburn tramp; you must also reserve your bunk space in advance should you wish to stay in Howden, Lake Mackenzie, Routeburn Falls or Routeburn Flats **huts**. Lake Mackenzie and Routeburn Falls are the two best-located and most popular huts on the track. Outside of peak season bookings are not required but a hut ticket must be purchased.

The **adult hut fee** in peak season (Oct-Apr) is NZ$45 and NZ$15 the rest of the year; the **camping fee** is NZ$15 in peak season but free at other times. Children and youths are also free for both hut and camping.

The huts are supplied with bunks, mattresses, wood stoves for heating, flush toilets, water supply and limited lighting. Gas stoves are provided during the peak season but are removed once this finishes, so make sure you carry portable cooking stoves and fuel if you choose to tramp outside of the summer months. Wardens are resident during the summer to check and validate hut passes and provide advice, daily weather reports and other necessary information.

**Camping** is allowed only at two designated sites, at Lake Mackenzie and Routeburn Falls hut, in a bid to minimise environmental damage to this fragile ecosystem. The soft peaty soils and slow-growing alpine vegetation are particularly prone to damage from insensitive camping. Advance bookings must also be made for tent pitches. The **emergency shelter** at the Harris Saddle and the shelters at either end of the track must not be used as overnight accommodation. There are two huts on the track that are solely for the use of **guided groups**.

These are located at Lake Mackenzie and Routeburn Falls. Independent trampers must not use these facilities.

## Maps

The *Routeburn and Greenstone Trackmap* (335–02) covers the whole track at 1:75,000 scale, which is more than adequate for the summer-season traverse of this area. A combination of Topomaps *Milford* (D40), *Eglinton* (D41) and *Earnslaw* (E40) also provide detailed coverage of the track. All of these can be purchased from DOC offices or information centres near the track.

## Distances and times

The 33km, well-maintained track can be tramped in either direction. However, by beginning at The Divide you climb quickly to Key Summit, which offers you magnificent vistas of the surrounding landscape and allows you to appreciate where you'll be tramping in the forthcoming days. You gain an immediate and dramatic impression of the effect glaciation has had on this area of South Island and can begin to appreciate the enormous power of ice on the move. The other benefit of walking in this direction is the long descent from Harris Saddle to Routeburn Falls, which can be tackled sedately and thus enjoyed more fully.

| | | |
|---|---|---|
| The Divide to Lake Mackenzie Hut | 12.5km | 4-5 hours |
| Lake Mackenzie Hut to Routeburn Falls Hut | 11.5km | 4-6 hours |
| Routeburn Falls Hut to Routeburn Shelter | 9km | 3-4 hours |

## TRACK DESCRIPTION

### The Divide to Lake Mackenzie Hut          12.5km/4-5 hours; Map 1

This first section allows you to gauge the scale and grandeur of the tramp you are undertaking, since you climb rapidly to a point where panoramic views unfold of the vast, snow-capped Darran Mountains, narrow Hollyford Valley and the harsh Humboldt Mountains.

The track begins at **The Divide** (532m/1745ft), the lowest east–west crossing of the Southern Alps. From the shelter at the car park, you climb steadily on a graded, well-tended surface that allows you to gain height quickly. Enclosed by silver beech, ribbonwood and fuchsia, you gain only glimpses of the surrounding landscape until, after 30-45 minutes, the track breaks out of the trees and arrives at the signposted junction for **Key Summit** (815m/2673ft). The views now are astonishing and are even better if you choose to drop your pack and climb the side path to the summit (919m/3014ft) itself. The path zigzags uphill through tussocks and scrub for 20 minutes before arriving at an alpine wetland area consisting of several small tarns and bogs. Please stick to the track and boardwalks here as the habitat is particularly fragile. Rushes, mosses, orchids, sundew, bog pine and other small herbs thrive amidst attractive, still tarns whose glassy surfaces reflect the jagged skyline. Views of the Darran Mountains, Pyramid Peak and Lake Marian to the north-west compete for your attention with those of the Hollyford Valley and the Humboldt and Ailsa mountains to the north-east and east respectively.

Having revelled in the views, return the way you came to the junction with the main track, from where the path descends gently along the flank of Key Summit, dropping 120m to arrive at **Howden Hut** and the lake that shares its name. The comfortable 28-bunk hut sits at the junction of the Routeburn and Greenstone tracks. It is possible to camp at the far end of the lake by following the Greenstone Track south for 20 minutes.

From the hut the Routeburn Track heads east, crossing **Pass Creek** before climbing gradually through a forest rich in ferns. Through gaps in the thick foliage you can make out the Lower Hollyford Valley, river and **Gunns Camp** to the north. Gunns Camp is a historic public works camp from the 1930s located in the Hollyford Valley. Families of the labourers building the Milford Road were housed here. It's now one of the only living records of that era. You can stay in simple huts here and there's also a small museum.

Having climbed 400m the track crosses a jumble of boulders at the base of **Earland Falls**. This thundering cascade plummets 80m from Lake Roberts and is an impressive spot to linger.

If the weather is fine the sunshine should guarantee a brilliant rainbow at the base of the falls. If it has been raining heavily or the falls are in flood, use the emergency bridge to cross further downstream.

The track continues north-west, hugging the cliffside as it edges across several avalanche paths, crosses **Sunny Creek** and after an hour emerges from the light forest in a natural clearing known as **The Orchard**, so called because the ribbonwoods growing here resemble fruit trees with their light green foliage and white hibiscus-like flowers. Camping is strictly prohibited at The Orchard.

The track then rambles along the treeline, breaking out of cover occasionally to reveal the Hollyford Valley far below you. After a precarious crossing of **Roaring Creek**, you descend 130m steeply through deep forest. Half an hour later, the track levels and having forded several small streams you pass the guided walks lodge to emerge on a small flat. The 48-bunk, two-storey **Lake Mackenzie Hut** enjoys a superbly tranquil location at the southern end of Lake Mackenzie, surrounded by soaring cliffs. There are only a handful of camping sites some 300 metres further on adjacent to the lake, owing to the fragile nature of the environment in this area. The perfectly clear emerald waters of Lake Mackenzie reflect the beautifully rendered Emily Peak (1820m/5970ft) and the other prominent summits of the Ailsa Mountains at the far end of the lake. A circuit around the lake makes a satisfying scramble. Even if cloaked in mist and low cloud the area has incredible charm, the muffling effect of the cloud merely adding to the stillness and eeriness that the mirror lake inspires.

## Lake Mackenzie Hut to Routeburn Falls Hut   11.5km/4-6 hrs; Map 2

This is the most spectacular section of the track. Climbing above the treeline the path edges along the Hollyford Valley before crossing into the Routeburn Valley, all the while providing some of the most sumptuous views of first Fiordland and then Mount Aspiring National Park.

Leaving Lake Mackenzie Hut, the track passes below the lake on a boulder-strewn trail. It then begins a series of steep switchbacks, climbing 300m through

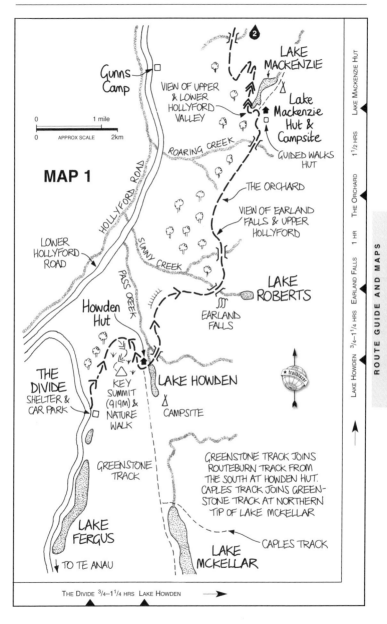

ROUTE GUIDE AND MAPS

LAKE MACKENZIE HUT

1½ HRS

THE ORCHARD

1 HR

EARLAND FALLS

¾–1¼ HRS

LAKE HOWDEN

THE DIVIDE  ¾–1¼ HRS  LAKE HOWDEN

tough, squat forest, bearded with mosses and lichens, to emerge well above the lake, sparkling in its forested valley, with views across the valley head to the finely shaped Emily Peak. The track continues to climb above the treeline, albeit more gently, finally rounding a spur to leave the valley and emerge on the steep, exposed Hollyford face.

On a clear day the immense views seen on this section are some of the most startling and impressive in New Zealand. As you sidle along the Hollyford face, beneath Ocean Peak (1848m/6061ft), you stare across at the muscular Darran Mountains where the skyline is rent by the impressive peaks of Mt Madeline (2537m/8321ft) and Mt Tutoko (2746m/9007ft). Directly below you the slope falls away sharply, dropping to the Hollyford River at the foot of the valley. This section is highly exposed and can be treacherous in high winds.

A bridge leads you over **Potters Creek** and an hour later passes a signpost that appears to point crazily off the mountainside. This is the junction with the particularly steep **Deadman's Track**, which leads to the valley floor and the Lower Hollyford Rd, 1km north of Gunns Camp. The main track narrows now and having clung to the cliff arrives at a series of steps. Rounding a bare knoll and wandering around several tarns you arrive at the **Harris Saddle Emergency Shelter** and the more modern guided walks shelter. This is a good spot to pause and catch your last views of the Hollyford Valley.

A short, steep track clings to the side of **Conical Hill** (1515m/4969ft), which looms above the shelter. The effort to scramble the additional 250m to the peak is well worth it, since the panoramic views are unparalleled. The slopes can be icy and slippery so beware whilst making the 30-minute ascent. Orange snow poles mark the route. Halfway up is an excellent view back over Lake Harris, while the panorama at the top encompasses the Darran Mountains, Humboldt Mountains, Richardson Range and the entire Hollyford Valley. However, if the weather is poor or there is low cloud shrouding the peak, you will be hard pressed to make out anything. The summit is also very exposed and prone to blustery winds in these conditions.

The main track crosses the Harris Saddle and turns into the **Routeburn Valley**. Easing through heaped mounds of moraine and rock bluffs it climbs above and around deep-blue **Lake Harris** (1225m/4018ft), a product of past glaciation. Carved out by glacier action, the lake fills an 800m by 500m (2624ft by 1640ft) depression. In winter it frequently freezes over although it is dangerous to try to walk on the ice. Often chunks of ice are still floating on the lake waters when the Routeburn Track opens in October. Fed by snowmelt and a stream issuing from Lake Wilson 1.5km away, its waters remain cold year-round.

The track peaks just beyond the lake before dropping into the **Harris Basin** to follow the left branch of the Routeburn across this pleasant alpine meadow. To walk through this meadow whilst the gentians, daisies, herbs and buttercups are in bloom is a treat. Over the course of an hour the track drops 180m to arrive at the **Routeburn Falls Hut**, immediately adjacent to a series of rock ledges over which the Routeburn rushes. It plunges through a series of cataracts, dropping 300m between the first of these to the grassy flats below.

ROUTE GUIDE AND MAPS

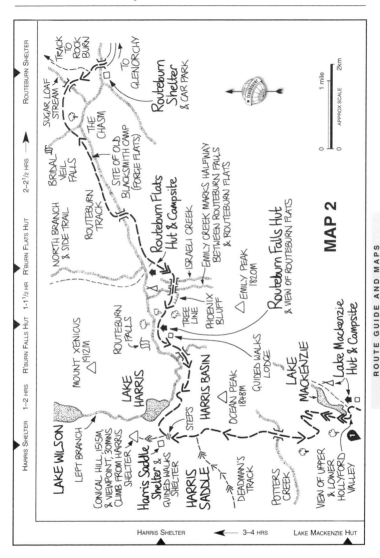

ROUTE GUIDE AND MAPS

MAP 2

TRACK TO ROCK BURN

TO GLENORCHY

Routeburn Shelter & CAR PARK

SUGAR LOAF STREAM

BRIDAL VEIL FALLS

THE CHASM

SITE OF OLD BLACKSMITH CAMP (FORGE FLATS)

NORTH BRANCH & SIDE TRAIL

ROUTEBURN TRACK

Routeburn Flats Hut & Campsite

ISRAELI CREEK

EMILY CREEK MARKS HALFWAY BETWEEN ROUTEBURN FALLS & ROUTEBURN FLATS

EMILY PEAK 1820M

Routeburn Falls Hut & VIEW OF ROUTEBURN FLATS

TREE LINE

PHOENIX BLUFF

ROUTEBURN FALLS

MOUNT XENICUS 1912M

LAKE HARRIS

HARRIS BASIN

GUIDED WALKS LODGE

LAKE MACKENZIE

Lake Mackenzie Hut & Campsite

LAKE WILSON

LEFT BRANCH

CONICAL HILL, 1515M, & VIEWPOINT, 30MINS CLIMB FROM HARRIS SHELTER

STEPS

OCEAN PEAK 1848M

Harris Saddle & GUIDED WALKS SHELTER

HARRIS SADDLE

DEADMAN'S TRACK

POTTERS CREEK

VIEW OF UPPER & LOWER HOLLYFORD VALLEY

Perched at the head of the valley, on the boundary between mountain forest and sub-alpine vegetation, the views from the deck of this 48-bunk hut are exceptional. Looking out over the silver beech-dominated forest, down the Routeburn Valley and across the surrounding Humboldt Mountains you can pick out the final day's track. The strong winds that bustle out of the Harris Basin have lowered the treeline in the falls area. Snow can lie here for months on end in winter and early spring, and temperatures can remain low even in summer.

Behind the Routeburn Falls Hut is a **guided walks lodge**. Camping is not allowed in the vicinity of this hut nor indeed in the Harris Basin.

### Routeburn Falls Hut to Routeburn Shelter      9km/3-4 hours; Map 2

The final section continues the gentle descent and allows you to appreciate the wild beauty of the area whilst also making you aware of the fragility of the land-scape and the damage that adverse weather conditions can inflict upon it.

Immediately behind Routeburn Falls Hut the track plunges back into the for-est and drops sharply. Stumbling through thick vegetation you arrive suddenly at an exposed cliff face, the site of a large landslip caused by several days of tor-rential rain in 1994. The rocks, mud and debris dislodged by the rain obliterated every tree in this section, leaving a broad, bare swathe cut into the forest. Looking up the hill, you can still see the path of the landslip. Down the slope over slowly regenerating vegetation you can see all the way to the valley floor.

The track passes back into the forest and edges around the substantial **Phoenix Bluff** before crossing a swing bridge over **Emily Creek**. It then bridges **Israeli Creek**, named in honour of an Israeli couple that got lost com-ing over a nearby untracked pass and spent some time on a ledge above the creek before being found. This is roughly the halfway point of the descent.

Having dropped 270m through silver and mountain beech forest, the path forks. The left-hand path leads to **Routeburn Flats Hut and Campsite** over-looking the river. Although less well situated than Routeburn Falls Hut, this compact 20-bunk hut is certainly quieter and there are still superb views of Mt Somnus and the Humboldt Mountains. There is an excellent side trip from this hut that follows the north branch of the Routeburn River to the head of the val-ley. Following route markers and cairns alternately through forest and boulder fields, you are treated to views of Mt Xenicus and Mt Erebus to the west and the Humboldt Mountains to the east. Once out of the bush there is a superb view of North Col directly ahead of you. It takes almost three hours to reach the head of the valley, but the deviation from the trail provides an interesting contrast to the rest of the Routeburn Track.

Back at the junction, the right-hand fork follows a level route through the trees adjacent to the Routeburn, crossing the river on a long swing bridge after half an hour. Passing above a gravel stretch alongside the river the track goes by tranquil **Forge Flats**, the site of a blacksmith's camp during the early con-struction of a bridleway in the 1870s, approximately halfway between Routeburn Flats Hut and Routeburn Shelter.

The track narrows and enters a steep-sided gorge where it passes above **The Chasm**, a narrow feature through which the water plunges over huge fractured grey sandstone boulders and tree trunks long since wrenched from the soil that appear to have been brutally tossed together by giant hands.

Finally the track crosses the small gorge gouged by **Bridal Veil Falls** and leaves the riverside for the forest. Having crossed **Sugar Loaf Stream** you return to the river bank, passing through an area of magnificent, stately red beech trees. There is a signposted detour that heads upstream to Sugar Loaf Pass, crosses into Rock Burn and loops back to the Glenorchy–Routeburn road via Lake Sylvan.

**Routeburn Shelter** is visible across the river but the track continues to a large swing bridge. Cross it, join the road and then double back to the shelter.

# Milford Track

*'The finest walk in the world'*   **Blanche Baughan** in an article for *London Spectator*, 1908

## INTRODUCTION

Fiordland is a haven of pristine wilderness and exhilarating, dramatic scenery in the far south-west of New Zealand, full of endless gradations of light and shade. The 53.5km Milford Track has been enabling trampers to experience this wilderness since 1889. The fairly easy four-day tramp is New Zealand's most famous Great Walk. It is justly renowned for its glacier-gouged valleys, its forests and alpine flower fields, ubiquitous waterfalls and towering peaks. It is a land of mystery and stillness that is disturbed only by the sound of streams and countless cascades. Once dubbed 'the finest walk in the world', it is undoubtedly one of the highlights of New Zealand.

Owing to its popularity, the Milford Track has developed into a highly regulated, stringently monitored tramp. Although this may frustrate and annoy some people, it does mean that inexperienced trampers can enjoy an exceptional mountain area without the attendant struggles usually associated with tramping in such an uncompromising landscape.

The Milford Track is a historic pathway. In many respects the track is a memorial to the early Maori who forged the trail over the pass. Although the current track is very different from the one the Maori used, it is still powerfully affecting to walk a similar route and see the same glorious landscape that has inspired and enriched generations.

## HISTORY

Early Maori referred to the south-west of New Zealand as Te Wahipounamu, 'The Place of Greenstone'. The Maori of Southland and Otago travelled the Milford Track south from Milford Sound, which they knew as Piopiotahi – a name derived from the piopio, a type of native bird – in search of this highly valued stone. A particular kind of pounamu (greenstone) was especially valued:

> ### The creation of takiwai
> Maori lore describes how Poutini, the spirit of pounamu, stole the wives of a man called Tamaahua. Distraught, Tama began searching for them. He travelled the length of South Island by canoe until he reached Fiordland. Passing Milford Sound he heard strange noises and paddled into the mouth of the sound. Here he found one of his wives transformed into translucent pounamu. As he cradled the cold body he wept openly. Tears ran down his face and splashed onto the stone, where they etched themselves into the pounamu, causing it to become flecked. This type of pounamu came to be known as *takiwai*, which literally translates as 'tear water'.

*takiwai* (see box above) is slightly softer than usual, and particularly beautiful. Highly prized for jewellery, it can be found around Milford Sound, principally at St Anne Point.

European explorers who arrived in the region in the mid-1800s learnt nothing of this established route and promptly set out to forge one.

The first permanent European resident of Milford Sound was Donald Sutherland, a native of Wick, Scotland, who arrived on a whaling boat in 1877 with the intention of prospecting for precious minerals. He quickly established himself in Milford, becoming known as the 'hermit of Milford Sound' and living here for over 40 years. He and John Mackay explored much of the area and were responsible for discovering Mackay Falls and then Sutherland Falls in 1880. Popular history records how they first found Mackay Falls and flipped a coin to see whose name should be attached to it. Mackay won, only for them to then stumble upon a vastly superior three-level waterfall several days later, which Sutherland gleefully claimed. Sutherland promptly publicised the discovery widely and somewhat inaccurately, claiming that the falls were over 3000 feet (almost 1000m) high. In 1888, he was commissioned to cut a track up the Arthur Valley from Milford Sound to the Sutherland Falls. At much the same time, the pioneer explorer and surveyor Quintin Mackinnon was employed to

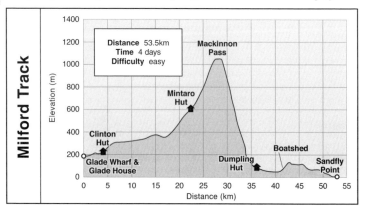

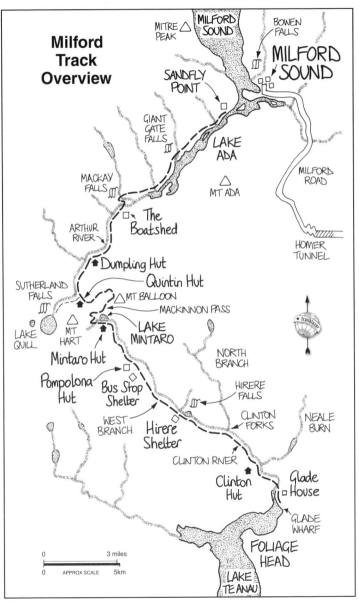

**Milford Track Overview**

MITRE PEAK △

MILFORD SOUND

BOWEN FALLS

MILFORD SOUND

SANDFLY POINT

GIANT GATE FALLS

LAKE ADA

MILFORD ROAD

MACKAY FALLS

MT ADA △

ARTHUR RIVER

The Boatshed

Dumpling Hut

Quintin Hut

HOMER TUNNEL

SUTHERLAND FALLS

MT BALLOON △

MACKINNON PASS

LAKE QUILL

MT HART △

LAKE MINTARO

Mintaro Hut

Pompolona Hut

Bus Stop Shelter

NORTH BRANCH

HIRERE FALLS

WEST BRANCH

Hirere Shelter

CLINTON FORKS

NEALE BURN

CLINTON RIVER

Clinton Hut

Glade House

GLADE WHARF

FOLIAGE HEAD

LAKE TE ANAU

0 — 3 miles

0 — APPROX SCALE — 5km

ROUTE GUIDE AND MAPS

### The creation of Milford Sound

South Island came into being when the four celestial sons of Rangi, the Sky Father, came to earth to inspect their father's new bride, Papa tua nuku, the Earth Mother (see p48). Whilst exploring the seas in a giant canoe, disaster struck and their canoe sank. As it sank so it turned to stone. The west side settled much higher than the east and the sons all rushed to the higher side in order to be safe. Tragically, they too were turned to stone and became high mountains. The eldest son, Aoraki, became Mt Cook and his three brothers, Raki-roa, Raki-rua and Raraki-roa became the three peaks nearby.

This new land needed to be sculpted so as to be fit for people to live on. The god Tu te Rakiwhanoa was sent to fashion the earth. His greatest labour was on the south-western coast of South Island. Beginning at the southernmost point of Fiordland he used an enormous adze to carve fiords out of the solid rock. His initial careless blows gave way to more calculated strokes as he progressed north. Eventually he came to Milford Sound, which proved to be the toughest of all. His immense toil here paid dividends and Milford Sound is truly his greatest masterpiece.

Whilst hacking out Milford Sound, Tu was visited by Papa tua nuku. She told him that the sides of the fiord were too steep to support people and asked him to carve out a landing place. To do this Tu created Te Wahi o Papatuanuku, 'The Place of Papatuanuku', at the head of the sound. Exhausted, he sank down to rest on Te Nohoaka o Tu, 'Tu's Seat', which is now known as The Devil's Armchair.

After its creation, Te Hine nui te po, the Goddess of the Underworld, visited Milford Sound. She was entranced by the beauty of the sheer walls and feared that people would want to live there forever. In order to drive people away she created a number of sandflies, Te Namu, and released them at Te Namu a Te Hine nui te po, which has come to be known as Sandfly Point.

cut a track up the Clinton Valley from the northern tip of Lake Te Anau. On 17 October, 1888, Mackinnon and Ernest Mitchell arrived at the head of the Clinton Valley and forged a path over the pass, entering the Arthur Valley.

With the establishment of a route and the continued advertising of the region's scenic attractions, including the falls, it was inevitable that people would flock to this area. Mackinnon became the first Milford Track guide, ferrying groups in his boat *Juliet* to the head of Lake Te Anau, from where he would escort them over the pass to Lake Ada. From here a second boat ferried them to Sutherland's residence in Milford Sound. In 1892, Mackinnon tragically disappeared during a storm on Lake Te Anau and was presumed drowned. The *Juliet* was found wrecked on the shores of one of the islands midway up the lake. A memorial cross now stands here. A stone memorial was also erected on the pass that now bears his name. In 1901 the government tourist department took over all facilities for the track, including the access ferry that brought people to the trailhead. Initially the government allowed only guided parties to use the track.

In 1908 the poet Blanche Baughan wrote an article about the Milford Track on behalf of the *London Spectator*. Rhapsodising about it, Baughan described the track in glorious detail. Her vivid prose is said to have so enraptured her editor that he chose to alter the title of her article to *The Finest Walk in the World*. The tag has since stuck.

The track was closed during both world wars. In 1935 as part of a Depression-era unemployment project, construction began on the Homer Tunnel which would provide Milford Sound with road access for the first time. The 1200m/3936ft tunnel was eventually opened in 1954. Trampers could now walk off the track at Milford Sound and catch transport back from there rather than having to retrace their steps. Then in 1952 Fiordland National Park was set up. At this time, the track was still open only to guided groups. In 1966, after protests, use of the track was extended to independent trampers too. New, separate huts were built for these 'freedom walkers'. The numbers of trampers using the track has continued to increase and a strict booking system has been introduced to cope with the demand for places. Careful management ensures that although massively popular it doesn't ever feel overcrowded.

## GEOLOGY

The Fiordland landscape has been manipulated and moulded by massive glaciers. The fiords are old glacial troughs, sculpted during the ice age at a time when sea levels were much lower and the glaciers themselves stretched beyond the current coastline. As the glaciers retreated, the sea flooded back into the mountain valleys, penetrating on average 20km inland.

Milford Sound is the northernmost of Fiordland's 15 fiords. Iconic Mitre Peak's walls plunge for 1600m/5248ft to the water. Beneath the surface they continue vertically down for a further 300m/980ft. The inner part of the fiord has been gouged the deepest, with the mouth of Milford Sound only about 100m/328ft deep. This is some of the most striking fiord scenery in the country.

The granite rocks that largely make up the landscape are sufficiently hardy to have retained the key features of glaciation. This is particularly evident in the U-shaped valley cross sections of the Clinton and Arthur valleys and the ice-gouged ledges and hanging valleys of tributary streams found all along the track.

The sheer cliff walls lend themselves ideally to the formation of waterfalls, of which there are an abundance. Plumes of plunging water are a feature of the track. The most famous are the Sutherland Falls, which plunge 580m/1904ft over three dramatic leaps, making it one of the highest waterfalls in the world.

## FLORA AND FAUNA

### Flora

Fiordland is consistently wet and enjoys heavy rainfall. This perpetual dampness supports a wide variety of vegetation. The early stages of the track receive marginally less rainfall than the latter ones. Consequently the Clinton Valley is dominated by beech forest. Silver, red and mountain beech proliferate, with broadleaf, hebe and fuchsia common on the exposed areas created by landslips.

As the track climbs to its high point on Mackinnon Saddle, the vegetation changes. Above the treeline is a band of sub-alpine scrub, featuring hardy grasses, tussocks and herb fields. Cushion plants made up of dozens of rosettes crouching shoulder to shoulder can also be found here. Small flowering plants including daisies and buttercups are usually evident only in summer. Beyond the pass the vegetation diversifies and thickens once more. Owing to the additional rainfall, the forests in the Arthur Valley are lusher. Silver beech, kamaki, miro and totara shield smaller plants, while mosses, lichens and ferns are all widespread.

## Fauna

The varied landscapes support a variety of different **birds**. Most common are the bellbird, rifleman, fantail, kereru, tomtit and bush robin. Kea and rock wren live above the treeline. Morepork and brown kiwi are less likely to be seen but may be heard calling at night. The fast-flowing Clinton and Arthur rivers are ideal for the rare blue duck, whilst mallards and shags also feed from them.

Unfortunately, introduced predators have adversely affected bird numbers. A low intensity stoat-trapping regime has been on trial in the Clinton Valley to see if it improves the chances of kiwi chicks reaching maturity. Stoats kill some 95% of kiwi chicks in their first year. A bonus of this programme is that the rare blue duck may benefit, since stoats also feed on their eggs. The traps extend from Glade Wharf to Mackinnon Pass. It is hoped that the steep-sided walls of the Clinton Valley will help to reduce the incidence of stoats reappearing in the valley from outside areas. Sadly, **sandflies** are to be found all along the track. They are most abundant adjacent to the rivers and at the aptly named Sandfly Point.

Brown and rainbow **trout** have also been introduced to the Clinton and Arthur rivers, both of which make excellent fishing spots if you are sufficiently stealthy and patient. You must have a current licence. The very high rainfall has also created a permanent freshwater layer on the surface of the sea in Milford Sound. Below this layer lies a concentrated 40m band of marine life flourishing on and around the sheer rock walls.

## PLANNING YOUR TRAMP

You have two options when tramping the Milford Track: go as part of a guided group or tramp it as an independent walker. The guided walk costs around NZ$2000. Staying in **private lodges** at Glade House, Pompolona and Quintin, all the heavy equipment, packs and food are transported for you; all you need to carry is a light daypack. Independent walkers will pay around NZ$280-350 for their Milford Track experience depending on where they return to after the tramp. The price of independence, though, is that you have to carry everything you might need and be fully self-sufficient.

### When to go

Fiordland is rightly famous for its high rainfall and changeable weather patterns. On average, over 7200mm of rain falls per year on Milford Sound. It is often joked that the Fiordland rainy season runs from January to December. Whilst this is slightly harsh, unpredictable weather patterns mean that low temperatures, strong winds, heavy rain and even snow can occur at virtually any time of year. Expect quantities of rain every month.

The Milford Track is the most highly regulated Great Walk. There is a definite season when it is 'open', running from late October to mid April. During that period the track is likely to be fully subscribed. For this reason it is essential that you book well in advance. The best time to tramp the track is probably **March**, when the temperatures are pleasantly warm and there may be fractionally less rainfall.

The track is open only in the summer season. In theory you *can* still tramp the track during winter, although you must arrange your own boat transport since the official launch doesn't run. This can be complicated and expensive. Furthermore, during the winter months snow can lie on the high ground for extended periods, which may make the track impassable. Mackinnon Pass can be extremely treacherous under snowy or icy conditions. This is an exposed alpine pass that can be buffeted by strong winds making it a dangerous place to be in adverse weather conditions.

Remember that 56 avalanche paths bisect the track between Glade Wharf and Quintin Hut. As the surrounding cliffs are so steep, avalanches often cannot be seen developing until they are plummeting towards the path. The risk is highest after prolonged periods of snow or rainfall, particularly in late winter and early spring, when avalanche and snow hazards can change rapidly from low to high. Several bridges are removed from the mid-Clinton Valley to Quintin Hut owing to the threat at this time to prevent their possible destruction. Flooding is also common after heavy rain, especially between Hirere Shelter and the Bus Stop in the Clinton Valley, and between the Boatshed and Poseidon Creek in the Arthur Valley.

All of this means that a winter crossing of the Milford Track should be undertaken only by well-equipped, experienced trampers.

### Sources of information

When it comes to booking your tramp, the simplest way is to do so via the **DOC website**, 🖳 www.doc.govt.nz, with its secure online booking facility that allows you to reserve your transport and accommodation well in advance. The website keeps track of how many tramping places are still available for each day and is updated regularly. It also leads you through all the transport options on offer so that you can book a complete package at the same time. This is a painless, easy way of securing a booking and is recommended as long as you are certain when you wish to undertake the tramp.

Should you wish to book your tramp in person, the best place to do this is the DOC counter in Fiordland Visitor Centre (see p214) on Lake Front Drive in Te Anau , which also sells all the necessary mapping and literature. Or you may wish to make your booking in Queenstown at the Information Centre, the DOC office or the adjacent Information and Track Centre; see p214 for details. Both can also provide information on reaching the trailhead at Glade Wharf.

### Getting to the trailhead

Because this tramp is highly regulated, you will need to organise your transport connections when you book your hut passes. The official package is likely to cost around NZ$150-200. This includes a shuttle bus and ferry ride to the start of the track, a ferry from the track end to Milford and then a return bus fare.

There is no direct road access to the Milford Track but instead it's most usually reached via a ferry from Te Anau Downs, 34km north of Te Anau, via the scenic Milford Rd. Tracknet (☎ 0800-483 2628 or 03-249 7777, 🖥 www.track net.net) departs from outside the Fiordland Visitor Centre at 9.45am and 1.15pm in time to make the 10.30am and 2pm ferry connection at Te Anau Downs operated by Real Journeys (☎ 0800-656 501, 🖥 www.realjourneys.co.nz). The ferry transports you the length of Lake Te Anau to Glade Wharf, the official start of the track. Both these services are best booked directly with DOC online at 🖥 www.doc.govt.nz or through the DOC office in Te Anau.

**At the other end of the track** a regular ferry service departs Sandfly Point at 2pm and 3.15pm for Milford Sound. This is the official option and can be booked through DOC in Te Anau or via the website. Buses can then be booked to take you onward to Te Anau, the Divide or Queenstown.

As an alternative, you can sea kayak from the track end into the sound for only a little extra. Contact Rosco's Milford Sound Sea Kayaks (☎ 0800-476 726, 🖥 www.kayakmilford.co.nz) or Fiordland Wilderness Experience (☎ 0800-200 434, 🖥 www.fiordlandseakayak.co.nz) for details.

From Milford Sound it is possible to return to Te Anau on the stunning Milford Rd. This extraordinary road passes through some of the most striking features of Fiordland. It is 119km long and takes around two hours to complete though as it is lined with scenic viewpoints it may take you much longer. Its tortuous path runs from the sound through the Homer Tunnel. This is a truly dramatic stretch of road. Passing under the Homer Saddle it emerges in an enormous cirque that has been carved by glaciers to resemble a steep-walled amphitheatre. From here it wends its way down the canyonesque Cleddau Valley into the Eglinton Valley and on to Te Anau.

## Local services

Because most of the transport packages that take you to the start of the track originate in Te Anau, the majority of trampers use this attractive town as their base. Small and busy, Te Anau is the tourist hub of the area and all your requirements can be met here with supermarkets, equipment shops and sports stores. Tourist information booths and the superb Fiordland Visitor Centre will help you to plan, book or otherwise organise your tramp. The DOC office is located in the visitor centre and can sell you maps, pamphlets and literature for the tramp. There are plenty of cafés, restaurants and bars spread throughout town and lots of accommodation; for details, see pp216-18.

At the end of the track there are far fewer amenities. There is a café-bar and a couple of places to stay in **Milford Sound**. *Milford Sound Lodge* (☎ 03-249 8071, 🖥 www.milfordlodge.com; see p215) is located slightly back from the Sound on the Milford Rd and has dorms, single and doubles as well as basic tent pitches available at reasonable rates.

## Huts and campsites

You must book the track accommodation well in advance; if you're after a specific date during the high season or are part of a big group you should try to book things up to six months ahead of departure. Note that **camping is strictly prohibited** anywhere along the Milford Track at all times. Each day a maximum of 40 independent walkers will be allowed to start the track and demand for these places is very high. It is possible to make bookings from early July for the following October–April season. This entails a degree more organisation and forethought than is necessary for any other Great Walk. **Hut passes** are issued for particular days and you must adhere to these dates. It is essential that you start the track on the stipulated date and stick to the four-day/three-night structure imposed. It is not possible to push on to the next hut since it will be full with the previous day's trampers. Likewise it is not possible to stay two nights in any hut since a second full contingent will be arriving the following day.

● **Independent cost during summer season**  Adult hut (three nights) NZ$135; child/youth hut (three nights) Free
● **Penalty fine for failing to pre-purchase or book a hut pass**  Up to 100% of adult rate regardless of age
● **Independent cost in off-season**  Adult hut NZ$15 per night; child hut Free

There are three **DOC huts** for independent walkers. Clinton, Mintaro and Dumpling huts are all large, excellent facilities. Bunks, mattresses, gas heating and stoves, water supply, flush toilet facilities and limited lighting are all provided during the summer season. Hut wardens will be on hand with radios to check tickets, issue weather forecasts and deal with any emergencies that may arise. They are also able to impose on the spot penalties for failing to show a hut pass. During winter the huts remain open but some facilities may not be available. Gas cookers, radios and heating fuel will not be provided. You may stay a maximum of two nights at any hut at this time.

Independent bookings should be made well ahead of departure via the official DOC website 🖳 www.doc.govt.nz, greatwalksbooking@doc.govt.nz or in person at the DOC office in the Fiordland Visitor Centre (see p214) in Te Anau. There are discounts available for some outdoor groups.

Guided packages should be organised through Ultimate Hikes (☎ 0800-659 255, 🖳 www.milfordtrack.co.nz).

## Maps

The best map for the track is the *Milford Trackmap* (335–01), which covers the route at 1:75,000 scale. The entire route is also covered by Topomaps' *Milford* (D40) and *Eglinton* (D41). All of these can be bought from DOC offices and information centres throughout South Island, such is the popularity and widespread appeal of the track.

## Distances and times

The Milford Track may be tramped in one direction only, from Glade Wharf to Milford Sound. It must be completed in four days and trampers must stay one night at each of the three huts provided along the track. This doesn't allow for very much flexibility and can be frustrating, especially on the very short first day. There are no options to push on to the next hut or to stay a second night in any of the accommodation, even to wait out bad weather.

The track is marked with mileposts along its entire length. It is obvious and well cut. The 53.5km tramp is not especially arduous, although the track can be rocky underfoot and quite uneven in places. However, some effort is required. The steep ascent of Mackinnon Pass and the long descent into the Arthur Valley can catch some people unaware, making the third day a slightly tougher proposition. You may be required to wade through floodwater several feet deep during or after heavy rain and to cross unbridged streams. You should expect to get muddy and have soggy feet – it's part of the Milford Track experience.

The distances and times listed below are for the independent walker's version of the track; guided groups stop at different points.

| | | |
|---|---|---|
| Glade Wharf to Clinton Hut | 5km | 1-1$^1$/$_2$ hours |
| Clinton Hut to Mintaro Hut | 6.5km | 5-6 hours |
| Mintaro Hut to Dumpling Hut | 14km | 5$^1$/$_2$-6$^1$/$_2$ hours |
| Dumpling Hut to Sandfly Point | 18km | 5$^1$/$_2$-6$^1$/$_2$ hours |

## TRACK DESCRIPTION

### Glade Wharf to Clinton Hut                 5km/1-1$^1$/$_2$ hours; Map 1

This short, easy day's tramp comes after a 30km ferry trip the length of Lake Te Anau that takes you into the heart of Fiordland. The ferry trip takes about two hours and allows you to savour the countryside as it slips past. Once you leave Te Anau behind, the mountains become more pronounced, closing in on both sides. As you round Foliage Head and finally enter the arm of the lake with Glade Wharf located at the far tip, you are truly isolated from civilisation. The journey also passes a series of small islands midway up the lake. One of these bears a cross, a memorial to Quintin Mackinnon who is believed to have drowned here when his ship foundered in a heavy storm. His body was never recovered although the wreck of his ship, the *Juliet*, was discovered washed up on the island's rocky beach.

Disembarking at the small **Glade Wharf**, you begin the tramp proper. The broad, even track leads into light beech forest alongside the clear, tranquil **Clinton River**. The track was originally cut so that packhorses could carry supplies to the huts. After 1km you emerge on a large grassy river terrace to pass by **Glade House**, a guided walks lodge. Just past this lodge the track crosses the translucent Clinton River on a swing bridge, the first and longest of nine swing bridges on the track. Sticking to the western bank of the river the path coils and curls upstream through increasingly dense, moss-draped silver beech forest. Just over 2.5km from the wharf you pass the site of Mackinnon's original hut, built in 1889, though there is little evidence of it any longer.

Almost 4km from Glade Wharf there is a good view back south-west to Dore Pass (1375m/4510ft), a tough high-level route over the Earl Mountains. Within 5km of the wharf the track passes a signposted junction that leads to a

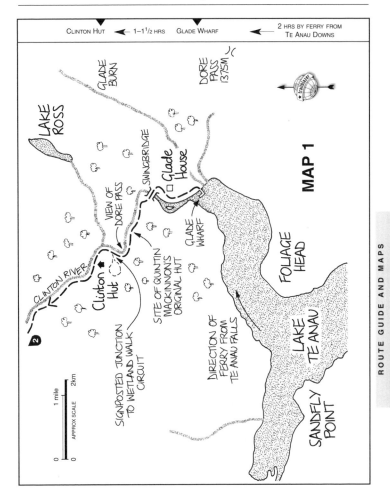

CLINTON HUT ◀— 1–1½ HRS    GLADE WHARF    2 HRS BY FERRY FROM TE ANAU DOWNS

GLADE BURN

DORE PASS 1375M

LAKE ROSS

SWINGBRIDGE

Glade House

MAP 1

VIEW OF DORE PASS

GLADE WHARF

SITE OF QUINTIN MACKINNON'S ORIGINAL HUT

CLINTON RIVER

Clinton Hut

FOLIAGE HEAD

DIRECTION OF FERRY FROM TE ANAU FALLS

LAKE TE ANAU

SIGNPOSTED JUNCTION TO WETLAND WALK CIRCUIT

SANDFLY POINT

2km
1 mile
APPROX SCALE
0
0

ROUTE GUIDE AND MAPS

short wetlands boardwalk (15 minutes return) before arriving at **Clinton Hut** ten minutes later. This pleasant 40-bunk hut is the obligatory first stop for independent trampers. Built in the late 1990s, it replaced the Clinton Forks Hut that was in danger of being swept into the Clinton River as a result of pronounced erosion of the riverbank. The facility is set in a purpose-built clearing, surrounded by high-sided mountains. Keas are often seen here, raucously competing for your attention.

## Clinton Hut to Mintaro Hut                     16.5km/5-6 hours; Map 2

This is a reasonably long, steady tramp to the head of the valley that gives you a better impression of the immensity of the Fiordland wilderness. Climbing gently, the track is increasingly pinched by the towering bluffs until it arrives at Lake Mintaro at the foot of the Mackinnon Pass. This section of the track is particularly prone to avalanches and the track crosses several slip sites, so you must be careful during periods of sustained or heavy rainfall.

The track continues to hug the western bank of the Clinton River as it climbs gradually through the lichen-covered **Black Forest**. All the beech trees here are of a similar girth and height, suggesting that they are all roughly the same age and have probably developed from seedlings together in the wake of a calamitous slip that levelled all the previous vegetation.

After 3km the track arrives at the confluence of the north and west branches of the Clinton River. This is the site of the old Clinton Forks Hut although a toilet is now all that remains of the original overnight accommodation. There are great views north up the north branch of the river to Mt Mitchelson (1939m/6360ft) but you turn west and follow the west branch.

A further 3km on the track passes through an area of regenerating scrub that clings to the mass of debris caused by an enormous landslip in 1982. The rocks, mud and trees caught up in the slip dammed the river and caused a lake to form behind it. Broken tree trunks and drowned vegetation stick out of the lake. The granite walls are particularly steep and after rainfall waterfalls spring from the cliff faces, dousing the luxuriant vegetation that hangs tenaciously to the rock. Every crease and fold in the mountains seems to hold a waterfall. Unsurprisingly, the section of track immediately beyond this point is prone to flooding.

One kilometre beyond the far eastern end of the lake is the Hirere Falls **guided walks shelter**. From here there are good views across the river to Hirere Falls, a shimmering band of water that plunges to the river through a series of arches and hollows.

The track continues up the valley, which widens slightly. After 1km you are able to see Mackinnon Pass for the first time, far ahead of you. From this distance the pass looks more akin to a vertical wall, solid and impregnable. There is a signposted side track that loops to **Hidden Lake** and back to the main track. The lake fills a depression created by an avalanche and sits beneath another waterfall at the foot of a steep, fluted cliff face.

The track goes on meandering north-west through further beech forest beneath the snow-capped peaks of Mt Fisher (1878m/6160ft) and Castle Mountain (2131m/6990ft). After 2.5km it passes the basic **Bus Stop Shelter**, which sits rather gloomily beside the track. Just beyond this is **Pompolona Hut**, the second guided walks overnight accommodation. The hut is named after a type of scone that Mackinnon used to cook for his early guided parties.

Beyond the hut the track climbs slightly and crosses a small spur. Just after the headland the forest opens up and the track descends slightly to cross a series of small streams. There is a **wooden bench** set on the edge of the forest,

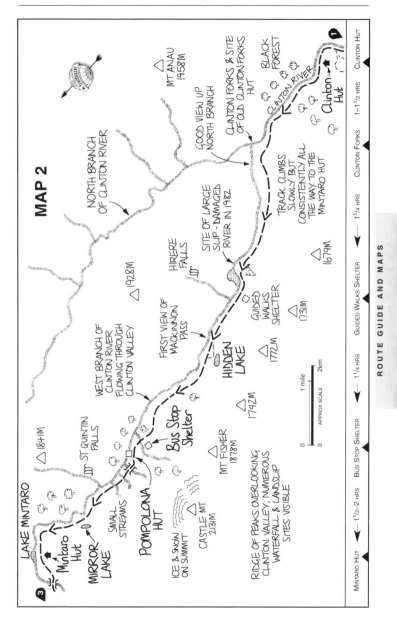

## MAP 2

MT ANAU 1958M

NORTH BRANCH OF CLINTON RIVER

CLINTON FORKS & SITE OF OLD CLINTON FORKS HUT

BLACK FOREST

CLINTON RIVER

Clinton Hut

GOOD VIEW UP NORTH BRANCH

SITE OF LARGE SLIP - DAMAGED RIVER IN 1982

TRACK CLIMBS SLOWLY BUT CONSISTENTLY ALL THE WAY TO THE MINTARO HUT

1928M

HIRERE FALLS

1679M

FIRST VIEW OF MACKINNON PASS

GUIDED WALKS SHELTER

1731M

HIDDEN LAKE

1772M

WEST BRANCH OF CLINTON RIVER FLOWING THROUGH CLINTON VALLEY

1792M

Bus Stop Shelter

LAKE MINTARO

ST QUINTIN FALLS

1841M

MT FISHER 1878M

SMALL STREAMS

POMPOLONA HUT

ICE & SNOW ON SUMMIT

CASTLE MT 2131M

RIDGE OF PEAKS OVERLOOKING CLINTON VALLEY; NUMEROUS WATERFALL & LANDSLIP SITES VISIBLE

Mintaro Hut

MIRROR LAKE

APPROX SCALE

0    1 mile

0    2km

**ROUTE GUIDE AND MAPS**

| ◀ | | ◀ | | ◀ | | ◀ | | ◀ | |
| --- | --- | --- | --- | --- | --- | --- | --- | --- | --- |
| Mintaro Hut | 1½–2 HRS | Bus Stop Shelter | 1¼ HRS | Guided Walks Shelter | 1¼ HRS | Clinton Forks | 1–1½ HRS | Clinton Hut | |

a far better, more attractive lunch stop than the Bus Stop Shelter if the weather is fine.

A series of basic bridges crosses small streams that swell incredibly after rainfall. Large boulders litter the trackside at these points, evidence of severe flooding and landslips. The track ascends past a fine viewpoint of St Quintin Falls.

The final section of the day's tramp sees the track gradient increase as it rises through dense, tangled forest for half an hour, before emerging at **Lake Mintaro**, which Mackinnon originally christened 'The Resting Place'. **Mintaro Hut** is set back slightly from the track and is the second hut for independent trampers. From here you are poised to tackle the pass. If you arrive early enough and the weather is fine, it is worth considering an ascent that afternoon. By leaving your pack at the hut you can climb the pass in around $1^1/2$ hours and may well enjoy excellent, clear views. The late evening light is striking and you can enjoy the stillness of the pass with fewer people around to disturb it.

### Mintaro Hut to Dumpling Hut                   14km/5$^1$/2-6$^1$/2 hours; Map 3

This is the toughest day on the track. Aside from the steep ascent of Mackinnon Pass, it includes a long, equally punishing descent into the Arthur Valley. This can be a long day, especially if you choose to include the $1^1/2$-2 hours round trip to Sutherland Falls. However, the rewards are well worth the effort.

The track drops down to **Lake Mintaro** and continues west alongside the river to a swing bridge built into a tree. Beyond this you climb steadily. Over a series of 11 switchbacks the track gains almost 400m to **Mackinnon Pass** (1073m/3519ft). On the fourth switchback you pass the 15 mile/24km post, which marks halfway in terms of distance climbed to the pass but not quite half in terms of height gained. At the sixth switchback you pass above the treeline to an area of alpine scrub while the eleventh brings you to the narrow top of the pass. As you climb there are fantastic views of the head of the valley and its scooped natural amphitheatre, a vast glacial cirque and the source of the Clinton River. Look the other way for Lake Mintaro and the Clinton Valley beyond.

Coming onto the ridge at the top, the track leads past a large 4m-high **stone memorial** built to commemorate Quintin Mackinnon's discovery of the route over the pass. On the exposed ridge you are better able to appreciate the grand scale of the place. There are glorious, expansive views in every direction: northwest you look over an 800m vertical drop – off which somebody has estimated it would take twelve seconds to fall to the bottom – to the forested valley to Quintin Hut; north-east are glorious views of the valley head and the Jervois Glacier beneath the impressive summit of Mt Elliot (2003m/6570ft); while to the south there are great views of the Clinton Valley. The sharp ridge itself runs west to east, joining Mt Hart (1782m/5845ft) to the west and the unlikely named Mt Balloon (1853m/6078ft) to the east.

The track leads across the narrow ridge above vertiginous drops, the views continuing to enthral and develop as you climb slightly and round a small knoll to reach the track's highest point (1154m/3798ft). It then descends past a series

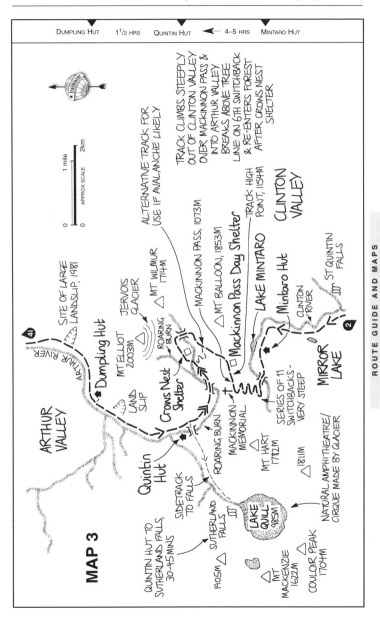

DUMPLING HUT  1½ HRS  QUINTIN HUT  ◄── 4–5 HRS  MINTARO HUT

MAP 3

TRACK CLIMBS STEEPLY OUT OF CLINTON VALLEY OVER MACKINNON PASS & INTO ARTHUR VALLEY BREAKS ABOVE TREE LINE ON 6TH SWITCHBACK & RE-ENTERS FOREST AFTER CROWS NEST SHELTER

ALTERNATIVE TRACK FOR USE IF AVALANCHE LIKELY

MACKINNON PASS, 1073M

MT BALLOON, 1853M

Mackinnon Pass Day Shelter

TRACK HIGH POINT, 1154M

LAKE MINTARO

CLINTON VALLEY

Mintaro Hut

ST QUINTIN FALLS

CLINTON RIVER

MIRROR LAKE

SERIES OF 11 SWITCHBACKS - VERY STEEP

MT WILMUR 1714M

JERVOIS GLACIER

ROARING BURN

MT ELLIOT 2003M

Dumpling Hut

SITE OF LARGE LANDSLIP, 1981

ARTHUR RIVER

LAND SLIP

Crows Nest Shelter

ROARING BURN

Mackinnon Memorial

MT HART 1782M

1811M

ARTHUR VALLEY

Quintin Hut

SIDETRACK TO FALLS

ROARING BURN

SUTHERLAND FALLS

QUINTIN HUT TO SUTHERLAND FALLS, 30-45 MINS

1905M

MT MACKENZIE 1622M

COULOIR PEAK 1704M

LAKE QUILL 985M

NATURAL AMPHITHEATRE/ CIRQUE MADE BY GLACIER

trailblazer

1 mile

APPROX SCALE

2km

0

0

of small tarns to the **Mackinnon Pass Day Shelter** (1069m/3506ft). If you are making the crossing in bad weather, this emergency shelter makes a welcome rest spot. The distinction between the two types of trampers is preserved even here, with the shelter divided between independent walkers and guided groups. Three earlier shelters have been blown off the pass in the past and the current incarnation clings precariously to its foundations. During the summer season gas rings are provided here. There is a toilet with an astounding view situated nearby.

Beyond the shelter the track begins to descend on a narrow, rocky ledge, edges around the flank of Mt Balloon and heads up the valley. There are frequently dozens of waterfalls leaping off the sheer cliffs above, the water coursing down the slopes. The track traverses around the head of the valley, crosses a sturdy bridge over the **Roaring Burn** and continues to drop, passing the **Crows Nest**, a guided group shelter and re-entering the forest where it drops steeply alongside the Burn. Steps and boardwalks have been built to help you negotiate the steep, unstable slopes. The plunging river, waterfalls and luxuriant forest are glorious to tramp amongst and on the descent there are good views of Dudleigh and Lindsay falls. Having lost 800m in height over 7km, the track reaches the foot of the mountain. A signposted junction leads left, crosses the Roaring Burn on a swing bridge to arrive at **Quintin Hut**, a guided group hut with an independent walkers shelter attached.

The 1-1½ hour return trip from here to **Sutherland Falls** is well worth making. The falls are the highest in New Zealand and amongst the very highest in the world. Leave your pack at the shelter and follow the clearly marked, rocky track as it climbs for 30-45 minutes through a natural tunnel of beech trees, ferns and fuchsia to the base of the falls. The 580m/1904ft drop comprises three giant leaps of, from top to bottom, 248m/815ft, 229m/751ft and 103m/338ft. The Maori gave the falls the descriptive name Ko Te Tautea Ka Tu, 'The White Thread Fixed against the Cliff'. They are a moving and impressive sight regardless of the weather. The sheer noise of them is sufficient to overwhelm your senses. If the water level is right it is possible to climb around the plunge pool at the base of the falls and then behind the cascading torrent. Take care if you attempt this since the rocks are extremely slippery. As you marvel at the falls, consider the achievement of William Quill, who climbed the sheer cliffs immediately adjacent to the falls in 1890. He discovered and christened Lake Quill, the feeder lake that fills a large glacial cirque above the falls.

From Quintin Hut the main track crosses back to the eastern side of Roaring Burn and heads north into the **Arthur Valley**. Edging alongside the river with good views back to the Sutherland Falls, after 2km you pass over the site of another large slip from 1978 and continue north-east. Further on the path becomes a raised boardwalk which clings to a cliff side. This continues until you arrive at **Dumpling Hut**, the final overnight stop for independent walkers. In good weather there's a decent plunge pool opposite the turn-off to the hut. The bank above the boardwalk is an excellent spot to see glow-worms after dark.

## Dumpling Hut to Sandfly Point     18km/5½-6½ hours; Map 4i & ii

This longish final section consists of a relatively gentle descent down the Arthur Valley. It is important to be conscious of the time on this final section since you must make your appointed rendezvous with the launch at Sandfly Point in order to be ferried to Milford Sound.

To begin, the track returns to the forest and follows the eastern bank of the Arthur River downstream. After 6km of shallow descent on well-graded trail, it then passes the **Boatshed**, a guided group shelter, and just beyond crosses the increasingly broad river on a large swing bridge. From the middle of the bridge there are good views up and down the valley. You then climb slightly to cross **Mackay Creek**, a tributary of the Arthur River. Shortly after the crossing point are the picturesque, multi-tiered **Mackay Falls** and the unusually shaped **Bell Rock**. Worn down by water and stones, the Bell Rock was smoothed and hollowed before being tumbled aside in a rock fall. Peer underneath it to see a hollowed-out space that is large enough to stand in. The track traverses a hill and returns to the riverbank, crossing two small swing bridges over **Poseidon Creek** as it goes.

ROUTE GUIDE AND MAPS

DUMPLING HUT    2–2½ HRS ➤ MACKAY FALLS    1¼–1½ HRS    POSEIDON CREEK    ¾–1 HR TO GIANT GATE FALLS (MAP 4ii)

All being well, you eventually arrive at **Lake Ada**, named by Sutherland after a Scottish girlfriend, where you mount a rocky ledge above it. The lake was formed by a massive landslip more than 900 years ago. Below the water level the drowned forest still stands. Long-dead beech trees are still visible in the depths. The track passes through a series of cuttings laboriously blasted out by work parties in the 1890s. There are sporadic views of the lake below.

Six kilometres beyond Mackay Falls, the track crosses a tributary on a swing bridge beneath **Giant Gate Falls** (Map 4ii) to a small clearing at the foot of the boulder cascade – an ideal lunch spot if the weather is good. Loiter here if you are ahead of schedule to meet your boat rather than endure the voracious sand-flies at the end of the track. The final section of the track skirts Lake Ada beneath the **Devil's Armchair** (1634m/5360ft). There are several small rapids at the far

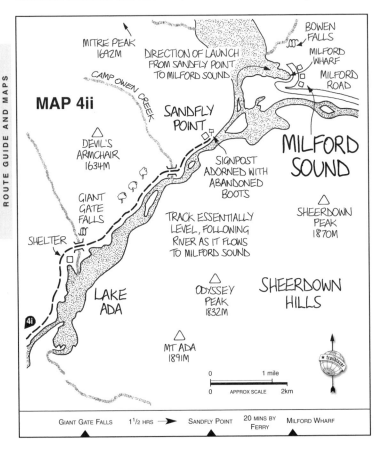

ROUTE GUIDE AND MAPS

MAP 4ii

MITRE PEAK 1692M

CAMP OWEN CREEK

BOWEN FALLS

DIRECTION OF LAUNCH FROM SANDFLY POINT TO MILFORD SOUND

MILFORD WHARF

MILFORD ROAD

SANDFLY POINT

DEVIL'S ARMCHAIR 1634M

SIGNPOST ADORNED WITH ABANDONED BOOTS

MILFORD SOUND

GIANT GATE FALLS

SHELTER

TRACK ESSENTIALLY LEVEL, FOLLOWING RIVER AS IT FLOWS TO MILFORD SOUND

SHEERDOWN PEAK 1870M

LAKE ADA

4i

ODYSSEY PEAK 1832M

SHEERDOWN HILLS

MT ADA 1891M

0      1 mile

0    APPROX SCALE    2km

GIANT GATE FALLS    1½ HRS →    SANDFLY POINT    20 MINS BY FERRY    MILFORD WHARF

❏ **Farewell from the Milford Track**
At Sandfly Point is a Maori farewell acknowledging those who have completed the
track and hoping that they travel on safely.

| | |
|---|---|
| *Nga manuhiri, kua takihaere i* | The visitors who travelled |
| *Te ara nei o ou matou tupuna, o te* | this pathway of our ancestors being |
| *Iwi Kai Tahu, Kati Mamoe me* | Kai Tahu, Kati Mamoe, Waitaha |
| *Waitaha hoki me ratou uri* | and their descendants of the area |
| *Tawhito katoa o tenei rohe* | Go in peace |
| *Haere i runga i te rangimarie* | Farewell farewell farewell. |
| *Haere Haere Haere Haere koutou* | |

end of the lake. This part of the track is prone to flooding during wet weather. In
dry conditions it is only 1¹/₂ hours from Giant Gate Falls to Sandfly Point.

Passing out of the forest the track crosses a grassy river flat and arrives at
the shelter by **Sandfly Point**. Just beyond the shelter is the jetty and the much
photographed 33¹/₂ mile sign, festooned with abandoned boots.

The launch departs here at 2pm and 3.15pm. It is a pleasant 20-minute ferry
trip out into Milford Sound. As the boat slips into the grand, brooding sound,
the unmistakable Mitre Peak (1692m/5550ft) distinguishes itself from the circle
of peaks to the north-west. Named by a sea captain because of its resemblance
to a bishop's mitre, it is a stunning final sight.

The ferry eases past Bowen Falls and docks at the Milford Wharf. From
here you can enjoy the exquisite, dramatic view laid out before you and reflect
on the tramp that you have just completed.

# Kepler Track

*From the moment my eyes rested on the snow-clad alps I worshipped their beauty and was
filled with a passionate longing to touch those shining snows, to climb to their heights of
silence and solitude, and feel myself one with the mighty forces around me. The great peaks
towering into the sky before me touched a chord that all the wonders of my own land had
never set vibrating, and filled a blank of whose existence I had been unconscious.*

**Freda Du Faur**, *The Conquest of Mount Cook*

## INTRODUCTION

The Kepler Track is unusual in that it was purpose-built as a Great Walk.
Constructed in 1988, the idea behind it was to offer an alternative to the overcrowded Milford and Routeburn tracks. Brilliantly conceived, it rivals both in
terms of dramatic scenery and high-quality tramping. Several infrequently used
tracks in the Kepler Mountains were fused together to create a 67km circuit that
could be readily accessed from Te Anau. The result was a very high standard
multi-day tramp through a variety of habitats, eminently worthy of its standing

ROUTE GUIDE AND MAPS

and inclusion as a Great Walk. Relatively straightforward, it can be completed in three to four days and as a consequence its popularity has soared.

The rewards of tramping the Kepler Track are many. Situated on the edge of the Fiordland wilderness, the track crosses spectacular mountain tops and links a host of disparate natural features.

## HISTORY

Unlike many other areas of New Zealand, very little is known about the pre-European history of the Maori in Fiordland. Aside from some evidence of seasonal occupation around the lakeshores and on some of the islands on both Lake Te Anau and Lake Manapouri, little else is certain.

The legendary Maori leader Rakaihautu is said to be responsible for naming the Great Lakes in Fiordland whilst exploring this area of South Island. During a period of sustained wet weather, he came across an attractive, sizeable lake that he christened Te Ana Au, meaning 'Cave of Rushing Water'. A little further south Rakaihautu discovered another beautiful lake, which he named Roto Ua, meaning 'The Lake where Rain is Constant'. Roto Ua has since come to be known as Lake Manapouri, derived from Manawapora meaning 'Sorrowing Heart', which was the original name of South Mavora Lake but was accidentally transferred to this lake by European cartographers. According to legend, the sorrowing heart belonged to a traveller caught on the lake waters by a sudden storm.

Before Europeans arrived in this part of New Zealand, Maori hunted and fished around the lower Kepler Mountains. Although archaeological evidence suggests that the Maori occupation of the area was seasonal, at least initially, villages were built adjacent to the Waiau River and next to Lake Te Anau. History also records that Brod Bay on the opposite shore to Te Anau was the site of a Maori battle in which the local chief Pukutahi was killed.

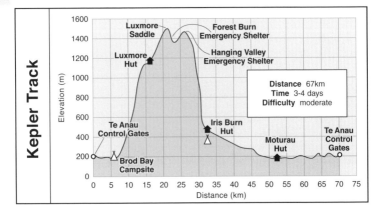

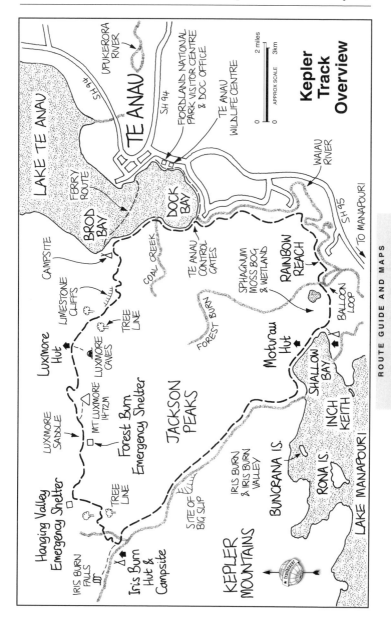

Assisted by their Maori guides, George Wera and Rawiri Te Awha, the European explorer Charles Nairn and William Stephen 'discovered' the lakes in 1852. Many of the early Europeans to drift into the area following its discovery were of Scottish extraction. One of the first was the Scottish surveyor James McKerrow. In two years of extensive work surveying Lake Te Anau, Manapouri and the Waiau River area, he named many of the landmarks still apparent today. Often misunderstanding or incorrectly translating the descriptive Maori names for many of the area's features, he tended to settle instead on more typically European names. The renowned missionary and explorer, Dr Livingstone, and head of the Royal Geographical Society, Sir Roderick Murchison, were honoured, as was the German astronomer Kepler. McKerrow's legacy is also apparent on some of the river names, including Awe Burn, Garnock Burn and Iris Burn. Other early Scottish settlers christened two of the islands in Lake Manapouri, Rona and Pomona, both of which are Orkney names.

Although much of the region was largely ignored by Europeans, early tracks were cut up onto Mount Luxmore by the runholder Jack Beer in order to provide access to summer pastures for his sheep. The Kepler Mountain tops were still farmed by Beer up until his death in 1930. Following his demise the land reverted to the national park. After World War II, hunters and climbers explored the area more fully and in doing so increased public interest in the region. In the 1970s a ski-field and funicular railway were proposed for Mount Luxmore but this idea foundered and was eventually abandoned.

Following various environmental assessments, the tourist department gave Fiordland National Park a substantial grant to develop a new track and establish accommodation huts along it. The Kepler Track was completed and officially opened in February 1988 as part of New Zealand's National Park Centennial Year celebrations. Due to its increased popularity and the continued boom in Fiordland's visitor numbers, the DOC launched a pilot booking system for the track for the first time in 2003.

## GEOLOGY

The Te Anau Basin has been in existence for tens of millions of years. Enclosed by granite mountain ranges and the Fiordland wilderness, it is a remote, rugged area. The base rocks here are hard metamorphic and plutonic rocks that were formed deep in the earth's crust and consequently erode very slowly. These base rocks are covered by younger, softer sediment. This is most evident at the limestone bluffs below Mount Luxmore.

The lowland areas surrounding the Basin are littered with glacial deposits that date back to the last ice age, some 15,000 years ago. Glaciers carved and gouged the fiords, deep U-shaped valleys and sheer mountains for many, many thousands of years. Lake Te Anau is the largest lake in South Island and the second largest in New Zealand. At 417m/1368ft deep, the lake bottom is at some points over 200m below sea level. Its deeply indented western shoreline ensures that its coastline is disproportionately large, totalling around 500km and making it the longest in New Zealand.

## FLORA AND FAUNA

### Flora

Fiordland benefits from a vast amount of rainfall. As a result, the area is covered in lush vegetation. The hard rocks that make up the region are covered in a layer of moss that acts as a natural sponge, holding moisture in the soil. This in turn supports a thick ground flora of ferns, lichens and smaller plants. Beech trees predominate, blanketing the valleys and clinging precariously to the steep cliff sides. Mountain, silver and red beech are all present, flourishing alongside well established podocarp forests comprising kamahi, miro, rimu and totara. As you climb higher, so silver beech becomes the most visible species. Above the treeline, snow tussocks, mountain daisies, gentians and various hardy alpine grasses exist.

At lower levels, particularly between Shallow Bay and Rainbow Reach, the terrain gives way to a series of **wetlands** and sphagnum moss **bogs**. These are very important habitats and provide a striking contrast to the other landscapes on the track. Acting as natural retainers for moisture, they never dry out. The peat soils release water in times of dryness. Although low in nutrients, some hardy plants survive here, having become especially adapted to living in a boggy environment. As well as sphagnum moss, celery pine, wire rush, bog pine, manuka and turpentine scrub all thrive. Carnivorous sundew plants also exist here, using specially designed sticking hairs to catch passing insects. Skeletons of victims may be seen trapped on the plants' bright red leaves. The striking, deep-blue sun orchid enjoys the open, well-lit environment that a wetland creates, although it often opens its petals only when the sun is shining.

### Fauna

The forests support a wide range of **birds**. Bellbird, tomtit, fantail, chaffinch, riflemen, kereru, tui and bush robin are all prevalent throughout the forest. The higher tussock-clad slopes are home to kea, pipit and rock wren. You may be lucky enough to hear morepork or brown kiwi calling at dusk around Mt Luxmore and Iris Burn huts. The waterways and lakes also support several species of duck. The rare blue duck can sometimes be found in the upper Iris Burn area, whilst paradise ducks and mallards can be found along the shoreline of Lake Te Anau. New Zealand scaup, shags and kingfishers also feed on the lake and Waiau River.

The area just north of the Kepler Mountains is the site for a remarkable recovery scheme. The flightless takahe was considered extinct in New Zealand for half a century, up until 1948 when several birds were discovered in the Murchison Mountains. The area was instantly set aside as a special reserve and an intense recovery scheme launched. Much time and effort has ensured that the takahe has escaped extinction, at least for the time being. However, there are still only around 200 birds in New Zealand, the majority of which can be found in this area. The Te Anau Wildlife Centre adjacent to Te Anau represents most people's best chance of viewing this endangered species.

ROUTE GUIDE AND MAPS

**Invertebrates** such as grasshoppers and dragonflies patrol the wetlands' edges. Glow-worms can be spotted beneath ferns and on forest banks. Less welcome is the presence of sandflies in the area, particularly along the lake shores. **Mammals** such as red deer, possums, hares, stoats and weasels have all been introduced to the region and have had a significant impact on the vegetation.

The waterways and lakes are well known for their concentration of brown and rainbow **trout** and make excellent fishing spots.

## PLANNING YOUR TRAMP

### When to go

The region is plagued by high rainfall and changeable conditions. The prevailing westerly winds come in off the Tasman Sea. These moisture-laden winds reach the natural barrier of the Fiordland Mountains and are forced to rise, cooling and depositing the moisture as rain or snow. Up to 9000mm of rain falls on the western section of the region. To the east, Te Anau lies in a rain shadow and consequently receives only 1200mm of rain per year.

Unpredictable weather patterns ensure that cold snaps, rain or even snow can occur at almost any time of year. The ideal time to tramp the track is between **early November** and **late April**. The warmest time of year is November to February, but with rainfall up to 200 days a year, dry spells can't be guaranteed. However, the lighter east and south-easterly winds during the winter months often bring more settled weather.

The section of track between Luxmore Hut and Iris Burn Hut traverses a series of exposed ridges. These can be treacherous stretches as the weather here can change very quickly. Strong winds up to 80km/h can lash the open slopes. If it is cloudy or misty at this altitude, special care must be taken on this section. It is imperative that you bring the correct clothing and equipment with you at all times of year because of the changeable weather.

### Sources of information

All pre-departure planning and preparation can be done in Te Anau. The excellent Fiordland National Park Visitor Centre (see p214) on Lake Front Drive will be able to help. Should you wish to make any bookings or gather any more material outside of Te Anau, the Queenstown DOC office and the two information offices can assist you (see pp214-5). Other DOC offices and information centres throughout Fiordland will also be able to aid you.

### Getting to the trailhead

The Kepler Track officially starts and finishes at the Lake Te Anau Control Gates at the southern end of the lake. This point is 4km from Te Anau itself. However, it is a pleasant, leisurely stroll around the attractive lake edge, which should take 45-60mins to complete. From the Fiordland Visitor Centre the lakeside track passes through the Te Anau Wildlife Centre, skirts the shoreline and arrives at the Control Gates.

If **driving**, follow SH95 south from Te Anau towards Manapouri. Just after the visitor centre is a well-signposted junction to the right. This will in turn take you to a car park a short walk away from the Control Gates. However, there is a free car park at the visitor centre that has the added appeal of being safer than the one at the trailhead. If you do not have your own transport, **shuttle buses** or **taxis** can be organised to drop or collect you either at the Control Gates or at Rainbow Reach swing bridge, which is 14km to the south of Te Anau, down a shingle track that branches off the Manapouri Rd. Contact Kepler Track Shuttle (☎ 03-249 7777, 🖳 www.greatwalksnz.com) or Top Line Tours (☎ 03-249 8059, 🖳 www.toplinetours.co.nz) for departure and pick-up times. **Hitching** on the road between Manapouri and Te Anau is relatively easy owing to the frequency of traffic.

There are also several **water-taxi operators** who will take you from Te Anau across the lake to Brod Bay. Contact Kepler Taxi (☎ 03-249 8364, 🖳 stevesaunders@xtra.co.nz) to book a space and check departure times. This is a good time-saving exercise, since it shortens this section by around $2^1/4$-$2^1/2$ hours. However, it does mean that you begin by climbing very steeply without a chance to really warm up.

### Local services
The most convenient access point for the Kepler Track is the town of **Te Anau**. This small, charming town straggles along the eastern shore of its eponymous lake and offers all the requisite facilities and amenities. Various supermarkets, equipment shops and sports stores stock a wide range of food and gear. Numerous travel agents and tourist information points throughout town will be able to help you organise or plan your activities, whilst the excellent Fiordland Visitor Centre and DOC office is beautifully situated on the lakeshore. Several cafés, restaurants and bars compete for your attention and business. A range of accommodation is also available; see pp216-18 for details.

The town of **Manapouri**, 21km south of Te Anau, also has an idyllic setting and most amenities.

### Huts and campsites
Advance bookings are now required for the peak summer season. You are strongly advised to book well in advance as the numbers are restricted and spaces limited. There are three large, well-appointed **DOC huts** on the track. Should you wish to stay at Luxmore, Iris Burn or Moturau huts you will need a **Great Walk pass**. There are stiff penalty fines for failing to buy a pass in advance. Bookings are not required during the much cheaper off-season from May to mid October. Check with DOC for the exact date of each season.

The **adult hut fee** in the peak season is NZ$45 and NZ$15 in the off season; the **camping fee** is NZ$15 in the peak season and NZ$5 at other times. Children and youth are free all the time.

The huts are all exceptionally well equipped with bunks, mattresses, wood stoves, gas cookers, flush toilet facilities and water supply. All the huts also have some limited lighting, provided by solar panels. Usually this means that the dining/cooking areas of the huts will be illuminated until 9.30-10pm. During the summer season a warden will be resident in each hut to check passes and provide daily updates on the weather. During the rest of the year there are no wardens and the cooking gas is disconnected. **Camping** is allowed only at designated sites at Brod Bay, Iris Burn and Shallow Bay. It's not permitted anywhere in the vicinity of Luxmore Hut or on the section of track between Mt Luxmore and Iris Burn Hut because of the exceptionally fragile nature of the alpine area, the dramatically changeable weather and the high risk of fire during summer.

Once above the treeline, the tops can be very exposed. After Luxmore Hut there are two **emergency shelters**. The basic structures at Forest Burn Saddle and Hanging Valley are simply designed to offer sanctuary from inclement weather. There are no bunks, mattresses or cooking facilities here and it is not permitted to stay in the shelters overnight, unless poor conditions dictate otherwise.

## Maps
The best map of the area is the *Kepler Trackmap* (335–09), which covers the route at 1:50,000 scale. The track is also covered by Topomaps' *Manapouri* (C43) and *Te Anau* (D43). All of these are available from the DOC office in Te Anau or the majority of information centres in the immediate area.

## Distances and times
The Kepler Track is a reasonably strenuous proposition. A decent level of fitness is necessary for the complete circuit, but sections of the track are ideal for day walks. The section from Rainbow Reach to Lake Manapouri is a simple proposal, whilst a return trip to Luxmore Hut is more challenging.

It is possible to tramp the track in either direction and there is little to choose between the two. Most people tramp anticlockwise, opting to ascend Mt Luxmore first. Despite this intimidating first day, it does mean that you are in the best place to gauge the weather the following day before beginning the traverse of the exposed tops. The day above the treeline and the descent to Iris Burn Hut can then be fully enjoyed, whilst a final evening at Moturau Hut beside Lake Manapouri makes for an enchanting conclusion to a remarkable tramp.

Although tramping clockwise begins with a gentle introduction, the arduous ascent from Iris Burn Hut to Hanging Valley Shelter is the steepest on the track. Even once you have reached the shelter, you are still some 10km from Luxmore Hut, your final rest spot. For this reason, I'd advise tramping anticlockwise.

| | | |
|---|---|---|
| [Te Anau to Control Gates | 4km | $3/4$-1 hour] |
| Control Gates to Luxmore Hut | 14km | $5^1/4$-6 hours |
| Luxmore Hut to Iris Burn Hut | 18.5km | 5-6 hours |
| Iris Burn Hut to Moturau Hut | 17.5km | 5-6 hours |
| Moturau Hut to Control Gates | 17km | $4^1/2$-$5^1/2$ hours |
| [Control Gates to Te Anau | 4km | $3/4$-1 hour] |

## TRACK DESCRIPTION
### Te Anau to Luxmore Hut                    **19km/6-7 hours; Map 1**
This is potentially a long, tough day. The majority of the section is spent climbing steeply up the flank of Mt Luxmore. However, the stunning views and quality of the forest that you tramp through are worth the trouble.

Most trampers begin by walking south from Te Anau on the level lakeside track that skirts the lake's southern tip and allows you time to clear your mind of urban distractions and focus on the wilderness tramp ahead. The track passes through the Te Anau Wildlife Centre, which makes for a charming diversion, before running around the lake to the Te Anau Control Gates. Just before the Control Gates is a viewpoint that offers superb views north, along the length of the lake with the rugged, mountainous western shoreline looming above you in stark contrast to the gentler opposite shoreline, which stretches away to the east.

Having passed through the Control Gates, the track proper begins by skirting **Dock Bay**. It meanders through red and mountain beech forest amidst scattered miro, rimu and kamahi, staying close to the shore. After about half an hour the track reaches a good picnic and swimming spot then turns north-west, still hugging the shoreline to pass through an area of very attractive forest full of tree and crown fern. Passing over a swing bridge at **Coal Creek** the well-graded path continues for about 3km through similar terrain before crossing a second stream to emerge at **Brod Bay**, the point at which the water taxi from Te Anau will also drop you. Here a swathe of white sand stretches temptingly in front of you. This is also a very good spot for swimming and makes a scenic campsite for those who made a late start from Te Anau or those who simply wish to enjoy the lakefront. Beware of the sandflies though.

About halfway along the beach is a signpost to Mt Luxmore, where you leave the shoreline and turn south-west. The track begins to climb the north-facing flank, gently at first but increasingly steeply. On a series of long switchbacks you ascend through the moss-covered forest. After climbing almost 400m there is a break in the trees and a good view back across the lake to Te Anau.

The track continues to climb steeply, gaining a further 150m to arrive beneath a series of towering, overhanging limestone bluffs (747m/2450ft). The bluffs are over 200m wide and up to 60m high, an imposing natural feature formed over millions of years. Boardwalks and steps have been built to take you around and then over this obstacle. The merciless ascent continues as the track climbs north-west towards the treeline, climbing a further 270m through stunted mountain and silver beech. Here the forest is denser and skeins of moss and old man's beard drip from gnarled branches like tattered lace. Edging around a bend, the track abruptly breaks out of the forest and climbs above the treeline. This heralds a truly stunning panoramic view of the Te Anau Basin. From this vantage point you can see most of Lake Te Anau to the north and east, Lake Manapouri to the south-west as well as the Jackson, Takitimu, Snowdon and Earl mountains.

Cresting several small rises the track undulates gently through an area of alpine tussocks and hardy grasses. All about are mountains, lakes and sky. The track follows a series of orange-topped snow poles that helpfully mark the track during bad weather conditions. About 45 minutes later you edge around a small bluff and arrive at **Luxmore Hut**. This spacious, split-level hut has 50 bunks and is located in a slight depression offering unparalleled views north over the tree canopy and Hidden Lakes, across the metallic gleam of the South Fiord waters some 900m/2950ft below, to the forbidding Murchison Mountains that rise steeply from the water's edge. The peaks of Mt Owen (1769m/5802ft) and

Black Cone (1679m/5507ft), separated by the intriguingly-named Mystery Burn, ought to be readily apparent. Behind the hut, to the west, is Mt Luxmore (1472m/4828ft) itself. At night, because you are above the treeline and removed from any real light pollution, this hut makes a spectacular spot for stargazing. Stand on the deck or just next to the hut for grandstand views of the Southern Cross, the Milky Way and a host of other constellations.

If you arrive early and the weather is good, you may wish to consider an ascent of **Mt Luxmore**. Although most people climb the summit the following day, if the weather report suggests deteriorating weather overnight it may make sense to leave your pack at the hut and do the 2-3-hour round trip that afternoon.

An interesting side trip from the hut leads south to the **Luxmore Caves**. Climbing above the hut along a ridge, the side track takes you to a series of caves some ten minutes from the hut. A staircase leads underground into a cave system that was formed by an underground stream. Although the cave appears to narrow rapidly, there is in fact about a 1km-long cave system here. By squeezing and stooping you can explore the first section of the cave. Be sure to take at least two light sources since it is impossibly dark without a torch and do make sure to tell the warden or someone at the hut your intentions as it can be treacherous underground.

### Luxmore Hut to Iris Burn Hut            18.5km/5-6 hours; Map 2

If the weather is good, this section can be a real highlight. Most of the day is spent above the treeline, gently traversing a series of exposed tops surrounded by outstanding views. The ascent of Mt Luxmore and the final descent to Iris Burn Hut are further highlights on this spectacular section.

It is well worth waking up early to catch the sunrise. Climb the slight rise behind the hut to witness the sun sneaking over the horizon, touching the peaks of the Murchison Mountains and illuminating the frequently cloud-filled fiord far below your vantage point. As the sunlight hits the alpine scrubland, the countryside turns red-gold and comes alive.

**ROUTE GUIDE AND MAPS**

---

**Colour section (following pages)**

● **C1** Maori carving in front of the marae at Tieke Kainga on the **Whanganui River Journey** (see pp148-172).
● **C2** Superb views north from the exposed alpine tops of the **Kepler Track** (see pp247-64).
● **C3** Trampers dwarfed by the cascading waters of Sutherland Falls on the **Milford Track**.
● **C4** Routeburn Flats from below Routeburn Falls Hut (**Routeburn Track**, pp209-28).
● **C5** The empty sands of Heaphy Beach on the **Heaphy Track** (pp194-208).
● **C6** Tongariro Northern Circuit (pp127-47) – **Top left**: Oturere Hut in the lee of Mount Ngauruhoe. **Bottom left**: View across the Lower Tama Lake and Tama Saddle to the northern flank of Mt Ruapehu. **Middle**: The classic andesitic cone of Mt Ngauruhoe looms above the volcanic dyke in Red Crater. **Right**: The Emerald Lakes.
● **C7 Top left**: View east across Lake Waikaremoana from Marauiti hut to the Panekiri Range (**Lake Waikaremoana Track**, pp110-26). **Bottom left**: Canoe beached beneath Tieke Kainga marae on the **Whanganui River Journey** (pp148-172). **Middle**: The symbolic Bridge to Nowhere straddling the Mangapurua Stream (see p168).
● **C8** Milford Track (pp229-46) – **Top**: The iconic, glaciated walls of Mitre Peak rise steeply from Milford Sound. **Bottom**: Looking north from the sheer-sided Mackinnon Pass.

C3

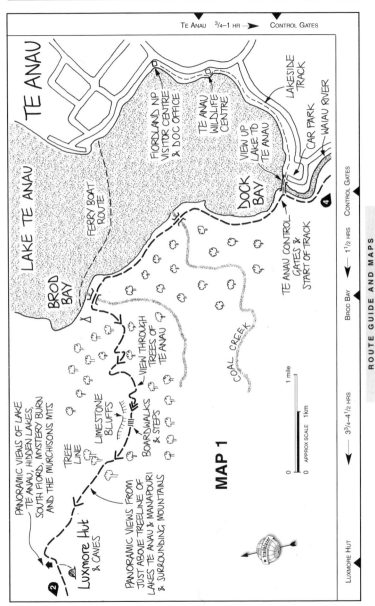

MAP 1

The warden will post a daily weather report early in the morning and you should wait to see this before setting out. If bad weather is forecast consider waiting at the hut for it to pass. If good weather is forecast, set out early to make the most of the spectacular scenery. Regardless of the weather, be sure to carry sufficient water since there are no streams along the early section of the track.

The track begins by climbing gently west. It gains about 150m, rising along a ridge towards the unnamed peak east of Mt Luxmore. It skirts around this peak amidst large blocks of rock that sparkle with crystals and mica before turning north. The rock jumble is a colourful mix of dark reds and blue greys, a visually striking palette. Rounding a spur, the track climbs a ridge before arriving at the **Luxmore Saddle** (1400m/4592ft).

Just beyond Mt Luxmore is a signposted junction. Leave your pack here and scramble the remaining distance to the trig point on the peak (1472m/4828ft). The panoramic view is breathtaking, showing you the tortured, broken topography of Fiordland to the north and west in contrast to the vast stretches of water to the south and east. The return trip takes around twenty minutes.

Having descended by the same route, continue west on the main track. This section is very exposed and frequently narrow. Beware of violent gusts of wind when crossing the Saddle and mind your footing. The track edges along the Saddle above steep-sided slopes, passing through herb fields and shrubland consisting of mountain daisies and grasses. The dramatic views of Forward Peak (1361m/4464ft) and the ridge leading to it are spectacular.

The track begins to descend gently, zig-zagging over loose scree until it reaches **Forest Burn Emergency Shelter** (1270m/4166ft). Beyond the shelter, the track negotiates a couple of rock outcrops and the bluff at the end of a ridge, with South Fiord and the Murchison Mountains visible beyond.

The narrow path climbs to a ridge crest and proceeds to rise and fall along the top for almost two hours. Skirting a rise, it eventually reaches **Hanging Valley Emergency Shelter** (1390m/4559ft). There are yet more vast Fiordland vistas comprising jagged peaks and shrub-filled valleys here and the spot makes an ideal lunch break. The track then turns south and follows a very narrow ridge for 2km. A guide wire has been fixed in some places to help you steady yourself on the sharp ridge crest while a series of steps drops you safely and swiftly on the steepest sections. As you descend this laddered and boardwalked section you begin to get your first views of the Iris Burn Valley and the Big Slip. An exposed knoll at the end of the ridge offers the best views.

From here the track turns west and quickly drops back into the forest. The trees close in and the views are lost as you zigzag tightly down the mountain, descending 400m in this fashion before crossing an attractive tributary of the Iris Burn Stream and edging along the side of this hanging valley. There is a short two-minute detour here to a small waterfall, which is pleasant as long as there has been at least some rainfall to swell it.

The track levels briefly before twisting and plunging a further 300m down the bush-clad face. Views from creek crossings and rock slip sites allow you to look down the broad Iris Burn Valley before finally emerging on the valley

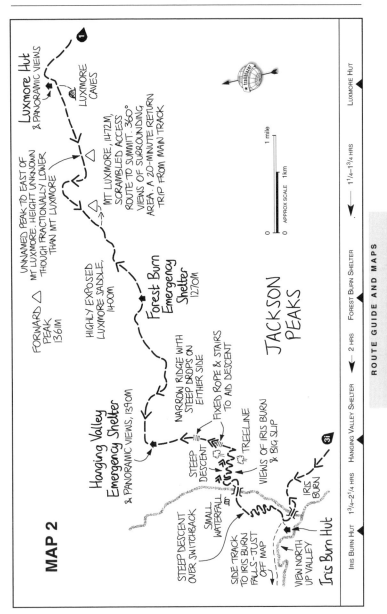

**MAP 2**

Luxmore Hut
& PANORAMIC VIEWS

LUXMORE CAVES

UNNAMED PEAK TO EAST OF
MT LUXMORE. HEIGHT UNKNOWN
THOUGH FRACTIONALLY LOWER
THAN MT LUXMORE

FORWARD △
PEAK
1361M

HIGHLY EXPOSED
LUXMORE SADDLE,
1140M

MT LUXMORE, 1472M,
SCRAMBLED ACCESS
ROUTE TO SUMMIT. 360°
VIEWS OF SURROUNDING
AREA. A 20-MINUTE RETURN
TRIP FROM MAIN TRACK

Forest Burn
Emergency
Shelter
1270M

JACKSON
PEAKS

Hanging Valley
Emergency Shelter
1390M
& PANORAMIC VIEWS

NARROW RIDGE WITH
STEEP DROPS ON
EITHER SIDE

FIXED ROPE & STAIRS
TO AID DESCENT

STEEP
DESCENT

TREELINE

VIEWS OF IRIS BURN
& BIG SLIP

IRIS
BURN

STEEP DESCENT
OVER SWITCHBACK

SMALL
WATERFALL

SIDE TRACK
TO IRIS BURN
FALLS—JUST
OFF MAP

VIEW NORTH
UP VALLEY

Iris Burn Hut

0    1 mile
0    1km
APPROX SCALE

Trailblazer

floor. **Iris Burn Hut** is located in a tussock-filled clearing. This large, 50-bunk hut is a pleasant, tranquil spot to rest after the day's exertions. There are good views up towards the head of the valley. A short side trip follows the Iris Burn upstream through the dense, mossy forest for twenty minutes to the dramatic Iris Burn Waterfall, set in an attractive clearing.

### Iris Burn Hut to Moturau Hut       17.5km/5-6 hours; Map 3i & ii

This is a much gentler day's tramp, meandering through the lush forest to emerge on the banks of Lake Manapouri, an idyllic location and a perfect spot to contemplate what has gone before.

The track begins by crossing a tributary of the Iris Burn and climbing a small knoll. It meanders through mixed forest and crosses another tributary before dropping into a large open area of regenerating vegetation. This large clearing was the site of the **Big Slip**, an enormous landslide that devastated the hillside to the west during a period of exceptionally heavy rain in 1984. Large boulders and piles of rock litter the valley bottom and the scar from the slip is still etched into the hillside, underlining just how unstable and fragile these cliffs can be. The clearing does, however, enable you to marvel at the grandeur of the mountains towering above you.

The track passes back into the forest and continues south-east alongside the river, crossing several more tributaries of the Iris Burn as it descends gently. Some $2^{1}/_{2}$-3 hours after leaving the Iris Burn Hut the track reaches **Rocky Point** (Map 3ii). There is a work camp here for track maintenance. The boulder-strewn inlet makes a good lunch spot.

Beyond Rocky Point the track climbs briefly, crosses a stream and descends once more to the Burn. The track sidles through a gorge and emerges at flats near the mouth of the river. As you begin to approach Lake Manapouri, the track turns east and cuts across a headland through beech and podocarp forest. The track rejoins the lake shore at **Shallow Bay**, skirting around the edge to **Moturau Hut**.

A lot of trampers walk out from Iris Burn Hut, skipping Moturau Hut. This is unfortunate since the latter is a slightly smaller hut, having only 40 bunks, and is frequently not full. The resulting tranquility can be in marked contrast to the bedlam that sometimes occurs in the larger, busier Iris Burn Hut. It is also fantastically located on the shores of **Lake Manapouri** and has splendid views west of the islands in the lake and the distant mountains.

The original name for Lake Manapouri was Moturau, a descriptive Maori name meaning 'Many Islands'. A mistake on an early map of the region wrongly labelled the lake Manapouri, itself a twisted version of Manawapora, the original Maori name for South Mavora Lake, literally meaning 'Sorrowful Heart'. Lake Manapouri is up to 440m/1440ft deep, making it the second deepest lake in New Zealand as well as the fifth largest. It has 34 islands. This vast expanse of water is used for generating electricity by New Zealand's largest power station. The lake water is assiduously controlled to ensure that it doesn't rise or fall beyond its natural level. If you stand on the tranquil shoreline you should see stunning reflections of the mountains, islands and Fiordland clouds.

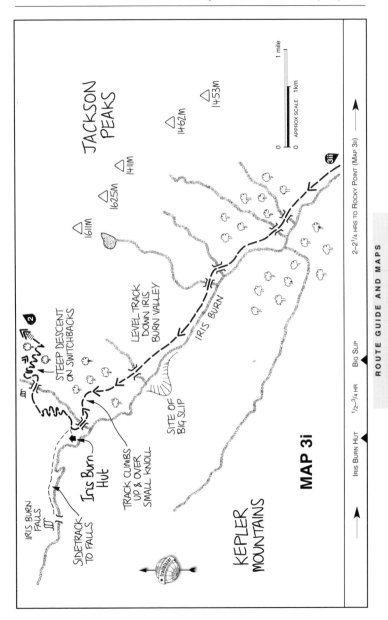

MAP 3i

JACKSON PEAKS

△1625M
△1611M
△1411M
△1462M
△1453M

STEEP DESCENT ON SWITCHBACKS

2

LEVEL TRACK DOWN IRIS BURN VALLEY

IRIS BURN

SITE OF BIG SLIP

Iris Burn Hut

TRACK CLIMBS UP & OVER SMALL KNOLL

IRIS BURN FALLS

SIDETRACK TO FALLS

KEPLER MOUNTAINS

3ii

0 APPROX SCALE 1km
0 1 mile

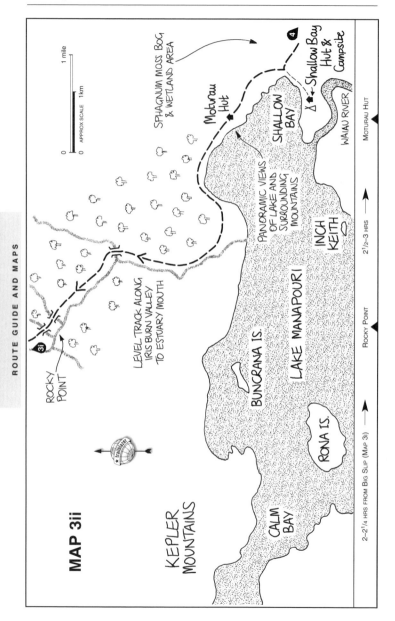

MAP 3ii

KEPLER MOUNTAINS

SPHAGNUM MOSS BOG & WETLAND AREA

Moturau Hut

Shallow Bay Hut & Campsite

SHALLOW BAY

WAIAU RIVER

ROCKY POINT

LEVEL TRACK ALONG IRIS BURN VALLEY TO ESTUARY MOUTH

PANORAMIC VIEWS OF LAKE AND SURROUNDING MOUNTAINS

BUNGRANA IS.

LAKE MANAPOURI

INCH KEITH

RONA IS.

CALM BAY

0    APPROX SCALE    1km
0                    1 mile

2–2¼ HRS FROM BIG SLIP (MAP 3i)    ROCKY POINT    2½–3 HRS    MOTURAU HUT

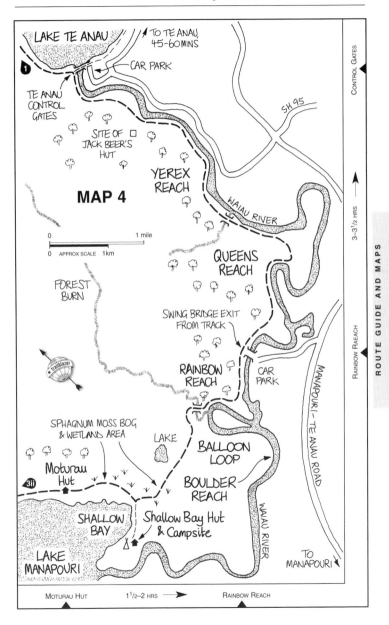

LAKE TE ANAU

TO TE ANAU, 45-60 MINS

CAR PARK

TE ANAU CONTROL GATES

SITE OF JACK BEER'S HUT

MAP 4

0 ———— 1 mile
0 APPROX SCALE 1km

YEREX REACH

SH 95

WAIAU RIVER

QUEENS REACH

FOREST BURN

trailblazer

SWING BRIDGE EXIT FROM TRACK

RAINBOW REACH

CAR PARK

SPHAGNUM MOSS BOG & WETLAND AREA

LAKE

BALLOON LOOP

Moturau Hut

BOULDER REACH

3ii

SHALLOW BAY

Shallow Bay Hut & Campsite

WAIAU RIVER

MANAPOURI - TE ANAU ROAD

LAKE MANAPOURI

TO MANAPOURI

CONTROL GATES

3-3½ HRS

RAINBOW REACH

ROUTE GUIDE AND MAPS

MOTURAU HUT    1½-2 HRS ➤    RAINBOW REACH

As you look out across the lake you can see (from left to right) the mouth of the Upper Waiau, Mt Titiroa (1710m/5608ft), the Hunter Mountains, the Turret Range, the Beehive, Leaning Peak (1476m/4841ft), the mouth of the Iris Burn, the Cathedral Peaks, the Kepler Mountains and the Iris Burn Valley along which the track leads. The islands scattered across the lake include (left to right) Inch Keith, Mahara, Holmwood, Pomona and Rona. It is an enchanting spot where the light changes frequently, shifting and illuminating different aspects of the view.

## Moturau Hut to Te Anau                22km/5¼-6½ hours; Map 4

This final section is a delightful, gentle tramp through thick forest. Although it is a fair distance from Moturau Hut to Te Anau, it is all on well-graded track. There are also several early exit points where you can catch a shuttle bus or taxi to whisk you back to the town, should you wish to finish before Te Anau.

Initially the track heads south-east around Shallow Bay. After a little less than 2km there is a signposted junction for Shallow Bay Hut, off to the right. Instead take the left-hand fork and head east on this final section.

After 1km the track passes through an area of wetland known as the **Sphagnum Moss Bog**. This amoeboid mire is centred on a small lake. Massive sheets of ice from the Manapouri Glacier once blanketed this area. As the glacier melted and retreated, so the meltwaters caused the deposited rocks to form dams, which now enclose this mire. A large block of ice was trapped here and eventually melted to create the depression now filled by this lake. Rich peat deposits provide the ideal base for sphagnum moss and various other plants to thrive. The bog can be several metres deep in places. The track crosses it on a series of boardwalks, both for your benefit and in order to protect the fragile landscape. A small viewing platform can be accessed on the edge of the lake.

The track skirts the moss bog and continues east, arriving at an old river terrace to cross the **Forest Burn** on a swing bridge just above its outlet into Balloon Loop, a pronounced meander in the **Waiau River**. The broad track continues to follow the Waiau River upstream for about 30 minutes along fertile terraces. The river continues to widen and several exposed bluffs give you good views up and down it. You finally emerge by a long swing bridge at **Rainbow Reach**. There is a shuttle bus service available from here to Te Anau during the summer.

The final section of track upriver from Rainbow Reach passes through an attractive stretch of forest. Having continued east, the track turns north and passes **Queens Reach**. It climbs slightly onto a river terrace and passes above a set of rapids. The track hugs the Waiau River as it passes **Yerex Reach** and the site of Jack Beer's old pioneer farm hut, which he occupied until 1930. Shortly afterwards the **Control Gates** are visible through the trees. The track curves through the forest and emerges at the Control Gates, from where it is a 45- to 60-minute gentle walk back alongside Lake Te Anau to the **Fiordland Visitor Centre**.

# Rakiura Track

*I must go over to New Zealand one day*  **A Stewart Islander**

## INTRODUCTION

Stewart Island offers trampers the chance to step back in time. Its remoteness has ensured that it remains largely unaffected by human activity. It is the least logged, burnt or developed of New Zealand's three main islands. Its forests give trekkers an idea of what much of southern New Zealand must have looked like once, before man arrived.

The 36km Rakiura Track is a moderately difficult tramp that offers you a brief introduction to the wilderness of Stewart Island. Usually completed in two to three days, it is best walked slowly so that you can appreciate what nature does when left to its own devices.

## HISTORY

Stewart Island has a rich history of both Maori and European settlement. Archaeologists have determined that as early as the 13th century tribes of Polynesian explorers travelled to the island in order to hunt moa. However, relatively few of these early Maori made Stewart Island their home, since it was impossible to grow kumara, sweet potato, their staple foodstuff. Instead they preferred to make annual trips to the main and offshore islands in order to hunt and gather muttonbirds, or titi, shellfish and eels. Hunting camps were established at several coastal sites including Port William/Potirepo and Freshwater River. These were accessed by outrigger canoe. This annual harvest still continues.

Captain James Cook and his crew were the first Europeans to sight the island in 1770. He mistakenly thought it was a peninsula connected to South Island and mapped it as 'South Cape'. This error went uncorrected for several

---

**The Land of the Glowing Skies**

Stewart Island's place in Maori folklore extends back to the discovery of New Zealand by the legendary Polynesian voyager Maui. Using South Island as a canoe he caught and hauled up a great flat fish that became North Island (see box p50). Stewart Island anchored the canoe and became known as Te Punga o te waka a Maui, 'The Anchorstone of Maui's Canoe'. It is more frequently referred to as Rakiura, which translates as 'The Land of the Glowing Skies'. This moniker is equally descriptive of both the island's spectacular blazing sunsets *and* its sunrises, not to mention the occasional night-time displays of Aurora Australis, the Southern Lights, which can be seen from here. To early Maori the island was also known more simplistically as Moutere Nui, the 'Big Island'.

decades until an American sealer OF Smith discovered Foveaux Strait in 1804. The strait was briefly known as Smith's Strait until it was renamed in 1809 after the then governor of New South Wales.

The island itself took its current European name from William Stewart, the first officer aboard the sealing vessel *The Pegasus*, which sailed from Port Jackson in 1809. Whilst the boat was in the large south-eastern harbour that now bears its name, Stewart began compiling the first detailed chart of the southern coast and eventually drafted the first map of the island in 1816.

European sealers arrived on the island in the early 1800s and by the mid 1820s had established the first mixed-race settlement at Sealer's Bay on Codfish Island off the north-west coast of Stewart Island. Sealing was replaced by whaling at the end of the 1820s. Small whaling stations were built on the island but never really evolved, although whaling continued until the 1920s.

Port William/Potirepo was the site of the early Maori settlement of Pa Whakataka. Both European sealers and whalers took advantage of its sheltered harbour. In 1866 gold was discovered here, on Magnetic Beach, but in insufficient quantities to support a sustained rush. The largest finds occurred between 1889 and 1894 in the mountains above Port Pegasus/Pikihatiti.

In 1864 Crown agents acting on behalf of the government negotiated terms for the sale and purchase of Stewart Island. A fee of £6000 was agreed, a small sum since it was considered that the island was of little or no value to the Maori. However, by the deeds certain Maori reserves were declared on the main island together with 21 'muttonbird islands', breeding grounds for the much-prized titi.

In 1861 sawmills opened at Kaipipi Bay in Paterson Inlet/Whaka a Te Wera. The timber-milling operation flourished for 60 years and at its peak supported 190 people. Today there is little evidence of their endeavours. In 1872 the government subsidised the relocation of a group of Shetland Islanders to Port William/Potirepo in order to develop the fledgling timber industry. The settlement was a failure, though, and all that remains is a handful of unlikely gum trees.

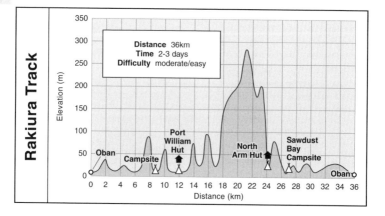

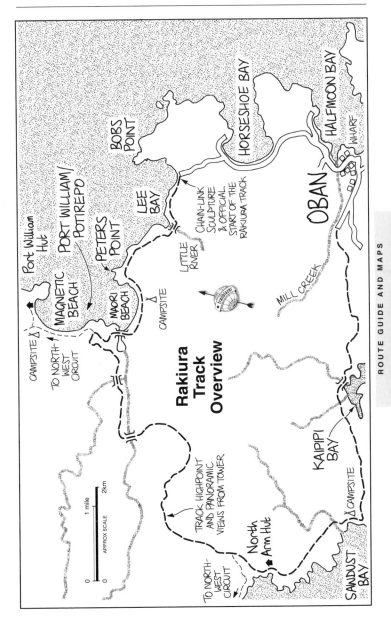

The discovery of tin in Pegasus Creek in 1888 led to a brief influx of people. A revival of interest in 1911 resulted in small developments until this industry also folded. Indeed, the only real industry to endure is fishing. In 1868 a deepwater oyster bed was discovered off the coast of Port Pegasus/Pikihatiti. Today fishing and marine farming feature heavily in the island's economy. Crayfish and paua are exported, whilst salmon and mussels are produced for export and the domestic markets. Blue cod is supplied to the New Zealand market.

The island's other major industry is tourism. Around 20,000 people visit Stewart Island to experience its wild landscapes. In March 2002, Stewart Island became New Zealand's fourteenth national park. Covering 1500 sq km, more than 90 per cent of the whole island, Rakiura National Park is New Zealand's fourth largest of the fourteen national parks and the first to be situated outside the two main islands.

## GEOLOGY

Stewart Island is New Zealand's third largest island. It is separated from South Island by Foveaux Strait, which is about 30km wide but comparatively shallow. Until the sea level rose after the end of the last period of glaciation, 10,000 years ago, the island was linked to the tip of South Island. As such Stewart Island is part of the enormous granite batholith that extends northwards into Fiordland. Complex peaks of coarse igneous rock rise to form the highest mountain on the island, Mt Anglem/Hananui, which reaches 980m/3214ft and bears the only traces of glaciation on the island. Rather than ice or glaciers, wind is the major shaper of land-forms here, such is the force of the constant prevailing west and north-westerly gusts. A process called 'exfoliation', whereby the granite is weathered, creates the spectacular bare domes that can be seen across the island. It is extremely rugged.

Other topographical features of note include the rounded foothills around Halfmoon Bay and the Paterson Inlet-Freshwater River depression that almost completely splits the island. Paterson Inlet is the island's largest harbour, extending 16km from the open sea and containing 20 islands. Stewart Island itself is surrounded by about 170 offshore islands and rock stacks.

The island tilts from west to east so that streams rising relatively near the west coast meet the sea to the east.

Stewart Island is infamous for its muddy bogs and deep sinking mires. This is a consequence of the quantity of rainfall that lands on the island and the island's poorly-drained soils. You must simply accept that you will most likely become caked in mud. Tread carefully around the larger wallows but be aware that the pungent, earthy mud will inevitably claim you.

## FLORA AND FAUNA

### Flora

Stewart Island is remarkable for its almost complete cover of natural flora. Rugged and windswept, it is mostly covered in dense forest and wetland vegetation. Low growing sub-alpine scrub clings to the mountainsides whilst podocarp-broadleaf forest extends to the water's edge. This is the preserve of the southernmost podocarp forest in the world. The forests mainly comprise rimu, kamahi, miro and rata, which protect a rich diversity of tree and ground ferns. At their 300m/985ft upper limit, hardy manuka and sub-alpine shrubs become dominant. Tussock grasslands and herb fields offer a dramatic contrast to the dense forest formed at lower altitudes. Stewart Island vegetation is unique in that beech, which dominates the rest of New Zealand's forests, is absent here. Biogeographers think this odd exemption is probably due to a combination of climate changes and glaciation. Because of the high rainfall, mosses and lichens thrive here, ensuring that the forest wears a permanent green mantle.

## Fauna
Stewart Island is also ecologically unique since it is largely free of predatory animals. Although some feral cats, possums and rats have reached the island, it is still free from stoats, ferrets and weasels. Consequently, forest **bird species** are able to thrive. The lack of large-scale land clearance for farming has also ensured that most ecosystems remain intact.

Around the coast muttonbirds, shags, mollymawks, cape pigeons and little blue penguins can be seen. A host of wading birds including oystercatchers, herons and dotterels inhabit the tidal flats. In the forests bellbirds, tui, fantails, parakeets and kereru are widespread. Grey warblers, weka, kaka, tomtits, saddlebacks and kakapo also exist here. After the silence of some mainland forests this can seem a noisy choral cacophony. Stewart Island kiwis are found throughout most of the island. Amongst their favourite haunts are the sand dunes of Mason Bay. Unlike their mainland relatives, Stewart Island kiwis are active during daylight hours as well as at night and can be seen nonchalant and absorbed, fossicking for invertebrates in the seaweed and kelp washed ashore. Here the shrill dawn chorus rings out all day. This is one of the largest of New Zealand's kiwi species and exists here in good numbers. The population is estimated to be around 20,000 birds. The island represents most people's best chance of seeing a kiwi in the wild. Should you spot one remember the following DOC guidelines in order to minimise disturbance to the bird: keep noise to a minimum, stay five metres from the bird at all times, do not chase it, do not shine bright light directly at it and do not use flash photography.

Other native **fauna** found on Stewart Island include short and long-tailed bats, lizards and geckos. Whitetail and red deer have been introduced to the island. Seals and sea-lions can sometimes be spotted off the coast. Because there are no trout on the island, the streams support **native fish** such as kokopu.

The islands that surround Stewart Island are largely free of pests. These islands offer important conservation opportunities in the battle to preserve endangered species. A degree of care and vigilance should ensure that they remain so. If you find yourself with a spare day in Oban take time to pop across to Ulva Island on a water taxi in order to experience the rich diversity of birdlife found on this protected, pest-free reserve. Tramp the narrow trails through thick native forest looking out for birds that you almost certainly won't spot elsewhere such as saddlebacks, yellowheads and brown kiwis, and check out the beaches for fur and elephant seals basking on the sand.

## PLANNING YOUR TRAMP

### When to go

Although this is the most popular Stewart Island tramp, the track will still feel empty in comparison to most of the other Great Walks since only about 1500-2000 people complete it each year.

Stewart Island's climate has an unfairly harsh reputation. Despite its southerly latitude, it is surprisingly mild with temperatures averaging 16.6°C in summer and 9.9°C in winter. It even enjoys occasional periods of settled weather. Annual rainfall of about 1600mm is only slightly higher than the national average. However, it does rain up to 290 days a year, ensuring that you get a little rain a lot of the time. The prevailing winds tend to be south-westerly, which means that the western coast receives a much higher annual rainfall. The only snowfall occurs on the summit of Mt Anglem/Hananui.

The island's reputation for remarkably changeable weather *is* justified, however. Rain can fall and then clear several times in the course of a day, so make sure that you are prepared for all eventualities. Good waterproof clothing is essential.

The track is open all year. The busiest season is from **December to April**. The ideal time is towards the end of this period when visitor numbers begin to dwindle and the weather remains potentially more stable. Unfortunately, due to the unpredictability of the weather patterns, no particular period can really be said to be better than another.

### Sources of information

Once you are on Stewart Island the best place to organise and book your tramp is the friendly, helpful DOC office in the **Rakiura National Park Visitor Centre** (☎ 03-219 0002 for the DOC desk or 03-219 0009 for the visitor centre, 🖳 stewartislandfc@doc.govt.nz), on Main Rd, Halfmoon Bay. The office is open weekdays 8am-5pm and weekends 9am-4pm.

**Oban Visitor Information Centre** (🖳 www.stewartislandexperience.co.nz), also on Main Rd, is open weekdays 8am-7pm and weekends 9am-7pm in summer, and 8am-5pm weekdays and 10am-noon at weekends for the rest of the year. The staff are very familiar with the island and can advise or answer any questions that you may have. They can also sell you all necessary mapping and information leaflets required to enjoy your tramp. **Stewart Island Visitor Information Centre** (☎ 03-219 1400, 🖳 www.stewartisland.co.nz) can be found at 12 Elgin Terrace.

Should you wish to book your tramp in advance, approach the **DOC** (☎ 03-214 4589, 🖳 invercargill@doc.govt.nz) office in Invercargill, which can be found on the seventh floor of the Cue on Don Building at 33 Don St and is open during the week from 8.30am-4.30pm. For other information regarding Stewart Island visit **Invercargill i-SITE** (☎ 03-214 6243, 🖳 www.invercargill.org.nz)

in the Southland Museum and Art Gallery at 108 Gala St, adjacent to the entrance to Queens Park. The visitor centre is open 9am-5pm on weekdays and 10am-5pm at weekends.

## Getting to the trailhead

Stewart Island can be reached by sea or by air. The Stewart Island Experience ferry (☎ 03-212 7660, 🖳 www.stewartislandexperience.co.nz) operates from Bluff to Oban up to five times per day in high summer and at least daily during the rest of the year. Fares cost NZ$51 each way. They will also arrange bus transfers from Invercargill, Te Anau or Queenstown to Bluff. It takes around one hour to cross the frequently stormy 30km Foveaux Strait but is a fabulous way to arrive on the island. You also have the chance to see plenty of seabirds during the crossing. **Stewart Island Flights** (☎ 03-218 9129, 🖳 www.stewartis landflights.com) operates from Invercargill to Oban three times a day. Although standard fares cost NZ$95/NZ$175 one way/return, a standby seat on this short 25-minute flight can prove to be almost as cheap as the ferry crossing. You should check directly with both operators for exact times and availability. The Invercargill Information Centre and even some hostels in Invercargill may be prepared to make bookings for you.

The Rakiura Track itself begins in **Lee Bay**, north of Oban and finishes at the end of the Kaipipi road, to the west of the town. Lee Bay is 5km from Halfmoon Bay, the home of Oban, via the attractive Horseshoe Bay. Most trampers walk this section of tarmac road. The Kaipipi road end is 2km from Halfmoon Bay on a sealed gravel road. Again, most trampers walk off the track and back into the settlement at Oban. If you prefer, it is possible to hitch or arrange a taxi to either end of the track.

## Local services

Only a very small stretch of Stewart Island's 755km coastline is touched by human habitation. There is barely 20km of road on the island compared to almost 250km of track. The tiny settlement of **Oban** (see map p273) consists of a scattering of houses in the bush around the attractive crescent of Halfmoon Bay. The majority of Stewart Island's 400 residents live here. Despite the increase in tourism it still feels quiet.

There is a DOC office and information centre, a small store, several cafés, restaurants and a pub. Although the small store is relatively well stocked it is more expensive than the equivalent on South Island so try to arrive fully equipped for your tramp. Remember, there are no banks or ATMs on the island so, although a number of businesses take credit cards, make sure to bring plenty of cash with you.

There is plenty of accommodation of various standards and prices but it can be surprisingly difficult to get a bed so make sure you book ahead during peak season. The DOC office keeps a daily list of which places still have vacancies and will phone around on your behalf should you arrive without having booked anything. The characterful, historic *South Sea Hotel* (☎ 03-219 1059, 🖳 www .stewart-island.co.nz; sgl/dbl NZ$65-100/85-110 depending on whether you want a sea view, motel units NZ$155) on Elgin Terrace offers standard accommodation at reasonable rates, whilst its public bar is the traditional meeting point on the island. On Ayr St the *Stewart Island Backpackers* (☎ 03-219 1114, 🖳 shearwater.inn@stewart-island.co.nz; camping NZ$10 per person, dorm NZ$24, sgl/dbl NZ$30/50) is a large hostel offering fairly basic but perfectly adequate dorm, single- and double-room accommodation. *Bunkers Backpackers* (☎ 03-2191 160, 🖳 www.bunkersbackpackers.co.nz; dorm/sgl/dbl NZ$25/45/70) on Argyle St has a comfy lounge and decent kitchen facilities. Should you prefer something more personal try the superb, cosy *Jo and Andy's B&B* (☎ 03-219 1230, 🖳 jariksem@clear.net.nz; sgl/dbl NZ$48/70), which sleeps just five in an old fashioned home full of welcoming touches and where you are offered traditional Southland hospitality.

Even more intimate are the two gorgeous, upmarket suites at *Sails Ashore* (☎ 03-219 1151, 🖳 www.sailsashore.co.nz; dbl first night NZ$635, subsequent nights NZ$405), which overlooks Halfmoon Bay and operates on a B&B basis. *Glendaruel B&B* (☎ 03-219 1092, 🖳 www.glendaruel.co.nz; sgl/dbl NZ$100-150/200), a ten-minute stroll from town overlooking Paterson Inlet, is run by very accommodating hosts and has a handful of en suite rooms, a guest lounge and covered balconies. Around 15 minutes east of town *Port of Call* (☎ 03-219 1394, 🖳 www.portofcall.co.nz; sgl/dbl NZ$300/385) is an attractive boutique B&B set on the edge of a cliff amidst native bush where there are also self-catering options in The Bach (NZ$300 per couple) and cottage (NZ$170 per couple). *Rakiura Retreat Motel* (☎ 03-219 1096, 🖳 www .rakiuraretreat.co.nz; units NZ$120-200) is set a little further away from the town centre on a hill overlooking the bay so has superb views as well as nicely maintained apartments.

For **food**, try the seafood chowder or blue cod on offer at the *South Sea Hotel* (see p271, NZ$20-30), which is also the island's only pub; *Just Café* (NZ$10-15) at 6 Main St serves home-baked cookies, cakes and filling snacks; the *Church Hill Café* (NZ$30-40) at 36 Kamahi Rd offers good-value lunches and good-quality evening meals from the country's southernmost stonegrill; or there's the cheap *Kai Kart* (NZ$5-20) on Ayr St where the exceptionally fresh, delicious seafood is served from a caravan. For a complete night out drop in on *Charliez* (🖳 www.charliez.co.nz), a cosy pizza den at 10 Main Rd with a superb little cinema, the Rakiura Theatre, right next door.

## Huts and campsites

The **huts** at Port William and North Arm have space for 24 and 26 people respectively but cannot be booked in advance. Bunks, mattresses, a stove for heating, toilet facilities and water are all supplied. **You must carry your own cooking gear and fuel**. A date-stamped **Great Walks pass** is necessary in order to stay in the huts. This must be pre-purchased from a DOC office or information centre. Wardens may be resident at each hut during the summer to check passes and will charge you a higher premium on the spot if you can't present one. There is a limit of two consecutive nights in any hut.

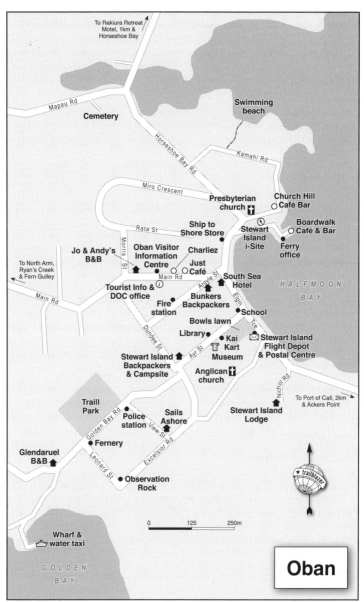

To Rakiura Retreat
Motel, 1km &
Horseshoe Bay

Mapau Rd

Cemetery

Swimming
beach

Horseshoe Bay Rd

Kamahi Rd

Miro Crescent

Presbyterian
church

Church Hill
Café Bar

Rata St

Ship to
Shore Store

Stewart
Island
i-Site

Boardwalk
Café & Bar

Ferry
office

Morris St

Jo & Andy's
B&B

Oban Visitor
Information
Centre

Charliez

Just
Café

Main Rd

Argyle St

South Sea
Hotel

HALFMOON
BAY

To North Arm,
Ryan's Creek
& Fern Gulley

Main Rd

Tourist Info &
DOC office

Fire
station

Bunkers
Backpackers

Elgin Tce

School

Dundee St

Bowls lawn

Library

Kai
Kart
Museum

Stewart Island
Flight Depot
& Postal Centre

Ayr St

Stewart Island
Backpackers
& Campsite

Anglican
church

Nichol Rd

To Port of Call, 2km
& Ackers Point

Traill
Park

Golden Bay Rd

Police
station

Sails
Ashore

Stewart Island
Lodge

View St

Glendaruel
B&B

Fernery

Leonard St

Excelsior Rd

Observation
Rock

★ trailblazer

0        125        250m

Wharf &
water taxi

GOLDEN
BAY

Oban

ROUTE GUIDE AND MAPS

There is no off-season on this track and prices apply year-round. The **adult hut fee** is NZ$15 and the **camping fee** is NZ$5. There is no charge for children or youths.

**Camping** is allowed only at the designated sites at Maori Beach, Port William and Sawdust Bay. Each site is also provided with a shelter, toilets and a water supply.

## Maps

The most useful map available for the Rakiura Track is the *Stewart Island National Park Map* (336–10) which covers the whole island at 1:150,000 scale. It also includes a more detailed 1:50,000 inset of the Rakiura Track itself. This is readily available from DOC offices and information centres throughout South Island. The Topomaps' *Halfmoon Bay* (E48) and *Ruggedy* (D48) also cover the track in combination.

## Distances and times

It is possible to walk the 36km track in either direction although most people prefer to start at Lee Bay and tramp anticlockwise. If you are completing the track in three days you can afford to amble along the beaches, revel in the forests' tranquility and indulge in some bird spotting. It also means that if the weather turns sour you have time to wait out the heavier rain.

Should you choose to complete the track in only two days, one of those days will be tough. Although it is possible to shorten the stretch from Oban to North Arm Hut by omitting the section of track that leads to Port William Hut and hence the need to backtrack, by doing so you will miss the idyllic Magnetic Beach and superbly situated hut at Port William. Better perhaps that you enjoy a shorter day's tramp to Port William, allowing yourself sufficient time to explore the area here fully, before pushing hard to cross the headland and return to Oban the following day.

| | | |
|---|---|---|
| Oban to Port William Hut | 12km | 4-5 hours |
| Port William Hut to North Arm Hut | 12km | 4³/₄-6 hours |
| North Arm Hut to Oban | 12km | 4-5 hours |

## TRACK DESCRIPTION

### Oban to Port William Hut         12km/4-5 hours; Map 1

This is a largely-level, gentle day's tramp which introduces you to some of Stewart Island's subtle charms, its craggy terrain and striking beaches.

Begin at the waterfront in front of **South Sea Hotel** and head north along Horseshoe Bay Rd, climbing over a headland and descending to the coast at **Horseshoe Bay**. Skirt the crescent bay until you reach its far end, turn left at this point and cross another headland until you emerge at Lee Bay.

The track proper begins here by passing through a specially commissioned **chain-link sculpture** that commemorates the creation of Rakiura National Park. The inspiration for the sculpture is drawn from the Maori creation story (see p50). The stylised anchor chain sculpture is secured firmly on land by a

ROUTE GUIDE AND MAPS

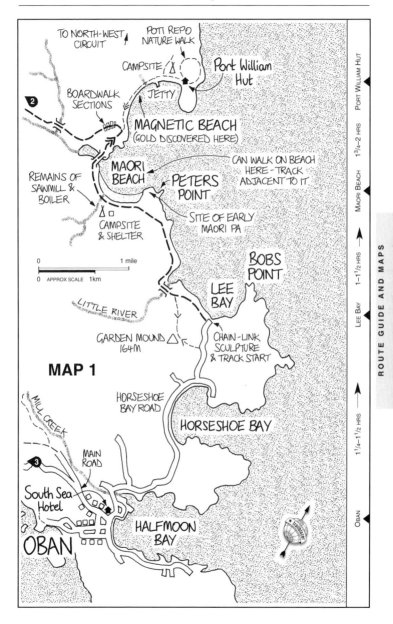

TO NORTH-WEST CIRCUIT

POTI REPO NATURE WALK

CAMPSITE

Port William Hut

BOARDWALK SECTIONS

JETTY

MAGNETIC BEACH
(GOLD DISCOVERED HERE)

MAORI BEACH

PETERS POINT

CAN WALK ON BEACH HERE - TRACK ADJACENT TO IT

REMAINS OF SAWMILL & BOILER

CAMPSITE & SHELTER

SITE OF EARLY MAORI PA

0        1 mile
0   APPROX SCALE   1km

BOBS POINT

LEE BAY

LITTLE RIVER

MAP 1

GARDEN MOUND 164M

CHAIN-LINK SCULPTURE & TRACK START

MILL CREEK

HORSESHOE BAY ROAD

MAIN ROAD

HORSESHOE BAY

South Sea Hotel

OBAN

HALFMOON BAY

PORT WILLIAM HUT

1¾-2 HRS

MAORI BEACH

1-1½ HRS

LEE BAY

1¼-1½ HRS

OBAN

ROUTE GUIDE AND MAPS

shackle but slips into the sea and vanishes beneath Foveaux Strait, a reminder of the spiritual and physical connections between Stewart Island and Bluff, the traditional stern post of Te Waka a Maui. The chain links also symbolise a history of inter-relationships that have given the people of Stewart Island a powerful sense of heritage and identity. Unfortunately, not everyone recognises this. The day after its unveiling a disgruntled local salmon-farm worker shot at the sculpture. The bullet indent is still visible at the top of the main arch.

From here the track passes through a small group of trees before emerging on the coast. The track hugs the coast, edging along beside wind-sheared kamahi and rimu groves. Fuchsia, supplejack and rata are also evident in the approach to the Little River estuary. This delightful spot features forest trees, sometimes loaded with summer blossom that overhang the calm waters and sandy beaches.

Crossing over the bridge, you now head inland, returning after 1km to the shoreline to round **Peters Point**, which used to be the site of an early Maori village. The point is named after Peter Garrotty who planned to grow strawberries in the area. Unfortunately the soil was too peaty in consistency. He tried to sweeten the soil by adding lime made by burning oyster shells. The surplus lime he produced he sold to other farmers and even shipped to New Zealand's South Island.

The track drops down to **Maori Beach** where there is a DOC shelter and campsite. Maori Beach itself is an attractive broad swathe of white sand, backed by small dunes and grasslands. The area has known human occupation since pre-European times and in the early 1900s it supported a sawmilling community. By 1920 a sufficient number of families lived here to merit the construction of a school, though the depression forced the closure of the sawmills and by 1931 all the mills and the school had shut. While a **rusting boiler**, hidden at the southern end of the beach by regenerating forest, is a reminder of these early days, today Maori Beach is the redoubt of little more than ghosts.

Walk the length of the beach slowly, foraging as you go. Skulls and vertebrae from the occasional stranded whale, shells and other flotsam litter the beach. Torn nets, sections of rope, battered bait-boxes and lost floats can also be found here. At the northern end of the beach a broad tidal stream is spanned by a swing bridge. From there, the track turns inland and begins to climb steeply, rising 150m. At the top of the climb is a junction that heads inland towards North Arm Hut. For now, continue north on the right-hand track, descending equally steeply to **Magnetic Beach**, where gold was discovered in small quantities in 1866. At low tide you can drop off the track and follow the beach round to **Port William Hut and Campsite**, which lie by a rickety jetty. At high tide there is an alternative track above the shoreline. By the campsite is a signposted junction for the section of the tough North-West Circuit that heads to Bungaree Hut.

Port William Hut is a very pleasant spot, situated on the former site of a Maori village. The clump of towering gum trees in front of the 24-bunk hut is all that remains of the doomed settlement of Shetland Islanders sent here in

1876. If you arrive early or have energy to spare there is a one-hour return nature walk that circles the headland. The **Poti Repo** ('Corner of Swamp') **nature walk** is a small, occasionally muddy track that loops through the forest. Supplejack, crown fern, coprosa and wheki are all marked, as are broadleaf, rimu, miro and kamahi. The track emerges on the northern edge of the headland with excellent views north all the way up the coast to Big Bungaree Beach and Gull Rock Point and back south to Bobs Point by the trailhead at Lee Bay. This is a dramatic, isolated spot, especially close to sunset when the sky tends to look moody and bruised.

## Port William Hut to North Arm Hut                 12km/5-6 hours; Map 2

This is the toughest day of the three, although it is still not *that* difficult. Relentlessly undulating track climbs to the tramp's high point, from where you can enjoy great views of the land that you have passed over as well as that which you are about to tackle.

This section begins with a retracing of steps for 2km. Head south along Magnetic Beach. At the end of the beach haul yourself up the knoll to the sign-posted junction with the main track. Take the right-hand fork. The track turns inland, heading westwards. This initial section has been planked to make progress easier. The track winds through the forest, over a small hill, before dropping to a pretty stream that runs into the sea at Maori Beach. The track runs alongside the stream, crossing a side creek on a swing bridge, before turning south and crossing a second swing bridge over the stream itself.

At this point the track begins to climb and fall repeatedly as it passes over several hills before turning west and crossing another side creek linked to the earlier unnamed stream. Stretches of well-maintained boardwalk alternate with muddy patches of track; jumbles of tree roots and fallen branches must be scrambled over. The track begins to ascend from here and does so for 2km until it reaches the bush saddle, the climb to the summit ridge passing through lush vegetation. Previously milled and regenerating podocarp forest gives way to rata and sub-alpine scrub. At the summit a signpost directs you to a **look-out point** (305m/1000ft), the highest point on the Rakiura Track, with views south of the dense forest canopy stretching down to shimmering Paterson Inlet/Whaka a Te Wera and beyond to the Tin Range. The panoramic views in other directions reveal just how rugged and broken is the island's topography. Forested ridges stretch away all around.

From here the track descends 3km through the forest. It passes a junction to Freshwater Landing Hut, part of the North-West Circuit, before emerging by the shoreline. Rounding a small inlet it arrives at **North Arm Hut**. This pleasant 26-bunk hut is located above North Arm Bay. Camping is not permitted here. Although much of the bay is too shallow to swim in, even at high tide, it is an attractive spot to loiter and catch the sunset. At low tide the water retreats a long way, exposing rocky coves, interesting rock formations and shellfish reef platforms that are well worth exploring.

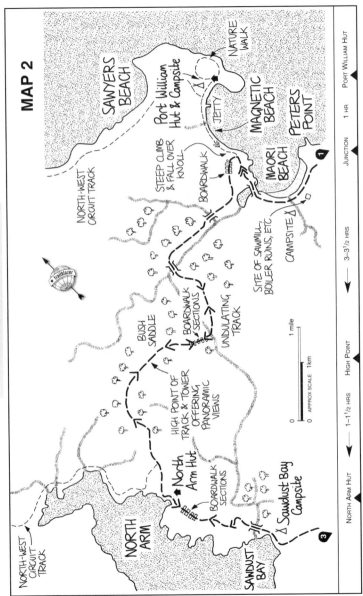

MAP 2

SAWYERS BEACH

NORTH-WEST CIRCUIT TRACK

STEEP CLIMB & FALL OVER KNOLL

BOARDWALK

Port William Hut & Campsite

NATURE WALK

MAGNETIC BEACH

JETTY

MAORI BEACH

PETERS POINT

SITE OF SAWMILL, BOILER RUINS, ETC

CAMPSITE △

*trailblazer*

BOARDWALK SECTIONS

BUSH SADDLE

UNDULATING TRACK

HIGH POINT OF TRACK & TOWER OFFERING PANORAMIC VIEWS

North Arm Hut

BOARDWALK SECTIONS

NORTH ARM

NORTH-WEST CIRCUIT TRACK

Sawdust Bay Campsite

SAWDUST BAY

0          1 mile

0    APPROX SCALE   1km

| ▶ Port William Hut | 1 HR | Junction ▶ | 3–3½ HRS | High Point ▶ | 1–1½ HRS | North Arm Hut ▶ |

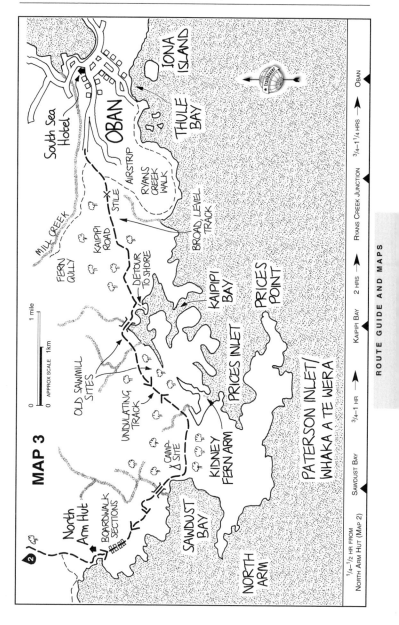

MAP 3

North Arm Hut

BOARDWALK
SECTIONS

SAWDUST BAY

NORTH ARM

OLD SAWMILL SITES

UNDULATING TRACK

CAMP SITE

KIDNEY FERN ARM

PRICES INLET

PRICES POINT

PATERSON INLET/
WHAKA A TE WERA

DETOUR TO SHORE

FERN GULLY

KAIPIPI ROAD

MILL CREEK

STILE

South Sea Hotel

OBAN

AIRSTRIP

RYANS CREEK WALK

BROAD LEVEL TRACK

KAIPIPI BAY

THULE BAY

IONA ISLAND

trailblazer

0          1 mile
APPROX SCALE   1km
0

¼–½ HR FROM
North Arm Hut (Map 2) ▶ Sawdust Bay  ¾–1 HR ▶ Kaipipi Bay  2 HRS ▶ Ryans Creek Junction  ¾–1¼ HRS ▶ Oban

**North Arm Hut to Oban**                    **12km/3³/₄-4³/₄ hours; Map 3**

The final section tracks along Paterson Inlet/Whaka a Te Wera before heading inland to Kaipipi Rd and on to Oban. It is a steady tramp on a reasonably level, well-maintained trail.

You begin by heading south on more boardwalk, climbing 90m over a forested hill and bypassing several headlands before descending to **Sawdust Bay**. Between 1914 and 1918 this was the site of a sawmill.

Midway along the bay is the official **Sawdust Bay Campsite**. This isn't a particularly good spot, set in the forest adjacent to the track. At low tide you can walk out on the mud-flats quite a long way. It is possible to see the vast mud-flats on the far side of the inlet around Freshwater River estuary. Sea grass and cockles grow on these extensive flats, which are important spawning grounds for fish. At low tide they become a haven for large numbers of wading birds that feed here.

You then turn inland, heading east to cross a headland over a bush saddle dominated by kamahi and rimu, rejoining the shoreline at **Kidney Fern Arm** to skirt around **Prices Inlet**. The track then passes a couple of sites of old sawmills that were working in the early to mid-1860s and each of which, at their height, employed around 100 people. Having dropped to Kaipipi Bay and crossed the pretty, fern-draped head of the inlet on a footbridge, you find, shortly afterwards, a small detour leading to the shoreline, which makes a good spot for a break or lunch.

Continuing to head east, the track now follows the old **Kaipipi Road** – the former logging road. At one time it was the busiest, best-kept road on the island and although its heyday has long since passed, the broad track is still in excellent condition and allows for good, steady-paced tramping.

After 2.5km you reach a stile. Beyond this is the signposted junction for **Ryans Creek Walk**, an attractive coastal stroll that hugs the shore as it heads south and then east to Thule and Golden Bay, to the south of Oban. The main path, however, continues to head east, arriving at **Mill Creek** and the junction to **Fern Gully**. Just after this, to the east, is the end of the **Kaipipi Road** which in turn becomes Main Road and leads right to the heart of Oban. A brisk 2km downhill stroll taking 30-45 minutes will deposit you back at the wharf in **Halfmoon Bay**.

# APPENDIX A: MAP KEYS

## Trail map key

| | | | | | |
|---|---|---|---|---|---|
| | Walking track | | Bridge | ♠ | Accommodation |
| | Road | | Sea | ⋏ | Campsite |
| | Steps | | River | PO | Post Office |
| | Slope | | Stream | † | Church |
| | Steep slope | | Crags or cliffs | ☏ | Public telephone |
| | Building or ruin | | | ❸ | Map continuation |

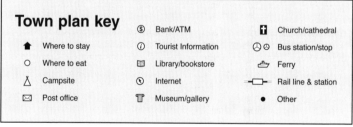

## Town plan key

| | | | | | |
|---|---|---|---|---|---|
| ♠ | Where to stay | $ | Bank/ATM | | Church/cathedral |
| ○ | Where to eat | ⓘ | Tourist Information | | Bus station/stop |
| ⋏ | Campsite | | Library/bookstore | | Ferry |
| ✉ | Post office | Ⓝ | Internet | | Rail line & station |
| | | ▥ | Museum/gallery | ● | Other |

# APPENDIX B: GLOSSARY OF MAORI TERMS

**adze** – axe/club, usually fashioned from greenstone
**ana** – cave
**ao** – cloud
**Aoraki** – Maori name for Mt Cook
**Aotearoa** – Land of the Long White Cloud (New Zealand)
**ara** – road or path
**awa** – river
**bach** – holiday home (pronounced 'batch')
**haka** – traditional war dance
**hangi** – earth oven made by digging a hole and steaming food over hot coals, a traditional Maori feast
**hapu** – sub-tribe/smaller tribal grouping (several hapu make up an *iwi*)
**Hawaiki** – traditional Polynesian homeland of the Maori
**heitiki/tiki** – carved, stylised grotesque/human figure
**hongi** – Maori greeting where two people press noses together
**iwi** – tribe/tribal group with common lineage
**kahurangi** – treasured possession
**kai** – food
**kai moana** – seafood
**kainga** – unfortified village/home
**kumara** – type of sweet potato
**mana** – prestige/status/authority
**manga** – stream
**manu** – bird
**Maori** – indigenous people
**Maoritanga** – Maori culture/'Maoriness'
**marae** – literally 'courtyard in front of a meeting house'. Focal point of a settlement. Has come to refer to any complex centred on a meeting house.
**mata** – headland
**Maui** – important figure in Maori mythology
**maunga** – mountain
**moana** – sea
**moko** – tattoo
**ngati** – 'people of'/'descendants of'; plural is *nga*
**nui** – great or big
**pa** – fortified village
**pakeha** – non-Maori/settler of European origin

**pounamu** – greenstone/type of jade
**powhiri** – traditional Maori welcome to a *marae*
**puke** – hill
**puna** – spring
**Rakiura** – literally 'Land of the Glowing Skies' ie Stewart Island
**rangi** – sky/heavens
**raro** – north
**roto** – lake
**taipo** – goblin
**tane** – man
**tangata** – people
**taniwha** – mythical water monster
**taonga** – something of great value, often passed down through generations
**tapu** – sacred/forbidden
**tara** – peak
**Te Ika a Maui** – literally 'The Fish of Maui' ie North Island
**Te Papa** – literally 'our place'/special container for holding treasured items
**Te Wahipounamu** – South Island
**tiki** – Maori pendant depicting a distorted human figure
**tohunga** – priest
**tonga** – south
**uru** – west
**wai** – water
**waka** – canoe
**whakapapa** – family tree
**whanau** – extended family
**whare** – house
**whenua** – land/country
**whiti** – east

# APPENDIX C: HUT ACCOMMODATION BOOKING

## The hut system

DOC has a network of more than 950 huts in National, Maritime and Forest parks. To stay in these huts you must purchase **backcountry hut tickets**, which cost NZ$5 each and can be brought from any DOC office. When you arrive at the hut, you simply date your ticket(s) and deposit them in the box provided. The huts fall into four categories. **Serviced huts** are the premier track accommodation and cost NZ$10 per night (ie two tickets). The exception are **Alpine Serviced huts** which cost NZ$20-35. They provide bunks or sleeping platforms, water, heating facilities, cooking facilities and possibly fuel. They may also be attended by a warden. **Standard huts** are more sparsely equipped, and cost NZ$5 per night. They provide bunks or sleeping platforms as well as toilet facilities and water supply. **Basic huts** are little more than a shelter or bivouac with limited facilities and are free to use. Most of New Zealand's tracks have serviced or standard huts on them. If you are going to do a lot of tramping on these back-country tracks, consider an annual hut pass (NZ$90). This entitles you to stay in serviced and standard huts throughout the year.

## Huts on the Great Walks

The Great Walks Huts constitute the fourth category and are an exception to the structure outlined above. To use the huts on the nine designated Great Walks during the peak season (generally October to April, see below), you must purchase a **Great Walks hut pass**. Other hut tickets and annual passes are not usable on these routes at this time. These hut passes must be purchased before you start the track or you will be charged a hefty fine.

The cost of each hut pass varies according to the popularity of the Great Walk in question. Prices start at NZ$15 per night for the Rakiura Track, rising to NZ$45 per night on the Routeburn, Kepler and Milford tracks. Children aged 17 or under can stay free of charge in the huts or campsites though. All relevant prices are quoted in the text for each of the routes.

Six of the Great Walks now operate an **advance booking system**, where the numbers of users are regulated and there are a maximum number of people allowed to start the track each day. These are the Lake Waikaremoana, Abel Tasman and Heaphy Tracks, where bookings are required all year round, and the Routeburn, Milford and Kepler tracks, where bookings are required only during the peak season from 1 October to 30 April. Your advance booking of a Great Walks Hut pass on these tracks guarantees you a bunk in the huts on the date specified. Owing to their popularity you may need not to have reserve dates available when you contact DOC to make your booking. On the other tracks, where numbers are not regulated, the huts operate on a first-come-first-served basis and you may find yourself sleeping on the floor if you arrive late and the hut is already full. Note, however, that you still need to buy a Great Walks hut pass in advance of your departure. But numbers are not restricted and effectively you are not booking a space, just paying your hut fees.

Outside the peak/summer season, when the tracks are much less heavily used, unserviced and not staffed by wardens, trampers may stay overnight in the huts by using **backcountry hut tickets**, as on the other NZ walks. The huts cost NZ$15 at this time.

| Track | Usual Peak Season | Booking required in high season |
|---|---|---|
| **Lake Waikaremoana** | Beginning of Oct to end of April | X (all year) |
| **Tongariro Circuit** | Late October to early June | |
| **Whanganui River Journey** | Beginning of Oct to end of April | |
| **Abel Tasman** | Beginning of Oct to end of April | X (all year) |
| **Heaphy** | Beginning of Oct to end of April | X (all year) |
| **Routeburn** | Beginning of Oct to end of April | X |
| **Milford** | Beginning of Oct to end of April | X |
| **Kepler** | Beginning of Oct to end of April | X |
| **Rakiura** | Beginning of Oct to end of April | |

# INDEX

**Page references in bold type refer to maps**

# TRAILBLAZER GUIDES – TITLE LIST

**www.trailblazer-guides.com**

SEA
TASMAN SEA

Hawera

Farewell
Spit

Collingwood    Takaka
HEAPHY                    ABEL TASMAN
TRACK                     COAST TRACK
Motueka          Wellington
Karamea          Picton
Nelson
Blenheim          COOK
STRAIT

Westport    Ariki

Punakaiki

Greymouth          Kaikoura

Hokitika

Franz Josef    △ Mt Cook/
Aoraki          Christchurch

Haast          Ashburton

Timaru

Milford
Sound    ROUTEBURN
TRACK
MILFORD    Wanaka
TRACK    Glenorchy    Tarras
Glade House
Queenstown          Oamaru
Lake
Te Anau
Lake
Wakatipu
KEPLER          Te Anau
TRACK
Lake
Manapouri          Gore          Dunedin

Clifden

Invercargill
Bluff
Foveaux          Strait
Solander
Island          RAKIURA
TRACK    Oban

Stewart
Island

SOUTH PACIFIC SEA

## New Zealand
### SOUTH ISLAND

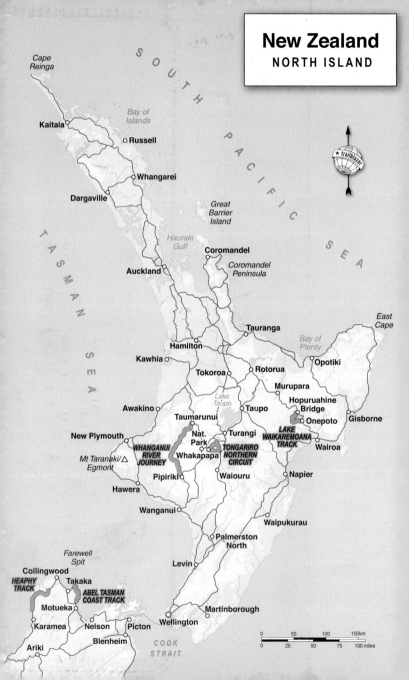

# New Zealand
## NORTH ISLAND

★ trailblazer

*Cape Reinga*

*SOUTH*

Kaitaia

*Bay of Islands*

○ Russell

*PACIFIC*

Whangarei

Dargaville

*Great Barrier Island*

*TASMAN*

*Hauraki Gulf*

Coromandel

*Coromandel Peninsula*

Auckland

*SEA*

Tauranga

*East Cape*

Hamilton

*Bay of Plenty*

Opotiki

Kawhia

Tokoroa

Rotorua

*SEA*

Murupara

*Lake Taupo*

Hopuruahine Bridge

Awakino

Taumarunui

Taupo

Onepoto

Gisborne

New Plymouth

Nat. Park

Turangi

*LAKE WAIKAREMOANA TRACK*

*WHANGANUI RIVER JOURNEY*

Whakapapa

*TONGARIRO NORTHERN CIRCUIT*

Wairoa

*Mt Taranaki/△ Egmont*

Pipiriki

Waiouru

Napier

Hawera

Wanganui

Waipukurau

Palmerston North

*Farewell Spit*

Collingwood

Levin

*HEAPHY TRACK*

Takaka

*ABEL TASMAN COAST TRACK*

Motueka

Martinborough

Karamea

Nelson

Picton

Wellington

Ariki

Blenheim

*COOK STRAIT*

0   50   100   150km
0   25   50   75   100 miles